The Illustrated Directory of

SPORTS
CARS

The Illustrated Directory of

SPORTS CARS

Graham Robson

MOTORBOOKS

A Salamander Book

First published in 2002 by Motorbooks, an imprint of MBI Publishing Company LLC, Galtier Plaza, Suite 200, 380 Jackson Street, St. Paul, MN 55101 USA

© Salamander Books, 2002

An imprint of Anova Books Company Limited

www.anovabooks.com

The information in this book is true and complete to the best of our knowledge. All recommendations are made without any guarantee on the part of the author or Publisher, who also disclaim any liability incurred in connection with the use of this data or specific details.

We recognize, further, that some words, model names, and designations mentioned herein are the property of the trademark holder. We use them for identification purposes only. This is not an official publication.

MBI Publishing Company titles are also available at discounts in bulk quantity for industrial or sales-promotional use. For details write to Special Sales Manager at MBI Publishing Company, Galtier Plaza, Suite 200, 380 Jackson Street, St. Paul, MN 55101 USA.

To find out more about our books, join us online at www.motorbooks.com.

ISBN 978-0-7603-1420-3

Credits

Project Manager: Ray Bonds
Designers: Interprep Ltd
Picture research: Mirco De Cet
Reproduction: Anorax Imaging Ltd
Printed and bound in: Italy

The Author

Graham Robson has been fascinated by cars – classic, modern, road, and sporting – for many years, in a career which began as an Engineering Graduate at Jaguar Cars in 1957. Along the way he also found time to compete in rallies all over Europe, to become Competitions Manager of Standard-Triumph in the 1960s, to join *AUTOCAR* magazine's technical staff, then to run the experimental and road proving departments at Chrysler UK Ltd. – before finally becoming an independent writer, historian, author and broadcaster in the 1970s. As one of the most prolific of all British motoring writers, he is a recognized authority on many classic marques, contributes to motoring publications around the world, can often be seen commentating at major classic and sporting events around the UK, and has now written well over 100 books, including several standard works on classic cars.

Acknowledgements

The publishers wish to thank the automobile manufacturers who have scoured their archives in order to provide photographs for this book, as well as the many private photographers and collectors, including in particular Mirco De Cet and Andrew Morland, as well as the motorsport photographic agencies, particularly LAT Photographic, London.

Additional captions

Front cover (top to bottom): Saleen S7, Ferrari F360 Modena, Mercedes-Benz 300SL.
Back cover: Pagani Zonda.
Page 1: Chevrolet Corvette.
Page2-3: BMW Z8.
Pages 4-5: Singer Nine.
Pages 6-7: Noble M12 GTO

Contents

Introduction

It was a real pleasure to choose the contents of this book, to be able to list legendary Bugattis, Ferraris and Porsches alongside less-well-known Panoz, Alpine-Renault and TVR types. It was our delightful task, to find a representative selection of the sports cars which have gladdened the hearts of drivers for at least a hundred years.

But it also meant that we had to make hard choices. First of all, of course, there was the joy of leafing back through history, to collect the details of a century of the some of the world's most exciting road-car machinery. But then we came up against two major problems. With a hundred years to cover, we had to find space for all the cars we thought should be included – and sideline many more – but the other was to decide what type of cars they were or are. Easy enough to decide, you might say. A Jaguar E-Type, a vintage Bentley and a Mazda MX-5 – well, obviously they are sports cars. But what about Porsches with roofs which can carry four people? Or those phenomenal cars built to win the World Rally Championship? And what about *any* tin-top Ferrari larger than the open-topped Dino brigade?

We knew that motoring enjoyment, and a certain character, should always be a factor, but was that enough? In the 1960s, nothing was quite so much fun as driving a Mini-Cooper S, and before the end of the century there were occasions when the best car to raise one's spirits was a four-wheel-drive, Subaru Impreza or Mitsubishi Lancer Evo, but were these sports cars? Vintage Bentleys with limousine bodies were not sports cars, even though the same chassis with a Vanden Plas tourer body most certainly was. What about an early Ford Mustang with every option in the performance book? And what should we make of the world's first Wankel-engined saloon, the NSU Ro80?

So, what is a sports car? Must it have only two-seats? Must it have an open top? Must it be used in motor sport? Must it have a unique chassis or mechanical layout? If that were so, almost every car built before 1900 would qualify. Difficult to decide, as I'm sure you will agree.

Maybe every motoring writer should be asked to answer that very question: what is a sports car? And every one of us, I suspect, would come up with a different answer. Look it up in a dictionary? This was some help, but not a total solution. One edition of the famous Oxford Dictionary merely says: 'a low-built, fast car', while a rather larger version includes the word 'open'.

We then looked around to see what other experts had concluded, from time to time, and found that they, too, had found difficulties. In the end we sat down with our lists, applied the ice-packs to our fevered brows, and decided what *we* would have liked to own, at the right time, in the right place.

There isn't much doubt where sports car motoring (enjoyable motoring, that is) really began. If you eliminate the idea of those bravely engineered Victorian devices that you see every year in a veteran car run, then the world's first sports car was probably the original Mercedes models which took the world by storm in 1901. The rivals which followed were invariably bigger, heavier and by no means as nimble, and almost inevitably they were costly and hand-built machines.

It wasn't until the 1910s and 1920s that designers learned to follow that wonderful adage for increasing performance: 'simplicate and add lightness', ▶

Below: Jaguar's E-Type is one of the world's most famous classic sports cars, matching performance with style, and oozing with glamour.

▶ which had already served aircraft engineers so well. It seems so obvious today, but to make cars go faster, they could either fit a more powerful engine – or they could build a lighter car. If they could build a much smaller, lighter car, it might even sell at a lower price, and the market might therefore expand.

By the 1930s, therefore, it wasn't only the rich who could buy sports cars. For the well-to-do, there were Frazer Nashes, Lagondas, and SS Jaguars, but for the salary earner there were new, stylish, and enjoyable little machines from MG, Singer, Fiat and others.

And then came the 1950s, that happy time when companies as diverse as MG and Chevrolet, Triumph and Fiat, Austin-Healey and Jaguar, all concluded that a sports car could still look, feel and sound right, even if it used the running gear from a saloon car under the skin. By this time, too, it didn't matter if a sports car had more than two seats, or its permanent roof kept the rain out in bad weather. Did anyone ever dare to suggest that a Porsche 911 was not a sports car? It had, after all, seats for four, and all but a tiny minority of the cars had permanent steel roof panels. And how many ordinary cars were accepted as sports car material purely because they had open tops? Have a look at a Triumph Dolomite Roadster of 1938/1939, and tell me what you think?

We were delighted to note that 'supercars' – and I'm sure I don't have to define what that means – have always been with us. For sure, that wasn't a breed which invented itself when the first Lamborghini Miura came along: what about the first 61/2-litre Bentleys of the 1920s? Or the Mercedes-Benz 540K?

Or the tool-room-built Pegaso Z102 of the 1950s?

Which brings me to the question of the passengers' comfort. Way back, to get a true sports car experience, you had to be ready to get cold, to get wet, and to be exhausted by wind, rain and noise. A rug, a waterproof, and a comprehensive tool kit were all things to be carried – if, that is, there was space inside the car. But not any more. Modern sports cars may reach 130-140mph with ease (and it's amazing how many of them can beat 155mph, which is nearly the magic 250kph in metric), and nowadays this can often be in air-conditioned comfort, with the sound system playing your favourite music. Along the way, you'll appreciate the near-silent exhaust system, the ride and handling, the traction, and the promise of secure anti-lock braking (though you hope you'll never need it).

The good news, too, is that sports cars are here to stay. Legislators may stifle fun in so many other ways, and they demand totally clean exhaust gases, but they cannot stop us having fun. By the time the world's oil threatens to run out (and it will not do that for many years to come), engineers will have developed alternative fuels. And more power. And better roadholding. And even more pleasing styles.

We are looking forward to it.

Below: Ferrari settled on its ideal sports car layout in the 1970s, with the Dino family, and retained it for the next thirty years.

AC Ace

Ace, Aceca, Ace-Bristol, Ace-Zephyr and Greyhound built from 1953 to 1964 (data for Ace-Bristol)

Built by: AC Cars Ltd., Britain.

Engine: Six cylinders, in line, in four-bearing, cast-iron block. Bore and stroke 66mm by 96mm, 1,971cc (2.60 × 3.78in, 120.3cu.in). BMW-inspired pushrod overhead valve operation, two valves per cylinder, operated by pushrod and rocker, exhaust valve by pushrod, pivot, cross pushrod and rocker. Single side-mounted camshaft. Aluminium cylinder head with downdraught siamesed inlet ports and three Solex carburettors. In standard tune, maximum power 105bhp. In further-modified form, 128bhp at 5,750rpm, and maximum torque 122lb.ft at 4,500rpm.

Transmission: Single-dry-plate clutch and four-speed synchromesh gearbox (with non-synchronised first gear) in unit with back engine. Open propeller shaft to chassis-mounted hypoid final drive. Exposed universally jointed drive shafts to rear wheels.

Chassis: Separate multi-tubular frame, relying on two main tubes for beam and torsional stiffness. Fully independent front and rear suspension, by traverse leaf springs and wishbones. Bishop cam steering. Coil spring suspension, plus rack-and-pinion steering on Greyhound. Telescopic dampers. Drum brakes on all wheels at first, but Girling front discs from 1957. Light-alloy coachwork on framework of light tubes – open two-seat (Ace), closed two-seat (Aceca), or closed 2+2 seater (Greyhound).

Dimensions: Wheelbase 7ft 6in (229), tracks 4ft 2in (127cm). Overall length Ace 12ft 8in (386cm), Aceca 13ft 4in (406cm), Greyhound 14ft 7in (444cm). Unladen weight Ace-Bristol sports car 1,850lb (838kg).

History: After years of making nothing but the 2-litre saloon design, AC

Right: Even prettier than the Ace two-seater was the Aceca coupé – sold with the light-alloy AC, or with the 2-litre six-cylinder Bristol engine. The styling was all-British, but looked Italian – a compliment to AC's car. Each car was hand-built around a twin-tube steel chassis, with transverse leaf spring all-independent springing. Maximum speed was up to 120mph.

surprised the world by announcing their new Ace sports car in 1953. Although the Ace retained the distinguished old 1,991cc engine, by now tuned to give 85bhp, the chassis and coachwork were startlingly modern. Inspiration was from John Tojeiro's Bristol-engined sports-racing car which raced in Britain in the early 1950s. Tojeiro, introduced to AC, was asked to productionise this chassis and specify the AC engine. With this superb Ferrari-like styling, the Ace went on sale in 1954. This chassis was rudimentary but strong with two main tubular longerons suitably attached to transverse leaf springs and lower wishbones. So low were the weight and the centre of gravity, that anti-roll bars were not needed to ensure good handling. Maximum speed was about 105mph in original form.

The very pretty fastback Aceca soon followed the Ace, and final work on the 40-year-old engine design produced a 105bhp power output. Demands from customers who wanted to race or rally their cars resulted in the BMW-based six-cylinder Bristol engine being offered. This could (and often was) urged to produce more than 140bhp, and made the Ace very fast indeed. In 128bhp production form a 120mph maximum speed was usual, and roadholding was as well balanced as ever. The AC engine was offered right up to the death of the Ace in the mid-1960s, but the Bristol unit was dropped in 1961, after which a few of the tuned 2.6-litre Ford Zephyr units were offered instead.

An interesting but unsuccessful diversion at Thames Ditton was that a long-wheelbase 'almost four seater' car, the Greyhound, was sold, but it was both too expensive and too unrefined to be a success. Before time finally caught up with the Ace it was transformed into the Cobra by the transplant of an American V8 engine. Sales of Cobras were so high that AC found they could fill their workshops with no difficulty, and the Ace models had to be discontinued in 1964.

AC Cobra

AC Cobra 260, AC Cobra 289, AC Cobra 427, AC Daytona Cobra (data for Cobra 289)

Built by: AC Cars Ltd., Britain, and Shelby American Inc., USA.

Engine: Eight cylinders, in 90-degree vee-formation, in five-bearing cast-iron block. Bore and stroke 101.6mm by 72.9mm, 4,727cc (4.00 × 2.87in, 289cu.in). cast-iron cylinder heads. Two overhead valves per cylinder, operated by pushrods and rockers from a single camshaft positioned in the vee of the cylinder block. Single carburettor. Maximum power 195bhp (gross) at 4,400rpm in standard form. Maximum torque 282lb.ft at 2,400rpm. Shelby-modified Mustang-type engines with up to 271bhp (gross) available to special order. Engine based on mass-production Ford of Detroit 4.2/4.7-litre unit.

Transmission: Single-dry-plate clutch, and four-speed all-synchromesh manual gearbox in unit with engine. Open propeller shaft to chassis-mounted Salisbury limited-slip final drive, with 3.45:1 ratio. Universally jointed exposed drive shafts to rear wheels.

Chassis: Tubular chassis frame, with two main longitudinal tubes and front and rear subframes supporting suspensions. Independent front and rear suspension by transverse leaf springs and lower wishbones (from 1965 by coil springs and unequal length wishbones). Steering by rack and pinion (by worm and sector on

14

first 125 cars built in 1962). Girling disc brakes to all four wheels. Wire wheels with 185 × 15in tyres.

Dimensions: Wheelbase 7ft 6in (229cm), track (front) 4ft 7in (140cm), track (rear) 4ft 6in (137cm). Overall length 13ft (396cm). Unladen weight 2,282lb (1,035kg).

History: American racing driver Carroll Shelby first approached AC Cars Ltd of Thames Ditton in autumn 1961, proposing that they should supply Ace body-chassis assemblies, for his Los Angeles based company to insert Ford V8 engines and transmissions. A prototype was completed early in 1962, and production of the first 100 cars began later in the year. Compared with that of the Ace, the chassis was much strengthened, as were the suspension components, and a more robust 4HA Salisbury back axle was fitted. These cars were shipped from Britain to California for American-sourced parts to be fitted. The first 75 cars were equipped with 4.2-litre (260cu.in) engines, and the first 125 with Ace-type worm-and sector steering. From the beginning of 1963 the 4.7-litre (289cu.in) V8 engine, and rack-and-pinion steering became normal.

Shelby raced Cobras with great success, evolving for 1964 the brutal but sensationally fast 'Daytona' coupé body. Thus equipped, the team won the 1964 World GT Championship. There were important changes in 1965. First, a major ▶

Left: The Cobra was unmistakable from any angle. This car has been fitted with tubular rear bumpers and roll-over hoop behind the driver's head.

▶ suspension redesign replaced the transverse leaf springing by a coal-spring and double-wishbone layout. Second, and more important, from mid 1965, all Shelby supplied cars had been fitted with the much bulkier 6.989cc Ford Galaxie-based V8 engine, with 345 bhp (gross) at 4,600rpm. At the same time, AC re-designated the smaller version an 'AC 289' and were allowed to sell these cars on the British and other markets. There was always confusion over names. AC insisted that the car was an AC, but Shelby badged it, and marketed it, as a Shelby American Cobra (and it was homologated in sporting form with that name). Later, and even more confusing, the cars became known as Ford Cobras.

Production of Cobras was suspended in 1968, after which AC produced a

Above: By the late 1960s, Cobras had taken on ultra-wide wheel arches, and fat tyres. Late 1990s examples had massive 355bhp engines.

long-wheelbase chassis version called the AC428, which was equipped with stylish and expensive Frua coachwork. The last of those cars was produced in 1973, but was not the end of the story. Under new management, the Cobra was re-introduced in 1983, as a 5-litre V8-engined Mark IV. Tiny numbers, re-creations of the original type, really, were then produced until the end of the century, along with a 355bhp supercharged version known as 'Superblower'.

AC 428

AC 428 open sports car, or fastback coupé, built from 1966 to 1973
Built by: AC Cars Ltd., Britain.

Engine: Ford-USA eight cylinders, in 90-degree vee, in five-main-bearing cast iron cylinder block. Bore and stroke 104.9 x 101.1mm, 7,016cc (4.13 x 4.00in, 428cu.in). Cast iron cylinder heads. Two valves per cylinder, operated by pushrods and rockers from camshaft mounted in vee of block. One Holley carburettor. Maximum power 345 (gross) bhp at 4,600rpm. Maximum torque 462lb.ft at 2,800rpm.

Transmission: Rear-wheel-drive, single dry plate clutch and four-speed manual gearbox, with remote control, centre gearchange. Optional Ford three-speed automatic transmission.

Chassis: Separate steel chassis frame, with tubular side members, tubular cross-bracing and fabricated stiffeners. Independent front suspension by coil springs and wishbones, independent rear suspension by coil springs and wishbones; telescopic dampers. Rack-and-pinion steering. Four-wheel. hydraulically-operated, disc brakes, with vacuum-servo assistance. 15in wheels, centre-lock wires, with 205-15in tyres. Separate light-alloy two-seater body shell by Frua of Italy, available as open-top Roadster, or as fast-back coupé.

Dimensions: Wheelbase 8ft 0in (244cm), front track 4ft 7.5in (140cm), rear track 4ft 8in (142cm). Overall length 14ft 6in (442cm). Unladen weight 3,145lb (1,426kg).

History: To follow up the success of the Cobra two-seater, AC moved on to building a larger and altogether more civilised car. Although it was based on a

long-wheelbase version of the Cobra's chassis and running gear, the AC 428 was a quieter, better equipped and altogether more versatile machine.

Mechanically there were two big improvements – one being to stretch the wheelbase by 6in/15.2cm, the other being to use Ford-USA's 428CID vee-8, which was less highly tuned and more flexible than the Cobra's sporty unit. Automatic transmission, which never has been tolerated in the Cobra, was an option, and the style was both more modern, and better equipped.

AC did not feel that they could design and produce their own high-standard coachwork, so the new car's two-seater body shells, in fact, came from Frua of Italy, either as fastback coupés or as open top derivatives. Because Frua was already supplying other European manufacturers, it was no surprise that these looked rather like the Maserati Mistrale of the day.

Not only was the character of the AC 428 totally different from that of the Cobra, but it cost a great deal more, so demand was always limited. Not as fast or sexy as a Ferrari, and without a long-established pedigree, this range only sold slowly. Production hold ups in acquiring bodies from Italy, nor several labour disputes, did not help, so the model was finally dropped in 1973 after only 81 cars had been made.

Below: British engineering plus American powerplant plus Italian bodywork unfortunately all added up to a nice-looking car that didn't sell well enough.

Alfa Romeo 6C Series

6C1500, 6C1750, 6C1900 models, built from 1927 to 1933 (data for 6C1750 Super Sport)

Built by: SA Italiana Nicola Romeo & C., Italy.

Engine: Six cylinders, in line, in cast-iron block, on separate four-bearing light-alloy crankcase. Bore and stroke 65mm by 88mm, 1,752cc (2.56in x 3.46in, 107.0cu in). Detachable cast-iron cylinder head. Two overhead valves per cylinder, operated directly via screwed-in tappets from twin overhead camshafts in cylinder head. Single horizontal carburettor with Roots-type supercharger at nose of crankshaft, or single updraught carburettor without supercharger. Maximum power (supercharged) 85bhp (gross) at 4,500rpm. Maximum power (unsupercharged) 64bhp (gross) at 4,500rpm.

Transmission: Dry multi-plate clutch and four-speed manual gearbox without synchromesh, all in unit with front-mounted engine. Direct control central gearchange. Propeller shaft enclosed in torque tube, connected to spiral bevel 'live' rear axle.

Chassis: Separate steel chassis frame, with pressed and tubular cross bracings, and channel section side members. Tubular front axle beam. Front suspension by semi-elliptic leaf springs. Rear suspension by semi-elliptic leaf springs and torque tube. Friction-type dampers. Four-wheel drum brakes, shaft and rod operated. Centre lock wire spoke wheels. 27 x 4.5in tyres. Coachbuilt two-seater open sports car body style, mostly by Zagato - light-alloy panels on wooden framing.

Dimensions: Wheelbase 9ft 0in (274.5cm), tracks (front and rear) 4ft 6.3in (138cm). Overall length 13ft 4in (406cm). Unladen weight (unsupercharged/supercharged) 1,985/2,030lb (900/920kg).

History: The triumphs of the Alfa Romeo P2 were still fresh in the minds of Alfa-Romeo directors when they asked Vittorio Jano to develop a new, much lighter car than the RL range. The brilliant Jano, whose fame at Milan had only really just begun, laid down a conventional chassis, but graced it with the first of a series of six-cylinder engines. Between 1927, when the first 6C1500 was actually delivered, and 1933, when it was finally overtaken by the even more noteworthy 8C series, this engine family was built in many guises, with single and twin overhead camshaft cylinder heads, with or without superchargers.

The 6C1500, which founded the range, originally had big six-seater bodywork, and its unsupercharged single-cam engine could produce a top speed of 70mph. The next step was to reveal the 6C1500 Sport, complete with twin-cam detachable cylinder head, and in 1929 this was further developed into the 6C1500 Super Sport, where light-alloy bodies were specified, and where the option of a supercharged engine made top speeds of 87mph with 76bhp.

All this, however, paled into insignificance when the beautiful 6C1750 models arrived, in which the same basic engines had larger cylinder bores and longer strokes, but were outwardly much the same as before. The Gran Sport and Super Sport models had outstandingly rakish two-seater short chassis bodies by Zagato or Touring: the supercharged Super Sport, with 85bhp, could reach more than 90mph.

The 'works' team drivers had the pick of the factory's expertise, which included providing them with engines having non-detachable cylinder heads cast in unit with the cylinder blocks, a ruse which allowed the supercharging to be boosted, and the maximum power to be raised to more than 100bhp (and top speed to about 106mph). Thus equipped, Tazio Nuvolari won the 1930 Mille Miglia in great style. Achille Varzi won the Targa Florio, and Nuvolari then went on to win the Tourist trophy race, which was held in

Above: Vittorio Jano designed a brand-new six-cylinder car for Alfa Romeo in the 1920s, and the 6C cars were built in Milan for seven years. This was the 1928 6C 1500 Super Sport (twin-camshaft) model.

Northern Ireland at the time.

Development of competition cars, however, was rapid, and from 1931 the 6C1750 model was supplanted by the even more exciting 8C2300 sports cars, but there was still a close connection, for these eight-cylinder engined cars had many engine components in common with the 6C1750 units. Jano having been instructed to lay down the new engine on just that basis.

In fairness, one should mention that unsupercharged, long-wheelbase, mildly tuned versions of this chassis and power train were always available, but somehow it was the very fast sports cars which always stole the headlines. Certainly the twin-cam cylinder heads, with valves opposed at 90 degrees, and with classically simple valve operation, set the standard followed by many other designers in the 1930s, and the basic design was used on all *eight*-cylinder Alfas built until the outbreak of war in 1939 as well. The 6C1750 Super Sport, of course, became so famous in Italy that in the 1960s *Quattroroute* (the Italian motoring magazine) sponsored the deign of a modern 'look-alike' car using current-model Alfa Romeo mechanical equipment. It says much for the 1920s type of Alfa Romeo that the modern car was not even thought to have as much character and appeal.

Even after the 8C2300 had been designed, introduced, and taken precedence over the 6C1750 cars, that was not quite the end of the story. Alfa Romeo realised that the 8Cs were too costly, and too esoteric, to appeal to every sportsman, and in 1933 they produced a series of 197 6C1900 GT cars, in which the famous six-cylinder engine was bored out to a capacity of 1917cc, and had a light-alloy twin-cam cylinder head, which was a material innovation for the type. It is not without significance that the bore and stroke of this engine was the same as that of the current 8C2600 Monza, for the policy of commonisation of moving parts was well developed at Alfa Romeo at this time.

The last 6C car of all was built in 1933, after which its place was taken by the new 6C2300, which had an entirely different twin-cam engine. Surviving cars are worshipped by every Alfa Romeo enthusiast.

Alfa Romeo 8C Series

8C models built from 1931 to 1939 (data for 8C2300 or 1931 – Spider Corsa version)

Built by: SA Alfa Romeo, Italy.

Engine: Eight cylinders, in line, in two four-cylinder light-alloy blocks bolted up to a ten-bearing light-alloy crankcase. Bore and stroke 65mm by 88mm, 2,336cc (2.56in × 3.46in, 142.5cu in). Two detachable light-alloy cylinder heads. Two overhead valves per cylinder opposed to each other at 90 degrees and operated by twin overhead camshafts and tappets screwed on to the valve stems. Single downdraught carburettor and Roots-type supercharger. Dry-sump lubrication. Maximum power 155bhp at 5.200rpm (165/180bhp at 5,400 in 1932/43).

Transmission: Multiple-dry-plate clutch, and four-speed manual gearbox (without synchromesh), all in unit with front-mounted engine. Direct action central gearchange. Propeller shaft enclosed in torque tube to spiral-bevel 'live' rear axle.

Chassis: Separate pressed-steel chassis frame, with tubular and sheet metal cross-bracing, and channel-section side members. Tubular front axle beam. Front and rear suspension by half-elliptic leaf springs and friction-type dampers. Four-wheel drum brakes, shaft and cable operated. 18in centre lock wire wheels 29 × 5.50 tyres.

Dimensions: Wheelbase 9ft 0.2in (275cm), front track 4ft 6.3in (138cm), rear track 4ft 6.3in (138cm). Overall length 13ft 5in (409cm). Unladen weight 2,205lb (1,00kg).

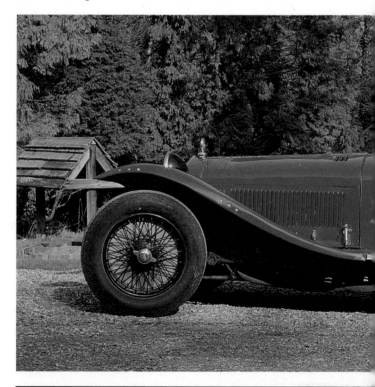

History: Vittorio Jano joined Alfa Romeo in 1923, and immediately began a design programme which led to the famous P2 Grand Prix cars, and to the use of twin-cam engines in the 6C1500 and 6C1750 series of cars. By the end of the 1920s Alfa's sports and racing cars were pre-eminent. To ensure continued domination, Jano then designed the legendary straight-eight twin-cam engine, which was to power the 8C cars throughout the 1930s and (in developed form) Alfa's Grand Prix cars for a number of years.

The engine was a constructional masterpiece, with two four-cylinder blocks and two cylinder heads on a common crank and crankcase, with camshaft drive by a train of gears up the centre of the unit. 8C2300 cars were tremendously successful sports cars in the early 1930s, and were speedily developed into the 8C2600 Monza sports-racing machines by the Scuderia Ferrari. The 2300 Monza and B-Type single-seaters had much in common, and the 8C2900 range (with the same basic engine, enlarged and made more powerful – up to 220bhp) kept the government-controlled Milan producers competitive. Production was always low, almost handbuilt, but Mussolini intended the cars as prestige machines, and not profit-makers and if every modern-day schoolboy yearns after a Ferrari, in the 1920s and 1930s he would have wanted an Alfa Romeo. A car needs no better epitaph than that.

Below: This famous 8C Alfa Romeo is a Monza, the ultra-special racing derivative, as driven by Tazio Nuvolari in the early 1930s. In this period Enzo Ferrari prepared the 'works' cars.

Alfa Romeo Alfetta GT/GTV6

Alfetta GT, GTV, GTV6, built from 1974 to 1987 (data for GTV6)
Built by: Alfa Romeo SpA, Italy.
Engine: Six-cylinders, in 60-degree vee formation, in four-main-bearing cas
aluminium cylinder block. Bore and stroke 88 x 68.3mm, 2,495cc (3.46 x 2.69in
152.3cu.in). Cast aluminium cylinder heads. Two valves per cylinder, opposed
to each other in part spherical cylinder heads, and operated by inverted bucke
tappets (and pushrod and rocker in case of exhaust valves), from single
overhead camshaft per cylinder head. Bosch L-Jetronic fuel injection
Maximum power 160bhp at 5,600rpm. Maximum torque 157lb.ft at 4,000rpm
[Also four cylinder engines, 1,570cc to 1,962cc, available with 109bhp a
5,600rpm to 130bhp at 5,400rpm.]
Transmission: Rear-wheel-drive, single-dry-plate diaphragm spring clutch and
rear-mounted five-speed all-synchromesh manual gearbox. Remote contro
central gearchange.
Chassis: Unitary-construction pressed-steel body/chassis structure, in two
door four-seater fastback body style by Ital Design. Independent fron
suspension by torsion bars, wishbones and anti-roll bar: De Dion rea
suspension by coil springs, radius arms, Watts linkage, and anti-roll bar
Telescopic dampers front and rear. Rack-and-pinion steering. Hydraulically
operated disc brakes at front and rear, with vacuum-servo servo assistance
Alloy, bolt-on 15in disc wheels. 195/60-15in tyres.
Dimensions: Wheelbase 7ft 10.5in (240cm), front track 4ft 5.5in (136cm), rea
track 4ft 5.5in (136cm). Overall length 13ft 9in (419cm). Unladen weight 2,668lt
(1,210kg).

**Below: Tens of thousands of Alfetta GTs and GTVs shared this smart
2+2-seater coupé style, which upheld the famous Italian maker's coupé
pedigree.**

Above: Giorgetto Giugiaro had a very sure eye for styling, producing this crisp GT shape on the mundane Alfetta saloon platform.

History: After years of developing the Giulia theme, Alfa Romeo finally evolved a brand-new mechanical layout for a new model that it called the Alfetta. This name was chosen because the new car had the same basic layout as the famous racing Alfa of the 1940s – its engine was at the front of the car, and its transmission was in unit with the final drive at the rear.

The Alfetta, of which the saloon was launched in 1974, and the smart fastback/hatchback sports coupé Alfetta GT followed in 1974, broke new ground in several technical respects. Not only was the famous twin-cam engine up front, with a five-speed gearbox integrated with the final drive, but it had a new torsion bar and wishbone front suspension layout, allied to De Dion rear suspension at the rear.

The style of the new saloon was neat and conventional enough, and had been carried out by Alfa Romeo itself, and although a shortened wheelbase version (by 4.3in/11cm) of the same platform was retained for the sporty version, styling had been left in the very capable hands of Giorgetto Giugiaro. Here was an Alfa which showed off all the expected features – the famous shield-shaped front grille, and the fastback 2+2-seater proportions we had known on previous Alfas – but one which was noticeably crisper, and more emphatic than anything seen before from Milan.

The original GT used a 122bhp/1.8-litre version of the twin-cam engine (a family which had already been in production for twenty years), and on the road it soon showed up splendid, well-balanced road manners. Apart from the lack of an open-top derivative (such cars were tested, but not put on sale), the only ▶

▶ real controversy came in the cabin, where the fascia layout looked very disjointed indeed.

Even in its first form, this was a 110mph car, but after two years, when more than 21,000 had already been produced, the original 1.8-litre version was swept away, to be replaced by two new versions, the 109bhp/GT 1.6 and the 122bhp/GTV 2000, which bracketed the original car's market. No more than minimal changes were made to the style, or the equipment, and – predictably enough – it was the 2-litre-engined GTV 2000s which sold best of all.

A very limited-production 'Turbodelta' version of the 2.0-litre car was also on sale in the early 1980s, though this 150bhp car was only produced as an indulgence, so that customers could go motor racing with highly-tuned 300bhp examples.

Alfa Romeo, however, were keeping the best until last, for it was not until the end of 1980 that the majestic GTV6 appeared, this effectively being a revised version of the GTV 2000 into which Alfa's magnificent new fuel-injected overhead camshaft 2.5-litre V6 engine had been squeezed. Here was a new company building block which produced 160bhp in this form – which was enough to push the GTV6's top speed up to 130mph – but which revved well, sounded wonderful, and was obviously ripe for further development in the

future. Which, indeed, it was, for revised examples were still being used in the early 2000s.

Not only was the sure-footed GTV6 the best of all these Alfetta types, but it also had many improvement to the suspension, larger and grippier tyres, cosmetic retouches all around, along with a revised and much smarter fascia/interior package, which made the car a whole lot more desirable than before. Maybe it had all the usual cabin ergonomic failings beloved of Italian designers (whose legs seemed to be short ...) but it was otherwise an extremely capable machine.

Faced with such a capable 'Big Brother', the smaller GTV 2000 died out in the early 1980s, the GTV6 then carrying on strongly, alone, until 1987. Between 1974 and 1987, and even though contemporary Alfas had a well-earned reputation for rust corrosion at an early age, more than 126,000 such machines were produced.

Below: GT versions of the Alfetta were available with four-cylinder twin-cam, or vee-6 engine power. All had front-mounted engines, though the gearbox was at the rear.

Alfa Romeo Giulia Spider

Giulia Spider, built from 1966 to 1993 (data for original 1600 Duetto of 1966)

Built by: Alfa Romeo SpA, Italy.

Engine: Four-cylinders, in line, in five-main-bearing light-alloy cylinder block. Bore and stroke 78 x 82mm, 1,570cc (3.07 x 3.23in, 95.9cu.in). Light-alloy cylinder head. Two valves per cylinder, opposed to each other in part-spherical combustion chambers, and operated by inverted-bucket tappets from twin-overhead camshafts. Two horizontal twin-choke Weber carburettors. Maximum power 109bhp at 6,000rpm. Maximum torque 103lb.ft at 2,800rpm.

Transmission: Rear-wheel-drive, Single dry plate, diaphragm spring clutch and five-speed all-synchromesh manual gearbox, with remote control centre gearchange.

Chassis: Unitary-constriction pressed-steel body/chassis structure, in two-seater sports style by Pininfarina.. Independent front suspension by coil springs, wishbones and anti-roll bar, Beam axle rear suspension by coil springs, radius arms and A-bracket location. Telescopic dampers at front and rear. Recirculating ball steering. Hydraulically operated disc brakes at front and rear, with vacuum-servo assistance. 15in wheels, bolt-on steel disc. 155-15in tyres.

Dimensions: Wheelbase 7ft 8.5in (235cm), front track 4ft 3.5in (131cm), rear track 4ft 2in (127cm). Overall length 13ft 11.5in (425cm). Unladen weight 2,295lb (1,041kg).

[Other versions had engines from 1,290cc to 1,962cc, with power between 89bhp at 6,000rpm and 132bhp at 5,500rpm. Overall length shortened to 13ft 6in (412cm) from 1969.]

History: By the mid-1960s, Alfa Romeo was adept at squeezing every possible version out of every one of its models. As with the Giulietta series, therefore, it aimed to turn the new larger-engined Giulia model into a complete family – of saloons, estate cars, coupés, special-bodied types – and open-top sports cars.

It took a little time, however. The original unit-construction Giulia saloon arrived in 1962, this being a slightly larger car than the Giulietta, with a similar

Below: Styled in the mid-1960s, and still looking good decades later, the Spider was a classic two-seater which upheld every Alfa Romeo tradition.

Above: From 1967 the Duetto was replaced by the 1750 Spider Veloce, and this later adopted a cut-off tail style.

suspension/running gear layout, though everything had been improved. Initially it had a 1.6-litre version of the now-famous small twin-cam engine, and a five-speed transmission was standard. By the time a shorter-wheelbase, Bertone-styled Sprint GT came on the scene in 1963, disc brakes for all four wheels had also been adopted.

The Spider, originally called Spider Duetto, had been styled by Pininfarina, who would also build the production body shells, and took shape on a yet-shorter version of the Giulia's platform; whereas the Spider ran on a 7ft 8 5in/235cm wheelbase, that of the saloon was 8ft 2.8in/251cm

The original style was small, neat, rounded, but with a rather long tail, and was fashioned purely as a two-seater. Originally built with a 109bhp version of the 1.6-litre twin-cam engine, the Duetto offered a top speed of up to 113mph, with all the dash, and all the brio, of such small Italian machines.

Right from the start the Duetto sold well – it was especially successful in the USA, where most sales would be captured over the years – but Alfa Romeo always had big plans to improve it, and make it more widely accessible. From late 1967 it was replaced by the more powerful 1750 Spider Veloce, where the Duetto name was dropped, and the engine was enlarged to 118bhp/1.8-litre, this car also getting a smart and sharply cut-off tail style for 1970.

Within a year of that, there was also the 1300 Junior, with 89bhp/1.3-litres, which also got the short tail for 1970, and from mid-1971 there came the definitive version, the 2000 Spider Veloce, which had the fully-expanded 132bhp/2.0-litre version of this splendid twin cam engine.

Even then (and this was so typical of Alfa Romeo, to whom change and the juggling of titles became a way of life) there was still time for two more versions of the Spider, known as the Junior 1300 and Junior 1600 Roadster, to be reintroduced in 1974. This was partly a reaction to the Energy Crisis which had just struck the automotive world, and partly a pragmatic way of covering all possible market slots with a still-attractive machine! Well over 5,000 cars a year were being built at this time, the bodies coming from Turin and being transported up the autostrada for final assembly in Milan.

By the 1980s, though, the 2000 Spider Veloce reigned alone, and would ▶

▶ continue to do so until the early 1990s. Although the engineering did not seem to advance to any great extent, Alfa Romeo and Pininfarina continuously kept on re-touching the decoration of the machine, and to look for novelties. Although few expensive-to-incorporate changes were ever made to the metal of the unit-construction body, there would be many changes and updates to the bumpers, the mouldings, the badging, and the cabin equipment.

From 1982 the Spider received a styling makeover, with a new nose/grille, a big chin spoiler at the front, and a rubberised flexible spoiler across the tail. Although many of the purists did not like what they saw, sales (particularly in the USA) perked up, and the same style would persist throughout the decade, even though the Spider was now the very last of the Guilia family to stay in being.

In 1990 there was still time for one more re-vamp, this time with a simplification of what had gone before. The front chin spoiler disappeared in

favour of a more rounded moulding, there was no sign of a rear spoiler, there were new side skirts which actually enhanced the looks, there was a new and rather rounded sheet metal tail, and once again the interior had been re-jigged, and made to look more modern.

This final version of the car was sold almost entirely in the USA, where its fuel-injected 2.0-litre engine was rated at 126bhp (or 120bhp if an exhaust catalyst was specified). The last cars of all, which still looked good (a huge credit goes to Pininfarina for this) were produced in 1993. In a 27-year career, more than 120,000 of all types had been manufactured.

Below: The original Spider, badged Duetto and sporting its long tail, is nearest the camera. The later model is at the rear. Both were smart two-seaters.

Alfa Romeo Giulietta Series

Giulietta, built from 1954 to 1964 (data for 1956 Sprint Veloce)
Built by: Alfa Romeo SpA., Italy.
Engine: Four cylinders, in line, in five-bearing light-alloy block/crankcase. Bore and stroke 74mm by 75mm, 1,290cc (2.91in × 2.97in, 78.7cu.in). detachable light-alloy cylinder head. Two overhead valves per cylinder, opposed to each other at 90 degrees in part-spherical combustion chamber and operated by inverted-bucket tappets from twin overhead camshafts. Two horizontal twin-choke Weber carburettors. Maximum power 90bhp at 6,500rpm. Maximum torque 87lb.ft at 4,500rpm.
Transmission: Single-dry-plate clutch and four-speed synchromesh manual gearbox, both in unit with front-mounted engine. Remote control central gearchange. Two-piece open propeller shaft to hypoid-bevel 'live' rear axle.
Chassis: Unitary-construction pressed-steel body/chassis unit, in two-door four-seat coupé style by Bertone. Independent front suspension by coil springs, wishbones and anti-roll bar. Repeat suspension by coil springs, radius arms and A-bracket. Telescopic dampers. Worm-and-roller steering. Four-wheel, hydraulically operated drum brakes. 15in pressed-steel bolt-on wheels. 155 × 15in tyres.
Dimensions: Wheelbase 7 ft 10in (239cm), track (front) 4ft 2.9in (129cm), track (rear) 4ft 2in (127in). Overall length 12ft 10.5in (393cm). Unladen weight 1,973lb (895kg).
History: The Giulietta series, born in 1954, was really Alfa's first attempt at mass-production, although the 1900 model had paved the way to this a few years previously. It was laid down specifically to be produced in many versions – four-door saloon, two-door coupé, and open Spider, and each and every one of the cars had a splendid and all-new twin-cam light-alloy engine. Until then, only Jaguar had put a twin-cam into true quantity production, but by the start of the 1960s Alfa Romeo had overtaken their figures. The 1,290cc engine was only the first of a magnificent pedigree and family of units – later expanded through 1600, 1800 to 2-litre versions, and forming the backbone of middle-class Alfa private car production. The Sprint came about as a result of a *muletto* car built by Bertone, and speedily adopted by Alfa Romeo. For years it was known as the most beautiful of all small GT cars, and was only surpassed by the bigger-

Below: Flawless when new, and still pleasing at fifty years old, the Bertone style on the original Giulietta GT.

Above: The Giulietta Spider, as styled by Pininfarina, was one of the purest and most classic sporting two-seater shapes yet seen. For the final years the cars gained a 1.6-litre engine, and a bonnet scoop.

Above: The mass-production Giulietta saloon appeared in 1955, and provided the platform for sporting versions of that model range.

engined Giulia GT which followed in the 1960s. Well over 150,000 Giuliettas of all types were built in ten years, which included some really fierce Zagato-bodied competition cars and more than 25,000 Sprint GTs and Veloces. The Giulietta was the car which changed Alfa's public image – before this they had made a few expensive cars, and after it they were to make a lot of middle-class thoroughbreds with world-wide appeal.

Alfa Romeo Spider/GTV

Alfa Romeo Spider and GTV, introduced in 1994 (data for 2.0-litre Spider version)

Built by: Alfa Romeo SpA, Italy.

Engine: Four cylinders, in line, in five-main-bearing iron cylinder block. Bore and stroke 83 x 91mm, 1,970cc (3.27 x 3.58in, 120.3cu.in). Aluminium cylinder head. Four overhead valves per cylinder, operated by inverted bucket-type tappets from twin overhead camshafts. Bosch fuel injection. Maximum power 150bhp at 6,200rpm. Maximum torque 137lb.ft at 4,000rpm. [144bhp/1,747cc 4-cyl, and V6 engines of 2.0-litre and 3.0-litres also available.]

Transmission: Transversely mounted engine and front-wheel-drive, single-dry-plate diaphragm spring clutch and five-speed all-synchromesh manual gearbox, in unit with engine. Remote control centre gearchange.

Chassis: Unitary construction steel body/chassis structure, in two-seater open Spider or closed coupé GTV styles. Independent front suspension by coil springs, MacPherson struts and anti-roll bar, independent rear suspension by coil springs, radius arms, anti-roll bar. Hydraulic telescopic dampers. Rack-and-pinion steering.with power assistance. Disc brakes at front and rear, with vacuum servo assistance, and ABS as standard. 16in bolt-on alloy wheels, 205/50-16in tyres.

Dimensions: Wheelbase 8ft 4in (254cm), front track 4ft 11in (150cm), rear

track 4ft 11.3in (151cm). Overall length 14ft 0.7in (428cm). Unladen weight 2,982lb (1,354kg).

History: Soon after Fiat took control of Alfa Romeo, for the 1990s it commissioned a new pair of sports cars – the front-wheel-drive Spider and Coupé. It was not before time, for Alfa's existing models were very old: the famous old rear-driver Spider, which would disappear in 1993, had originally been launched in 1966.

But what type of car should the new-generation Spider be? There was much debate, but in the end pragmatism came before sentiment, and the new cars were based on a mass-production front-wheel-drive platform. This had already been finalised for the new Fiat Tipo/Lancia Dedra family cars, and proved to be amazingly versatile, and suitable for the job.

These new cars, therefore, were the first-ever sporting Alfas to have front-wheel-drive and transversely-mounted engines – though the styling never actually betrayed this. Right from the start there were to be twin two-seater machines which would re-cycle a pair of famous Alfa model names – a fixed roof coupé called GTV, and an open-top model to be called Spider. With a long life predicted for them, both had conventional steel, unit-construction structures.

This was always a corporate, rather than purely an Alfa, project, confirmed ▶

Left: The new 1990s-generation of Alfa Romeo Spider featured a transversely mounted engine and front wheel-drive.

▶ by the fact that the packaging and shaping of the cars was carried out by Enrico Fumia of Lancia, with help from the independent styling house Pininfarina. Although there was much specialisation, and tuning to Alfa's own requirements, engines and gearboxes, too, would come from the Fiat-Lancia-Alfa Romeo 'parts bin'.

Mechanically the two cars would be identical and would eventually share the same choice of engines and transmissions. Their basic style was totally shared too, the differences only being obvious above and behind the passenger doors. In spite of having to accommodate transverse engines, the designers still managed to provide a long and swooping nose, complete with a symbolic Alfa Romeo shield let into the front of the bonnet panel: the use of a sharply rising body panel crease along the flanks was an instant recognition point too.

Compared with earlier Spiders and GTVs, of course, the running gear was all new – the use of front-wheel-drive saw to that. For the first time on such an Alfa, for instance, there was independent rear suspension, neatly packaged with coil springs and multi-link location.

The major novelty, though, came in the nose, where there was to be a choice of four-cylinder or vee-6 engine power. The vee-6 was the latest 202bhp/3-litre version of Alfa Romeo's own celebrated power unit, but the 'four' was a modern 'twin-spark' Fiat corporate unit of 2.0-litres, this one having 16-valves, twin Lanchester-style counter-rotating shafts to improve the balance,

Above: The 1994-generation Spider featured front-wheel-drive, but the smart style completely hid this away. A fixed-head coupé version was also available.

and a rousing 150bhp. Both were matched to a five-speed transmission.

Here was the founding of a new sports car dynasty at Alfa Romeo. Traditionalists moaned about a loss of pedigree (but, then, traditionalists always do ...) but those who drove the cars realised that they were faster, better built, and at least equal in handling to any Alfa which had gone before. The new cars were comfortable and well-specified, their character was well up to expectations, and they soon built up a big following.

The two-engine line-up, though, was only a start. By the end of the decade there were no fewer than five different choices of engine in the line-up. Not only had an 'entry-level' 144bhp/1.8-litre 'four' been added, but there were two versions of a new type of vee-6, this having twin overhead camshafts and an even more charismatic character and delivery than before.

By the early 2000s the rumour was not only that this would be the final version of the famous Alfa vee-6, but that a new generation of front-wheel-drive Spider was also being developed. By this time, though, Alfa enthusiasts were so enthusiastic about the front-wheel-drive Spiders which had occupied the late 1990s that they were looking forward to the future with great interest.

Alfa Romeo SZ

Alfa Romeo SZ sports coupé. Along with RZ open version, built from 1989 to 1993

Built by: Alfa-Lancia Industriale S.p.A., Italy.

Engine: Eight cylinders in 90-deg vee, five-bearing cast alloy cylinder block. Bore and stroke 93 × 72.6mm, 2,959cc (3.66 × 2.86in, 180.6cu.in). Two light alloy cylinder heads. Two valves per cylinder, operation by single overhead camshaft per head. Bosch/Alfa electronic fuel injection. Maximum power 210bhp (DIN) at 6,200rpm. Maximum torque 181lb.ft at 4,500rpm.

Transmission: Rear-wheel-drive, single dry plate diaphragm spring clutch and five-speed all-synchromesh manual gearbox, all in unit with front-mounted engine. Remote-control, central gearchange.

Chassis: Unitary-construction pressed-steel body-chassis unit skinned in ICI methacrylic composite skin panels. Independent front suspension by coil springs, wishbones, telescopic dampers and anti-roll bar. De Dion rear suspension by coil springs, angled radius locating arms, Watts linkage and telescopic dampers. Rack-and-pinion steering, with hydraulic power assistance. Four-wheel disc brakes. Cast alloy 16in wheels, 205/55-16in (front) and 225/55-16in (rear) tyres.

Dimensions: Wheelbase 8ft 2.8in (250.9cm), front track 4ft 9.6in (146.4cm), rear track 4ft 8.1in (142.6cm). Overall length 13ft 3.8in (405.9cm). Unladen weight 2,778lb (1,260kg).

History: For Zagato, the specialist body-building concern which manufactured the body shell of the astonishing SZ sports coupé, this was a project made in heaven. Blessed by Alfa Romeo, who needed a short-run headline raiser at this stage of its history, there was no commercial risk and, in a way, the more outrageous the car looked, the better. Conceived in 1987 as a statement of its character, of its engineering genius, and its love for all things automotive, the new car was based on existing Alfa Romeo underpinnings – the 75 saloon – but had an entirely fresh steel body shell.

Not meant to be practical, not meant to be timeless, but meant to be a fun car for those who could afford it, the SZ was always placarded as a limited-

Above right and below: No-one ever called the Zagato-constructed Alfa Romeo SZ classically beautiful, but it was certainly brutal, unmistakeable, and appealing. Later cars were also available with a convertible style.

production machine. Starting in 1989, only 1,000 of the coupés would be produced and, although we did not know it at the time, when that run had been completed and sold, they would be followed by a convertible derivative, of which only 800 were built.

The style was, and always will be, controversial, for it flew in the face of almost everything Alfa Romeo was doing at the time. Built up on a short (98.8in/251cm) wheelbase platform, the new car had a bluff nose, a waistline which rose consistently towards the tail, slab sides and a fastback cabin profile. Not only that, but the details were, in many ways, bizarre – six small rectangular headlamps, no visible door handles and a freestanding rear aerofoil. The facia/instrument panel, at least, was conventional, well-equipped, and stylish.

Some loved it, some hated it, but when questioned Zagato merely replied politely that it was an Alfa project for which they had been hired to build production machinery. They were ideal for this task, they said, because the shell itself was a low-volume unit, and many of the skin panels were in high-tech composites, which needed a specialist to make, fettle and fit them together.

Under the arresting skin, the running gear was closely based on that of the 75 saloon, with the same pressed-steel platform. Like the highest-performance

version of that car, there was a silky, high-revving and very effective V6 engine up front, while the five-speed transmission was at the rear, in unit with the final drive. As with several existing Alfa Romeos, there was De Dion rear suspension, which meant that the wheels were linked by a stout tube, but that the transaxle was mounted to the floorpan.

But, forget the looks for a moment, and consider how the SZ performed. Fast in a straight line (in spite of the unpromising-looking body shape it could beat 150mph), it was a true driver's car, with awesome grip, and a great feel. Much of the chassis development, after all, had been influenced by Alfa's current 75 racing saloons, so this was expected.

The mark of a great car is not what is the immediate public reaction, but what reputation it acquires over the years. The SZ, and the convertible RZ, therefore, seem to be safe, for they are now highly prized machines.

Allard

Allard J, K, L, M and P models, built from 1946 to 1955 (data for J1)
Built by: Allard Motor Co. Ltd., Britain.
Engine: Ford-manufactured, eight cylinders, in 90-degree vee formation, in three-bearing cast iron cylinder block. Bore and stroke 78 x 95.25mm, 3,622cc (3.07 x 3.75in, 221cu.in). Two cast iron cylinder heads. Two side valves per cylinder, directly operated from single camshaft mounted in centre of vee of cylinder block. Solex downdraught carburettors. Maximum power 85bhp at 3,800rpm. Maximum torque 150lb.ft at 2,000rpm. [Later cars were sometimes supplied with 3,917cc/100bhp Ford V8 engines. Cars supplied to the USA without engines sometimes used Chrysler or Cadillac V8 engines.]
Transmission: Rear-wheel-drive, single-dry-plate clutch and three-speed manual gearbox (no synchromesh on first gear), with remote control, cenrre, gearchange.
Chassis: Separate steel chassis frame, with box section side members, and pressed cross-braces. Independent front suspension by swinging half axles, transverse leaf spring and radius arms. Rear suspension of .beam rear axle by transverse leaf spring and radius arms. Lever-type hydraulic dampers. Marles steering. Drum brakes at front and rear: no servo assistance. 16in steel disc wheels. 6.25-16in tyres. Open two-seater bodywork, with light-alloy panelling on wood framing.
Dimensions: Wheelbase 8ft 10in (269cm), front track 4ft 8in (142cm), rear track 4ft 4in (132cm). Overall length 14ft 0in (427cm). Unladen weight 2,450lb (1,111kg).
History: Sydney Allard was a London-based racing and trials enthusiasts, who built a series of Ford-UK based Allard Specials in the 1930s. His Ford-franchised garage spent the war years repairing military vehicles, and in 1946 he set out to use the empty spaces by building Allard cars. The first production Allards

Below: The fastest and most charismatic Allards were the open-wheel J2 and J2X types of the early 1950s. The fastest of all had Cadillac V8 engines.

Above: Allards came in several shapes and sizes – this being the 3.9-litre V8 K2 sports car of 1950-1952.

were delivered in that year, and production would peak in the early 1950s.

Original types were based on a simple chassis design, which featured Ford V8 parts (engine, transmission and rear suspension), with a crudely simple type of swing axle independent front suspension which also used Ford parts. Bodies – two-seater J1 or K1, and four-seater L1 tourer - had different wheelbases, but were mechanically the same, the bodies being large, bulbous, and made very simply indeed with much aluminium in their construction.

The long swooping bonnet, and the 'waterfall' front grille were features – as was the rumbling, extrovert character provided by the side-valve Ford V8 engines. Before long the original cars were joined by the M-Type drop-head coupé, and by the big four-seat P1 saloon, and production rose to more than 300 cars a year, colossal by Allard's original hopes. There would even be a slow-selling Safari estate car in the 1950s.

Allards sold well in export markets (they were simple to maintain, and versatile in their appeal). Allard, in fact, was happy to supply them with larger-capacity (Mercury-manufactured) 3.9-litre engines, and many of these were also equipped with the Ardun engine conversion.

The first out-and-out Allard sports car, the J2, came along in 1950, not only on the shortest of all the chassis, and with coil spring front suspension and de Dion rear suspension, but with a 4.4-litre Ford V8 engine, and an ultra-simple two-seater body style in which separate cycle-type wings were fitted. Many of these cars were supplied to North America without engines, where knowledgeable enthusiasts then fitted powerful and modern overhead-valve Chrysler or Cadillac V8s. Although the J2 could look alarming on a circuit – because of the suspension layout. its front wheels took on significant positive camber when being cornered hard – it was very fast, and very successful.

Coil spring front suspension was soon added to other Allards, though the style ▶

► never changed. This, however, was only an interim step forward, as the much more advanced J2X type, complete with a new, and lighter, tubular chassis frame and a 5.4-litre Cadillac V8 engine as standard, went on sale in 1951. Except for the P1, which Sydney Allard himself drove to win the Monte Carlo rally in 1953, the J2X was the most famous of all Allards.

The new frame, the seven inch rearward repositioning of the engine, and the successful use of De Dion rear suspension, all hidden by the same J2 two-seater style, made this a brutally fast and competent sports car, though no-one would ever describe it as carefully or tastefully made. Even so, in motorsport, a bravely driven J2X could often beat the Jaguars and even the Ferraris which it met in sports car races.

The X-Type frame was eventually adopted under all surviving V8-engined Allards, though as the availability of cheaper, mass-produced cars built up the demand for this individually-made machine faded away. Later models featured an 'A'; for 'Allard' front grille motif, but the basic style of 1946 was never discarded .

Although Allard tried to progress by launching the much-smaller Palm Beach model in 1952, this was a not a success. The last of the big vee-engined models, the K3 touring two-seater, was produced in 1955.

Below: The Allard Palm Beach of 1952-1955 had a choice of four-cylinder or six-cylinder Ford-UK engines.

Alvis 12/50

12/50 SA to TJ, built from 1923 to 1932 (data for SA type of 1923)
Built by: Alvis Car and Engineering Co. Ltd., Britain.
Engine: Four cylinders, in line, in three-bearing cast-iron block. Bore and stro
68mm by 103mm, 1,496cc (2.68 4.06in, 913cu.in). cast-iron cylinder head. Tw
overhead valves per cylinder, operated by pushrods and rockers from sing
side-mounted camshaft. 5.35:1 compression ratio. One Solex carburett
Engine originally derived from the first side-valve Alvis power unit, introduced
1920. Power output about 50bhp minimum (each engine power tested befo
fitting). SC type had 1,598cc (97.5cu.in) engine. TE, TG and TJ types had 1,645
(100.4cu.in) engine. All other types retained basic engine.
Transmission: Four-speed manual gearbox, without synchromesh, separate
from engine by short shaft. Right-hand gearchange. Live spiral-bevel axle, fu
floating type.
Chassis: Simple separate chassis, with pressed-steel channel-sectic
members, and pressed cross members. Half-elliptic front and rear springs. N
dampers. Ribbed drum brakes, mounted only on rear wheels. Worm-and-whe
steering with adjustable steering column. Dash-mounted petrol tank, gravi
feed to engine. Two-seat lightweight sports bodywork normal. Many oth
options available (including saloon coachwork on later models).
Dimensions: Wheelbase 9ft 0.5in (275cm), track (front and rear) 4ft 2
(127cm). Overall length 12ft 9in (389cm).
History: The Alvis car was inspired by T. G. John, who set up his own compar

n Coventry in 1919. The very first Alvis was dubbed a 10/30 model – which meant 10 British RAC-rating horsepower, and about 30 developed horsepower. Deliveries of this simple, but well-engineered, side-valve car, with its 1,460cc engine, began in 1920. Development, mainly through races and trials, was swift. The 10/30 soon became the 11/40, then the 12/40, and briefly the overhead-valve 10/30hp Super Sports.

The 12/50 Alvis, the first of a famous line of light sporting cars, arrived in 1923 to replace the Super Sports 10/30. Its power unit was a shorter-stroke/larger-bore version of that engine, aimed at giving more power and higher-revving capabilities. The pedigree of this model stretches from 1923 to 1932, when it was finally superseded by more modern designs. Although the chassis received little development in that time, the engine was persistently updated and made more powerful. Cars in factory-sponsored and private hands achieved great success in motor racing of the period.

Over the years there were at least eight basic body types, of which the most famous was undoubtedly the 'duck's back' shell with polished aluminium panelling. In 1931/32 the 12/50 was joined by the 12/60 type, basically the same car but having a more powerful engine with twin SU carburettors, close ratio gears, and more comprehensive equipment.

Below: Everybody loved the duck's back Alvis 12/50s, which were typical of the best in vintage sports cars.

Amilcar C-Series

C-Series cars, built from 1920 to 1929 (data for CGSS model)
Built by: Sté Nouvelle pour l'Automobile Amilcar, France.
Engine: Four cylinders, in line, in two-bearing cast-iron, block/crankcase. Bore and stroke 60mm by 95mm, 1,074cc (2.36in × 3.74in, 65.5cu.in). detachable light-alloy cylinder head. Two side valves per cylinder, operated by single side mounted camshaft, via finger placed between stem and camshaft. One updraught Solex carburettor. Maximum power up to 35bhp at 4,500rpm. Optional supercharged version, with 40bhp at 4,500rpm.
Transmission: Multi-plate clutch, running in oil, and three-speed manual gearbox (without synchromesh) all in unit with engine. (Four-speed gearbox on last few built.) direct-acting central gearchange. Propeller shaft in torque tube to spiral-bevel 'live' rear axle.
Chassis: Separate pressed-steel chassis frame, with channel-section side members, fabricated and tubular cross-bracing. Forged front axle beam. Front suspension by half-elliptic leaf springs. Rear suspension by quarter-elliptic leaf springs. Friction-type dampers. Four-wheel drum brakes, rod and steel-strip operated. 27in centre-lock wire wheels. 27 × 4.00in tyres.
Dimensions: Wheelbase 7ft 7in (231cm), track (front and rear) 3ft 7in (109cm). Overall length 12ft (366cm). Unladen weight 1,200lb (544kg).
History: The Amilcar was a typical post-war French *voiturette*, or 'light car', in that it combined a tiny engine with minimal chassis and body weight to provide economical and amusing transport for the new motorists who could not afford anything bigger. Many such firms bought all their components from proprietary manufacturers, but Amilcar at least managed to design and build their own four-cylinder water-cooled engines.

The company was set up by Emil Akar and Joseph Lamy, and it is interesting to conjecture how the near-anagram of Amilcar's name evolved from those two people. Design was in the hands of Edmond Moyet, and André Morel worked

Below: A typically-detailed example of the Amilcar of the 1920s, with its light and functional wings, and the spare wheel fixed to the bonnet side.

Above: The 1920s Amilcar C4 inspired many other sporting styles in the 1930s.

tested, and raced for the new firm. Amilcar was really founded from the ruins of the pre-war Le Zèbre firm, for whom Morel and Moyet had worked, and the cars were made in the old factory, near Paris.

The original product, first seen in 1920, was the Type CC, the basis for all four-cylinder cars to come in the 1920s. Its engine was small (903cc) and side-valve, while its rudimentary chassis had quarter-elliptic leaf springs at front and rear. The original car was so simple that in true 'cycle car' guise it had a straight-bevel final drive, without even a differential; this was later amended. The CC was normally a two-seater and strictly a touring car, weighing not more than 950lb (431kg) complete. From 1922 the range began to expand.

First along was the C4, with a longer chassis and enlarged 1,004cc engine, which could take four-seater bodies, while the CS was a rather more sporting version of the CC, with 985cc. The CS3, on the other hand, was a three-seater, where the third passenger could be accommodated in a dickey seat hanging over the tail. Most cars were built with the Petit Sport body – a narrow two-seat open shell, with a pointed tail and cycle type or combined wings with the running boards.

By 1924 a more sporting Amilcar still had evolved, directly as a result of the events contested by the factory in preceding years. The CGS (GS meaning 'Grand Sport') was a direct development of the CS, but had a bored-out 1,074cc engine, much improved brakes, a strengthened and lengthened chassis, and half-elliptic front springs. Ricardo had redesigned the head, which was now made of aluminium, and even though the CGS was quite a lot heavier than previous Amilcars it could still reach 75mph. Pressure lubrication was a great engine advance (splash lubrication had been normal up to then).

The CGS was good and sold well, but Moyet had even more exciting developments in mind. For 1926 he revealed the CGSS – the 'Surbaissé' model, so named because it had a lowered chassis frame and radiator. The power output had again been increased – to between 30 and 35bhp, and before the end of the model's run it was even given a four-speed gearbox. A few of the cars were built with Cozette superchargers, and such a model won the 1927 Monte Carlo Rally outright. Amilcar's problem, as with most of the other 'light car' builders, was that they were not sufficiently capitalised to change and update their cars frequently. By the end of the 1920s, whatever the increase in ▶

▶ performance that had been achieved, they were still very much of an ear
vintage design, and indeed a survivor of the 'light car' age which seems to hav
all but disappeared. Competition from quantity-production builders (like Citroë
in France, for instance) intensified, and their prices were much lower tha
Amilcar could manage.

Although their days as *voiturette*-manufacturers were over in 1929, they ha
already introduced parallel touring-car models. Between 1923 and the m

1930s, a series of touring cars – the Type Es, Js, Ls, Gs (almost an alphabet of models) were on offer, some of them with six-cylinder models. Even so, nearly 4,700 of the CGS/CGSS sports cars were built in only five years, and rather more than 6,000 of the touring C-Series four-cylinder cars.

Below: By 1920s standards, the French Amilcar was a smart and purposeful little sports car. This C4 was a compact and pleasing machine.

Arnolt-Bristol

Arnolt-Bristol, built from 1954 to 1961

Built for: S. H. Arnolt Inc, USA.

Engine: Bristol-manufactured, six cylinders, in line, in four main bearing cast iron cylinder block. Bore and stroke 66 x 96mm, 1,971cc (2.60 x 3.78in, 120.3cu.in). Aluminium cylinder head. Two overhead valves per cylinder, opposed to each other in part-spherical combustion chambers, operation by pushrods and rockers (plus cross pushrods for exhaust valves) from a camshaft in the cylinder block. Three downdraught Solex carburettors. Maximum power 130bhp at 5,500rpm. Maximum torque 128lb.ft at 5,000rpm.

Transmission: Front engine, rear-wheel-drive, single dry plate clutch and four-speed synchromesh manual gearbox, without synchromesh on first gear, all in unit with engine. Remote control centre floor gearchange.

Chassis: Separate steel chassis frame, with steel box section cross-bracings and reinforcements. Independent front suspension by transverse leaf spring and wishbones, suspension of beam rear axle by logitudinal torsion bars, radius arms and A-bracket. Telescopic hydraulic dampers. Rack-and-pinion steering. Drum brakes at all four wheels. 16inbolt-on steel wheels, with 5.50-16in tyres. Steel/aluminium bodyshell, on steel framing, by Bertone of Italy, in open two-seater sports car style, or as fastback hardtop.

Dimensions: Wheelbase 8ft 10.2in (244.5cm), front track 4ft 3.8n (131.7cm), rear track 4ft 6in (137.2cm). Overall length 13ft 11.7in (426cm). Unladen weight from 2,050lb (930kg).

History: S. H. 'Wacky' Arnolt of Chicago had already sold a number of special-bodied MGs with Bertone coachwork, which he called 'Arnolt-MG' types, when he decided to go further. As an important personality at Bertone (where he was vice-

president), he then decided to go one better.

Having done a deal with the small, high-quality, Bristol company in England, he decided to match the Bristol 404 chassis with a more powerful Bristol engine, a special body style by Bertone, and to sell these cars exclusively in North America. The result was a curvaceous and very attractive two-seater whose only drawback was its necessarily high price.

Because Bristol was then a subsidiary of the notable Bristol Aeroplane Co., and the engine was an update on the pre-war BMW 328 sports car unit (Bristol had liberated this as 'post-war reparations'!), the Arnolt-Bristol had a very well-made and highly-regarded chassis. The engine, of course, was also fitted to post-war Frazer Nash cars, and to many British race cars. Here was a car which not only looked good, but handled well, went fast, and was carefully put together when new.

Most of these cars were supplied as open-top two-seaters, there being three varieties, of which the 'Bolide' was a stripped out version suitable only for sports car racing, though Arnolt could also supply a very smart fastback fixed-head coupé variety of the same style.

In a seven year career, the Arnolt-Bristol sold only slowly, at a high price, but it was universally admired by many other automotive lovers who could not raise the money. The last cars of all were produced in 1961, when Bristol finally stopped making the BMW-derived engines, though the very last example was not produced (from spare parts) until 1964, A total of 142 Arnolt-Bristols were manufactured.

Below: The fastest of all Arnolt-Bristol models was the Bolide, a stripped-out version of the road car, only really suitable for sports car racing.

Aston Martin (1920s and 1930s)

Aston Martin sports cars, 1.5-litre type, built from 1927 to 1935 (data for Mk II of 1932)

Built by: Aston Martin Ltd., Britain.

Engine: Four cylinders, in line, in three-main-bearing cast-iron cylinder block. Bore and stroke 69.3 x 99mm, 1,495 cc (2.73 x 3.90in, 91.3cu.in). Cast iron cylinder head. Two valves per cylinder, operation by single overhead camshaft mounted in cylinder head. Two horizontal SU carburettors. Maximum power 73bhp at 4,750rpm. Maximum torque not quoted.

Transmission: Front engine, rear-wheel-drive, single dry plate clutch and four-speed manual gearbox, without synchromesh. Remote control, centre floor gearchange.

Chassis: Separate steel chassis frame, with channel section side members, tubular and fabricated cross-bracing and reinforcements. Front suspension of beam front axle by half-elliptic leaf springs, suspension of beam rear axle by half-elliptic leaf springs. Friction-type dampers. Worm-type steering. Drum brakes at front and rear. 18in centre-lock wire wheels, with 5.25in tyres. Various body styles, all of aluminium body panelling on wooden skeletons, some as open top roadsters. [Many different body styles, including drop-head coupés and saloons, also available.]

Dimensions: Wheelbase 10ft 0in (304.8cm), front track 4ft 4in (132cm), rear track 4ft 4in (132cm). Overall length 14ft 5in (439.5cm). Unladen weight 2,526lb (1,145.5kg).

▶

Below: The vintage/thoroughbred Aston Martins looked good from every angle, all being low, squat and oozing character.

Above: Even in the mid-1930s, when the Aston Martins became Mk IIs, they kept to their traditional style, with cycle-type wings and ultra-hard suspension.

▶ **History:** Today's Aston Martins share no more than a name with the vintage and thoroughbred types built in the 1920s and 1930s. These, nevertheless, were the founders of a famous dynasty.

The first Aston Martins, known as the 'Lionel Martin' types, started things off in 1914, but bankruptcy intervened in 1925. A new company, rather precariously financed by A. C. Bertelli, then revived the business, which was based at Feltham, in Middlesex. From 1926 to 1939, this resourceful, skilful, but only sketchily equipped concern produced a series of tautly engineered, character-loaded, sports and touring cars, all of which shared the same type of handbuilt single overhead camshaft engine. Until 1935 all these were 'Bertelli' 1.5-litre units, after which the capacity went up to 2.0-litres.

All such Astons were characterised by their low, lean chassis, with the characteristic radiator style that became so well known. All had stiff, short-travel half-elliptic leaf spring suspension and very direct steering, their brakes being mechanically operated. The engines proved to be so receptive to tuning that a series of successful racing types were built. Unsurprisingly, they were expensive – a typical two seater of the period costing at least three times that of an equivalent MG – though there was a good choice of body styles, long and ▶

Right: The Ulster model of the 1930s was named after a particular motor racing success for the marque, and had this smart two-seater body style.

Below: The Ulster version was everyone's favourite. Although very rare, many such cars survive into the twenty-first century.

Below: EML 129 was the last-ever 'Bertelli' Speed Model, with a two-litre engine and a fine record in motorsport.

▶ short chassis, open and closed.

After a total of 129 cars had been built, a new Second Series came along (much improved, with a better gearbox, and with renewed finance from Sir Arthur Sutherland), the 'International' and 'Le Mans' model names now being legendary. Third Series cars followed in 1934, by which time engines had up to 73bhp, and the styles (still stuck in 1920s fashions) began to look old-fashioned.

By the time the last 1.5-litre types had been made, 425 had been sold, and

Above: Modified in later years – the road wheels on this car are certainly smaller now, than they were – the short-chassis 1 1/2-litre types were, and are, very desirable.

the 2-litre type which followed added another 174 to that total. After World War II, the company was taken over by David Brown, but after a series of changes in the 1970s and 1980s, it came and has stayed under Ford control.

Audi TT Quattro

Audi TT Quattro roadster and coupé, introduced in 1998 (data for 225 model)

Built by: Audi AG, Germany.

Engine: Transversely mounted, four cylinders, in line, in five-main-bearing cast iron cylinder block. Bore and stroke 81 x 86.4mm, 1,781cc (3.19 x 3.4in, 108.7cu.in). Light-alloy cylinder head. Five valves per cylinder, operated by inverted bucket-type tappets, from twin overhead camshafts. Bosch fuel injection and KKK turbocharger. Maximum power 225bhp at 5,900rpm. Maximum torque 206lb.ft at 2,200rpm.

Transmission: Front engine, four-wheel-drive, single-dry-plate diaphragm spring clutch and six-speed all-synchromesh gearbox, remote control, centre gearchange.

[A 180bhp front-wheel-drive version of this design was also available.]

Chassis: Unitary construction steel body/chassis structure available in open Roadster or fastback coupé style. Independent front suspension by coil springs, MacPherson struts, wishbones, and anti-roll bar, independent rear suspension by coil springs, wishbones and anti-roll bar. Hydraulic telescopic dampers. Rack-and-pinion steering, with power assistance. Disc brakes at front and rear, with servo assistance, and ABS.17in cast alloy wheels, with 225/45-17in tyres.

Dimensions: Wheelbase 7ft 11.6in (243cm), front track 5ft 0in (153cm), rear track 4ft 11.3in (150.5cm). Overall length 13ft 3in (404cm). Unladen weight 3,076lb (1,395kg).

History: Although Audi and VW had been sharing components, sometimes even body shells, since the 1970s, it was not until product-enthusiast Dr. Ferdinand Piech took control of the company in the 1990s that this mix-and-match process intensified. Not only was Seat and Skoda added to the stable of marques, but corporate engines and platforms began to be blended at a frenetic pace.

To understand the ultra-sporting Audi TT, therefore, one had to dig deep to find its origins. Under that sleek, rounded skin, the platform was closely based on that of the front-wheel-drive VW Golf hatchback (and therefore related to that of the Audi A3 family car), all the suspension and chassis components evolved from those two cars, while the chosen four-cylinder engine was a logical development of the five-valves-per-cylinder Audi unit.

Although there was to be a front-wheel-drive version of this product, the ▶

Below: Under the TT's sleek two-seater skin is a transversely mounted engine in the nose, and front wheel drive.

▶ real secret behind its appeal was that it was also to be available with four-wheel-drive, and a magnificent 225bhp engine. Years of experience with this, and earlier engines, had allowed Audi to meld a five-valve cylinder head, which was unique among mass-production car makers at the time, with turbocharging, to offer 126bhp/litre, and an impressively wide and flat torque curve. This, no question, had to be one of the most flexible of all mini-Supercars.

Even so, all that power without the security of drive through four wheels might have been difficult for the chassis to handle, but since Audi's four-wheel-drive experience stretched back into the late 1970s, and the TT's system had been perfected in the A3, there were never any qualms about choosing it.

It was the rounded looks of the TT, a concept of which was shown in 1996, which immediately sold it to sports car lovers. Even at that early stage, different variations on the same theme – an open-top roadster and a fastback coupé – were exhibited, and although early production was confined to hardtops, it was always clear that both types would be made available before long. Even Porsche – mightly Porsche – must have worried that the TT might become a competitor to its own new rear-drive-only Boxster.

Open or closed, here was a sinuously shaped little two-seater which seemed to spell out 'function' rather than 'image'. Chunky wheel arch

Below: The TT was available as a fastback coupé or a Spider, all types being based on the A3/VW Golf chassis platform.

Above: In the 1990s, Audi intended the cabin of the new TT to be compact, purposeful, and full of information. There is an airbag in the steering wheel hub.

extensions covered the massive wheels, there was little overhang at front and rear, nor were there any separate, unsightly, bumpers. Yet because there was a definite family resemblance to other, less sporty, cars in the range, no-one was ever likely to mistake the TT for any other make of car. The interior, though, was unique, and very attractive, with its simple round dials, easy to understand controls, and that marvellously chunky steering wheel. Here was a car which spelt out: 'don't mess with me' – and would always deliver.

Independent road tests proved that point, for the 225bhp version could reach no less than 145mph – and this, please note, from only a 1.8-litre engine – and could annihilate almost all its opposition on any journey which put a premium on torque, traction, and general agility. The TT, in other words, was an amazingly nimble machine —the short wheelbase, compact dimensions and the four-wheel-drive all saw to that ▶

▶ – which never seemed to be taken aback by poor conditions.

Although it was never a cheap car – the 225bhp TT had to fight, head-to-head, with the Mercedes-Benz SLK, and cost more than Alfa Romeo's appealing new GTVs and Spiders, for instance – it had one unique selling factor – the quattro factor.

Below: Because early TTs had rather skittish roadholding, Audi specified
a rear spoiler to help trim the chassis performance. This view shows just
what a compact little car the TT actually was, for front and rear
overhangs were tiny.

Austin Healey 100

Austin-Healey 100 BN1 and BN2, built from 1953 to 1956
Built by: British Motor Corporation (BMC), Britain.
Engine: Four cylinders, in line, in cast iron cylinder block. Bore and stroke 87.3 x 111.1mm, 2,660cc (3.44 x 4.37in, 162.3cu.in). Cast iron cylinder head. Two overhead valves per cylinder, operated by pushrods and rockers from camshaft in cylinder block. Two semi-downdraught SU carburettors. Maximum power 90bhp at 4,000rpm. Maximum torque 144lb.ft at 2,500rpm.
Transmission: Rear-wheel-drive, single-dry-plate clutch and three-speed all-synchromesh manual gearbox, with Laycock overdrive on top and second gears. (BN2 models have a four-speed gearbox, with overdrive on top and third gears). Centre floor gearchange.
Chassis: Separate steel chassis frame, with box section side and reinforcing members, and with steel body inner structure welded to it on assembly. Independent front suspension by coil springs, wishbones and anti-roll bar, suspension of beam rear axle by semi-elliptic leaf springs and Panhard rod. Hydraulic lever arm dampers. Cam-and-peg steering. Drum brakes front and rear, no servo assistance. 15in centre-lock wire wheels, 5.90-15in tyres. Two-seater steel open sports car body (some aluminium panels), with optional, removable, hardtop.
Dimensions: Wheelbase 7ft 6in (229cm), front track 4ft 1in (124cm), rear track 4ft 2.75in (129cm). Overall length 12ft 7in (383.5cm). Unladen weight 2,150lb (975kg).
History: Donald Healey's little car-making concern had been producing rather expensive Riley-engined cars from 1946, but it was 1952 before he was able to consider making a new model which would be smaller, simpler to build, and would sell at a lower price.

After discussions with Austin, and Tickford, the bodybuilders, he planned a smart new two-seater, which would use Austin A90 running gear in a specially designed structure. The design of the new 'Healey 100' featured a sturdy box-section chassis to which the load-bearing parts of the body would be welded on assembly, though some of the skin panels were to be aluminium. Because it had a smooth, low-slung style, it looked certain to beat 100mph.

Only one car was built before the 1952 :London Motor Show, where BMC's Leonard Lord liked it so much that he immediately took over the design, arranged for it to be called 'Austin-Healey', and prepared for mass-production in

Below: The original 100 style was for a two-seater, where wire-spoke wheels were standard, and the doors had removable side screens.

Above: The 100M of 1954 to 1956 featured a 110bhp/2.6-litre engine, and was fitted with a louvred bonnet and a bonnet holding-down strap.

1953. Instead of being produced in small numbers at the Healey factory in Warwick, BMC now prepared to build up to 100 cars every week at its vast Longbridge plant, where Austin cars were built in big numbers.

The secret was in the way the production cars came together, for chassis frames were produced by a Midlands specialist, body/chassis structures were completed, painted and trimmed by Jensen Motors in West Bromwich, and the engines and running gear were provided, 'in house', by Austin at Longbridge.

The original cars, always known as BN1s, which was their BMC chassis prefix, went on sale in mid-1953, with unmodified 90bhp engines mated to a three-speed gearbox and Laycock overdrive; because this device was arranged to work on top and second gears, the BN1 effectively had a five-speed gearbox, and matched its 103mph top speed with very brisk acceleration.

From the summer of 1955, though they would only be on sale for one year, the BN2 took over, this having a four-speed instead of a three-speed transmission, though overdrive was still retained, this model eventually being replaced in the summer of 1956 by a substantially-different update, the six-cylinder-engined BN4 (which was the predecessor of the 3000).

Both BN1 and BN2 models were fast, sleek, and surprisingly tuneable, which made them ideal for use in motorsport. Unhappily they had a fault (their only real one) in that they rode too close to the ground, which made them ideal for circuit racing, but not at all useful for the rough-and-tumble of European rallying. There was, however, never a complaint about their looks, or their behaviour, for apart from the usual British habit of being rather under-cooled and under-developed for the hottest North American climates, they were excellent export machines.

In 1953 and 1954 Healey developed a successful series of 'Special Test Cars' for racing, and record breaking, there being two developments from this process. One was that the '100M' kit was evolved, in which cars could be provided with 110bhp versions of the engine, and improved handling, while the other was that just 50 very special aluminium-bodied 100S types were built in 1955. The 100S had a special 132bhp version of the engine, which made it a formidable 'class car' in production sports car racing.

This, the original Austin-healey, did marvellous things for BMC, who had been striving, for years, to match MG's traditionally-styled TDs with a new model which the Americans would like as much, and it also freed Donald Healey from the constant financial worries which had dogged him throughout the life of the 'Warwick' Healeys. A total of 14,684 such cars were produced.

Austin-Healey 3000

3000 models BN7, BT7, BJ7 and BJ8, 1959 to 1967, also 100-6 models BN4 and BN6, 1956 to 1959 (data for BJ8)

Built by: British Motor Corporation Ltd., Britain.

Engine: Six cylinders, in line, in four-bearing cast-iron block. Bore and stroke 83.3mm by 88.9mm, 2,912cc (3.28in × 3.5in, 177.7cu.in). Cast-iron cylinder head (aluminium on competition cars). Two overhead valves per cylinder, operated by pushrod and rocker from side-mounted camshaft. Two SU carburettors. Maximum power 148bhp (net) at 5,200rpm. Maximum torque 165lb.ft at 3,000rpm.

Transmission: Single-dry-plate clutch, and four-speed synchromesh manual gearbox (without synchromesh on first gear), remote control central gearchange. Optional overdrive on top and third gears. Open propeller shaft to hypoid-bevel 'live' rear axle.

Chassis: Separate steel chassis frame, with box-section side members, box and pressed cross brace and cruciform members. Welded to steel body after manufacture. Independent front suspension by coil springs, wishbones and anti-roll bar. Rear suspension by half-elliptic leaf springs and radius arms. Piston-type hydraulic dampers. Cam-and-peg steering. Disc front brakes and drum rear brakes hydraulically operated 15in steel disc or optional centre-lock wire spoke wheels. 5.90 × 15in tyres. Steel sports car body style, with tiny 'plus 2' seats behind front bucket seats. Optional hardtop. Body/chassis units built by Jensen.

Dimensions: Wheelbase 7ft 7.7in (233cm), track (front) 4ft 0.7in (124cm), track (rear) 4ft 2in (127cm). Overall length 13ft 1.5in (400cm). Unladen weight 2,460lb (1,116kg).

History: Donald Healey's Healey 100 was the result of an unofficial competition set up by Sir Leonard Lord in 1952. The rules were that mainly BMC components should be used; BMC would sponsor the winner. MG and Jensen were losers. The

Below: Six-cylinder cars had longer wheelbases and some models were available with two-seater or 2+2-seater cabins: this is 2+2 model.

Above: In the 1950s and 1960s the most exciting of all Austin-Healey 3000s were the 'works' team competition cars, prepared at the MG works at Abingdon. They had light-alloy bodies and powerful (210bhp) tuned engines. They were equally at home in the roughest of rallies or in long-distance road races (above: Paul Hawkins/Timo Makinen in the Targa Florio). Brute strength and noise were features.

first Austin Healeys had four-cylinder 2.6-litre engines, and these were made between 1953 and 1956. Chassis and bodywork were designed by Geoffrey Healey and his father Donald. The car was a great export success, and racing versions (the 100S – 'S' for Sebring) achieved great things in 1954/5. When supplies of the old 'four' ran out, the car was re-engined as a 'six' with the new BMC 'C' series 2.6-litre unit.

Three years later, in 1959, the engine was enlarged to 2.9-litres, and the Austin-Healey 3000 was born. In the next eight years there were four distinct types of 3000 but illogically enough the last one, with its wind-up windows, walnut facia and most powerful engine, was called the Mk III! If the 3000 had faults they were that it was too low-slung, too coarse and too cramped to be totally successful. It was, however, a real man's sports car and in final tune was capable of over 120mph. The 'big Healey', as it was always affectionately known, was a ▶

▶ formidable rally car, winning Alpine and Liège-Sofia-Liège rallies, and it dominate the GT categories for many years. As a racing car it was too standard to be outright winner, but properly prepared, it was just about unbreakable. Nea 43,000 '3000s' were built, and the car was forced off the market at the end of 19 by United States legislation rendering continued production uneconomic.

A car like the 3000 could never have been planned, but merely evolved, those who loved it, and conceived it, thought of more and more enhancemen By the late 1960s, no doubt, it badly needed better ventilation, more performanc and a serious re-style, but its character could not be improved.

Replicas, or re-creations, were attempted in the 1980s and 1990s, thou designer Geoff Healey would not sanctify them with his approval. Although th looked similar, and had bigger, more powerful, engines, the essential charact was missing. Now, as earlier, there was no substitute for the real thing.

Right: Although a 2+2 seat cabin was offered, there was really very littl space behind the front bucket seats. These cars retained the same fasc style from 1952 to 1964.

Below: The first 3000 appeared in 1959, and had a 2.9-litre six-cylinder engine. Such 'wobbly' grille mesh was a feature on all Austins of the late 1950s.

Ballot RH Series Eight

**RH Eights built from 1927 to 1932 – 2.6, 2.8 and 3.0-litre versions (data
3.0-litre RH3)**
Built by: Etablissements Ballot, France.
Engine: Eight cylinders, in line, in cast-iron block, with detachable nine-bear
aluminium crankcase. Bore and stroke 68mm by 105mm, 3,050cc (2.68in × 4.13
186cu.in). Light-alloy cylinder head. Two valves per cylinder, operated by sin
overhead camshaft, drive by skew gears and shaft at rear of engine. Vertical valv
in flat faced cylinder head. Single updraught Zenith twin-choke carburettor.
Transmission: Twin-plate clutch in unit with engine. Four-speed man
gearbox without synchromesh, also fixed to engine. Sliding gears at fir
constant mesh gears on last batch of cars built. Direct action cen
gearchange. Open propeller shaft to spiral-bevel 'live' rear axle.
Chassis: Separate steel chassis frame, with channel-section main si
members and tubular and pressed cross bracing. Half-elliptic leaf springs at fro
and rear. Forged front axle. Hydraulic lever arm dampers. Worm-and-r
steering. Rod-operated four-wheel drum brakes, with vacuum-servo assistan
31in centre-lock wire wheels, fitted with 31 × 5.25in tyres. Several coachwo
versions to choice, from Belgian/European specialists.
Dimensions: Wheelbase 10ft 10.5in or 11ft 10in (331cm or 261cm). Trac
(front and rear) 4ft 5in (135cm). Overall length depending on coachwc
Unladen weight (chassis only) 2,520lb (1,143kg).
History: Before 1914, Ballot in Paris specialised in the manufacture of car a
stationary engines. From 1918, Edouard Ballot decided to extend his compan
prestige by making and selling complete cars. First he engaged Ernest Henry
1913/1914 Peugeot fame) to design eight-cylinder and four-cylinder racing ca
The first Ballot road car was the 2LS, really a slightly civilised racing two-sea
and this was followed in 1923 by the 2LT type. The 2LT introduced Ballo
particular and notable engine/cylinder layout, where the overhead-cam opera
in-line valves operated in a flat head with Heron-type bowl-in-piston combust
chambers. The 2LT was supplemented by the 2LTS in 1925, which had m
conventional combustion chamber arrangements and rather more performar
in 1927, however, Ballot decided to push up their offerings even more –
specification, performance and price.

Although they catalogued a 2-litre 'six' at the beginning of 1927 this
never went into production. In its place, at the Paris show of 1927, came t
eight-cylinder, 2.6-litre Model RH Ballot. Its chassis followed the 2LT's lir
closely, although the wheelbase was considerably lengthened. The engi

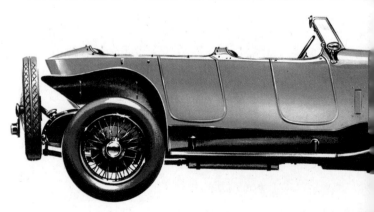

bove: A feature of the RH Eights was its magnificent eight-cylinder ngine, with 'Heron' combustion chambers and an overhead camshaft. he long wheelbase encouraged splendid and elegant bodies.

1ore closely related to the Heron-headed 2LT 'four' than to the 2LTS 'four', 1itially had a cylinder bore of 63mm, and a capacity of 2,618cc, but to improve 1e performance when heavy coachwork was fitted this was twice increased – o 66mm in 1928 and to 68mm for 1930. The RH had a beautifully and flexibly 1ned engine, which made the car an aristocrat among French machines, with a 1ther flexible chassis which sometimes caused grievous harm to the none-too-gid bodies of the day.

In 1932, like so many other makers of exclusive cars, Ballot ran into financial 1fficulties, and were soon taken over by Hispano-Suiza. That was really the end f Ballot cars as we know them. A new model produced in Paris and badged as Ballot HS26 was, in fact, a 4.6-litre small-scale replica of Spanish Hispano 1odels. Even this car reverted to type and became a Hispano-badged machine efore long.

elow: Striking in style and advanced in engineering, the Ballot Type 2LT as a fine vintage car. This body was by Legache-Glaszmann of France. he car preceded the legendary 'Eights'.

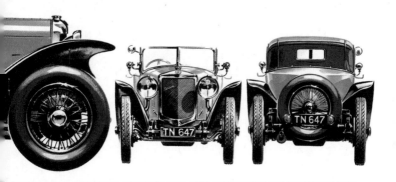

Bentley 3-litre

3-litre models built from 1921 to 1928 (data for short-wheelba 'Standard')

Built by: Bentley Motors Ltd., Britain.

Engine: Four cylinders, in line, in five-bearing cast-iron block and light-al crankcase. Bore and stroke 80mm by 149mm, 2,996cc (3.15in × 5.87 183cu.in). non-detachable cast-iron cylinder head. Four valves per cylinc operated by rockers from a single overhead camshaft. Camshaft driven vertical shaft and gears from nose of crankshaft. Two SU carburettors af 1924, single Smith carburettor up to that date. Maximum power 80 to 85b depending on time.

Transmission: Single-dry-plate, inverted cone clutch, slightly separated fr four-speed unsynchronised gearbox. Remote control right-hand gearchan Open propeller shaft to spiral-bevel 'live' rear axle.

Chassis: Separate steel chassis frame, with channel-section side members a angled and tubular cross bracing. Half-elliptic leaf springs for front and r suspension. Forged front axle beam. Hartford-type friction dampers. Worm-a wheel steering. Rear-wheel drum brakes (up to 1923), four-wheel drum bra (after 1923), without servo assistance. Centre-lock wire wheels, several s changes between 1921 and 1928. Initial tyre fitments 820 by 120 ty Coachwork to choice; cars supplied from Bentley Motors as rolling chassi sports, touring or saloon styles.

Dimensions: Wheelbase 9ft 9.5in (298cm), tracks (front and rear) 4ft (142cm). Overall length 13ft 3in (404cm). Unladen weight (depending coachwork) from 2,800lb (1,270kg).

History: W. O. Bentley had already made his name as an importer of Frer DFP sports cars before World War I, and for his BR air-cooled rotary aero-eng

designs during it, when he decided in 1919 to make a car of his own design. The 3-litre, first seen at the 1919 Olympia Motor Show, and first sold in 1921, was the first of his legendary strain. Indeed, it is true to say that the 4½, 6½ and 8-litre cars (if not the unsuccessful 4-litre) are all recognisably descended from the 3-litre. Chassis engineering was conventional in every way. Interest, and praise, was always reserved for the engine. Massively built, tall and elegant in the Edwardian style, it was near-unique in having four-valves per cylinder and gave the bulky cars a sparkling performance.

Even though the firm was always under-capitalised (it was close to bankruptcy at least three times in the 1920s), Bentley himself eventually agreed to a Le Mans racing programme, to speed development and to provide publicity. The three-litre in 'lightweight' open guise won the race in 1924 and 1927. Cars also raced with distinction in the Tourist Trophy Race (second in 1922) and at the Indianapolis 500 Miles Race (where Hawkes's car averaged 81mph).

Bentley was so confident of his engineering that a five-year guarantee was given on the mechanical items in the car. Three-litres were in production for seven years, in several basic guises and in three wheelbase lengths. The Speed Model, with tuned-up engines, arrived in 1924, and following the development of the 4½-litre Bentley (the engine being an amalgam of 3-litre and 6½-litre 'six' design thought) a number of common parts were specified. There were three distinct sets of gearbox ratios. Chassis price, at first, was £1,100 (usually raised to about £1,400, depending on the coachwork chosen), but by 1924 the long-wheelbase 'Standard' chassis had been reduced to £895. This long-wheelbase chassis was the most popular – 765 being sold – while 513 of the Speed Model were produced. In total, 1,619 3-litre Bentley's were built. The car was finally replaced by the 4½-litre.

Left: The Bentley 3-litre established the massive and impressive style for which all vintage Bentleys would be famous.

Bentley 4¹/₂-litre

Bentley 4 ¹/₂-litre models, built from 1926 to 1931 (data for original model)
Built by: Bentley Motors Ltd., Britain.
Engine: Four cylinders, in line, in cast iron block on top of a six-main-bearing aluminium crankcase. Bore and stroke 100 x 140mm, 4,398cc (3.94 x 5.51in, 268.5cu.in). Cast iron cylinder head integral with the block. Four valves per cylinder, slightly opposed in narrow vee, operation by rockers and tappets from a single overhead camshaft, itself driven by an eccentric drive/connecting rod arrangement from the crankshaft. Two horizontal SU carburettors. Maximum power 104bhp. Other details not quoted.
Transmission: Front engine, rear wheel-drive, inverted cone dry clutch, separated from a four-speed manual gearbox with no synchromesh; remote control right-hand gearchange.
Chassis: Separate steel chassis frame, with channel section main side members, channel, fabricated and tubular cross-bracings and reinforcements. Front suspension by beam front axle and half-elliptic leaf springs, rear suspension of beam rear axle by half-elliptic leaf springs. Friction dampers front and rear. Worm-type steering. Drum brakes at front and rear, operated mechanically by rods, cranks and levers. 32.5 x 5.25in tyres on 21in centre-lock wire wheels. Choice of four- or five-seater, open Tourer and closed saloon body styles, mainly in aluminium/steel panelling on wood frame skeletons.
Dimensions: Depended on chosen bodywork. Typically, wheelbase 10 ft 10in (330cm), front track 4 ft 8in (142.2cm), rear track 4 ft 8in (142.2cm). Overall length 14 ft 4.5in (438cm). Unladen weight 3,416lb (1,549kg).
History: Here was the archetypal sports car for which British vintage motoring was famous. Big, stocky, powerful, but with essentially simple engineering, the Bentley 4¹/₂-litre was *the* car for the wealthy sportsman to use in the 1920s. As motoring fashions changed in the 1930s, the 4¹/₂ fell out of favour, but in the later years of the twentieth century it once again came to be worshipped as an icon of British motoring.

It used to be said that W.O.Bentley only ever designed one car, and that the entire 'W.O.' range was carefully evolved from it. In many ways – particularly that of chassis design, and body construction - that was so, for each model was closely related to the next, but there were intriguing differences between the engines of all five different 'W.O.' models.

The 3-litre of 1921 had been the original, but in 1925 a vast and immensely impressive 6¹/₂-litre type had also appeared. The 6¹/₂ not only had a larger and more solid chassis, but it also featured a new six-cylinder engine.

One year later, in 1926, Bentley then announced the 4¹/₂-litre model, which was really an amalgam of the earlier types. Although the chassis size, in general, was like that of the 3-litre, the 4¹/₂-litre model had a new four-cylinder engine which was no more and no less than a close relation of the 6¹/₂ litre. The two engines, in fact, were amazingly alike, and used many common components. Not only did they share the same bore and stroke dimensions (100 x 140mm/3.94 x 5.51in), but they also had the same locomotive-like method of driving the cylinder-head-mounted camshaft from the crankshaft, by three tightly packaged connecting rods and eccentrics.

Although the engine itself was something of a monument (it was never a high-revving unit, nor particularly smooth), it developed truckloads of torque, with the sort of character once described affectionately as a 'great bloody thump'. Even though the motor car itself was heavy, the engine was so robust that it helped deliver very high performance. 90mph being possible, which was vastly impressive at a time when the average family car cruised at no more than 40mph.

Above: The Bentley badge, and the radiator it sat on, was one of the most famous motoring trade marks of the 1920s.

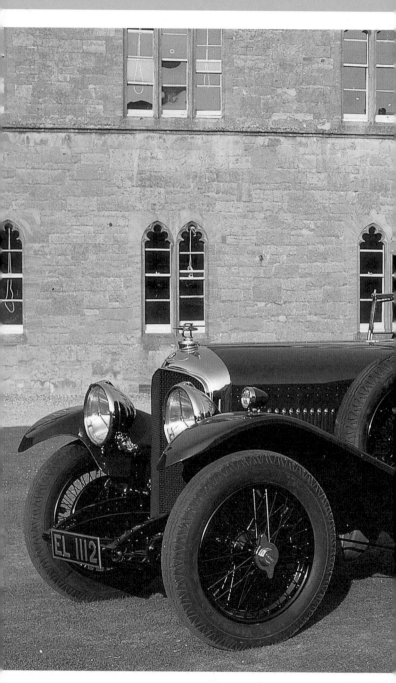

Above: A 4 1/2-litre Bentley with open four-seater sports car bodywork was the epitome of fast vintage motoring.

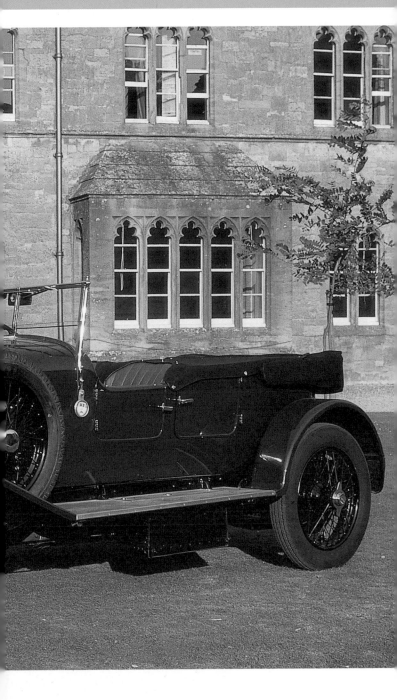

► No wonder, then, that Bentley chose this model as its 'works' car for the 24 hour race at Le Mans, which it won, most convincingly, in 1928. Interestingly, in 1930 the racing driver Sir Henry Birkin inspired the private-enterprise birth of the supercharged 4½-litre, though 'W.O.' would have little to do it, and assembly of road cars was always carried out elsewhere.

Everything about the 4½-litre was big, and impressive. There was, of course, the lofty radiator, the proud stance of the bodywork (many of these cars had an open-top Vanden Plas four-seater tourer style), the high gearing, the sheer delicious feel, and weight, of the controls. The 4½, in fact, could not have been more different from other small sporty cars of that period, for it felt, looked, and was immensely solid, and reassuring to drive.

By later standards, of course, the brakes were always a limiting factor, and it helped to have experience when handling the gearchange (the lever of which was placed on the right of the seat, close to driver's right leg), but this was a machine with a massive presence, capable of long journeys, fast journeys and – above all – pleasing journeys.

Because this was a handbuilt car with unique engineering it was, of course, an expensive car, which limited sales to wealthy customers. In five years, just 662 cars were built, along with 55 of the 'Blower' variety.

Below: The 4$^1/_2$-litre Bentley engine was a sturdy long-stroke design, with single overhead camshaft valve gear, and lots of low-speed torque.

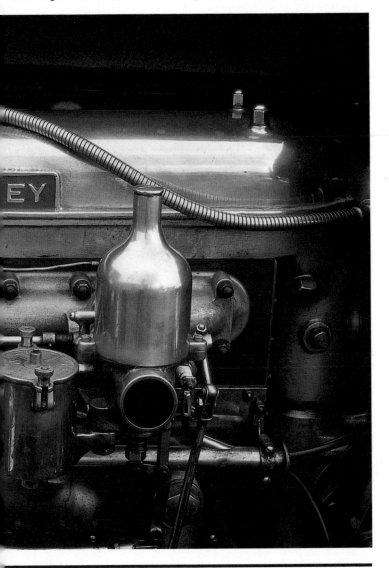

Bentley 6½-litre 'Speed Six'

Speed Six built from 1928 to 1930
Built by: Bentley Motors Ltd., Britain.
Engine: Six cylinders, in line, in light-alloy block with non-detachable cylinder head. Bore and stroke 100mm by 140mm, 6,597cc (3.94in × 5.51in, 402.5cu.in). Four valves per cylinder, operated by bifurcated rocker (inlet valves) or individual rockers (exhaust side) from single overhead camshaft. Three-throw coupling-rod drive and gear from nose of crankshaft. Twin plugs, one each side of cylinder head, under the manifolding; ignition by twin magnetos (coil and magneto supply in tandem later fitted). Twin horizontal SU carburettors. Compression ratio 5.3:1. Maximum power 180bhp at 3,500rpm with 'single port' block.
Transmission: Single shaft-operated dry-plate clutch. Four-speed unsynchronised gearbox, separately mounted, with right-hand gearchange. Open Hardy Spicer propeller shaft to spiral-bevel rear axle, of optional 3.54 or 3.85:1 ratio. Either 'C' Type or straight-cut gear 'D' Type gearboxes fitted.
Chassis: Channel-section side members in steel, liberally cross braced, conventionally over-slung at rear. Half-elliptic leaf springs front and rear, with worm-and-sector steering. Cable-operated self-wrapping drum brakes. Outside handbrake, sports car bodies only. Coachwork to choice – saloon, coupé, or open sports.
Dimensions: Wheelbase 11ft 8.5in (357cm), 12ft 8.5in (387cm), or 11ft (335cm) to choice (short wheelbase on Le Mans version only). Front and rear track 4ft 8in (142cm). Overall length 15ft 1in to 16ft 7in (460cm to 505cm) depending on wheelbase length and coachwork. Unladen weight between 4,480lb and 5,040lb (2,031 and 2,286kg).

Below: Built in 1929, this Speed Six had a touring body by Vanden Plas, who used to build Le Mans coachwork for the Bentley factory. This car had four separate doors, and a windscreen for the rear seat passengers, which could still be used with the hood erect.

Above: Ettore Bugatti might have christened the vintage Bentley as the 'fastest Lorry in the World', but this was pure jealousy. Heavy, high-geared, with a rumbling exhaust note, the Speed Six was a superb sports car of its day, with a natural cruising speed of at least 80mph.

▶ **History:** The 'Speed Six' is probably the most famous of all W. O.'s Bentleys. In factory drivers' hands, these cars won twice at Le Mans (in 1929 and 1930) – with Chairman Woolf Barnato in the winning car on each occasion, at Brooklands and in minor races elsewhere. Their domination of sports car racing was so complete that entries from other teams declined sharply.

Bentley's advanced six-cylinder engine, developed from but by no means the same as the original 'four' in design, was conceived in 1924, and the standard 6½-litre Bentley was put on sale at the end of 1925. Originally it had been a 4½-litre 'six', but it was found to be lacking in power and torque.

The 'Speed Six', with a chassis intended for sporting use if necessary, followed in 1928, and was produced until 1930, when it was replaced by the magnificent Bentley 8-litre. In all 545 6½-litre cars were built of which an exclusive 182 were 'Speed Sixes'.

Like others of the period, the car was massively strong and heavy. Even with the 180bhp engine, the Speed Six's normal maximum speed was no more than 92-95mph.

The engine's overhead camshaft drive was complex and unique, with triple eccentric coupling rod operation, thought by 'W. O.' to be more reliable than either chain or gear-drive systems. The cylinder head, as with all such Bentleys, was non-detachable and in unit with the cylinder block.

Built almost regardless of cost (the new car price, depending on coachwork,

Above: 6½-litre Speed Six Bentleys came in most shapes and sizes. This example has rakish two-seater styling and looks lower than in fact it is.

was between £2,300 and £2,500), the engineering was painstakingly thorough. There was a vast petrol tank (up to 43 gallons – 195 litres – on the race cars), and even the electron alloy oil sump held more than five gallons.

Although the car was magnificent in build and in durable performance, the company which made it was always financially insecure. Perhaps Bentley had the worst of bad luck when they chose the depths of the depression to upgrade the car to the very exclusive 8-litre; within a year of this launch the company was in liquidation.

Left: In later life, 6 1/2-Bentleys came in all shapes and sizes, this race-modified car being ready for the start of a VSCC event at Silverstone.

Bentley Hunaudières project car

Bentley Hunaudieres project car, shown in 1999
Built by: Bentley Motors Ltd., Britain.
Engine: VW-manufactured, 16 cylinders, in 72-degree 'W' formation (two narrow angle V8s, opposed at 72-degrees), in aluminium alloy cylinder block. Bore and stroke 89 x 80.3mm, 7,998cc (3.5 x 3.16in, 488cu.in). Two light-alloy cylinder heads. Four valves per cylinder, operation by twin overhead camshafts per cylinder head. VW electronic fuel injection. Maximum power 623bhp at 6,000rpm. Maximum torque 561lb.ft at 4,000rpm.
Transmission: Mid-engine, four-wheel-drive, dry plate diaphragm spring clutch and five-speed automatic transmission, all in unit with engine and final drive assembly. Remote control centre floor gearchange.
Chassis: Lamborghini Diablo-sourced multi-tubular and reinforced steel separate chassis frame, with composite (including carbon fibre and Kevlar) two-sweater closed coupé body shell. Independent front suspension by coil springs, wishbones and anti-roll bar, independent rear susension by coil springs, wishbones and anti-roll bar. Telescopic hydraulic dampers. Rack-and-pinion steering with power assistance. Disc brakes at front and rear, with vacuum servo assistance. 18in bolt-on cast-alloy road wheels, tyre dimensions not revealed.
Dimensions: Wheelbase 8ft 8.3in (265cm), front track 5ft 8.4in (173.8 cm), rear track 5ft 4.8in (164.5cm). Overall length 14ft 6.4in (443cm). Unladen weight: not quoted..

Below: The Hunaudières was a fine project car, built on the bare bones of a Lamborghini chassis, but was never meant for production.

History: To quote the famous North American advertising maxim – here was a classic case of 'Don't sell the sausage, sell the sizzle'. Bentley's Hunaudieres project car of 1999 was never meant to go on sale, but was meant to raise the marque's image in the market place. VW, who had recently taken control of Bentley, wanted the world to realise that a change of image was imminent – and they achieved this objective.

The Hunaudiéres (the name was lifted from a section of the Le Mans race track, where vintage Bentleys had starred so often) was no more than a statement of ability, not intent – a statement which was meant to prove that Bentley stylists and designers could, and would, produce different cars from the sumptuous saloons and limousines for which recent Bentleys had been noted.

The one-off super-coupé which starred at the Geneva Motor Show in March 1999 was a big, impressive, and smooth mid-engined two-seater which, if it had gone into production, would have broken almost every road car record. Not only in power – which came from a 620bhp 8.0-litre/W16 engine – but in all other details, it would have set new standards.

Because Bentley had become part of the VW-Audi empire, this car had been built up on the four-wheel-drive structure of a Lamborghini Diablo VT (Audi controlled that company), but the engine was the ultimate statement of the 'building block' approach which would see the same basic layout of narrow angle vee-6s related to W8s, and even to W12s before the end of the century.

The style, though, was all to Bentley's credit. Small by existing Bentley standards, but large as sporting coupés go, it sat on the Diablo VT's chassis, in a rounded, sexy and amazingly up-market manner, complete with British Racing Green bodywork, the famous Bentley badge on the nose, and a mesh grille ▶

which, once again, harked back to Bentleys of long ago.

Yet it was not for sale, nor ever intended to be so. At a stroke, however, made the world's public sit up and think. Maybe, just maybe, there would be true sports car in Bentley's future?

Above: We can all dream – this was Bentley's way of showing us that it was quite capable of building a Ferrari-beating Supercar in the late 1990s.

Berkeley

Berkeley sports car, built from 1956 to 1961 (data for B95 model)
Built by: Berkeley Cars Ltd., Britain.
Engine: Royal Enfield manufactured, two cylinders, parallel twin air-cooled motor cycle type, in two-bearing aluminium crankcase, and finned cylinder block. Bore and stroke 70 x 90mm, 692cc (2.75 x 3.54in, 42.2cu.in). Aluminium cylinder head. Two valves per cylinder, opposed to each other in part-spherical combustion chambers, operation by pushrods and rockers from a camshaft in the crankcase. One horizontal Amal carburettor. Maximum power 40bhp at 5,500rpm. Maximum torque 43lb.ft at 4,000rpm. [Berkeleys were also built with other two-cyl and three-cyl air-cooled engines, from 15bhp to 45bhp.]
Transmission: Front-engine, front-wheel-drive, multi-plate clutch and four-speed manual gearbox with dog-type engagement and final drive by chain. Remote control centre gearchange.
Chassis: Separate platform chassis frame, of aluminium structural members and bonded glass-fibre, topped by two-seater open top sports car body style in glass-fibre. Removable bubble-top and fastback hardtop body types also available. Independent front suspension by coil springs and wishbones, independent rear suspension by coil springs and swing axles. Hydraulic telescopic dampers. Worm and nut steering. Drum brakes at front and rear. 12in bolt-on steel disc wheels, with 5.20-12in tyres.
Dimensions: Wheelbase 5ft 10in (178cm), front track 3ft 6.5in (107.9cm), rear track 3ft 6in (106.7cm). Overall length 10ft 5.5in (319cm). Unladen weight 887lb (402kg).
History: This strange little car was conceived in Britain by a company which had previously made trailer caravans. Laurie Bond, a designer who had already evolved the Bond three-wheeler economy cars, was invited to produce a sport

Above: All Berkeleys had air-cooled motorcycle engines, this unit being a three-cylinder Excelsior power unit.

car: his brief was that its chassis should use known and existing caravan structural techniques, it should use cheap and cheerful motorcycle engines, and that it should be very low-priced.

Bond's design, therefore, used a platform chassis in a mixture of aluminium members and stiffening, along with glass-fibre, and that an appealing little glass-fibre body shell should be moulded to that. The secret, though, was that air-cooled motorcycle engines and their related gearboxes were to be fitted up front, ahead of the line of the line of the front wheels, powering the final drive of those front wheels by chain.

The trim and general detailing of these cars is best described as cheap-and-cheerful, but they were appealing. Early types, with tiny twin-cylinder two-stroke 322cc Anzani engines, only had 15bhp, and struggled to reach 60mph, but a 30bhp/492cc two-stroke Excelsior was better (nearly 80mph was possible), even if they had difficult in competing against Austin-Healey's new Sprite.

The four-stroke Royal Enfield engined B95 and B105 engines, complete with a square-grilled nose and exposed headlamps, were altogether more sporty, for they were at least 12in/30cm shorter and 500lb/227kg lighter than the Sprite. Even so, no-one ever seemed to achieve the 100mph that the company promised for the 50bhp/B105 model. Although the front-wheel-drive handling was secure, and they were relatively brisk, these cars were really to crudely detailed, and unrefined, to survive. The last of about 2,000 such cars were built in 1961.

Left: All Berkeley sports cars had front-wheel-drive, and a derivative of this neat little two-seater body style. The fastest of all had 700cc engines.

BMW 328

BMW 328 and Frazer Nash-BMW (data applies to both cars)

Built by: Bayerische Motoren Werke AG., Germany.

Engine: Six cylinders, in line, in four-bearing cast-iron block. Bore and stroke 66mm by 96mm, 1,971cc (2.60in × 3.78in, 120.3cu.in). Two overhead valves per cylinder, with inclined operation in part-spherical combustion chambers. Unique pushrod valve operation: inlet valve directly operated by pushrod and rocker, exhaust valve by pushrod, pivot, cross pushrod and rocker. Single side mounted camshaft. Aluminium cylinder head with downdraught siamesed inlet ports and three Solex carburettors. Maximum power 80bhp (DIN) at 4,500rpm.

Transmission: Single-dry-plate clutch and four-speed manual gearbox (synchromesh on top and third gears), with direct control gearchange. Open propeller shaft to spiral-bevel 'live' rear axle.

Chassis: Separate frame, of ladder-type construction, main members of steel tubing, and cross members of box or tubular sections, independent front suspension by transverse leaf spring and lower wishbones. Rear suspension by half-elliptic leaf springs. Hydraulic dampers all round. Rack-and-pinion steering. Four-wheel hydraulically operated drum brakes. 16in pressed-steel disc brakes with four-pin drive and centre-lock fixings. 5.50 × 16in tyres. Two-seat sports bodywork of alloy panelling on ash frame in nearly every case. Cabriolet version with fold-down hood, also available.

Dimensions: Wheelbase 7ft 10.5in (240cm), track (front) 3ft 9.4in (115cm), track (rear) 4ft (122cm). Overall length 12ft 9.5in (390cm). Unladen weight (sports body) 1,700lb (771kg).

History: The BMW 328 was the final flowering of a series of designs initiated in 1933. Kernel of the family of cars was a splendidly detailed six-cylinder engine (which was later fitted with unusual valve gear), a rigid tubular chassis, quite unlike most European designs of the 1930s, and independent front suspension, at a time when this was considered expensive and unpredictable. The engine first appeared as a 1¼-litre unit

Above: Three of these beautiful, special-bodied 328s were prepared for the Mille Miglia race of 1940, taking third, fifth and sixth places.

Below left: The original BMW 328 started a revolution in sports car style and engineering, which would surely have progressed further if war had not intervened. The engine had a clever form of valve gear invented by Dr. Fiedler, and was later used in post-war Bristol and Frazer Nash cars.

then in the Type 315 and 319 cars in 1½-litre form.

The Type 328 was a sports car pure and simple, designed to be smooth, look smooth, and have impeccable road manners – this, at a time when sports cars were normally harsh, crudely equipped and rather spartan. Body styling included faired-in headlamps and flowing integrated lines, which were all ahead of their time. BMW developments from this car undoubtedly inspired William Lyon's thinking on car shapes for his Jaguars of the 1940s.

The Type 328 was announced in 1936, and was distinguished by its unique cylinder head and valve gear. A part-spherical combustion chamber and good breathing were considered essential, but Dr. Fiedler, the designer, was ordered to stick with one side-mounted camshaft. He solved the restriction brilliantly by inventing the extra cross-pushrod arrangement to operate the inclined exhaust valves, and he arranged for the inlet port to enter the cylinder head from the top of the engine, with the carburettors atop that. The only disadvantage was that the engine, in total, was quite tall. BMW styling, however, could easily accommodate this.

Apart from its striking styling, the car was also equipped with a full undertray to improve aero-dynamics. Original cars had a hidden spare wheel, but most have the familiar part-recessed spare on the tail panel. The British BMW concessionaires AFN Ltd., imported the car as the Frazer Nash-BMW, and proved its worth with a 101 miles in a one-hour run at Brooklands in 1937. The last production cars were built in 1940, before German war production caused all private car building to cease. In all, 461 328s were built and the engine was adopted in post-war years by Bristol for their 400 and 406 models.

BMW 507

507 model, built from 1956 to 1959
Built by: Bayerische Motoren Werke AG., Germany.
Engine: Eight cylinders, in line, in 90-degree vee-formation, in five-bearing lig
alloy block. Bore and stroke 82mm by 75mm, 3,168cc (3.23in × 2.95
193.3cu.in). Two detachable light alloy cylinder heads. Two overhead valves p
cylinder, operated by pushrods and rockers from single camshaft mounted
centre of cylinder block 'vee'. Two down-draught twin-choke Solex carburetto
Maximum power 150bhp (net) at 4,800rpm. Maximum torque 127lb.ft
2,500rpm.
Transmission: Single-dry-plate clutch and five-speed, synchromesh man
gearbox (without synchromesh on first gear) both in unit with front-mount
engine. Central gearchange. Open propeller shaft to hypoid-bevel 'live' rear ax
with optional limited-slip differential.
Chassis: Separate pressed-steel chassis frame, with box-section side membe
and tubular cross-bracing. Independent front suspension by torsion bars a
wishbones. Rear suspension by torsion bars, radius arms and Panhard r
Telescopic dampers. Pinion-and-sector steering. Four-wheel, hydraulica
operated drum brakes. 16in bolt-on or centre-lock pressed-steel disc whee
6.00 × 16in tyres. Two-seat open sports or hardtop coachwork.
Dimensions: Wheelbase 8ft 1.5in (248cm), track (front) 4ft 8.7in (144cm), tra
(rear) 4ft 8in (142cm). Overall length 14ft 5in (439.4cm). Unladen weight 2,53
(1,147kg).
History: As a logical development of their 501 saloon car series, BMW marr
a shortened version of that chassis with the developed 3.2-litre V8 engi
which had become optional, and clothed the result in an outstandingly attract
two-seater sports car body style. Under the skin, the separate four-spe
gearbox of the saloons had given way to a new five-speed box in unit with t
engine and the rear suspension was both revised and improved. Overall des

Above and below: Perhaps the loveliest of all BMWs – pre-war or post-war – was the 507 of the 1950s. It had a 3.2-litre vee-8 engine, and could reach 140mph.

is attributed to Dr. Fiedler, who takes credit for the pre-war Type 328, and apart from its high price the Type 507 was a worthy successor. Maximum speed was between 135 and 140mph, with acceleration and stability to match. Although the 507 looked ideal for use as a competition car, the factory never entered it in any events, and private owners were too impressed by its looks and its high standard of finish and equipment to abuse it in this way. Two hundred and fifty-three BMW 507s were built.

BMW Z1

BMW Z1 open sports car, built from 1986 to 1990

Built by: BMW AG, Germany.

Engine: Six cylinders, in line, in cast-iron cylinder block. Bore and stroke 84 75mm, 2,494cc (3.31 × 2.95in, 152.2cu.in). Light alloy cylinder head. Two valv per cylinder, in narrow vee, operation by single overhead camshaft, rockers a inverted bucket tappets. Bosch/BMW fuel injection. Maximum power 170b (DIN) at 5,800rpm. Maximum torque 164lb.ft at 4,300rpm.

Transmission: Rear-wheel-drive, single-dry-plate diaphragm spring clutch a five-speed all-synchromesh manual gearbox, all in unit with front-mount engine. Remote-control, central gearchange.

Chassis: Unitary-construction pressed-steel body-chassis unit, in two-dc roadster style, with slide down passenger doors. Independent front suspensi by MacPherson struts, coil springs, lower wishbones, telescopic dampers a anti-roll bar. Independent rear suspension by coil springs, multi-links a wishbones, telescopic dampers and anti-roll bar. Rack-and-pinion steering, w hydraulic power assistance. Four-wheel disc brakes with ABS. Cast alloy 16 wheels, 225/45-16in tyres.

Dimensions: Wheelbase 8ft 0in (243.8cm), front track 4ft 8in (142.2cm), re track 4ft 9in (144.7cm). Overall length 12ft 10.5in (392.4cm). Unladen weig 2,948lb (1,337kg).

History: Why build a one-off testbed if you can build thousands, sell them a profit, and part-pay for the programme? That, it seems, is what BMW thoug when they decided to put the Z1 roadster on the market in 1986. It was no big programme, and in four years only 8,000 such cars would be sold, bu made its point.

Conceived early in the 1980s, the Z1 was a two-seater roadster with uniq and surprising features. Not only did it have a six-cylinder engine (when a mo sporty 'four' might have been expected), but there was a novel type of re suspension, and very novel construction features.

Below: BMW's first mass-market two-seater, the Z1, had passenger doors which, when opened, slid downwards into the sills.

Above: In many ways the Z1 was a styling forerunner of the later Z3, though this was the only BMW to adopt such a cowled-headlamp type of nose.

Starting, first, with the body, where the novelties were clear, BMW styled a neat by unexciting two-seater roadster – unexciting, that is, until one found that the doors did not open in the conventional manner, but retracted downwards, into the capacious sills, actuated by electric motors and toothed belts. The body shell itself was also equipped with an extra composite-fibre sandwich underfloor, which added to the rigidity, but while there was a familiar MacPherson strut suspension up front, this was the very first BMW to be equipped with what the company called its 'Z-axle'. 'Z' for what? – all we needed to know was that there were coil springs and an anti-roll bar, plus a complex system of upper and lower transverse and semi-trailing links to guide the movements of the wheels, and that this gave dramatically better grip, traction and roadholding than any of the semi-trailing cars which had previously come out of Munich.

Power was by the same 2.5-litre/170bhp six-cylinder engine which was already being used in 3-Series and 5-Series saloons, still with only a single overhead camshaft and two valves per cylinder in part-spherical combustion chambers. Backed by the same close-ratio five-speed gearbox also found in those cars, it was a satisfactory, if understated, way to produce a top speed of 136mph.

It was difficult to know quite what BMW intended the Z1 to achieve, for although its model name suggested that it was to be the first of a family of 'Z' cars – which it was – it was never backed up by anything as radical. Not quite as fast as expected, not quite as startlingly styled as it might have been, it was nevertheless a distinctive machine with all the right BMW credentials – the familiar kidney nose, the smooth and near-silent engine, the immaculate build quality, all backed by the huge self-confidence (don't say 'arrogance' please. . .) for which BMW was famous.

It was, above all, an ideal test bed for the new Z-axle, for this layout would soon be applied in other, mass-production, BMWs, proving conclusively that the days of tail-happy cars from Munich were over. The Z1, in other words, did its job. It never generated a huge demand, so when production ended in 1990 BMW concluded that it had all been worth it. The Z3, which followed in the 1990s, was a much more conventional car.

BMW Z3

BMW Z3 family, introduced in 1995 (data for original 1.9-litre)
Built by: BMW AG, USA.

Engine: Four cylinders, in line, in five-main-bearing cast iron cylinder bloc
Bore and stroke 85x 83.5mm, 1,895cc (3.35 x 3.29in, 115.7cu.in). Light all
cylinder head. Four valves per cylinder, in narrow vee angle, operation by buck
tappets from twin overhead camshafts. Bosch fuel injection. Maximum pow
140bhp at 6,000rpm. Maximum torque 133lb.ft at 4,300rpm. [Z3 models al
sold with 1.9-litre 4-cylinder, 2.0, 2.2, 2.5, 2.8, 3.0, and M-Type 3.2-litre s
cylinder engines.]

Transmission: Front engine, rear-wheel-drive, single dry plate diaphrac
spring clutch and five-speed all-synchromesh manual gearbox, all in unit w
engine. Remote control centre floor gearchange.

Chassis: Unitary construction combined steel body/chassis structure, w
steel body shell in two-seater open Roadster or sporting estate coupé sty
Independent front suspension by coil springs, MacPherson struts and anti-r
bar, independent rear suspension by coil springs, semi-trailing arms and anti-r

Below: The curvaceous BMW Z3 was a well-equipped open-top two-seat
which was sold with a wide range of four- and six-cylinder engines.

Above: All Z3s shared this smooth and nicely detailed fascia/instrument panel, which had been laid out with the American market in mind.

bar. Telescopic hydraulic dampers. Rack-and-pinion steering, with power assistance. Disc brakes for all four wheels, with vacuum servo assistance, and ABS as standard. 15in bolt-on cast alloy road wheels, with 205/60-15in tyres.

Dimensions: Wheelbase 8ft 0.3in (244.6cm), front track 4ft 7.5in (141.1cm), rear track 4ft 8.2in (142.7cm). Overall length 14ft 10.5in (402.5cm). Unladen weight 2,567lb (1,164kg).

History: After taking a strategic decision to set up a factory in the USA, BMW opened a plant in South Carolina in 1995. The very first product to stream out of this 'green-field' plant was a two-seater sports car named the Z3. Later, this machine was joined by other models (of which the four-wheel-drive X5 was the most numerous), yet the Z3 was so closely linked with South Carolina that it was always known as the 'American BMW'.

As ever, this ever-expanding German company had been clever in mixing and matching all its assets. Accordingly, although it was never obvious at a casual glance, the Z3 was based on the entire platform and suspension of an existing BMW hatchback, the 3-Series Compact. Although it took years for the strategy to emerge, it was evident that the new car could, and would, use most of the four-cylinder and six-cylinder engines already being used in 3-Series (and some 5-Series) touring cars as well.

The platform of the new Z3, therefore, was a straightforward pressed-steel structure, in which there was MacPherson strut front suspension, and the latest (and, as it turned out, final) derivative of BMW's semi-trailing link independent rear end. This was all hid by a rounded two-seater sports car, whose fold-back soft-top, flamboyant curves, and sumptuously equipped interior all ▶

▶ had a distinctly Transatlantic flavour. This was emphasised by the level of equipment, which included full air conditioning as an option, automatic transmission as an option on all but the least-powerful types, and such costly (but much sought-after) options as suspension traction control, and wider, more flamboyant, alloy road wheels.

In the usual pragmatic manner, BMW took time to build up, flesh out, and enlarge this range – though within five years this process was completed. After starting with the least powerful versions – the USA-specification 1.8-litre only had 116bhp and a single-overhead camshaft engine – the more advanced twin-cam 'fours' were added to the range, silky-smooth twin-cam 'six' units followed, while the most broad-shouldered type of all, the 325bhp M Roadster derivative, followed in 1999.

The original Z3, previewed in 1995, but on sale in 1996, gained enormous publicity by being used by the 'James Bond' character in the latest film, *Goldeneye*, though this was no more than a cameo role which told us nothing about its performance. Sales were confined to the USA at first, and did not follow on in Europe until 1997, but by this time the model was well established.

As one might expect from BMW, and especially of a sports car built in the USA, the Z3 was a rather soft-handling, flexible, and civilised machine – one, in fact, which not everyone seemed to like. In particular, it seems, there were complaints about the high-speed handling, which was compromised by the use

Above: Not only did BMW make the Z3 as an open-top two-seater, but as this coupé, which was really a sports hatchback.

of the Compact's old-fashioned type of rear suspension.

BMW listened politely to all such comments, but did little to re-design the car, for it was selling very well indeed, and soon built up an impressive reliability record. Instead the company concentrated on bringing forward more and more derivatives, so that soon there seemed to be a Z3 for every corner of the market.

Whereas the latest six-cylinder versions, and the facelifted types introduced in 2000 (which had a more broad-hipped rear stance) were always successful, the sporting-hatchback type of 1998, known as the Z3 Coupé, was less so: it might have been even more practical, with a great deal of stowage space behind the seats, but it did not look as neat as the Roadster, and consequently did not sell as well.

Even so, BMW's big gamble, that of producing a new sports car in North America, to suit North Americans, paid off handsomely. The 100,000th Z3 was built before the end of 1997, after which sales settled down to more than 50,000 units a year. Well before the new-generation Z3, forecast to arrive in 2003, could appear, BMW would have sold more than 300,000 original Z3s.

BMW Z8

BMW Z8, introduced in 2000
Built by: BMW AG, Germany
Engine: Eight cylinders, in 90-degree vee, in five-main bearing alloy cylinder block. Bore and stroke 94 x 89mm, 4,941cc (3.70 x 3.50in, 301.6cu.in). Two cast alloy cylinder heads. Four valves per cylinder, in narrow vee location, operation by bucket tappets and twin overhead camshafts per head. Bosch fuel injection. Maximum power 400bhp at 6,600rpm. Maximum torque 368lb.ft at 3,800rpm.
Transmission: Front engine, rear-wheel-drive, single dry plate diaphragm spring clutch and six-speed all-synchromesh manual gearbox, all in unit with engine. Remote control, centre floor gearchange.
Chassis: Aluminium space frame chassis structure, with aluminium body shell in open roadster two-seater style. Independent front suspension by coil springs, MacPherson struts and anti-roll bar, independent rear suspension by coil springs, multi-link location and anti-roll bar. Telescopic hydraulic dampers. Disc front and rear brakes, with vacuum servo assistance, and ABS as standard. 18in bolt-on cast alloy road wheels, with 245/45-18in (front) and 275/40-18in (rear) tyres.

Dimensions: Wheelbase 8ft 2.6in (250.5cm), front track 5ft 1.1in (155.2cm), rear track 5ft 1.8in (157cm). Overall length 14ft 5.2in (440cm). Unladen weight 3,495lb (1,585kg).

History: Occasionally, just occasionally, BMW produced a car which appealed to its designers, rather than to the product planners and accountants who ran this German business. The Z8 was a perfect example. There was no logical reason why it should ever be put on sale – but BMW did so, anyway.

The inspiration behind the Z8, they say, was the 507 of the 1950s, another BMW which evolved due to emotion, and not to logic. In 1993 it was only a chance meeting with an old 507, present at a BMW boss's retirement party, which reminded others of its appeal. In due course, and when spare time and money became available, the idea of designing 'a new 507' took shape.

The first Z8 concept car was shown as a concept car in the late 1990s, when enthusiasts could see not only that there were some visual clues to the old-type 507, but that in performance it would certainly match, and probably beat, the current 8-Series. But it was never meant to be an 8-Series replacement – for that car had been a smooth, closed, coupé, whereas the new Z8 was meant to be a brawny, characterful, open-top two-seater.

More importantly, by BMW standards the Z8 was meant to be a simple car. If ever there could be a BMW equivalent to a Dodge Viper or a Chevrolet Corvette, this was it. Here was a car which BMW expected to be driven hard, so tyre-stripping acceleration, a bellowing character, and no-nonsense equipment and behaviour were all built in as standard.

Although artists could detect a few minor visual similarities to the 507, the Z8's engineering was totally different. Although the drive line itself was familiar – BMW's famous 400bhp 32-valve 4.4-litre V8, and its six-speed transmission had already found a home in the M5 super-saloon – there was an entirely new chassis. This was a sturdy aluminium space frame structure, which pared great chunks of weight out of the all-up weight, though the steel body shell did little more to help that.

Even though it was a big car, heavy, wide and somehow bulky in its character, it looked, and was, a very fast car. If clever electronics had not kicked in to limit the top speed to 'only' 155mph/250kph, it might certainly have gone on to reach 180mph/290kph. It could reach a thundering 100mph from rest in a mere 11 seconds – though it was best never to calculate the fuel consumption, which was rarely better than 18mpg (Imperial).

Like the Z3, which was 'little brother' in some ways, the cockpit had several rather 'retro' touches – there was metal rather than plastic, and no wood, ▶

Left: Although different in every detail, BMW's Z8 took some styling cues from the 1950s-Type 507.

▶ in the fascia display, for instance, but this was still a car which offered all the usual 'toys' for well-off customers. Not only ABS braking, of course, but traction control (which could be switched off if the driver wanted to shred his tyres), and satellite navigation. Sports cars, indeed, had come a long way since the stark niceties of the 1920s.

In spite of the publicity gained by a cameo appearance in a 'James Bond' film (*The World is Not Enough*, where its fate was to be filleted by huge circular saws!), BMW never set out to built a lot of Z8s, for this was always meant to

be a very limited-production machine; BMW had ensured that its chassis was time-consuming to make, and the car's assembly lengthy and complicated. Only ten cars could ever be made in a day – which equated to little more than 2,500 every year – though in the early 2000s the signs were that demand was higher than this.

Below: BMW's Z8 featured a brutal late-1990s style, which hid an advanced aluminium space frame chassis.

Bricklin SV-1

Bricklin SV-1, built from 1974 to 1975
Built by: Bricklin Vehicle Corporation, USA and Canada.
Engine: AMC-manufactured, eight cylinders, in 90-degree vee, in five-main bearing cast iron cylinder block. Bore and stroke 103.63 x 87.38mm, 5,896cc (4.08 x 3.44in, 360cu.in). Two cast iron cylinder heads. Two overhead valves per cylinder, operation by pushrods and rockers from one camshaft in the cylinder block vee. Single downdraught four-choke Motorcraft carburettor. Maximum power 220bhp at 4,400rpm. Maximum torque 315lb.ft at 3,100rpm.
Transmission: Front engine, rear-wheel-drive, single dry plate diaphragm spring clutch and four-speed all-synchromesh manual gearbox, in unit with engine. Remote control, centre floor gearchange. Optional Chrysler three-speed automatic transmission.
Chassis: Combined steel chassis frame and body shell support structure, with box section side members, and main reinforcements, all in unit with body shell made of acrylic sheet/glass-fibre panelling, in two-seater fastback coupé style. Independent front suspension by coil springs, wishbones and anti-roll bar, suspension of beam rear axle by half-elliptic leaf springs. Telescopic hydraulic dampers. Recirculating ball steering, with power assistance. Front disc, rear drum brakes, with vacuum servo assistance. 15in bolt-on cast alloy road wheels, with GR60-15in tyres.
Dimensions: Wheelbase 8ft 0.5in (244cm), front track 4ft 10/3in (148cm), rear track 4ft 9in (144.5cm). Overall length 14ft 10.5in (453.5cm). Unladen weight 3,517lb (1,595kg).
History: Experience tells us that cars with gullwing doors never sell well. The Mercedes-Benz 300SL was too costly, and the DeLorean DMC-12 was not a very good car. Then there was the Bricklin SV-1, which flared briefly in the 1970s, eventually bankrupting its promoter, and doing untold harm to the state

of New Brunswick, Canada.

Malcolm Bricklin was a self-styled USA-born hustler, who seemed to be able to sell anything – he once sold 30,000 'bankrupt stock' Lambretta scooters in 60 days – who decided to build and sell his own-brand car in the 1970s.

Designed for him by Marshall Hobart, the Bricklin SV-1 (SV = Safety Vehicle) was a front-engined/rear-drive machine with a unique chassis, and odd, rather angular, styling. After casting round, Bricklin chose to use American Motors running gear, the result being a typical American sporty car with a big rumbly vee-8 up front, and a choice of manual or automatic transmission.

The solid 'bird-cage' like steel structure (which included a roll-over bar behind the two seats) was to be covered by body panels made of acrylic sheet backed by GRP-reinforced epoxy resin, in what was claimed to be an ultra-safe safety construction. The style was somewhat Corvette-like (the performance was claimed to be at that level too), though it featured lift-up 'gullwing' doors, which everyone agreed were *not* safe in a roll-over accident!

By hyping the new design before it was ready (John DeLorean must have taken lessons in later years ....), Bricklin persuaded the New Brunswick government to back a factory there, and launched a car which was still badly built, and detailed.

Early cars were built in summer 1974, but the car's ability never matched the hype, and with sales dragging slowly, the business went into receivership in September 1975. In spite of attempts to revive and improve it, with Ford V8 power, nothing could done, and only 2,897 such cars were ever completed.

Below: The Bricklin looked neat, if a little gauche by 1970s standards. Like the Mercedes-Benz 300SL, it had lift-up 'gullwing' doors.

Bugatti Type 49

Bugatti Type 49 models, built from 1930 to 1932
Built by: Automobiles E.Bugatti, France.
Engine: Eight cylinders, in line, in cast iron block, with nine-main-bearing light alloy crankcase. Bore and stroke 72 x 100mm, 3,257cc (2.83 x 3.94in 198.7cu.in). Fixed cylinder head. Three overhead valves per cylinder (two inlet and one exhaust), operation by adjustable rockers from single overhead camshaft. Single updraught Schebler carburettor. Maximum power and maximum torque not quoted.
Transmission: Front engine, rear-wheel-drive, with dry plate clutch and four-speed manual gearbox, without synchromesh, in unit with engine. Centre direct-acting, gearchange.
Chassis: Separate steel chassis frame, with channel-section main side members, tubular and fabricated cross-bracings. Forged front axle beam, and front suspension by half-elliptic leaf springs, suspension of beam rear axle by reversed-cantilever quarter-elliptic leaf springs, and torque rod from axle to frame. Friction type dampers. Worm-and-nut steering. Four wheel drum brakes, rod and cable operated. Bolt on cast-alloy road wheels, or centre-lock wire wheels, with 5.25-28in tyres. Wide choice of Bugatti-made open and closed bodywork, aluminium and steel on light skeleton.
Dimensions: Wheelbase 10ft 7in (323cm), front track 4ft 2in (127cm), rear

track 4ft 2in (127cm). Overall length 13ft 9in (419cm). Unladen weight (chassis only) 2,150lb (975kg).

History: Bugatti started with his own definite ideas of what a car should be and spent the 1920s and 1930s merely refining the same idea. A Bugatti, for instance, should never use a six-cylinder engine, nor should it have independent suspension. It should, on the other hand, always retain the same type of 'horseshoe'-style radiator, and be built almost without thought of in-life ease of maintenance.

The Type 49, a much more 'touring' Bugatti than many of its predecessors, was the last of this line, and therefore the most highly developed. It was the amalgam of design experience, and actual evolutionary components, and is really notable as being the very last single-overhead camshaft Bugatti.

The general engine layout was very much the same as in previous models, but in this case the camshaft drive was taken up the centre of the engine, and the crankshaft was built up from two pieces.

The first eight-cylinder Bugattis dated from 1921 and were for motor racing, but the first 'production' eight – the Type 30 – had followed in 1922. The Type 38 replaced it in 1926, and the same basic chassis from that car was then used in the Types 40, 43, 44 and 49 models which followed. The 49's single-cam engine stemmed from the new unit of 2,991cc which had first been seen in the

Type 44, and was related in many ways to the smaller, unsupercharged, versions of the racing 35 family.

Even so, the Type 49 exhibited many splendid examples of the art of producing Bugattis in small quantities, among which the delicately styled coachwork, the magnificent, slab-like, sculptured engine, and the unmistakable blend of mechanical noises were the most obvious. Engine smoothness was noteworthy, partly because the crankshaft ran in no fewer than nine main bearings.

Front and rear suspension were in traditional Bugatti style, with front springs passing through the axle beam in the Bugatti racing car tradition. There was no nonsense with silent gearboxes, nor with a soft ride, neither of which were thought necessary by Ettore Bugatti himself. This was a car in which the suspension layout which had proved itself in 1920s motorsport was therefore standardised once again, and would continue throughout the 1930s. To those who complained, ▶

Left: The Type 49 was so typically Bugatti in so many ways, including the use of the horseshoe shape of radiator, and with beam-axle front suspension.

▶ Bugatti would merely dismiss them as people who did not understand.

The car was capable of more than 80mph without showing signs of temperament, and was also a docile town car too, there being a wide choice of bodywork, which included very popular two-door sporting drop-head coupé types. It was also a pleasure merely to look at the engineering, the general layout of the car, and the detail of the specification, though apparently not a pleasure to contemplate servicing the engine, which could be complex, and was always expensive.

To many, a Bugatti like this was a paradox, neither technically advanced, nor ultra-refined, expensive but not totally exclusive, and built by a man who ruled his empire in Alsace by whim, rather than by logic. But Bugattis were all thought to be works of art, its clientele was totally committed to the French machine's character, and none of the 470-customers seemed to complain!

Below: By some Bugatti standards, the Type 49 was a conventional car, but still a fine late-vintage sporting machine.

Bugatti Type 57

Type 57, 57C, 57S and 75SC (data for Type 57SC)

Built by: Automobiles E. Bugatti, France.

Engine: Eight cylinders, in line, in six-bearing block, with cast-alloy crankcase bolted to it. Bore and stroke 72mm by 100mm, 3,257cc (2.83in × 3.94in, 198.7cu.in). Fixed cylinder head. Two overhead valves per cylinder, opposed to each other at 90 degrees included angle in part-spherical combustion chamber and operated by finger-type rockers from twin overhead camshafts. Single updraught Zenith carburettor. Maximum power about 175bhp at 5,500rpm.

Transmission: Twin-dry-plate clutch and four-speed manual gearbox (without synchromesh) in unit with engine. Direct-acting central gearchange. Open propeller shaft to spiral-bevel 'live' rear axle.

Chassis: Separate steel chassis frame. Pressed channel-section side members, with tubular and fabricated cross bracings. Forged front axle beam, drilled through for lightness. Front suspension by half-elliptic leaf springs. Rear suspension by reversed-cantilever quarter-elliptic leaf springs and torque rod from axle to frame. Worm-and-nut steering. Friction-type dampers. Four-wheel drum brakes, rod and cable operated. Centre-lock wire wheels. 5.50 × 18in tyres (front), 6.00 × 18in (rear). Variety of Bugatti-supplied coachwork, open or closed or from coachbuilders.

Dimensions: Wheelbase 9ft 9.5in (298.5cm), tracks (front and rear) 4ft 5in (135cm). Overall length 13ft 3in (404cm). Unladen weight (chassis only) 2,100lb (952kg).

History: There is little doubt that although the 'Royale' is the most famous of all Bugattis, the Type 57 series is the most popular. And very deservedly so. Introduced in 1934 and running through until the outbreak of war in 1939, in all its forms it sold to the tune of 710 cars. It was designed almost entirely by Jean Bugatti (son of Ettore), and was almost entirely new. Even the twin-cam engine, with bore and stroke of the single-cam Type 49, was quite unlike earlier twin-cam 'eights' (as used in the Type 50s and 51s), because its cams were driven by a train of gears at the tail of the crankshaft and cylinder block. The gearbox had constant-mesh gears, and at first it was even intended to give the front axle

Below and right: One of the most extraordinary of many exotic Bugattis was the Type 57SC Atlantic coupé. Few were made at Molsheim, and only three are now in existence. The supercharged engine produces well over 150bhp, and top speed is at least 110mph.

Above: Bugatti's Type 57 chassis, with its straight-eight twin-cam 3.3-litre engine, was probably the finest Molsheim car of all. The British drop-head coachwork contrasts sharply with the famous Bugatti radiator. The car had a very simple chassis, hard sprung.

▶ a measure of independence between its wheels, although Ettore Bugatti himself forbade that.

There were several variations. The original Type 58 was in production until 1936, and was followed in 1937 by the Series 2 cars with engine improvements including rubber mountings. The Series 3 cars arrived at the end of 1938 with hydraulic brakes and telescopic dampers as the major changes.

The Type 57S ('S' for Sport) was announced in 1935, had a tuned engine with dry-sump lubrication, and a modified chassis frame, lowered to allow sleeker bodywork to be offered. The 57C version had a supercharged engine producing at least 200bhp, and the combination of this engine and the 57S chassis gave rise to the 57SC the peak (in most people's opinions) of Bugatti's excellence. Cars with this engine and sports or coupé bodywork could beat 100mph by a wide margin – a good one might touch more than 120mph. Both cars were withdrawn in 1939 as they were becoming too expensive to

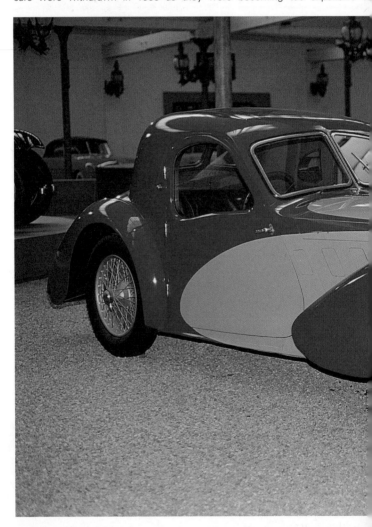

manufacture, although the 57 and 57C continued to sell well.

Perhaps more sensational even than the chassis was the type and nature of coachwork fitted, some Bugatti-made, and some by outside specialists. The Atlantic coupé, a true fast-back car with pronounced dorsal fin, was the most bizarre of all, and was both rare and effective. The chassis was long enough for four-door saloons to be built (almost impossible on other Bugattis) which makes the 57 chassis very versatile indeed. It was the last of all production cars from Molsheim, as production never got under way again after the war.

Below: Artists would normally argue that a vertical radiator clashed with the swooping lines of such cars - but in the case of a Corsica-bodied Bugatti Type 57 there were no such complaints. Two seats and a 110mph top speed - bliss by any standards in the late 1930s.

Caterham (Lotus) Seven

Originally Lotus Seven Series 3, from 1973 Caterham Super Seven, introduced in 1968 (data for 1980/1990s Caterham Super Seven)

Built by: Caterham Car Sales Ltd., Britain.

Engine: Large variety of four-cylinder proprietary power units – Ford, Vauxhall, Rover and others, 1,300cc – 2,000cc (79.4 cu.in to 122 cu.in). Power outputs ranging from 72bhp (DIN) to 175bhp.

Transmission: Rear-wheel-drive, single-dry-plate diaphragm spring clutch and four-speed/five-speed or six-speed all-synchromesh manual gearbox (depending on engine employed), all in unit with front-mounted engine. Remote-control, central gearchange.

Chassis: Separate multi-tubular chassis frame, with light-alloy two-seater body shell. Independent front suspension by coil springs, wishbones, telescopic dampers, anti-roll bar. De Dion rear suspension by coil springs, radius arms, transverse stabiliser, telescopic dampers. Rack-and-pinion steering. Front disc brakes, rear drum (or disc, depending on the engine specification) brakes. Pressed steel or cast alloy road wheels, 13, 14, 15 or 16in, tyres according to wheels and engine specification.

Dimensions: Wheelbase 7ft 4.6in (225cm), front track 4ft 5.9in (137cm), rear track 4ft 4in (132cm). Overall length 11ft 1.0in (338cm). Unladen weight depending on engine and specification 1,142 – 1,383lb (518 – 627kg).

History: Colin Chapman began his motor industry career in the 1940s by buying and selling used cars, operating on the fringe of London's notorious Warren Street market place. From there he progressed to building Austin Seven-based specials, which he personally drove in sporting trials and in sports car racing. Early in the 1950s (but only as a part-time occupation) he started marketing the very first Lotus 'production' car, the Lotus 6, which had a multi-tube chassis frame, and which was sold in kit form so as not to attract British purchase tax. In 1957, with Lotus's original reputation established in sports car racing, and with a more advanced multi-purpose two-seater sports car in mind, he replaced the Lotus Six by a more advanced (but still stark) two-seater, the Lotus Seven.

Then, and later, the Seven was everything that most contemporary sports cars from larger makers were not. Because of its complex but efficient multi-tube chassis frame, it was very light. Like every Lotus, it had good roadholding and (depending on the engine chosen) it could be very rapid indeed. Because it was sold in kit form, with very few creature comforts, fixtures or fittings, it was also very cheap to buy. Within the limits of the mass-production (bought-in) items which had to be fitted to the front suspension, and the use of a proprietary back axle beam, it also rode and handled very well indeed. Those with experience suggested that it was the nearest thing to a motorcycle on four wheels that could be imagined.

Although a Seven could be, and mostly was, used on the public road, its real stamping ground was on the race track, where it could usually dominate its engine size class because of its light weight and splendid roadholding. There were even cases where the Seven was banned from certain championships, which it would otherwise have dominated.

The original Seven was a commercial success, so Lotus introduced the Seven Series 2 in 1960, this having a modified (and stiffer) chassis frame, modified bodywork and many other details, while there were more complex rear-axle location methods. Not only that, but a number of Standard and Triumph 'building blocks' were now used in the suspension, along with a Triumph Herald steering rack. Modern Ford overhead-valve engines were also used.

Then, from 1968, the Series 3 Seven appeared, this forming the

Above: Each and every Lotus/Caterham Seven shared the same basic style, complete with starkly-trimmed cockpit, and long flowing front wings, but a multitude of different engines was available, some as powerful as 175bhp.

template of what would eventually become the Caterham Super Seven, and used a Ford rear axle. Blended into the mixture as before was a series of larger and more powerful Ford overhead-valve engines, these being the first sevens which could regularly reach, and exceed, 100mph. It wasn't long, too, before Lotus's own twin-cam engine, as used in Elans and Ford Escort twin-cams of the period, became an option. The Series 3 was the definitive Seven, for it had front disc brakes as standard, better (though still minimalist) equipment, and a large, ever-growing, list of optional extras. Before long Lotus was supplying five cars every week.

From 1970 Lotus then produced the Series 4, which was different in many ways, for it had a glassfibre instead of an aluminium body shell, and was more obviously 'styled' than before. Because of this, however, additional customers began to shy away. It was not long before Lotus (or, in particular, Colin Chapman) began to lose interest in the car – the streamlined sports-racers and the sleek little Elans and Elan Plus Twos were so much more exciting and, it seemed, easier to sell – but before the company could bring itself to discontinue the range, a saviour turned up.

Lotus dealers Caterham Cars, and their boss Graham Nearn, were so enthused about the Seven that they took over all the rights – marketing, development *and* production – and set about reviving the range. From 1973, Nearn took responsibility for the entire operation, speedily dropping the unloved Series 4, and reintroducing the Series 3, with a new name – Caterham Super Seven. Such a car, and its descendants, then remained in production, selling more and ever more readily, for the rest of the century.

By 2000 the Seven had taken on the mantle of a more advanced 'Morgan', for the pedigree had been on the market for 43 years, the visual link between 1957 and 21st century types was obvious, and there was ▶

▶ absolutely no sign of demand drying up. Along the way, assembly had be
moved, first from Hethel (Norfolk) to Caterham, south of London, a
eventually to Dartford in Kent, and almost every component had either be
improved, changed, or superseded by something new. The style, thoug
was (and probably always will be) recognisably the same.

As a Caterham, the Seven gradually, but persistently, became mc
sophisticated, took on more engine options, and (whisper it quietly) becar
more practical. It was a lengthy, gradual, but seemingly logical busine
with each change and improvement following on from the last.

Although four-cylinder in-line engines were always used (there being no space for other configurations to be employed in that narrow engine bay), by the 1990s the Ford engine monopoly had been lost, for Caterham not only fitted many cars with 16-valve twin-cam Vauxhall units (of the type found in Astra GT/E types), but also the light and advanced Rover K-Series engine (as

Below: This particular Seven was built in 1983, the style having been unchanged for more than 20 years - and it would still be unchanged in the 2000s.

▶ used in the hottest 200s and 400s, and of course in the MG MGF sports c
These were always matched with appropriate four-, five- or (latte
even six-speed transmissions, often with special clusters, or comple
assemblies like those from companies such as Hewland, and
performance of 175bhp/six-speed examples can be imagined.
In the 1980s, ways were found of re-packaging the chassis tubes around
cockpit (there were no passenger doors, of course) to allow the seats
move back and provide more leg space, while a De Dion rear suspens
was made available from 1984. Although the car was eventually put throu

Above: All Caterham Sevens evolved from this earlier type of Lotus Seven, which went on sale in the late 1950s.

he toughest of all tests – the German TUV tests – it was never necessary o change it fundamentally, which explains why production was higher than ver in the 1990s, and why the same style, the same vision – cramping soft op, and the same lack of doors persisted throughout.

A 1960s icon, and a 1970s marketing phenomenon, the Caterham Seven ad become an important sports car symbol by the end of the century.

Chevrolet Corvette

Corvettes, built from 1953 to date (data for 1963 Stingray)
Built by: Chevrolet Motor Co., United States.
Four engines – 250, 300, 340 and 360bhp versions – available for 1963. T
following is typical of the 360hp tune.
Engine: Eight cylinders, in 90-degree vee-formation, in five-bearing cast-in
block/crankcase. Bore and stroke 101.6mm by 83.5mm, 5,363cc (4.0in × 3.25
327cu.in). Two detachable cast-iron cylinder heads. Two overhead valves p
cylinder, operated by pushrods and rockers from single camshaft mounted
centre of cylinder block 'vee'. Rochester fuel injection. Maximum power 360b
(gross) at 6,000rpm. Maximum torque 352lb.ft at 4,200rpm.
Transmission: Single-dry-plate clutch and four-speed, synchromesh man
gearbox, both in unit with front-mounted engine. Remote-control cent
gearchange. Open propeller shaft to hypoid-bevel final-drive unit with limite
slip differential. Exposed fixed-length drive shafts to rear wheels. Optio
torque converter and three-speed Chevrolet automatic transmission.
Chassis: Separate pressed-steel chassis frame with box-section side memb
and boxed cross bracing. Independent front suspension by coil sprin
wishbones and anti-roll bar. Independent rear suspension by transverse le
spring. Lower wishbones and fixed length drive shafts. Telescopic dampe
Recirculating-ball steering. Four-wheel, hydraulically operated drum brakes, w
vacuum-servo assistance. 15in centre-lock cast-alloy disc wheels. 7.10/7
15in tyres. Open or closed glassfibre bodywork.
Dimensions: Wheelbase 8ft 2in (249cm), track (front) 4ft 8.3in (143cm), tra
(rear) 4ft 9in (145cm). Overall length 14ft 7.3in (445cm). Unladen weight 3,25
(1,474kg).

Above: The original Corvette style of 1953 was simple, effective, and distinctive. Note – no bumpers, and only two headlamps.

Below: First-generation Corvettes were open-top two-seaters, with a wrap-around screen and a glass-fibre body style. They soon became America's favourite.

▶ **History:** Chevrolet's interest in two-seater sports car motoring in modern times dates from 1951, when styling chief Harley Earl was beginning to think about such machines; the first mock-up of a new two-seater car to be called 'Corvette' was completed in 1952. General Motors rushed it into production at the beginning of 1953 and it became a cult-car, North America's only domestic two-seater sports car, except for the less rorty Thunderbirds of the mid 1950s, ever since. In 1953, apart from its short wheelbase and generally sporting looks, its only technical innovation was the glassfibre body-shell – used mainly to save time in tooling between the decision to go ahead and first deliveries. Since 1953, however, there have been four basic styles of Corvettes – including the first bulbous machines of 1953 to 1962, the Stingray machines of 1962 to 1967, and the even-more Europeanised cars of 1967 to 1984. There have been persistent rumours of a new mid-engined Corvette to replace the last of the classic front-engined cars, but this has not yet progressed beyond the status of a motor show 'special' as far as the public is concerned.

The first Corvettes had in-line six-cylinder 'Blue Flame' engines, but the first V8 engine option arrived in 1955. This was speedily followed by fuel injection in 1957, four-speed transmission and limited-slip differential and yet other engine tunes – all optional. The Stingray had a dramatically shaped fastback option, with all-independent suspension (the rear certainly inspired both by the Arkus-Duntov racing 'specials' *and* the Jaguar E-type suspension); four-wheel disc brakes were available from 1965. Bigger and better engines culminated in the 7-litre unit of 1966 (in later years the engines were enlarged and softened at the same time to look after exhaust-emission limitations). Although the latest cars have probably been the most popular, it was the Stingrays which gained most plaudits, and nearly 118,000 cars were built in its production run, rather less than half of these being the coupés. In its most powerful guise, the maximum speed was way over 150mph. Sales were rock solid throughout the 1970s, the

Above: The Stingray, launched in 1963, was the first Corvette to offer a choice between open-top roadster or fastback coupé.

pedigree then being re-defined with a new generation car in 1984. American buyers, it seemed, would always want to buy the glassfibre-bodied two seater Corvette, whose 50th anniversary was approaching in 2003.

Left: The new-generation Chevrolet Corvette Stingray arrived in 1962, complete with 'flatfish' front-end style, and pop-up headlamps. This was the first Corvette to use independent rear suspension.

Chevrolet Corvette

Third-generation Chevrolet Corvette, built from 1983 to 1996 (data for ZR1 of 1990)

Built by: Chevrolet Division of General Motors, USA.

Engine: Eight cylinders, in 90-degree vee, in five-main-bearing light alloy cylinder block. Bore and stroke 99 x 93mm, 5,727cc (3.90 x 3.66in, 350cu.in). Two light-alloy cylinder heads. Four valves per cylinder, in narrow-angle opposed vee, operation by inverted bucket tappets and twin overhead camshafts per cylinder head. GM electronic fuel injection. Maximum power 375bhp at 5,800rpm. Maximum torque 370lb.ft at 4,800rpm. [Corvette also sold with long-lasting overhead-valve 5.7-litre V8 engines, from 205bhp (original 1984) to 305bhp (from 1992), to 334bhp (1996), all with choice of five-speed manual or GM automatic transmission, and with Targa Roadster body style.]

Transmission: Front engine, rear-wheel-drive, single dry plate diaphragm spring clutch and six-speed all-synchromesh manual gearbox, all in unit with engine. Remote control, centre floor gearchange.

Chassis: Separate pressed steel chassis frame, with aluminium sub-frame for engine/transmission assemblies, topped by two-seater body shell in glass-fibre composite, Targa-type coupér. Independent front suspension by plastic transverse leaf spring, wishbones, and anti-roll bar, independent rear suspension by transverse plastic leaf spring, wishbones and anti-roll bar. Adjustable telescopic hydraulic dampers. Rack-and-pinion steering with power assistance. Disc brakes at front and rear, with power assistance, and ABS as standard equipment. 17in bolt-on cast-alloy wheels, with 275/40-17in (front) and 315/35-17in (rear) tyres.

Dimensions: Wheelbase 8ft 0.2in (244.3cm), front track 5ft 0in (152.4cm), rear track 5ft 2.0in (157.5cm). Overall length 14ft 10.5in (453.4cm). Unladen weight 3,519lb (1,596kg).

History: By the opening of the 1980s, the existing Corvette was seen as a disappointment, no longer fast enough, stylish enough, or capable enough to match its imported opposition. GM therefore started again, not only by producing a brand new and very capable chassis, but with an ultra-smooth two-seater body style, whose coupé had a lift-off Targa-style panel above the occupants.

It was this style, which was subject to regular updates both in power and in equipment, which took the Corvette safely forward into the mid-1990s. In its early years, it was selling at the rate of 40,000 cars a year, though this figure gradually fell away in the 1990s.

Although the new car was nearly nine inches shorter than the model it replaced, and had a two-inch shorter wheelbase, and was up to 250lb/113kg lighter than before, it was wider, lower, had a more roomy passenger compartment, and looked bang up to date. Here was a new Corvette which did not merely look bulbous and overdecorated, for it had a long, wide, and graceful style, with a sharply-detailed nose, a no-compromise two-seater cabin, and the option of the Targa-style coupé body, or one which could be run as a Roadster, with the soft-top folded away. As ever – and this was traditional with the Corvette – the body shell was made from glass-fibre, with assembly taking place at St Louis, Missouri.

By tradition the Corvette had been built with the same type of 'small block' ('small', that is, by North American standards) V8 engine since 1956 and for the new model, sure enough, an up-dated 5.7-litre was standardised. To show, too, how committed it was to providing genuine sports car motoring, Chevrolet also provided the new model with manual transmission – whereas the last of the old type had had only automatic transmission.

Until the ZR1 variety arrived in 1990, all Corvettes of this generation were built with the familiar, long-established, 350CID pushrod V8. Initially it was rated

Above: In 1984 the new-generation Corvette had remarkably smooth lines: with repeated up-grades, this successful model would be produced until 1996.

▶ at 205bhp, though that power would be pushed up over the years, so that by the 1990s even in the most basic Corvette the same basic push-rod unit would turn out a stunning 305bhp.

This radically different type of Corvette also used a brand-new welded skeletal steel chassis frame, which GM liked to call a 'perimeter frame-birdcage' structure, while as an integral part of this the front-mounted engine/transmission combination was rigidly attached to the differential by an aluminium 'backbone'. This made the whole car feel more rigid, more all-of-a-piece than ever before, and the pundits loved it.

They loved it even more in 1990 when the very special Corvette ZR-1 was launched, this car having a special alloy Lotus-designed vee 8 engine in which there were twin-cam cylinder heads and four-valves per cylinder. Even with all its settings damped down for it to meet the latest exhaust emission and engine noise regulations, this was a 375bhp unit. Along with a new six-speed manual transmission, this two-seater coupé (a Roadster version was never available) could reach 175mph, making it the fastest series-production Corvette of all time.

Although the ZR-1 quite dwarfed the performance of the pushrod-engined Corvette – with 375bhp against the 245bhp which was the rating at that time, it could hardly fail –but as it was at once much more expensive to buy, and more tricky to maintain, sales were always limited. American buyers, it seemed, still preferred their performance to be cheap and cheerful, so that Joe's Lube bay in Smallville, Mid-West could look after it without having to open the Manual.

Once the pushrod Corvette engine had reach 305bhp, the writing was on the wall for the ZR-1, which was therefore dropped in 1995: the entire range was replaced by yet another family of Corvettes in the winter of 1996/1997.

Below: By North American standards the two-seater Corvette was always a small motor car, though always impressive and always very fast. ZR1 types had 375bhp V8 engines.

Above: Corvettes have always been two-seaters, and this 1980s-1990s generation was always available for a coupé or convertible style.

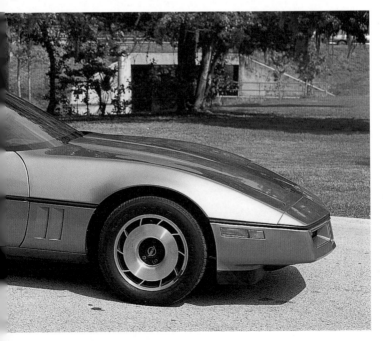

Daimler SP250 ('Dart')

Daimler SP250 sports car, built from 1959 to 1964
Built by: Daimler Co. (Jaguar Cars from 1960), Britain.
Engine: Eight cylinders, in 90-degree vee formation, in five-main-bearing cast iron cylinder block. Bore and stroke 76.2 x 69.85mm, 2,548cc (3.00 x 2.75in, 155.5cu.in). Aluminium cylinder heads. Two overhead valves per cylinder, operation by pushrods and rockers from a camshaft in the vee of the cylinder block. Two semi-downdraught SU carburettors. Maximum power 140bhp at 5,800rpm. Maximum torque 155lb.ft at 3,600rpm.
Transmission: Rear-wheel-drive, single-dry-plate clutch and four-speed manual gearbox, no synchromesh on first gear, all in unit with engine. Remote-control central-gearchange. Optional three-speed automatic transmission.
Chassis: Separate steel chassis frame, with box-section side members, channel and tubular cross-bracings. Independent front suspension by coil springs and wishbones. Rear suspension of beam axle by semi-elliptic leaf springs. Telescopic front dampers, lever arm hydraulic rear dampers. Cam and lever steering. Disc brakes at front and rear. 15in wheels, steel disc or centre-lock wires. 5.90-15in tyres. Separate glass-fibre body shell, 2+2-seater, as open Roadster, or with optional removable hardtop.
Dimensions: Wheelbase 7ft 8in (233 cm), front track 4ft 2in (127cm), rear track 4ft 0in (122cm). Overall length 13ft 4.5in (408cm). Unladen weight 2,220lb (1,007kg).
History: Daimler's short-lived SP250 two-seater sports car represented a complete change in design policy for the long-established Coventry concern. Before this, their only sporting connections had been through special roadster, drop-head coupé, and high-performance saloon derivatives of normal touring cars, mostly built rather heavily, and at a high price. The typical Daimler, up to this time, had been a limousine used by the aristocracy, or even for Royal duties.

The decision to build a two-seater sports car came about after a cataclysmic change of management, and because the new managing director, Edward Turner, was a brilliant designer of motorcycle engines.

The new car, which Daimler wanted to call the 'Dart' until Dodge

128

Above: Much of the Daimler SP250's engineering was inspired by the Triumph TR3A. This was the 'traditional-British' type of instrument panel.

Left: The Daimler SP250 was unmistakable from any angle. Fins at the rear, and twin exhaust pipes, were easy recognition points.

complained that it held the trade mark rights to that name, had a chassis and suspension layout which was unashamedly and admittedly copied from that of the Triumph TR3A (both cars were built in Coventry, England), as was the gearbox.

The engine, however, was a 90-degree vee-8 of 2,548cc, whose valve gear owed much to Turner's previous experience with Triumph motorcycle units, and was soon joined at Daimler by a similar but altogether larger 4.5-litre V8 which ▶

▶ would find a home in the Daimler Majestic Major saloons and limousines of the 1960s.

Production was always likely to be limited, and though Daimler could buy in chassis frames from suppliers, and could machine its own engines and transmissions, it could not afford to produce an all-metal body shell. It was therefore decided to use glass-fibre construction (Daimler would build their own shells- they already had experience in their bus and truck division): the style was distinctly controversial – in fact the prototypes seemed to have smoother and more acceptable shapes than the production cars which followed.

The new car, still badged 'Dart', was announced in the spring of 1959, but assembly of SP250s did not begin until late 1959. It was immediately apparent that the body shell lacked stiffness, and that build quality was lacking, so a series of improvements were later rushed through. ''B'' and 'C' specification improvement packages were aimed at correcting problems, which included a tendency for the doors to fly open on original cars, when they were being driven around corners on undulating or unmade surfaces.

Even so, the engine was a great success, very powerful, smooth and economical, so the SP250 soon made a reputation as a fine performer, adequately filling a market gap between the Triumph TR3A and the Jaguar XK150/E-Type sectors. Like the TR3A with which more drivers were familiar,

the ride was hard and basic, almost in the vintage style in the way the wheels tended to hop about, but the engine refinement was never in doubt, nor was the 121mph top speed. At this time, too, the SP250 was one of the few sports cars to have the option of automatic transmission.

If Daimler had continued under BSA ownership, the SP250 might have had a long-term future (a replacement body style was already being assessed in the early 1960s), but when Sir William Lyons's Jaguar concern took over the marque in 1960, its future was always in doubt. Jaguar eventually killed it off, as not being refined enough, or well enough built according to its own standards. Jaguar was, in any case, too committed to the E-Type to consider persevering with any other two-seater.

Although the engine soon found a home in Jaguar's own Mk II saloon body shell, to give birth to the Daimler V8-250 saloon, which enjoyed a successful career throughout the 1960s, company policy decisions soon brought an end to sports car production at Daimler. After 2,650 of these individualistic two-seaters had been produced, assembly ended in 1964.

Below: The SP250's body was made from glass-fibre mouldings. The low-mounted grille featured a wide-angle 'V' to emphasise the use of a V8 engine.

Datsun 240Z

Datsun 240Z, 260Z and 280Z models, built from 1969 to 1978 (data for 240Z)
Built by: Nissan Motor Co. Ltd., Japan.
Engine: Six cylinders, in line, in seven-bearing cast-iron block. Bore and stroke
83mm by 73.7mm, 2,393cc (3.27in × 2.90in, 146cu.in). Cast-iron cylinder head
Two overhead valves per cylinder, operated by single overhead camshaft. Twin
side-draught constant-vacuum SU carburettors. Maximum power 151bhp
(gross) at 5,600rpm. Maximum torque 146lb.ft at 4,400rpm.
Transmission: Single-dry-plate clutch and five-speed all-synchromesh manual
gearbox, in unit with front-mounted engine. Central, remote-control gearchange
Open propeller shaft to chassis-mounted hypoid-bevel final drive. Exposed,
universally joined drive shafts to rear wheels.
Chassis: Unitary-construction pressed-steel body/chassis unit, in single fixed-
head three-door body-style. Independent front suspension by MacPherson
struts and an anti-roll bar. Independent rear suspension by MacPherson struts
and lower wishbones. Rack-and-pinion steering. Servo-assisted brakes, front
discs and rear drums. 14in pressed-steel disc wheels. 175 × 14in tyres.
Dimensions: Wheelbase 7ft 6.5in (230cm), track (front) 4ft 5.5in (136cm), track rear
4ft 5in (135cm). Overall length 13ft 7in (414cm). Unladen weight 2,300lb (1,043kg).
History: Datsun, like other Japanese car makers, have prospered mightily since
1945. With the accent firmly on export, they eventually developed a series of
attractive sporting cars. The Datsun Fairlady, with its rigid back axle and MGB-

like styling, was successful enough, but in 1969 Datsun's successor to it, the 240Z, was unveiled. It combined striking good looks (reminiscent, some say, of Jaguar's E-Type), with typical Japanese-car reliability, and good performance. In a way, in American eyes it effectively replaced the Austin-Healey 3000. Whereas the big Healey had been killed by USA legislation, the 240Z was designed to meet and beat the same rules.

It began to sell well at once, being sold as a Nissan in some markets and as a Datsun in others. The factory launched it into a competition programme, and its successes included a win in the East African Safari in 1971. Later, in the modern idiom, its engine, which, incidentally was shared with other Nissan/Datsun saloons, was enlarged, and other versions were developed. The 240Z became the 260Z, and subsequently – for North America in particular – the 280Z was developed. The closed two-seater coupé was later joined by a longer wheelbase 2+2 version. Both cars sold in large numbers until 1978, when they were replaced by the 280CX, which had a new body shell and style.

Below: Datsun's 240Z sports coupé family was a long-running success story. Sold in huge numbers for nine years (in 2.8-litre form, only in the USA), the Datsuns were real muscle cars, and the engines made exciting noises. This is Tony Fall driving a Castrol-sponsored 240Z on the 1972 RAC Rally.

De Dietrich 24/28HP

24/28hp models, built from 1903 to 1905
Built by: De Dietrich et Cie, France.
Engine: Four cylinders, in line, in two pairs of cast-iron blocks with light-alloy water
jackets and two-bearing light-alloy crankcase. Bore and stroke 114mm by 130mm
5,308cc (4.49in × 5.12in, 324cu.in). Fixed cylinder head. Two overhead valves pe
cylinder, inlets in one line and exhausts in another, operated by pullrods and rockers
from two camshafts mounted in crankcase. Single up-draught carburettor
Maximum power about 30bhp.
Transmission: Cone clutch in unit with front-mounted engine. Separate mid
positioned four-speed manual gearbox (without synchromesh). Remote-contrc
right-hand gearchange. Final drive by chain, from sprockets on transmission cross
shaft to sprockets at rear wheel hubs. Bevel differential inside rear of transmission
case.
Chassis: Separate chassis frame, with wood/steel side members (steel applied as
flitch plates) and tubular cross members. Forged front axle beam. Front and rea
suspension by semi-elliptic leaf springs. No dampers. Worm-and-nut steering. Foo
brakes acting on drum mounted on sprocket cross shaft at side of transmission

Hand brake by brake bands on drums at rear wheels. Bolt-on artillery-style wheels.
Dimensions: Wheelbase 7ft 8.3in (234.5cm), tracks (front and rear) 4ft (122cm). Overall length 11ft 0.3in (336cm).

History: This manufacturer of railway rolling stock first built cars in 1897 which were licence-built Bollees. From 1902 De Dietrich began to build more conventionally laid out machines, with water-cooled four-cylinder engines of Turcat-Méry design. In the same year he employed the 19-year-old Ettore Bugatti to design the well-known 24/28 De Dietrich. This car was similar in layout to the Turcat-Mérys, but had a new type of engine where the valves were all overhead and the cylinder head was integral with the block (always a Bugatti hallmark). Valve operation was by pullrods rather than by pushrods. The transmission layout – a cone clutch, a massive separate gearbox, cross-shaft final drive and chain drive sprocket to the back wheels, was absolutely typical of the period, and it needed Renault and other influences to convince the firm they should adopt shaft drive later. Bugatti left De Dietrich in 1904 and a year later the cars were renamed Lorraine-Dietrichs to emphasise their French ancestry. The last Lorraine car of all was built in 1934.

Left: Even in stripped 1903 racing guise, the De Dietrich looks massive and impressive. The car was designed by a youthful Ettore Bugatti.

DeLorean DMC-12

DeLorean DMC sports coupé, built only in 1981 and 1982
Built by: DeLorean Motor Company, Northern Ireland.
Engine: Renault unit, six cylinders in 90-degree vee formation, and four bearing light-alloy cylinder block. Bore and stroke 91 × 73mm, 2,849cc (3.58 × 2.87in 174cu.in). Two light-alloy cylinder heads. Two valves per cylinder, in line operation by single overhead camshaft per head, and inverted bucket tappets Bosch K-Jetronic fuel injection. Maximum power 132bhp (DIN) at 5,500rpm Maximum torque 153lb.ft at 2,750rpm.
Transmission: Rear-wheel-drive, single-dry-plate diaphragm spring clutch and five-speed all-synchromesh manual gearbox, all in unit with rear-mounted engine. Optional automatic transmission. Remote-control, central gearchange.
Chassis: Separate backbone-style pressed-steel chassis frame, topped by a glassfibre body shell with stainless-steel skin panels. Independent front suspension by coil springs, wishbones, telescopic dampers, anti-roll bar Independent rear suspension by coil springs, semi-trailing arms and wishbones telescopic dampers and anti-roll bar. Rack-and-pinion steering. Four-wheel disc brakes. cast-alloy wheels, 14in front, 15in rear, with 195/60-14in (front) and 235/60-15in (rear) tyres.
Dimensions: Wheelbase 7ft 11in (241.5cm), front track 5ft 2.5in (159cm), rear track 5ft 3in (160cm). Overall length 14ft 0in (426.5cm). Unladen weight 2,745lb (1,245kg).
History: In so many ways the DeLorean was a great car, but its reputation will always be tainted by the seedy organisation which built it. It was, after all, the first car to be built with stainless steel body skin panels, and the first (and so far only) series production car to have been built in Northern Ireland. The man who conceived it, though, was later convicted of multi-million pound fraud, and nothing can rescue it from that.

John DeLorean achieved great things at General Motors – he ran the entire cars and trucks divisions in the early 1970s – before being eased out. Conceiving

Below: Only Mercedes-Benz had ever before used 'gullwing' action passenger doors, which DeLorean specified as one of the selling points on the DMC-12.

Above: The DMC-12's smart, sharp-edged Giuigiaro style was so well-proportioned that the true location of the V6 engine - in the tail - was disguised.

his own specialist sports car, with a rear-engined layout and lift-up gull-wing doors, and having it styled by Giugiaro of Italy, he then spent years hawking it around the world before persuading the British government to back him, in a new enterprise, in Northern Ireland. At this point he hired Lotus to convert his bright idea into a practical two-seater.

Starting in 1978, Lotus re-designed everything, effectively developing a larger version of the Esprit's backbone chassis, where the Renault V6 engine was, by edict from DeLorean himself, in the tail, behind the line of the rear wheels. The body, its style freshened up by Giugiaro, was made by Lotus's famous VARI glassfibre process, and clad in natural finish stainless steel skin panels.

By mid-1980 the design was complete, by the end of the year the brand-new factory at Dunmurry came falteringly to life, and from 1981 sales began. At first there were heady claims, that more than 20,000 cars a year would be assembled, and that there were long waiting lists in the USA, where all original cars were sold, but these were as unsubstantial as the profits being made. Here was a car always surrounded by hype, by smokescreens which covered company finances and inter-personal feuds – in other words a difficult birth. The company's own spokesman could not generate a favourable press, and DeLorean's own arrogant (and, as it now seems, shifty) demeanour did not help.

Observers were ready to give the DMC-12 a favourable reception if its behaviour matched its original launch, and its looks, for everyone was agreed that it looked attractive, if a little sharp-edged for the styling trends of the period. Worries about the practicality of the lift-up gullwing doors were suspended (but what would happen if a car was inverted in an accident ?), though it soon became clear that maintenance of the stainless steel panelling was always going to be problematical.

There was another problem. Although the DMC-12 handled well enough (though its tail-heavy weight distribiution had to be tackled by the fitment of wider-seation rear tyres), it was at once larger and less powerful than originally hoped. Impressive to look at, it could only accelerate to 60mph in 10.5 sec, and its top speed was no more than 109mph – neither of which was a match for the Porsches which DeLorean himself aimed to displace.

By 1982 stocks of unsold cars were piling up, both in the USA and in Northern Ireland, so deliveries to other countries never began. Eighty cars a day had been built in late 1981, but by the spring of 1982 it was all over, the company was wound up soon afterwards, and various fraud cases ensued. Only 8,000 cars were ever built.

Delage Series D1 and Grand Prix Cars

D1 models, all forms, built from 1923 to 1928 (data for 1928 model)
Built by: Automobiles Delage, France.
Engine: Four cylinders, in line, in cast-iron cylinder block with five-bearing light alloy crankcase. Bore and stroke 75mm by 120mm, 2,121cc (2,95in × 4.72in 129.4cu.in). Detachable cast-iron cylinder head. Two overhead valves per cylinder operated by pushrods and rockers from single camshaft mounted in side of crankcase. Single up-draught Zenith carburettor. Maximum power 38bhp (gross) at 2,400rpm.
Transmission: Multi-dry-plate clutch and four-speed manual gearbox (without synchromesh), both in unit with front-mounted engine. Direct-acting central gearchange. Open propeller shaft to spiral-bevel 'live' rear axle.
Chassis: Separate pressed-steel chassis frame, with channel-section side members and tubular and pressed cross bracing. Forged front axle beam. Front and rear suspension by semi-elliptic leaf springs. Worm-and-nut steering. Four-wheel, shaft-and-cable operated drum brakes. Centre-lock wire wheels. 820 × 120mm tyres. Opening touring, sporting or saloon car coachwork to choice.
Dimensions: Wheelbase 10ft 6in (320cm), tracks (front and rear) 4ft 5in (135cm). Overall length 13ft 10in (422cm). Unladen weight 2,100lb (952kg).
History: The first Delages were runabouts with conventional shaft drive and single cylinder 6½-horsepower engine supplied by De Dion. Delage soon became interested in motor sport and second place in the French Coupes de

Above and below: Mainstay of the Delage range in the 1920s was the versatile D1 series. The original D1 was a gentle little 2.1-litre touring car, but successive D1S and D1SS types were fiercer and more sporting. Logically enough the first 'S' was for Sports, and the second 'S' for Super. The D1SS is the car most people admire – and (above) examples are still raced in vintage events. Below: The 1924 D1SS Tourer was an impressive machine.

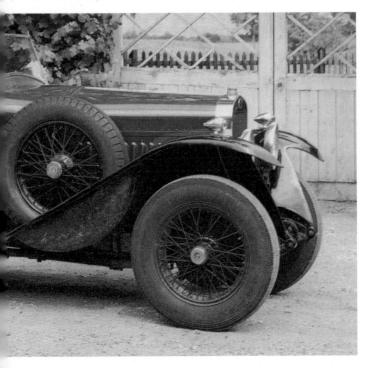

▶ Voiturettes in 1906 was followed by an outright win in 1908. With the rac
'bug' well and truly established, he was to be building Grand Prix cars e
before World War 1, and all-conquering machines in the 1920s. By then he
engaged the noted designer Lory to design first an impressive 2-litre V12 eng
and later a very successful 1½ -litre straight eight. His cars also held the La
Speed Record for a short time.

At the beginning of the 1920s there were big six-cylinder Delages, but
company's mainstay – neither as visually exciting, nor as fast, as the luxury c
or the racing cars – was the D1 series. This car was laid out on more pract
and more simple lines, but it was not made spindly or weak in the proce
Indeed, a car built around the D1's frame was used in hill-climbs and sprints v
nothing less than a 5.1-litre Type CO engine! The D1, as announced, wa
gentle and reliable four-cylinder car, with a 2.1-litre engine and such mechan
niceties as overhead valves (side-valve layouts were still 'conventional'
cheaper machines), a four-speed gearbox and four-wheel brakes. Cruising spe
might have been no more than 50mph and maximum speed between 65 a
70mph, but the cars exhibited impeccable handling, great reliability and
course used the noble radiator design which classed them as relatives (eve
they were considerably cheaper) of the luxurious 'sixes', and even of the rac
Delages.

Delage was quite unable to leave a production car alone if it was not sport
enough for him, so the D1S of 1924/25 evolved. The 'S' was for sport
('Sportif' in French) and the cars, built near Paris, backed up this title to so
extent. They were given a much shorter wheelbase (9ft 9in in place of 10ft 6
which did wonders for the handling and the weight, centre-lock 'Rudge' w
wheels, different gearbox ratios, bigger valves and an altered camshaft for
engine and a narrow and distinctive radiator. That was still not enough
Delage, however. Next along, in 1925, was the D1SS model, with the SS in t
case denoting Super Sports. This had all the D1S features, with a lowered a
lightened chassis, close-ratio gears, from 1926, and other details. Even so
look at production figures shows that the basic D1 was much the most popu
with more than 9,000 sold in five years, whereas only 983 D1S/D1SS cars w
built over the same period. There were other variants too – the D1C bein

igh-chassis' device intended for 'Colonial' conditions (442 sold) – and between
926 and 1929 there were the DM/DMS/DMN cars, all of which were based on
1 engineering and fitted with six-cylinder 3.2-litre engines, very closely related
) the four used in the D1s. The D1's engine was eminently tuneable, as the
)bhp boasted by the D1SS proved, and if it had not been for Delage's
redilection for ever-larger and more luxurious machines, sporting or
eremonial, that pedigree would have served the French company well into the
930s. perhaps even ensuring survival.

HE DELAGE GRAND PRIX CARS – 1926/27

the 1920s Albert Lory designed two wonderfully complex and successful
cing Delages. The vee-12 cars of 1923/25 were a miracle of effective
omplication – by 1925 they were developing 195bhp at 7,000rpm, in super-
harged form from two litres. The next series, built especially for the short-lived
½-litre 'formula' had simpler, but still very powerful 1,488cc straight-eight
ngines. The first chassis frames were too flexible, and road-holding was not a
rong point, and although the team won the 1926 British GP at Brooklands, and
ok second place at San Sebastian, they had one glaring fault – the hot exhaust
pe was carried past the driver's elbow and effectively 'cooked' him during a
ng race. For 1927 the engines were re-designed, with the exhaust system on
e left, and in this guise Robert Benoist won five major events that year. With
vin blowers and two Zenith carburettors, the engines produced a phenomenal
70bhp at 7,000rpm – the best yet achieved in terms of specific output. There
ere four of these cars, one of which was bought, developed and raced with
reat success by Dick Seaman in 1936. Even in the 1940s the engines were
sed in other racing cars.

**elow: Like the D1 in spirit but entirely special in engineering were the
elage Grand Prix cars of the 1920s. There were 2-litre vee-12 cars in
923/25, and the straight-eight 1½-litre machines (shown here) in
926/27. They were winners, but early cars cooked their drivers – note
e exhaust pipe!**

DeTomaso Pantera

DeTomaso Pantera, built from 1971 to 1994 (data for GTS model)
Built by: DeTomaso Automobile S.p.A, Italy.
Engine: Ford-USA-manufactured, eight cylinders, in 90-degree vee formati
in five-main-bearing cast iron cylinder block. Bore and stroke 101.6 x 88.9m
5,763cc (4.0 x 3.50in, 351.0cu.in). Cast iron cylinder heads. Two overhe
valves per cylinder, operated by pushrods and rockers from one camsh
mounted in the cylinder block. One downdraught four-barrel Holley carburet
Maximum power 350bhp at 6,000rpm. Maximum torque 333lb.ft at 3,800rp
Transmission: Mid-mounted engine, rear-wheel-drive, single dry pl
diaphragm spring clutch and five-speed all-synchromesh manual gearbox, w
remote control, centre floor gearchange.
Chassis: Unitary construction combined steel body/chassis structure, w
two-seater steel body shell in fastback coupé style. Independent fr
suspension by coil springs, wishbones and anti-roll bar, independent r
suspension by coil springs, wishbones and anti-roll bar. Rack-and-pin
steering. Disc brakes at all four wheels, with vacuum servo assistance. 1
bolt-on cast alloy wheels, with 285/40-15in (front) and 345/35-15in (rear) tyr
Dimensions: Wheelbase 8ft 3.0in (251.5cm), front track 4ft 11.5in (151c
rear track 5ft 2.1in (157.7cm). Overall length 14ft 0in (427cm). Unladen wei
3,219lb (1,480kg).
History: For years the Argentine-born Alejandro DeTomaso had built race ca
one-offs and small-run road cars, but it was the Ford V8-engined Mangu
which put him on his way to fame. Ford-USA liked what they saw, and
involved with its successor.

When a new model called the Pantera was shown in the 1970 New Y
Show, ready for production in 1971, its significance was not in styling,

**Below: Late-model Panteras had their styling somewhat revised (by
Marcello Gandini), but the basic mid-engined proportions were retaine**

**bove: Over the years, the fascia/instrument display of the Pantera was
radually tidied up – but this was never more than a strict two-seater.**

ngineering, but that it was being exhibited by Ford-USA. In a complicated deal
hich eventually involved Ford-USA buying the Ghia styling house from
eTomaso, the Detroit monolith agreed to market this fast and sexy-looking
alian-built mid-engined machine, through their Lincoln-Mercury chain.

The Pantera was based around a unit-construction pressed-steel shell. As
ith the mid-engined Maserati Bora/Merak model with which it was
ontemporary, this was possible with simple and limited tooling, due to the
alian expertise in this 'supercar industry'. However, although construction was ▶

▶ by DeTomaso, the style had been worked up by Ghia before this company v
sold to Ford.

Because Ford wanted to sell this car in sizeable numbers, they
provided much cost-reducing advice. This resulted in a standard Galaxie-si
pushrod V8 engine being chosen, though the choice of mid-rear engine loca
(where the engine was in unit with the transmission) meant that a ZF fi
speed transaxle had to be specified in the tail.

This was a big and brawny car by any Italian standards, for compared w
the Ferrari Boxers and Lamborghini Countachs with which it would compe
the Pantera used cast iron and pressed steel where its rivals would
aluminium castings and pressings. If this reduced costs and complicatic
though, Ford thought it could cope with this.

The chassis specification was much as expected of this era, with wishbc
independent suspension at front and rear, a weight distribution biased towa
the tail, and with the roadholding balanced out by the use of wider-section r
tyres. Compared with that of most other supercars of the period, there seem
to be generous two-seater accommodation, even for a fair amount of lugga
to be carried.

In spite of the 'soft' engine tune on which Ford insisted, the Pantera v
easily capable of exceeding 160mph, this being achieved with the minimum
fuss, though with a typically North American, as opposed to Italian, V8 bell
of exhausts.

To pander to the tastes of the North American customers the equipm
level was much more 'touring' then 'sporting', and for the period it was qu
amazing to find that every Pantera came with full air conditioning.

Although the numbers certainly added up – the Pantera could alwa
deliver the advertised performance, all backed up by a great deal of Italian st

Above: Hidden away under the skin of the Pantera was a mid-mounted Ford V8 engine, latterly with 350bhp.

Below: As face-lifted by Marcello Gandini in 1990, the Pantera retained a shovel-nose, and big air intakes for the cooling radiators.

and braggadocio – it had been rushed into service with a minimum of testing, and early examples seemed to suffer from all manner of reliability and deterioration problems. It wasn't long before reports of premature body corrosion, of water leaks into the cabin, of electrical problems, and of lapses in quality control were all borne out in practice.

Customers were angry, Lincoln-Mercury dealers were in despair, and Ford-USA was soon infuriated, for here was a car which looked so fabulous, performed like a true Supercar, but could not always keep on doing so for unlimited periods. Nor was it merely an American problem, for Panteras sold in Europe could also be seen to behave in the same way.

Having sold about 4,000 cars in the USA, Ford then pulled the plug on the project, and cast the Pantera to the winds. DeTomaso, amazingly, elected to keep it in production, and although sales fell to below 100 cars a year, the model carried on, gradually developed and improved, until 1994. The most powerful of all, in later years, pushed out no less than 350bhp.

Dodge Viper

Dodge Viper sports car, built from 1992 to 2002 (data for original specification)

Built by: Chrysler Corporation, USA.

Engine: Ten cylinders, in 90-degree vee formation, in six-bearing light-alloy cylinder block/crankcase. Bore and stroke 101.6 × 98.6mm, 7,997cc (4.00 × 3.88in, 488cu.in). Two light-alloy cylinder heads. Two valves per cylinder, overhead and in line, operation by pushrods and rockers from a central camshaft in the vee. Maximum power 400bhp (DIN) at 4,600rpm. Maximum torque 450lb.ft at 3,200rpm.

Transmission: Rear-wheel drive, single-plate diaphragm spring clutch and six-speed all-synchromesh manual gearbox, all in unit with the front-mounted engine. Remote-control, central gearchange.

Chassis: Separate chassis frame, with box section main members, and cross-bracing. Pressure-moulded plastic composite bodyshell. Independent front suspension by coil springs, wishbones, telescopic dampers and anti-roll bar. Independent rear suspension by coil springs, wishbones, telescopic dampers and anti-roll bar. Rack-and-pinion steering, with power-assistance. Four-wheel disc brakes with vacuum-servo assistance, but no ABS anti-lock. 17in cast-alloy wheels, 275/40-17in (front) and 335/35-17in (rear) tyres.

Dimensions: Wheelbase 8ft 0.2in (244.3cm), front track 4ft 11.6in (151.4cm), rear track 5ft 0.6in (154cm). Overall length 14ft 7.1in (445cm). Unladen weight 3,200lb (1,452kg).

History: Without the drive and enthusiasm of Bob Lutz, the legendary Viper would never have been built. Lutz, an all-time car enthusiast, and ex-Ford at the very highest level, became Chrysler's president in the late 1980s. Along with Lee Iacocca, his exuberant chairman, and with gleeful help from Carroll Shelby, he helped the Viper move from Good Idea, to concept car, to production machine and, finally, to motoring icon.

First shown in 1989, as a one-off concept, the Viper eventually went on sale in 1992, a car inspired by the career of Shelby's 1960s Cobra (which Iacocca had

Below: AC Cobra influence, if not shared parts, was found in the Viper (hence the choice of name), which had a simple chassis, a hugely powerful engine and lightweight body construction.

Above: The Viper's sensational styling hid a 400bhp V10 engine, a six-speed gearbox, and all-independent suspension. Those side-mounted exhaust pipes meant business.

always loved, and which also explains the serpent's name which was chosen), and in general layout as near to a direct descendant as possible. Like the Cobra, it combined a two-seater layout with a massively powerful engine, an outrageous character, and colossal performance. Americans had loved the Cobra in the 1960s, and a new generation loved the Viper in the 1990s.

Although the styling of the plastic-bodied two-seater shell (by Tom Gale of Chrysler's own design studios) was outrageous enough – deep skirts along the flanks, exhaust pipes poking out through them, scoops behind the front wheels to pull hot air out of the engine bay, and originally only one colour, bright red – this all hid a perfectly conventional (by USA standards) separate steel chassis frame, though this had all-independent suspension, fat tyres and the ability to hold the road well in most conditions.

The secret of the Viper's appeal was in its engine, a huge 8-litre V10, the like of which no American car lover had ever seen before. Deep down, in its origins, there was a cast iron engine intended for use in Chrysler Corporation trucks, but this was a specialised, all-aluminium, version of the same which had been evolved with the aid of Chrysler's then-associate company, Lamborghini, still with overhead valve gear, but much more ambitiously tuned, with fuel injection, fabricated exhaust manifolds, and every feasible performance trick. With a dry sump lubrication system, it produced a bellowing 400bhp – and not even Chevrolet's Corvette XZR-1 could match that. The performance – which included a top speed of nearly 160mph – was at a level very few would ever experience, but the potential, the traffic light kudos, and the general threatening character, all made it a matchless prospect.

Most original Viper owners always used their cars with the top open, though wimps could use a rather flimsy soft-top (which was almost a Surrey top, in view of the large and functional roll-over hoop behind the seats) if it rained. All of them loved the six-speed Borg Warner transmission which allowed them to produce engine booming noises at every opportunity. With no automatic transmission option, this was a uniqiue American car for the period.

Sales, as expected, were steady – thousands rather than millions, every year – but market appeal was improved by the arrival of the fastback GTS Coupé in 1993. Further even-higher-powered types were raced with success, and sold in small numbers. A new generation of Viper was launched in 2002.

Ferrari 250GT Berlinetta

250GT series, built from 1953 to 1964 (data for 1959 Berlinetta)

Built by: SEFAC Ferrari, Maranello, Italy.

Engine: 12 cylinders, in 60-degree vee-formation, in seven-bearing light-alloy block/crankcase. Bore and stroke 73mm by 58.8mm, 2,953cc (2.86in × 2.31in, 180.2cu.in). Two detachable light-alloy cylinder heads. Two overhead valves per cylinder, opposed to each other in part-spherical combustion chambers and operated by rockers from single overhead camshaft per cylinder head. Three down-draught twin-choke Weber carburettors. Maximum power 260bhp (net) at 7,000rpm.

Transmission: Twin-dry-plate clutch and four-speed, synchromesh manual gearbox, both in unit with front-mounted engine. Remote-control central gearchange. Open propeller shaft to hypoid-bevel 'live' rear axle.

Chassis: Separate multi-tubular chassis frame, with large-section side members and tubular cross bracing. Independent front suspension by coil springs, wishbones and anti-roll bar. Rear suspension by half-elliptic leaf springs and radius arms. Lever-arm hydraulic dampers. Worm-and-wheel steering. Four-wheel hydraulically operated disc brakes. Centre-lock wire wheels. 175 × 400 tyres.

Dimensions: Wheelbase 7ft 10.5in (240cm), track (front) 4ft 5.3in (135.4cm), track (rear) 4ft 5.1in (135cm). Overall length 13ft 7.5in (415cm). Unladen weight 2,400lb (1,088kg).

History: Ferrari's first attempt at building a Gran Turismo car was the 250 Europa of 1953, but unlike all its descendants this model was powered by the large Lampredi-designed V12. The 250GT, which followed in 1954, reverted to the original Colombo V12. The chassis was Ferrari-conventional, being built up of large-diameter tubing, and there was a front-mounted all synchromesh gearbox and a live rear axle located by leaf springs and radius arms. The Berlinetta cars (much lighter than production two-seater coupés) began to appear in the mid

Above: Inevitably the 250GT range was stretched – the original 250GT 2 + 2 was a Farina-styled 1960 model.

1950s and were intended for competition purposes. The name has been applied indiscriminately to *all* 250GTs, particularly those with short wheelbases, although the true Berlinettas, which became famous in GT racing, were built from 1959 to 1962, with that distinctive body by Scaglietti. Steel-bodied versions of these cars, rightly, became legendary and about 80 were made all in all. Out of the Berlinetta, of course, came the 250GTO, which was a pure competition car, and the 250GT Lusso, which was a pure road car. Successor to all of them, of course, was the smooth 275GTB, with its axle-mounted gearbox and 'rope-drive' propeller shaft. The 250GT cars, however, are those which truly signify Ferrari's change from being a racing car maker to being a production car maker.

Below: The final flowering of the 250GT pedigree was the graceful Lusso, of which 350 were built between 1962 and 1964.

Ferrari 275GTB and GTB/4

Ferrari 275GTB and 275GTB/4, built from 1964 to 1968 (data for 275GTB/4)
Built by: Ferrari S.p.A., Italy.
Engine: Twelve cylinders, in 60-degree vee formation, in seven-main-bearing cast alloy cylinder block. Bore and stroke 77 x 58.8mm, 3,286cc (3.03 x 2.31in, 200.0cu.in). Two light-alloy cylinder heads. Two valves per cylinder, opposed in part-spherical combustion chambers, and operated by inverted bucket tappets and twin overhead camshafts per head. Six downdraught Weber dual-choke carburettors. Maximum power 300bhp at 8,000rpm. Maximum torque 217lb.ft at 5,500rpm. [275GTB models, 1964 – 1966, had 280bhp engines with single-overhead-camshaft cylinder heads.]
Transmission: Front engine, rear-wheel-drive, single dry plate diaphragm spring clutch, and rigid torque tube, to five-speed all-synchromesh manual gearbox mounted in unit with the rear axle. Remote control, centre floor gearchange.
Chassis: Separate steel chassis frame, with tubular main side members, tubular and fabricated stiffeners and cross-braces. Independent front suspension by coil springs, wishbones and anti-roll bar, independent rear suspension by coil springs, wishbones and anti-roll bar. Hydraulic telescopic dampers. Worm and sector steering. Disc brakes at all four wheels, with vacuum servo assistance. 14in centre-lock cast alloy road wheels, with 205-14in tyres. Light-alloy/steel fastback two-seater coupé body style by Pininfarina or (275GTS) two-seater open Spider style.
Dimensions: Wheelbase 7ft 10.4in (240cm), front track 4ft 7.2in (140cm), rear track 4ft 7.8in (141.7cm). Overall length 14ft 5.6 in (441cm). Unladen weight 2,490lb (1,129kg).
History: The 275GTB which arrived in 1964 to take over from the long-running 250GT family, was really the first Ferrari to be produced by series-production methods, and always with the same body styles. It was much more than this, though, for it ushered in a new wave of Ferrari road-car thinking, in chassis and

Below: As ever, the 275GTB was styled for Ferrari by Pininfarina, and was a natural progression from the 250GT Lusso which it replaced.

Above: In the mid-1960s, no other high-performance car was as seductive as the 275GTB. Hidden away was a new high-tech. chassis and a 3.3-litre V12 engine.

transmission terms. Apart from the engine itself, almost every aspect of the 275GTB had been newly developed, and would have a considerable life ahead of it.

The designation 275GTB, incidentally, indicated the type of car and its engine, Each cylinder of the V12 engine measured 275cc, GT meant 'Gran Tourismo', and 'B' stood for Berlinetta, which in Italian might have meant 'small saloon', but in Ferrari terms meant 'very fast closed car'! It might have been a closed car, by the way, but by any other standard of measurement this was an out and out sports car.

The arrival of this model coincided with major expansion of the factory, for the 275GTB was intended to sell in larger quantities than previous Ferrari road cars. The basis of the design was a multi-tube chassis frame, of a type favoured by several contemporary Italian car makers of that period on to which a choice of two bodies could be mounted. The 275GTB was a low-nosed, closed coupé, while the 275GTS (S for 'Spider') which followed was an open two-seater, both of them having been styled by Ferrari's favourite consultant, Pininfarina.

Apart from its, as expected, overhead camshaft V12 engine – which had been enlarged to 3.3-litres, and produced no less than 280bhp in standard form (more power was available, for use in motorsport, to special order) - the core of the new design was its drive line and suspension layout. For the first time in a Ferrari road car, the transmission was separated from the engine. Whereas the ▶

▶ V12 was up front, the five-speed gearbox was at the rear, mounted in unit with the chassis-mounted final drive. At first the two were connected by a slim but solid propeller shaft with a single centre steady bearing, but from 1966, to improve on this, the connection was changed for a solid light-alloy torque tube linking engine to transmission, with the propeller shaft inside it. This, incidentally, not only cured any tendency for the transmission to vibrate, but added considerable stiffness to the rather shallow chassis frame.

The use of a rear-mounted transmission meant that independent rear suspension was essential, this being a double wishbone layout with remarkably similar geometry to that of the front suspension.

By any standards this was a magnificent new road car, whose looks were backed up by a 153mph top speed, by a snarling engine note, and by that indefinable Ferrari character that every opponent wished they could bottle, and re-use. Then, and for many years to come, this was seen as one of the world's supreme front-engined road cars.

The great got even better in 1966, too, when 275GTB became 275GTB/4. This was done by providing the engine with twin-overhead-camshaft cylinder

heads (these had already been race-proved in other V12-engined models), which raised the image stakes yet further, for the engine power had been raised to no less than 300bhp. This, and the use of the latest long-nose body style, made a great car into a positive icon of ultimate performance motoring, a status which the 275GTB/4 has never lost.

To the driver who could afford to buy one (and, these days, their classic car value is still way up in the stratosphere), the 175GTB was a gorgeous, unbeatable car. The 275GTS, useful in only the best of climates, had its own admirers, of course, but it was this peerless, 155mph Ferrari, which seemed to have it all.

Later GTS types had engines of up to 4.4-litres, though the engineering and the looks were unchanged. All in all, there were 806 275GTBs, and 320 GTS types, these being built in four short years.

Below: Only a two-seater, but with a new chassis frame, all-independent suspension, and a 3.3-litre V12 engine – the 275GTB was a magnificent Supercar.

Ferrari 365GTB4 Daytona

Daytona model, built from 1968 to 1974

Built by: SEFAC Ferrari, Maranello, Italy.

Engine: Twelve cylinders, in 60-degree vee-formation, in seven-bearing cast alloy block/crankcase. Bore and stroke 81mm by 71mm, 4,390cc (3.10in x 2.79in, 268cu.in). Two detachable light-alloy cylinder heads. Two overhead valves per cylinder, inclined to each other in part-spherical combustion chambers and operated by inverted-bucket tappets from twin overhead camshafts per cylinder head. Six down-draught twin-choke Webe carburettors. Maximum power 352bhp (DIN) at 7,500rpm. Maximum torque 318lb.ft at 5,500rpm.

Transmission: Single-dry-plate clutch in unit with front-mounted engine. Torque tube and enclosed propeller shaft to combined gearbox/differential transaxle. Five-speed, all-indirect, all-synchromesh manual gearbox, and hypoid-bevel differential with limited-slip device, all chassis mounted. Exposed, universally jointed drive shafts to rear wheels.

Chassis: Separate multi-tubular steel chassis frame, with light-alloy closed two-seater coupé coachwork by Scaglietti. All independent suspension coil springs, wishbones and anti-roll bars, with telescopic dampers. Worm-and-nut steering. Four-wheel, hydraulically operated ventilated disc brakes, with vacuum servo assistance. 15in centre-lock cast-alloy road wheels. 215/70VR15in tyres.

Dimensions: Wheelbase 7ft 10.5in (240cm), track (front) 4ft 8.5in (143.5cm), track (rear) 4ft 8in (142cm). Overall length 14ft 6in (442cm). Unladen weight 3,530lb (1,600kg).

History: To replace the long-running 250GT production cars, with their conventional mechanical layout and obligatory V12 engines, Ferrari launched the 275GTB in 1964. This was improved to become the 275GTB4 in 1966.

Below: When launched in 1968, the Daytona set new standards in several areas, notably in performance, and in its startling looks. Speeds of 170mph+ were always possible, and were achieved with huge panache.

Above: Until the 1990s, the Daytona was the last, the fastest, and the greatest of all Ferrari's front-engined V12s. Its performance matched its looks.

Although it remained true to the traditions, with front-mounted V12 engine and two-door two-seater coupé body, it had a multi-tubular chassis frame, all-independent coil-spring suspension and the five-speed gearbox in unit with the chassis-mounted differential.

There was little doubt that the four-cam 275GTB4 (with the final stretch of the original Colombo-type engine) was one of the fastest cars in the world, but Ferrari was not satisfied. In the autumn of 1968, his engineers had produced the delectable 365GTB4 Daytona car, which did everything that the now obsolete 275GTB4 could have done, but also had the massively powerful four-cam 4.4-litre engine and dramatically styled body (by Pininfarina) constructed as usual by Scaglietti. The 275GTB4's basic chassis and mechanical layout were retained, including the rear-positioned gearbox. However, the front and rear wheel tracks were wider and the shovel-nosed shape, with its hidden headlamps, was more shapely even than before. With all that power, the Daytona was tremendously fast. Its maximum speed was between 175 and 180mph, it could break almost any limit in the world in its 86mph second gear, and beat 140mph in fourth! Without any doubt it was the world's fastest production car, faster even than the Lamborghini Miura, in the six years it was on sale. Yet the whole business of going fast was carried out in exemplary Ferrari manner, with refinement to suit the high price, and the most amazingly flexible engine, as one had come to expect from the Maranello-built products.

The only way for the car to be significantly improved would have been to make it faster, or even more docile, but Ferrari was not interested in half-measures. He had decided that the Daytona should be the last of his front-engined super-car two-seaters and from 1974 it was deposed by the wickedly attractive mid-engined Berlinetta Boxer, with a new flat-12 power unit, also of 4.4-litres. To drive a Daytona was a truly memorable and exciting experience.

Ferrari Boxer/Testarossa family

Ferrari Boxer and Testarossa family built from 1971 to 1996 (data for original Boxer 365GTB4/BB)

Built by: SEFAC Ferrari, Italy.

Engine: Twelve cylinders, in horizontally opposed formation, in seven-main-bearing cylinder block/crankcase. Bore and stroke 81 x 71mm, 4,390 cc (3.19 x 2.79in, 267cu.in). Light-alloy cylinder heads. Two valves per cylinder, opposed in part-spherical combustion chambers, and operated by inverted bucket tappets from twin overhead camshafts per cylinder head. Four downdraught triple-choke Weber carburettors. Maximum power 344bhp at 7,200rpm. Maximum torque 302lb.ft at 3,900rpm. [512BB had 5.0-litre/360bhp, Testa Rossa had 5.0-litre/390bhp, 512TR had 5.0-litre/428bhp, F512M had 5-litre 440bhp engines.]

Transmission: Mid-mounted engine, rear-wheel-drive, single-dry-plate diaphragm spring clutch and five-speed all-synchromesh manual gearbox, in unit with engine and final drive. Remote control, centre floor gearchange.

Chassis: Separate multi-square-tube steel chassis frame, with square-section main side members, tubular and fabricated cross-bracings and reinforcements, with steel (some aluminium panels) body shell in two-seater fastback coupé style. Independent front suspension by coil springs, wishbones and anti-roll bar. Independent rear suspension by coil springs, wishbones and anti-roll bar. Telescopic hydraulic dampers. Rack and pinion steering. Disc brakes at all four wheels, with vacuum servo assistance, but no ABS. 15in cast alloy centre-lock road wheels, with 215-15in tyres.

Dimensions: Wheelbase 8ft 2.5in (250cm), front track 4ft 11in (150cm), rear track 5ft 0in (152cm). Overall length 14ft 3.7in (436cm). Unladen weight 3,197lb (1,450kg).

History: Once Lamborghini had launched the mid-engined Miura, a response from Ferrari was inevitable, though it was not until 1973 that the first 365BB GTB4/BB (which everyone immediately nicknamed 'Boxer' because of the layout of its flat-12 engine) went on sale.

Central to the entire design was the 340bhp 4.4-litre engine, which shared its bore, stroke and general cylinder head dimensions with the old Daytona

Below: The mid-engined Ferrari Boxer used a flat-12 power unit mounted behind the seats, originally of 4.4-litres, later of 5.0-litres.

Above: Although it was much larger, the flat-12-engined Boxer looked remarkably like the smaller Dino 308GTB.

though the horizontally-opposed layout was exactly like that of the entirely different engines being used by Ferrari's F1 cars of the period.

By any standards – Ferrari's, or the rest of the world – the Boxer family was unique. Not only was there a tyre-strippingly powerful flat-12 engine between the cabin and the rear wheels, but the transmission was actually under it. Although the sight of a boxer engine/transmission/final drive unit was enough to send every automotive enthusiast into raptures, the fact is that this inevitably placed the engine quite high off the ground, which did little for the roadholding.

Except for its mid-engined package, the rest of the car was pure contemporary Ferrari, for there was a multi-tube chassis, a sinuous two-seater coupé style by Pininfarina, and all-independent coil spring suspension, there being steel, some light alloy and even some glass-fibre in the panelwork.

Although the original Boxer was searingly fast, it seems that the body shape was not quite as slippery as that of the old Daytona, so its top speed was slightly reduced – and in spite of its colossal performance there were always slight reservations about its roadholding because of the bulky and rather high-mounted engine.

Even so, Ferrari persisted with this chassis layout for the next two decades, a period in which the engine was repeatedly improved (it would finally be a 440bhp 5-litre), in which the style was changed completely once, then modified twice thereafter, and in which several thousand sales were achieved. Intriguingly, although there was nothing to be ashamed of, this was a period in which Ferrari never admitted to production figures in detail.

The 512BB of 1976 looked the same, but had a 5.0-litre engine with 360bhp and more torque, while the 512BBi of 1981 had fuel injection. However, even though this was now a 170mph car, and more than 2,000 had been sold, Ferrari ▶

▶ thought it could do better. Three more derivatives then followed:

Testarossa: Eleven years after the original Boxer went on sale, Ferrari unveiled the sensationally styled Testarossa, which had a wider, more sharply styled body (which was distinguished by the flamboyant strakes along the flanks that guided cooling air into the engine bay), and wider wheel tracks, which helped to improve the roadholding. Engine power had once again been boosted – this time to 390bhp – though the top speed was still stuck at 170mph. If only because of its amazing looks, the Testarossa was a huge and permanent success, but Ferrari was convinced that there was more to come.

512TR: The result was the 512TR of 1992, which at first glance looked like no more than a revised Testarossa. Visually, at least, this was so, though there was a new nose, though among the many mechanical improvements were a lowered and lightened engine (now with 428bhp), better brakes, bigger wheels

and a revised instrument package. With a 180mph top speed this was an utterly convincing supercar.

F512M: Ferrari, however, decided to make one further derivative, in the last of a long and distinguished line. The F512M which arrived in 1994 was yet another re-touching of a famous shape, this time with different nose and tail detailing, included headlamps exposed behind plastic covers, and with an engine boosted to 440bhp. Like its predecessors, the F512M had a formidable presence and, with its 185-190mph top speed, and 0-100mph acceleration in just ten seconds, it was a wonderful way of bringing the career of this, the last-ever of Ferrari's mid-12-cylinder-engined pedigree, to an end.

Below: From 1984, the Testarossa took over from the Boxer, on the same basic mid-flat-12-engined chassis. The strakes on the side channelled fresh air into the engine bay.

Ferrari Dino 206GT and 246GT

Dino 206GT and 246GT, built from 1967 to 1973 (data for 246GT)

Built by: SEFAC Ferrari, Maranello, Italy.

Engine: Six cylinders, in 65-degree vee-formation, in four-bearing cast-iron block, transversely mounted behind driving compartment. Bore and stroke 92.5mm by 60mm, 2,418cc (3.64in × 2.36in, 147.5cu.in). Light-alloy cylinder heads. Two valves per cylinder inclined to each other, in part-spherical combustion chambers and operated by inverted-bucket tappets from twin overhead camshafts per bank. Three down-draught twin-choke Weber carburettors. Maximum power 195bhp (DIN) at 7,600rpm. Maximum torque 166lb.ft at 5,500rpm.

Transmission: Single-dry-plate clutch and train of transfer gears to five-speed all-synchromesh manual gearbox, mounted in unit with, but behind and below the cylinder block. Remote control central gearchange. Hypoid-bevel final drive unit, with limited-slip differential at rear of gearbox. Exposed, universally jointed drive shafts to rear wheels.

Chassis: Fabricated tubular and sheet steel load-bearing chassis frame, with steel and light-alloy welded to it on assembly. Light-alloy skin panels, in two-seat coupé or spider construction. Engine/transmission unit behind driving compartment. All-independent suspension, by coil springs, wishbones, anti-roll bars and telescopic dampers. Rack-and-pinion steering. Four-wheel hydraulically operated disc brakes, with vacuum servo assistance. 14in bolt-on cast-alloy road wheels. 205VR14in tyres.

Dimensions: Wheelbase 7ft 8.2in (234cm), track (front) 4ft 8.1in (142cm), track (rear) 4ft 7.1in (140cm). Overall length 13ft 9in (420cm). Unladen weight 2,400lb (1,088kg).

History: Ferrari's first mid-engined road car came about because of a desire to go racing in the 1967 Formula Two (which meant that engines had to be 'production' based), and because they were already committed to supplying such engines to Fiat for the same validation purpose. Mid-engined Dinos

Above: The classic lines of the Ferrari Dino, by Pininfarina. Coupe or Spider versions were built. First cars had mid-mounted 2-litres, later 2.4-litres.

entirely different from the road cars, were raced in 1965 to 1967, but the first true prototype was shown in 1967.

Styled by Pininfarina, the original car had a longitudinally mounted engine, but all production cars had the now-familiar transverse engine location shared by the Lancia Stratos. The first batch of Ferrari Dinos used 2-litre engines with cast-alloy cylinder blocks, but from the end of 1969 this was replaced by a cast-iron block unit of 2,418cc. Incidentally, the cylinder dimensions are identical to those of Grand Prix Ferraris of the late 1950s, the engines being very closely related. Apart from the engine, the rest of the Dino was all new, and the luscious styling was startlingly unique.

In spite of its racing origins the Dino was a thoroughly practical road car, fast enough (about 140mph maximum speed) for almost everybody, and had remarkable roadholding powers. It was replaced in 1974 by the new and larger 308GTB car, with a new V8 engine.

Left: The lines effectively hide the mid-mounted engine position. The car was small, with impeccable road manners.

Ferrari Dino 308/328 family

Ferrari Dino 308/328 family, built from 1973 to 1988 (data for original 308GT
Built by: Ferrari S.p.A, Italy.
Engine: Eight cylinders, in 90-degree V8 formation, in five-main-bearing ligh
alloy cylinder block. Bore and stroke 81 x 71mm, 2,926cc (3.19 x 2.80
178.6cu.in). Two light alloy cylinder heads. Two overhead valves per cylinde
operated by inverted bucket tappets from twin overhead camshafts per cylind
head. Four downdraught twin-choke Weber carburettors. Maximum pow
250bhp at 7,700rpm. Maximum torque 210lb.ft at 5,000rpm.
Transmission: Transversely-mounted engine, rear-wheel-drive, single-dry-pla
diaphragm spring clutch and five-speed all-synchromesh manual gearbox, all
unit with engine, with remote control, centre floor gearchange.
Chassis: Separate multi-tube steel chassis frame, with tubular and fabricate
steel reinforcements, clad in a steel and light-alloy two-seater coupé
removable roof coupé body (some glass fibre panels on early car
Independent front suspension by coil springs, wishbones and anti-roll ba
independent rear suspension by coil springs, wishbones and anti-roll ba
Hydraulic telescopic dampers. Rack-and-pinion steering. Disc brakes at all fo
wheels, with vacuum servo assistance. 14in cast-alloy, bolt-on wheels, wi
205/70-14in tyres.
Dimensions: Wheelbase 7ft 8.1in (234cm), front track 4ft 9.9in (147cm), re
track 4ft 9.9in (147cm). Overall length 14ft 6.2in (443.5cm). Unladen weig
2,748lb (1,246kg).
[328 models had similar 3,185cc V8 engines. Mondial 8 of 1980 was a longe
wheelbase, 2+2 version of the same chassis.]
History: Although the end of the Dino 246 family was mourned, the vee-
engined range of Dinos which took over were a genuine improvement. Large
more versatile and even more practical than before, they set up a 'mediur
sized' Ferrari line which persisted until 1988.

I must be cautious, of course, in calling them all Ferraris, for in theory
least, those built until 1975 were plain 'Dinos'. Even though few enthusias

Below: The 308GT4 of 1973 was the first and (as it turned out) the only
Ferrari road car to be styled by Bertone. Tightly packaged 2+2 seating
was provided.

Above: The vast majority of 308-derived cars were two-seaters, this being a GTS, in which the roof panel could be removed.

followed his lead, Enzo Ferrari had always insisted on this, and the badging of the cars was appropriate.

Although the general layout of the much-loved old Dino 246 had been retained – there was a multi-tubular chassis, and a transversely-positioned, mid-mounted engine driving the rear wheels – every detail had been changed. In particular there was the new 90-degree vee-8 engine, with twin overhead camshafts per bank, which shared many common components – bore stroke, pistons, connecting rods and valve gear, for instance – with the Daytona's V12 power unit – and which was originally a 2,926cc unit. In typical Dino and Ferrari fashion, the type number – 308 – reflected the use of a 3.0-litre engine and eight cylinders.

The very first 308, in fact, was an oddity, the 308GT4, which had a lengthened wheelbase, and a rather angular 2+2-seater cabin by Bertone, but Ferrari normality was restored in 1975 with the launch of the shorter, sexier, and altogether more attractive Pininfarina-styled two-seater 308GTB, where 'B' stood for 'Berlinetta'. This car, which had glass-fibre body panelling at first, was a genuine successor to the 246, and sold well from the start. Then, and later, it could always be distinguished by the scoops along the top of the doors, which fed cooling air into the engine bay behind the seats.

Before long a 308GTS variety ('S' for Spider) was added to the range, this being a model which looked almost the same, except that a Targa-type roof panel could be removed, and stowed, for warm days to be enjoyed with the top side open, and it was at this juncture that glass-fibre was abandoned in favour of conventional steel panelling.

Except for being retouched in visual detail, these two models would be the backbone of Ferrari's range until 1989, and from 1980 they were also joined by a longer-wheelbase 2+2 version called the Mondial ('world'), which really took over where the short-lived 308GT4 had left off.

Over the years, and as North American exhaust emissions legislation began ▶

▶ to bite, Ferrari fought a continuous battle to maintain its power output, needing new features such as fuel injection, four-valve heads and capacity enlargement to beat progressive strangulation.

Original 2.9-litre types had 250bhp (there was also an Italy-only 208GT with a 170bhp/2.0-litre engine), and then from 1981 there was the 214bhp 308GTBi, which used Bosch fuel injection. In 1982 the cars became 308GT QV, where QV stood for 'Quattrovalvole' (the Italian for 'four valve), and when horsepower went back up to 240bhp.

Finally, in 1985, the ultimate revision saw the model name change once again, this to 328GTB and 328GTS, the reason being that the engine had been enlarged to 3,185cc, and at the same time the peak power went up further, 270bhp at 7,000rpm.

In all this time, apart from the use of different wheels, and some decorative

mendment to air intakes and other detail, the basic body style was not hanged, so that it would still be easy to confuse a 1975 308GTB with a 1988 28GTB – and vice versa.

There was no question that this was always a very popular and successful ar. Early examples had been capable of 154mph, and although the heavier mid-980s 328GTB could still not reach 160mph, it accelerated faster, and was together more civilised in the process. Not bad at all for a 'baby Ferrari'!

By the time the last cars of all were produced, almost 23,000 of this edigree had been sold, and developments of the engine were still being used the early 2000s, in modern Ferraris such as the F360 Modena.

elow: What price 150mph motoring with the roof of a 308GTS
moved? Who cared – for this was a Ferrari!

Ferrari F40

Ferrari F40 sports coupé, built from 1987 to 1992
Built by: Ferrari S.p.A., Italy.
Engine: Eight cylinders, in 90-deg formation, in cast-alloy cylinder blc
crankcase. Bore and stroke 82 × 69.5mm, 2,936cc (3.23 × 2.74in, 179cu.in). T
light-alloy cylinder heads. Four valves per cylinder, in narrow vee-ang
operation by twin overhead camshafts and inverted bucket-type tappe
Weber-Marelli fuel injection and twin IHi turbochargers. Maximum pov
478bhp (DIN) at 7,000rpm. Maximum torque 425lb.ft at 4,000rpm.
Transmission: Rear-wheel-drive, diaphragm spring clutch and five-speed
synchromesh manual gearbox, all in unit with mid-mounted engine. Remc
control, central gearchange.
Chassis: Separate tubular/fabricated steel chassis frame, topped
Kevlar/carbon fibreglass-fibre body shell. Independent front suspension by
springs, wishbones, telescopic dampers, anti-roll bar. Independent
suspension by coil springs, wishbones, telescopoc dampers, and anti-roll
Rack-and-pinion steering. Four-wheel disc brakes, no servo assistance. Ca
alloy 17in road wheels, 245/40-17in (front) and 335/35-17in (rear) tyres.
Dimensions: Wheelbase 8ft 0.5in (245cm), front track 5ft 2.8in (159.4cm), r
track 5ft 3.2in (160.6cm). Overall length 14ft 3.6in (435.8cm). Unladen wei
2,425lb (1,100kg).
History: As every Ferrari enthusiast knows, the F40 model was designed a
fortieth anniversary model, to commemorate the birth of Ferrari road cars
1947, and to offer the very best, the very latest, and the most astonish
combination of Ferrari engineering that was possible at the time. Within
years of its launch, the F40 was superseded by other, more exuberant, Ferra

**Right: Once seen, never forgotten, the F40 had a low, ground-hugging,
front end, complete with NACA-type air intakes. The vast rear spoiler
was visible from all angles.**

**Below: Although the F40 was a road car, it was equipped as if motor
racing was planned - hence the figure-hugging Sparco seats and full-
harness safety belts.**

t somehow it has never lost its reputation as the most exciting Ferrari road car all time.

By comparison with some of its so-called rivals, in 1987 the F40 might have en considered unadventurous – no four-wheel-drive, no ABS brakes and no phisticated suspension systems, for instance – yet it offered an abundance of eer excitement. Preposterously fast (nobody seriously contested Ferrari's im that it would exceed 200mph), achingly beautiful, and blessed with the rt of in-built charisma that stopped traffic at two hundred paces, the F40 didn't ed any more equipment or a higher specification to make its point.

Without taking five years to design and develop the new car, and without ing end-to-end whizz-bang high technology, Ferrari intended only to provide e fastest Ferrari so far, in its rawest form. They succeeded, totally. Having ade 1,200 F40s in five years, they would close the production line and ignore still bulging order book. Customers, they decided, would have to wait for other 'limited-edition' Ferrari in the mid-1990s – if the company could be thered to make one.

The F40 was a direct descendant of the limited-production 288GTO, with a more power, and more obviously unique styling. Whereas the 288GTO had en derived from the 328GTB of the period (it looked very similar, even though e engine/transmission layout had been re-aligned), the F40 went its own, ▶

▶ glorious, way. It was, above all, a light machine, for whereas the Porsche 9 which some might consider to be a rival tipped the scales at no less th 2,977lb/1,350kg, the more starkly presented F40 weighed no more th 2,425lb/1,100kg, which was a massive saving. Less weight equated to high performance and, if anyone cared, potentially better fuel economy.

The chassis was essentially a tubular steel structure, which a incorporated bonded composite panels to endow greater rigidity and torsic stiffness. Ferrari reckoned that this was three times as rigid as a conventio steel frame would have been, but weighed perhaps 20 per cent less. There v tubular steel all around the passenger compartment, to provide a safety cag

This Supercar was so characteristically Ferrari (and, in some ways, v typically rough-and-ready finishing to some joints and assemblies), in which twin-turbocharged four-camshaft 90-degree V8 engine was mounted amidsh behind the two-seater cabin, driving the rear wheels through a five-spe transmission. To get the sort of power they required – 478bhp in this case – to keep the weight down, Ferrari engineers developed the 288GTO's V8 a sta further (and, let us remember, this V8 had its original roots in the 308GTB of mid-1970s). Keeping to the twin turbocharger layout – the F40, in fact, using Japanese IHi turbo for each bank of four cylinders – the engine was enlarged 2,936cc, further developed in detail, and eventually rated at 478bhp at a rous 7,000rpm. Although the 288GTO had produced 400bhp, up to that time no ot Ferrari road car unit had pushed out anything like the same power. Although engine, the transmission, the rock-solid artisan-engineering tubular chassis the all-independent suspension were all a logical development of what had g before, it was the body style, its construction and the materials used wh were so very advanced.

With the exception of the Testarossa of 1984, almost all previous Ferr had been rounded, sinuous, creatures (not machines, you understand, creatures), with sweeping lines over their wheels and their passenger cab Not the F40. Here was a two-seater coupé whose lines had been suggested Pininfarina, but whose detail had then been finalised after many hours of w tunnel testing.

The shell itself was made up of 12 pieces of Kevlar/carbon fibre/glassfi composite material – strong and light, so that the F40 could perform at its be

Below: In spite of having a 478bhp/2.9-litre engine, the F40 was quite compact car, its two-seater cabin being ahead of the turbocharged V8 engine. That spoiler was functional, not for decoration.

Above: The F40 was tightly but expertly packaged, with the turbocharged V8 engine behind the seats. Up front there was space only for the spare wheel - and a toothbrush. Note the huge width of rear tyres.

At the front it had a squared-up, almost flat, shovel-like nose, with a deep spoiler to channel air in the required direction. Headlamps were behind lift-up flaps, while there were two discreet NACA ducts in the 'bonnet' panel to channel fresh air to the interior. Air intakes for the engine bay were at the sides, 328GTB/288GTO-like, though detailed differently, and at the rear there was a large, full-width, fixed-incidence transverse aerofoil, the better to trim the high-speed handling. The cabin itself was pure two-seater, the roof blending sweetly into a tinted Perspex cover over the exposed engine, and liberally slatted to provide cooling.

It went as well, even better, than everyone expected. In a straight line, where excellence was expected, it always delivered – raucously, in a full-blooded way, time and time again. At speed it was as stable as hoped for – no high-speed journey, even on a limit-free German autobahn, ever caught out an F40 – and on twisty going it was sure-footed up to enormously high limits. The big disparity in tyre sections – 235/40 section at the front, and road-roller width 335-/35 section at the rear – saw to that. All this, allied to race-proved independent suspension, steering that was remarkably light even though there was no power assistance, and the sort of response that only professional racing drivers could treat as familiar, made it irresistible.

Even as the new century opened, the F40 was probably still the most desirable, the most spine-tingling, Ferrari of all, and one only has to look at the proven performance to see why. Maybe to experience the 200+ top speed was an academic wish, but the thrill of sprinting from rest to 100mph in a mere 8.8 seconds could make up for all that (current hot hatchbacks such as the Peugeot 205GTI and the Golf GTI were just hitting 60mph as the F40 sprinted past 'the ton').

So, what if the interior trim was stark, and the ground clearance flinched at every road hump in the world? What if it was almost impossibly expensive to insure, and costly to service? This was an F40, and this was the best.

Ferrari F50

Ferrari F50, built from 1995 to 1998
Built by: Ferrari S.p.A, Italy.
Engine: Twelve cylinders, in 65-degree vee formation, in seven main-bearing light-alloy cylinder block. Bore and stroke 85 x 69mm, 4,698cc (3.35 x 2.72in, 286.8cu.in). Two light-alloy cylinder heads. Five valves per cylinder, operated by inverted bucket tappets from twin overhead camshafts per cylinder head. Bosch Motronic fuel injection. Maximum power 513bhp at 8,000rpm. Maximum torque 347lb.ft at 6,500rpm.
Transmission: Mid-mounted engine, rear-wheel-drive, dry-plate clutch and six-speed all-synchromesh manual gearbox, in unit with engine and final drive. Remote control, centre floor gearchange.
Chassis: Separate carbon fibre chassis tub, with carbon fibre body shell in two-seater open-top style and removable roof panel. Independent front suspension by coil springs, wishbones and anti-roll bar, independent rear suspension by coil springs, wishbones, anti-roll bar. Electro/hydraulic telescopic dampers, with

adaptive ride control. Rack-and-pinion steering, no power assistance. Disc brakes at all four wheels, with vacuum servo assistance, but no ABS. 18in centre-lock cast-alloy road wheels, with 245/35-18in (front) and 335/30-18in (rear) tyres.

Dimensions: Wheelbase 8ft 5.6in (258cm), front track 5ft 3.8in (162cm), rear track 5ft 3.1in (160cm). Overall length 14ft 8.4in (448cm). Unladen weight 2,712lb (1,230kg).

History: How could Ferrari possibly replace the sensational F40? With the F50 of course, but it took more than four years of patient development, and some very expensive engineering, to finalise a car which would do even more.

As far as the customer was concerned, first cost would not be important, so Ferrari was never constricted in what it could do. Even so, to develop a two- ▶

Below: Ferrari's F50 was a step up from the F40, complete with a sinuous carbon-fibre body, and much F1-derived engineering under the skin.

▶ seater sports car, the F50, which was really an extension of early-1990s single-seater F1 thinking, was brave indeed. This time, too, it would one of Ferrari's always-traditional V12 engines, instead of a turbocharged V8.

Also brave was president Luca de Montezemolo's decision to reduce F50 production to precisely 349 – for it was later thought that far too many F40s (1,311, in fact) had been produced, to devalue that particular currency.

Like the F40, the F50 was meant to be a no-holds-barred mid-engined two-seater, which would drive its rear wheels, where performance would come before comfort, and where style would definitely come before practicality. The major advances, though, were in the looks of the new model, and how it was to be built.

For the new car Pininfarina, as ever, produced an absolutely stunning style, this being altogether more rounded, more delicate and somehow less threatening in its aspect than the F40 had always been. Naturally it had a low nose and a high tail, naturally there was a transverse rear aerofoil, and naturally there were big air intakes in the flanks, but this time the roof of the cabin was arranged to lift off, 'Targa' style: most F50s, it seems, were bought and driven in warm climates where weather protection was not needed!

The key to the whole car was its extensive use of carbon fibre, for the loadbearing chassis was in that material, so were the body panels, and even details like the gear lever knob used the same material. The body shell also included elements of Kevlar and of Nomex honeycomb.

Such levels of F1 technology were repeated in the engine and transmission. The engine, no less, was a de-tuned and productionised version of the 65-degree V12 used in the F1 Ferrari of 1990. This was one of the famous five-valve power

Above: The F50's sleek body style hid a mid-mounted 513bhp V12 engine of a type once used in the company's F1 cars.

units which had been further developed during the decade, but were about to be made obsolete in the single-seaters by a new V10.

In the F50 road car its capacity was pushed out from 3.5-litres to 4.7-litres, with peak revs reduced from 14,000rpm to a mere 8,500rpm, but with a (normally aspirated) peak power output of no less than 520bhp. Not only was this new V12 more powerful than the F40 (by 42bhp), but it drove a car of the same weight, so no one ever doubted claims of 202mph top speeds.

Behind the engine, too, was a new ultra-close-ratio six-speed transmission, the gear change had the sort of visible 'gate' for which all such Ferraris were famous, and the passengers sat in highly shaped carbon fibre seats to remind them exactly of what they were occupying. Ferrari refused to include power-assistance for the steering, and there was no ABS to the colossal Brembo brake discs. Rear suspension, in true F1 style, was by rocker-type coil spring/damper units, which were mounted on top of the transmission.

Even so, and in spite of there being no provision for sound equipment to be included, all this visible carbon fibre hid practical features to make the car more saleable especially in the USA), such as full air conditioning and careful airflow management in, around and through the front of the car.

By any standards this was a simply stunning Ferrari, which out-ranked anything which the Italian company had previously tackled. There was a waiting list even before the F50- went on sale, one which remained even when the model was withdrawn, as planned, after the 349 had been produced.

Ferrari F355

Ferrari F355 sports coupé and cabriolet, built from 1994 to 1998
Built by: Ferrari S.p.A., Italy.
Engine: Eight cylinders in 90-deg V8 formation, in five-main-bearing light-alloy cylinder block/crankcase. Bore and stroke 85 × 77mm, 3,496cc (3.35 × 3.03in, 213.4cu.in). Two light alloy cylinder heads. Five valves per cylinder (three inlet, two exhaust), operation by twin overhead camshafts per head, with inverted bucket-type tappets. Bosch/Ferrari fuel injection. Maximum power 380bhp (DIN) at 8,250rpm. Maximum torque 268lb.ft at 6,000rpm.
Transmission: Rear-wheel-drive, diaphragm spring clutch and six-speed all-synchromesh manual gearbox, all in unit with mid/rear-mounted engine.

Remote-control, central gearchange.
Chassis: Separate multi-tubular steel, with reinforcements, chassis frame, clad
in steel-and-light alloy two-seater body shell. Independent front suspension by
coil springs, wishbones, electronically adaptive telescopic dampers, anti-roll bar.
Independent rear suspension by coil springs, wishbones, electronically adaptive
telescopic dampers, anti-roll bar. Rack and pinion steering, with speed-sensitive ▶

**Below: Mid-V8 engine, style by Pininfarina, and a potential top speed of
more than 180mph made the F355 irresistible. If you could afford it, of
course.**

▶ power assistance. Four-wheel disc brakes, with power asistance, and ABS. Cast-alloy 18in road wheels, 225/40-18in (front) and 265/40-18in (rear) tyres.

Dimensions: Wheelbase 8ft 0.5in (245cm), front track 4ft 11.6in (151.4cm), rear track 5ft 3.6in (161.5cm). Overall length 13ft 11.3in (425cm). Unladen weight 3,135lb (1,422kg).

History: If the F40 was Ferrari's best-ever road car, so called, the F355 which arrived in 1994 was a contender for the best civilised, all-purpose, two-seater from the same stable. The two cars could not have been more different. The F40 was all about performance, and brushed aside many creature comforts, whereas the F355 was the all-can-do two-seater which could be fast or slow, could be driven in cities or on the highways, and would appeal to thousands.

Ferrari's 'small' V8 family had been founded in 1973 with the 308GTB, and progressed to the 328GT, which had then been supplanted by the 348tb of 1989. The F355 replaced the 348tb, and built on the previous reputation. The displaced 348tb had been good, but by Ferrari standards not quite good enough, particularly in its performance and its on-the-limit roadholding. For the F355 (note the new type of model naming policy) Ferrari aimed to improved on that.

Although the chassis, complete with its 96.5in/245cm wheelbase, was much as before, there had been development changes everywhere. The engine, too, while still the same basic 90-degree V8 (and thus related to that of the F40), was 3,496cc instead of 3,405cc, had brand new cylinder heads with the fashionable five valves per cylinder which Ferrari F1 V12s were already using – and produced no less than 380bhp at 8,250rpm.

Because the F355, with its new, rounded, but somehow understated styling, was smaller than the 512TR (the reworked Testarossa, which was still being made) it was a faster, and better car in all respects – and this with 'only' 3.5-litres, and with only eight cylinders. It was no wonder that road testers raved the moment they were let loose in it, and why the customers' queues soon built up.

This time, it seemed, Ferrari had thought of everything. Not only was this the fastest V8-engined 'everyday' Ferrari so far, but it also seemed to be the most complete. The style, by Pininfarina, was smooth and understated (no side strakes this time, unlike the 348tb), but this time it incorporated a smooth undertray to improve aerodynamic performance still further. Traditionalists saluted the return of circular tail lamps, while others wanted to know why there were no extravagant spoilers.

To match the 380bhp there was a new in-line close-ratio six-speed transmission (not even the F40 had had one of those), where the claimed top speed was 184mph, but where you could also beat 150mph in fifth. Acceleration was just as ferocious as expected, though the 265/40-section rear tyres did their very best to keep wheelspin in check.

The F355's most impressive feature was its completeness, for this was a car with roadholding as good as its performance, with looks matched to its equipment, with superlative power-assisted steering, sensitive brakes, ABS to take away all the pain and the worry, and a cabin in which (not always possible in earlier Ferraris, by the way) one could also relax.

Perhaps it was as well that the flat-12 Testarossa-based cars were already in their last manifestation, for the F355 surely out-gunned them in every respect. It was only when the 360 Modena came along in 1999 that we all realised that improvements were possible, after all.

Below: The F355 was powered by a 380bhp/3.5-litre V8 engine, with twin overhead camshafts and five valves per cylinder.

Ferrari F360 Modena

Ferrari F360 Modena, introduced in 1999
Built by: Ferrari S.p.A, Italy.
Engine: Eight cylinders, in 90-degree vee formation, in five-main-bearing light alloy cylinder block/crankcase. Bore and stroke 85 x 79mm, 3,586cc (3.35 x 3.11in, 219cu.in). Two light alloy cylinder heads. Five valves per cylinder (three inlet, two exhaust), operation by twin overhead camshafts per head, with inverted bucket tappets. Bosch Motronic fuel injection. Maximum power 400bhp at 8,500rpm. Maximum torque 275lb.ft at 4,750rpm.
Transmission: Mid-engine, rear-wheel-drive, single-dry-plate diaphragm spring clutch and six-speed manual gearbox, all in unit with engine and final drive Remote control centre floor gearchange.
Chassis: Separate multi-tube Alcoa aluminium space frame chassis, with alloy/steel body shell in two-seater sports coupé style. Independent front suspension by coil springs, wishbones and anti-roll bar, independent rear suspension by coil springs, wishbones and anti-roll bar. Hydraulic/electronic telescopic dampers with adaptive ride control. Rack-and-pinion steering, with power assistance. Disc brakes at all four wheels, with vacuum servo assistance, and ABS as standard. 18in bolt-on cast alloy road wheels, with 215/45-18in (front) and 275/40-18in (rear) tyres.
Dimensions: Wheelbase 8ft 6.3in (2600cm), front track 5ft 5.7in (167cm), rear track

Below: The F360 Modena was the latest in a long line of fabulous mid-V8-engined Ferraris, this time with 400bhp and a 185mph top speed.

Above: Although by no means extrovert in looks, the F360 Modena was instantly recognisable, and gained great respect from everyone else on the road.

5ft 3.6in (161.5cm). Overall length 14ft 8.2in (447.7cm). Unladen weight 3,191lb (1,447kg).

History: Whenever Enzo Ferrari was asked if he had a favourite Ferrari, he would always smile wolfishly and retort: 'The next one!' Progress at Maranello, he implied, was continuous, so today's Ferraris were always superior to their ancestors, while tomorrow's dream machine would take over in good time.

Accordingly, although it was easy enough to state that in 1999 the new F360 Modena was probably the most capable road car the company had ever built, we may be sure that they were already looking forward to improving on it in future years.

By any standards, however, the F360 had a formidable task – which was not only to improve on the well-loved F355, but also to be yet another fine two-seater to use a further-developed version of that robust V8 engine which had first appeared in 1973. Here was an engine which had improved mightily over the years, for in 1973 it had been a 240bhp/2,926cc power unit: now, in 1999, it pushed out a resounding 400bhp from 3,586cc.

Although the F355 and F360 types looked visually similar (and so they should, for Pininfarina had produced both these beautiful body styles), they were very different under the skin. From F355 to F360, in fact, Ferrari had ▶

▶ made a big jump in technology and in construction. Whereas the F355 had been the last of the old brigade, with its multi-tubular chassis frame, and with a body shell made largely of pressed steel, the F360 used a completely fresh aluminium structure, this being described as an aluminium chassis/space frame, clothed and wrapped in an aluminium shell.

Aluminium, indeed, seemed to be everywhere for, like BMW and Jaguar, Ferrari had also embraced the idea of aluminium forgings for its suspension wishbones, the wheels were also in aluminium, as was the casing of the transmission. One important change in the mid-engined layout was that cooling radiators were now in the nose, in each front corner, rather than in the engine compartment.

The importance of this was not that the car could look different (in fact it was a logical visual improvement on the F355), but that it could be equally rigid but lighter, than before. The shape, too, had been evolved with a purpose, for this new car not only had a larger and more comfortable cabin than the F355 but at high speeds it developed four times the downforce of its predecessor.

Under the skin, in fact, there was much which looked familiar, but which was different. The V8 engine, for instance, was only slightly up-graded from the F355, and was now to be supplied in 400bhp/3,586cc tune. Since that enlargement had involved only a 2mm increase in stroke, it was assumed that

the bore size was already at its limit, and that this would probably be the final 'stretch' of a much loved engine.

But 400bhp, from a normally aspirated engine, was sensational stuff, so it was no surprise to learn that with a brand-new six-speed gearbox, this could be a 185mph car. Ferrari advances in performance were continuous, it seems, for only ten years earlier they would have need 5.0-litres to guarantee so much power, in a bigger car (the Testarossa) – which would not have achieved the same levels of performance.

There was no doubt, therefore, when Ferrari said that its ambition was for the F360 to outsell its ancestors – and that was going to be a real challenge. Nearly 17,000 two-seater versions of the 308/328GTB types had been sold, and almost 10,000 of the F355s had immediately preceded the F360 Modena.

Ferrari standards, indeed, had changed considerably in three decades. In that time, the 'entry-level' Dino had enlarged from 2.4-litres to 3.6-litres, its power output from 195bhp to 400bhp.

'And if they can do this with a "small" car,' one expert commented, 'just think what they could do with a full-sized one!'

Below: Announced in 1999, the F360 was the first Ferrari road car to use a new-generation of aluminium space-frame chassis.

Fiat 508 Balilla

**Type 508 and 508s, side-valve and overhead-valve, built from 1932 to 193?.
(data for 508S overhead-valve)**

Built by: Fiat SpA., Italy.

Engine: Four cylinders, in line, in three-bearing cast-iron block. Bore and stroke
65mm by 75mm, 995cc (2.56in × 2.95in, 60.7cu.in). Cast-iron cylinder head. Two
overhead valves per cylinder, operated by pushrods and rockers from single
side-mounted camshaft. Zenith down-draught carburettor. Maximum power
36bhp at 4,400rpm.

Transmission: Single-dry-plate clutch and four-speed manual gearbox
(synchromesh on top and third gears), both in unit with engine. Central direct-
acting gearchange. Open propeller shaft to spiral-bevel 'live' rear axle.

Chassis: Separate steel chassis frame, with channel-section side members, and
cruciform bracing. Forged front axle beam. Half-elliptic leaf springs at front and
rear and friction type dampers (hydraulic on earlier 508 models). Worm-and-
wheel steering. Four-wheel, hydraulically operated drum brakes. Separate drum
handbrake on transmission, behind gearbox. 17in bolt-on wire wheels 4.00 ×
17in tyres. Coachwork to choice, on 508, but 508S built as two-seat sports car.

Dimensions: Wheelbase 7ft 6.5in (230cm), tracks (front and rear) 3ft 10in
(117cm). Overall length (depending on coachwork) about 12ft 10.8in (368cm).
Unladen weight 1,300lb (590kg).

History: Fiat's all-new Balilla model was launched in 1932, at the very depth of
the depression years. Fiat were well-protected against economic disaster (with
90 per cent of the Italian market), but could not afford to make another bad car
after the Type 514, which had failed. The 508 was typical in most ways of the
small family machine developed to expand the European market in the 1930s
with a one-litre engine, strictly conventional mechanical layout and lightweight
construction. Fiat, better than most, engineered their car well, made it reliable
and somehow ensured that it was interesting to drive. The original 508 had

**Below: Because it had a separate chassis, the Balilla could be sold with
several different body styles. Original 1932 types, usually known as
'Spider Lusso', had twin exposed spare wheels and rather upright lines.
By 1935, though, the car had become a 508S, with overhead valves, and
there was a fastback coupé body style too. This illustration shows the
typical two-seater open sports car style which went so well with that
final engine. The pronounced tail fin (which had no aerodynamic
function) was a 1930s fashion. Although only about 2,000 508S
models were made, some licence-built in France and Germany,
they were well-loved machines.**

Above: The Balilla's nose, with a rounded radiator shape, and twin high-mounted headlamps, gave it a cheeky and endearing frontal aspect.

marginally shorter wheelbase than the later 508S and a side-valve engine, but otherwise the specification remained mainly settled for five years. 'Balilla', incidentally, means 'plucky little one' and had rather sinister connotations with a Mussolini/fascist youth movement.

The 508S, built first as a side-valve car, but from 1934 with an overhead-valve conversion of the same basic 995cc engine, arrived in 1933 and eventually made its name in trials, rallies, and even in endurance racing. Class for class it was very competitive, although it was overshadowed by such exotic machinery as the supercharged MG Magnettes. Cars sold in Britain were usually given British two-seater bodywork, of which a recognition point was usually the pronounced tail-fin behind the cockpit. One very desirable version of the car was the *berlinetta aerodinamica,* a fastback coupé with attractive flowing lines; maximum speed was raised, but the car was not much faster overall than open versions. A bald look at the specification tells us little about a Balilla's charm, except that it had an unusually 'short stroke' and small-capacity engine for the period. Somehow it was much more of a small car than a scaled down battle cruiser, and handled accordingly. All in all, about 2,000 508S were built, and a few were licence-made by Simca in France and by NSU in Germany.

Fiat 1200/1500/1600S Cabriolet

Fiat 1200/1500/1600S family, built from 1959 to 1966 (data for original 1200)

Built by: Fiat SpA, Italy.

Engine: Four cylinders, in line, in three-main-bearing cast iron cylinder block. Bore and stroke 72 x 75mm, 1,221cc (2.83 x 2.95in, 74.5cu.in). Aluminium cylinder head. Two overhead valves per cylinder, operated by pushrods and rockers from a camshaft in the cylinder block. One downdraught Weber carburettor. Maximum power 58bhp at 5,300rpm. Maximum torque 61lb.ft at 3,000rpm. [Later models had 1.5-litre/72bhp, 1.5-litre twin-cam/80bhp and 1.6-litre twin-cam/90bhp engines.]

Transmission: Front engine, rear-wheel-drive, single-dry-plate clutch and four-speed synchromesh manual gearbox, with no synchromesh on first gear, all in unit with engine. Remote control, centre floor, gearchange.

Chassis: Unitary steel body/chassis structure, topped by two-seater sports car body style by Pininfarina. Optional removable steel hardtop. Independent front suspension by coil springs, wishbones and anti-roll bar, suspension of beam rear axle by half-elliptic leaf springs and anti-roll bar. Telescopic hydraulic dampers. Worm and roller steering. Drum brakes at all four wheels. 14in steel disc wheels, bolt on, with 5.20-14in tyres.

Dimensions: Wheelbase 7ft 8.1in (234cm), front track 4ft 0.5in (123cm), rear track 3ft 11.9in (121cm). Overall length 13ft 2.7in (403cm). Unladen weight 1,994lb (904kg).

Above: There was always a choice of engines in these Fiat Cabriolets –
either a mass-produced Fiat unit, or a twin-cam OSCA engine.

Below: All the 1200-1600S Cabriolets of the 1960s shared this smart fascia
style, so much more up-market than their British and Italian competitors.

History: Although everyone remembers the 124-based Fiat
Spiders of the 1960s and 1970s, it was the 1200 and 1500
Cabriolets that preceded them which really introduced
sporting Fiats into the world market.

By the late 1950s Fiat, which was (and still is) Italy's largest
car-maker, was expanding its range in all directions, and to
improve its image it needed to put a sporty model on sale.
The 8V had been too costly, and too rare, while the early
Pininfarina-styled roadster based on the 1100 platform had
been ungainly.

From 1959, though, all that would change, for a new car
which not only used the platform of the latest 1200 saloon,
but which had very smart new Pininfarina styling came on
the scene. The new car not only looked sleek, and was nicely
detailed, but it featured wind-up windows, and was much
more boulevard than its bow-windscreened predecessor: its
name – 1200 Cabriolet – immediately signalled the type of
equipment and weather equipment, which was fitted.

The first cars used a 58bhp/1,221cc pushrod engine, which
guaranteed 90mph, but the twin-cam engined 1500S which
soon followed (the engine was by OSCA, which was owned
by the Maserati family) was a more formidable machine, with
a 105mph top speed.

These were the two cars on which Fiat then developed the
final versions in 1962/1963 – the 1500 (which had a
72bhp/1.5-litre engine) and the 1600S (which had a
90bhp/1.6-litre version of the OSCA power unit), both of
which, when matured, had five-speed gearboxes. Although ▶

▶ the 1600S exuded glamour, it was more expensive, so it was the pushrod 15⬚ which took all the sales. The reputation of these cars was still growing in 196⬚ when they made way for the even more successful 124-based cars. More th⬚ 37,000 of this family had been built in seven years.

Above: Invited by Fiat to style a new, small, but image-boosting 2+2-seater Cabriolet, Pininfarina did a superb job. Every car had wind-up windows. A hardtop was optional too. The looks were back-up by speed and power, and also healthy sales for a few years.

Fiat 124 Spider

Fiat 124 Spider, built from 1966 to 1982. Pininfarina Spiders built fro
1982 to 1987 (data for original 1.4-litre)
Built by: Fiat SpA, Italy.
Engine: Four cylinders, in line, in five-main-bearing cast iron cylinder bloc
Bore and stroke 80 x 71.5mm, 1,438cc (3.15 x 2.82in, 87.5cu.in). Cast all
cylinder head. Two overhead valves per cylinder, operated directly by invert
bucket tappets from twin camshafts in the cylinder head. One downdraug
Weber carburettors. Maximum power 90bhp at 6,000rpm. Maximum torq
80lb.ft at 3,600rpm. [Later models had 1.6-litre/110bhp, 1.8-litre/118bhp a
2.0-litre/87bhp (USA market only). Pininfarina took over manufacture, rebadgi
the car, in 1982, making a 122bhp/2.0-litre version for European sale.]
Transmission: Front engine, rear-wheel-drive, single dry plate diaphrag
spring clutch and five-speed all-synchromesh manual gearbox, all in unit w
engine; remote control centre floor gearchange.
Chassis: Unitary construction steel body/chassis structure, with two-sea
open top steel sports car body style, by Pininfarina. Independent fro
suspension by coil springs, wishbones and anti-roll bar, suspension of bea
rear axle by coil springs, radius arms and Panhard rod. Hydraulic telescoj
dampers. Worm and roller steering. Disc brakes at all four wheels, with vacuu
servo assistance. 13in wheels, bolt on steel disc, with 165-13in tyres.
Dimensions: Wheelbase 7ft 5.8in (228cm), front track 4ft 5in (134.5cm), re
track 4ft 4in (132cm). Overall length 13ft 0.4in (345cm). Unladen weight 2,08:
(945kg).
History: Designed originally to replace the earlier 1500 and 1600S Cabrio
models, and to sell in much larger quantities, the closely related 124 Sp
Coupé and Spider cars evolved into some of the most long-running a

uccessful sporty cars ever to be put on sale by Fiat. Although the four-seater
oupé was finally discontinued in 1975, the open-topped two-seater, continually
pdated and modified, was produced until 1982, after which Pininfarina took it
ver, and re-badged it, for several more seasons.

Both types were based on the platform an important new family car, the
24. Although this originally had a perfectly conventional overhead-valve four-
ylinder engine, a twin-cam version was already planned, and would power the
oupé and the Spider throughout their careers.

The Sport Coupé, with its rather angular, but appealing, four-seater cabin,
ad been shaped by Fiat themselves, whereas the open-top Spider was
eveloped by Pininfarina, who also contracted to produce the painted
odyshells at first. As with most such Italian models, the Spider's floor pan was
horter than that of the saloon (and, therefore, of the Sport Coupé), but it was
ever meant to be more than a two-seater and its proportions looked exactly
ght. Hidden away was a beam rear axle, but this was well-located, and there
vere four-wheel disc brakes to add to the appeal.

The first Spider which, to British and many North American eyes, looked
ke a rather more chic and stylish derivative of the MGB, went on sale in 1967,
nd was originally fitted with a 90bhp/1.4-litre version of the twin-cam engine,
nd a five-speed gearbox. Quick, but rather frantically high-revving, it could
each 106mph, but more was expected of it in the future.

The first update came in 1969, when a long stroke version of the engine,
e 110bhp/1.6-litre, was specified, and even though North American ▶

**elow: Although the 124 Spider was based on the 124 saloon's platform,
was a neat little two-seater sports car, whose career lasted 21 years.**

▶ regulations took their toll of power, this was suddenly a more versatile mach
In 1972 a good sports car became even better when the 118bhp/1.8
version of the same engine arrived, and for years this was the limit of
Spider's improvements for Europe.

Solely for sale in North America, the Spider 2000 came along in 1978,
being accompanied by facelift style changes to the bodywork and to
interior. Although exhaust emission rules choked the power back to 87bhp,
the top speed to only 102mph, it was now available with the optio
automatic transmission, and sales remained steady for some time. From 1
Bosch fuel injection and an up-date was standardised and peak power cra⌄
back to 103bhp.

To increase the car's appeal in that market, the North Amer
concessionaire also developed a turbocharged version for the early 19
which had 120bhp and better performance, but was too costly to sell wide

In 1982 Fiat then made the starling decision to pull out of sports
manufacture, so Pininfarina then picked up the rights for building the entire

Above: In 21 years, the only style changes made to the 124 Spider's body were to add 'power bulges' in the bonnet panel.

and re-badged it as the Pininfarina Spider instead. Cars thus badged carried on selling steadily, but not sensationally, in the USA until 1987, though no major technical innovations were ever introduced.

One result of Pininfarina taking over the project was that a 2-litre model called the Spider Europa was finally made available in Europe after all, this having a Bosch injected/122bhp version of the engine which had been in use in USA-market cars since 1978/1979. This, though, was merely a coda to an amazingly long career.

At peak, in the late 1970s, well over 15,000 Spiders were being sent to North America every year where this model was always a great success. All in all, there were 190,546 Fiat-badged 124 Spiders, so with (never revealed) Pininfarina production in the 1980s, the 200,000 figure must surely have been reached.

Fiat X1/9

Fiat X1/9, built from 1972 to 1989 (data for 1500 model)
Built by: Fiat SpA, Italy.
Engine: Transversely-mounted four cylinders, in line, in five-main-bearing c
iron cylinder block. Bore and stroke 86.4 x 63.9mm, 1,498cc (3.40 x 2.5
91.4cu.in). Light alloy cylinder head. Two overhead valves per cylinder, opera
by inverted bucket tappets from single overhead camshaft in cylinder he
One downdraught Weber carburettor. Maximum power 85bhp at 6,000rp
Maximum torque 87lb.ft at 3,200rpm.
Transmission: Transversely mounted mid-engine, rear-wheel-drive, single
plate diaphragm spring clutch and five-speed all-synchromesh manual gearb
all in unit with engine. Remote control, centre floor gearchange.
Chassis: Unitary construction combined steel body/chassis structure, with tv
seater coupé/removable roof panel body style by Bertone. Independent fr
suspension by coil springs and MacPherson struts, independent r
suspension by coil springs and MacPherson struts: telescopic hydra
dampers. Rack-and-pinion steering. Disc brakes at all four wheels. 13in whe
bolt-on cast alloy, with 165/70-13in tyres.
Dimensions: Wheelbase 7ft 2.75in (220cm), front track 4ft 5.4in (135.5c
rear track 4ft 5.2in (135.5cm). Overall length 12ft 6.75in (383cm). Unlac
weight 2,010lb (911.5kg).
   [The X1/9 was originally made with a 75bhp/1.3-litre engine, and four-spe
gearbox, to 1978. Bertone took over complete assembly from 1982.]
History: When the X1/9, so neatly and crisply styled by Bertone, appearec
1972, it made all previous sports cars look out of date. Shaped around a n

**Below: Even though it had an engine mounted behind the seats, and
was a short car, the X1/9 had a comfortable and well-equipped cockpi**

Above: Some X1/9s were race-prepared, to take part in 1.5-litre 'production sports car' events. For comparison, that is a standard road car in the background.

steel structure, which featured a transverse engine and gearbox mounted behind the seats, but ahead of the line of the rear wheels.

The X1/9 (this was a project code carried forward to production) was a replacement for the little 850, with a neat little pressed-steel monocoque, which was not shared with any other model. A feature of the two-seat accommodation was that the roof panel could be removed, and stowed, and that there were *two* stowage areas – one up front, one in the extreme tail. To extract the spare wheel, it had to be removed through the passenger cabin, and a side door!

Fiat's secret was that it utilised a lightly modified version of the Fiat 128's front-wheel-drive package, which included a brand-new, overhead-cam, short-stroke engine. This needed little more than a revised gearchange, and modified suspension, to suit it for sporting use behind the cabin. Space efficient MacPherson strut suspension at front and rear added to an appealing, and convincing, package.

Early X1/9s used a 75bhp/1.3-litre engine, with a four-speed transmission, but the definitive type, which was announced in 1978, used an 85bhp/21.5-litre engine and a five-speed gearbox, which delivered 106mph in great style and comfort, though at this time some of the purity of the original style was lost.

Although premature rusting problems abounded, the X1/9 was so cute, so handleable and so practical that it always sold well. As with the 124, Fiat washed its hands of the X1/9 in 1982, after which Bertone completely took over manufacture, and carried on making the unchanged 1500 until 1989. At least 180,000 cars were built in seventeen years.

►

Above: Bertone's style on the X1/9 was so delicate that the mid-mounted engine position, behind the seats, is not at all obvious.

Fiat Barchetta

Fiat Barchetta, introduced in 1995
Built by: Fiat SpA, Italy.
Engine: Four cylinders, in line, in five-main-bearing cast-iron cylinder block. Bore and stroke 82 x 83mm, 1,747cc (3.23 x 3.27in, 106.6cu.in). Aluminium cylinder head. Four overhead valves per cylinder, operated by inverted bucket-type tappets and two overhead camshafts. Hitachi fuel injection. Maximum power 130bhp at 6,300rpm. Maximum torque 121lb.ft at 4,300rpm.
Transmission: Transversely mounted engine and front-wheel-drive, single dry plate, diaphragm spring clutch and five-speed all-synchromesh manual gearbox, in unit with engine. Remote control centre gearchange.
Chassis: Unitary construction steel body/chassis structure, in open-top two-seater style. Independent front suspension by coil springs, MacPherson struts, anti-roll bar, independent rear suspension by coil springs, trailing arms, anti-roll bar. Telescopic hydraulic dampers. Rack-and-pinion steering with power assistance. Front and rear disc brakes, with hydraulic vacuum servo assistance and optional ABS. 15in cast alloy wheels. 195/55-15in tyres.
Dimensions: Wheelbase 8ft 0in (244cm), front track 4ft 7.5in (141cm), rear track 4ft 7.5in (141cm). Overall length 12ft 10.3in (392cm). Unladen weight 2,328lb (1,056kg).
History: The Mazda MX-5, it seems, had a lot to answer for. Although Mazda admitted it was a retro restatement of the MG Midget theme, the MX-5, in turn,

Above: Barchettas had a tightly packed two-seater cabin, naturally with an airbag packaged into the hub of the steering wheel.

inspired a series of imitations. The two most notable, and successful, were MG's MGF, and the Fiat Barchetta.

For purely financial reasons Fiat had fallen out of love with sports cars, for they had dropped the X1/9 and 124 Spiders in 1982 when these cars no longer made money for them. It was not until the mid-1990s – and spurred on, some say, by their purchase of Alfa Romeo – that they thought again.

By this time Fiat not only owned Alfa Romeo, but Lancia, and were also in control of Ferrari. Logic, therefore, suggested that a new Fiat sports car should not attempt to sell in the same market as any of those marques. Having searched for the gap, therefore, Fiat found it towards the budget-price end of spectrum, and elected to develop a two-seater which would undersell any Alfa – and which could compete, head on, with the Mazda MX-5.

To do this, and to make such a ▶

Left: The rounded lines of the Barchetta made it look even smaller than it actually was . The engine was shared with the Alfa Spider of the period, but every other detail was special.

▶ project pay, management had to dig deeply into the corporate 'parts bin', and elected to build up a new open-top two-seater on an existing transverse-engine/front-wheel-drive floorpan. This was found under the latest Fiat Punto, which had made its debut in 1989, and was available with four-cylinder engines from 54bhp to 133bhp. For the new sports car, however, Fiat chose to shorten the pan by no less than 6.7in/17cm and of course to specify new-style road wheels so that no-one would recognise the source. As on the Punto, there was independent suspension at front and rear, with disc brakes all round, though the rack-and-pinion steering had no power assistance.

For its theme, Fiat chose to develop a 'Barchetta' style ('barchetta' means 'little boat' in Italian, and has always been attractive to sentimental Italians because of much earlier Ferrari visual connections), which meant that this new car had a simple, compact, rounded shape, smoothly detailed without bumps or obvious gouges or holes. The nose was long, though the tail was very short, and four headlamps were hidden away under plastic cowls.

The Barchetta's real novelty was that it was the very first Fiat to use a new

Above: The Barchetta featured a transversely mounted four-cylinder engine, and front-wheel-drive – not at all obvious from this angle.

family of engines – in this case a 16-valve, twin-cam, 1,747cc power unit – of a type which had already been previewed in the new-generation Alfa Romeo Spider and which would soon find itself in several other Alfas, Fiats and Lancia. For the light (2,328lb/1,056kg) Barchetta it produced 130bhp, and was matched to a five-speed transmission.

Like the Mazda with which it was a natural competitor, by modern standards the Fiat was a simple, no nonsense Roadster. Not only that, but with a claimed top speed of 125mph there was plenty of performance with which to match its looks, and the front-wheel-drive handling was taut and well-balanced.

If there was a problem with this car, it was that Fiat did not back it by pushing a performance image, or a motorsport programme. Some enthusiasts also wondered how it would have performed if the larger, 2-litre, version of this new engine had been fitted, but their dreams were never satisfied.

Ford Mustang

Mustang, built from 1964 to 1968, six-cyl and V8 models (data for 289cu.in
Built by: Ford Motor Co., United States.
Engine: Eight cylinders, in 90-degree vee-formation, in cast-iron cylinder block
Bore and stroke 101.6mm by 72.9mm, 4,727cc (4.0in × 2.87in, 289cu.in). Two
cast-iron cylinder heads. Two overhead valves per cylinder, operated by
pushrods and rockers from single camshaft mounted in cylinder block 'vee'
Downdraught four-choke Ford carburettor. Maximum power 271bhp (gross) a
6,000rpm. Maximum torque 312lb.ft at 3,400rpm.
Transmission: Single-dry-plate clutch and four-speed all-synchromesh manua
gearbox, both in unit with engine. Central remote-control gearchange. Oper
propeller shaft to hypoid-bevel 'live' axle. Optional limited-slip differential
Optional three-speed Ford automatic transmission with torque converter.

Below: These views of the Mustang show that the original cars had striking styling, but still found space for four full-size passengers. The car was a 'tourer' in every way, and was raced and rallied in the standard saloon car categories. Mustangs won the Tour de France in 1964, hundreds of races all over the world, and were a virility symbol to American youth of the 1960s. Through the years it grew up gradually but recent cars are smaller and slower, with European power trains. This convertible has the optional 289cu.in high-performance vee-8 engine, special wheels and tyres. Softer versions had six-cylinder engines and rather less performance. More than a million Mustangs sold in the first three years.

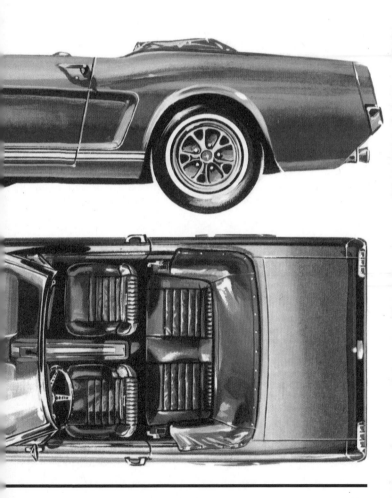

▶ **Chassis:** Unitary-construction, pressed-steel body-chassis unit, sold as open tourer four-seater, closed two-door coupé, or with fastback closed coupé style. Independent front suspension by coil springs, wishbones and anti-roll bar. Rear suspension by half-elliptic leaf springs. Recirculating-ball steering with power assistance optional. Four-wheel, hydraulically operated and servo-assisted drum brakes, with optional front discs. 14in pressed-steel disc wheels.

Dimensions: Wheelbase 9ft (274cm), track (front) 4ft 8in (142cm), track (rear) 4ft 8in (142cm). Overall length 15ft 1.6in (461cm). Unladen weight from 2,925lb (1,327kg) depending on equipment and bodyshell.

History: Ford's Mustang can probably thank the first very sporting Thunderbirds for its birth. The T-Bird, a two-seater at first, soon grew up and became a much larger car. By the early 1960s, with compact cars popular and sporting motoring again important to Ford, a place for a 'small' sporting machine developed. By European standards, of course, the Mustang has never been small – in original production form it was more than 15ft long, which is Aston Martin size, and bulkier than any sporting Jaguar. By Detroit standards, however, it was a very neat little package.

The production car was launched in April 1964, but had already been trailered by other prototype 'Mustangs' for the company to gauge reaction. The mid-engined car (the engine being a German V4) made public in 1962 was far too sophisticated for Ford to build in quantity and was made purely as a 'taster'. Mustang II, revealed at the US Grand Prix in the autumn of 1963, was still a non-production car, but since it was closely based on a prototype Mustang and redecorated lightly, its impact on the public was important. The public liked it and Ford went ahead to build the cars.

Chief of the Mustang project was Lee Iacocca, who was no innovative designer, but was sporting minded and already had the successful development of the compact Ford Falcon to his credit. It was therefore no surprise that the Mustang was such an enjoyable car to drive. It was more of a surprise that it could be persuaded to become a winner on the race tracks, but this was mostly because of the very imaginative list of high-performance options made available The car used many Falcon components, including the basic engines and

Below: For 1968 the Mustang received its first major re-style, becoming longer, smoother and more expensive. This was the fastback 2+2 GT.

Above: The original Mustang of 1964 was craggily styled, but struck a chord with America's affluent young, offering high performance at low first cost.

transmissions, and in true Detroit style there was a vast range of choice right from the start. One option much discussed, and even pictured in 1964, was an independent rear suspension for racing, but this was never proceeded with, and all Mustangs had to rely on the very basic half-elliptic leaf spring layout for location.

Engines ranged from the cheapest and least powerful straight six of 2,781cc to the highest-performance V8 of 4,727cc. The difference in power was from 101bhp to 271bhp, and shows the spread of owners' preferences for which Ford was aiming. By 1966, indeed, two tunes of sixes and five tunes of eights had already been listed, and as the years went by this choice widened. Cars could have manual or automatic transmission, drum or disc brakes, manual or power-assisted steering, soft or hard-tops, 13in or 14in wheels, extra instruments, special colour schemes and many other options.

Mustangs were successful in factory-sponsored teams almost at once, and their biggest early win was in the 1964 Tour de France where two cars prepared in Britain finished first and second overall, the winning car being driven by Peter Procter. As a racing 'saloon' car (for the Mustang was ideally dimensioned to satisfy international regulations), it was only ever beaten by other and even more special Fords, usually the lightweight Falcons. No young man, or young-at-heart man in North America could live until he had owned a Mustang, with the result that 400,000 were sold within twelve months, and the first million sales were notched up in 1966. Engine tuners like Carroll Shelby hurried to market their own special Mustangs (Shelby's was the GT350 and was very fierce indeed), while the 'add-on' accessory suppliers made a good living with special customising kits. The Mustang was an aggressively marketed runaway success in North America and (because of its reasonable size) was well-received in other countries. So much so, in fact, that Ford did not need to go for an important restyling operation until 1968. With that move, the Mustang, like the Thunderbird before it, began to move 'up-market' and to put on weight and bulk. Apart from the 5-litre 'Boss' of the late 1960s, it became less of a sporting car and more of a virility symbol. It was completely redesigned in the early 1970s and Mustang II was a much smaller, simpler and slower car.

Ford RS200

Ford RS200 sports coupé, built in 1985 and 1986

Built by: Ford Motor Co. Ltd., Britain.

Engine: Four cylinders, in line, in five-main-bearing light-alloy cylinder block. Bore and stroke 86 × 77.62mm, 1,803cc (3.39 × 3.06in, 110cu.in). Light alloy cylinder head. Four valves per cylinder, in narrow vee, operation by twin overhead camshafts and inverted bucket tappets. Ford/Bosch fuel injection and AiResearch turbocharger. Maximum power 250bhp (DIN) at 6,500rpm. Maximum torque 215lb.ft at 4,000rpm. Tune-up kits in 300bhp, 350bhp and 450bhp were all optionally available.

Transmission: Four-wheel-drive, AP Racing type of diaphragm spring clutch and five-speed all-synchromesh manual gearbox, all in unit with mid-mounted engine. Remote-control, central gearchange.

Chassis: Unitary-construction body-chassis unit, based around aluminium honeycomb/carbon fibre composite/steel tub, with integral steel roll cage, and glassfibre body skin panels. Independent front suspension by double coil springs, wishbones, telescopic dampers, anti-roll bar. Independent rear suspension by double coil springs, wishbones, telescopic dampers, and anti-roll bar. Rack-and-pinion steering, with optional power assistance. Four-wheel disc brakes, with hydraulic power assistance, but no ABS. Cast-alloy 16in road wheels, 225/50-16in tyres.

Dimensions: Wheelbase 8ft 3.6in (253cm), front track 4ft 11.1in (150.1cm), rear track 4ft 11in (150cm). Overall length 13ft 1.5in (400cm). Unladen weight 2,607lb (1,183kg).

History: Although rallying's Group B formula lasted only a few years, it inspired the birth of some remarkable four-wheel-drive monsters. The prettiest by far, though not the most successful in the sport, was Ford's RS200. Because only 200 such cars had to be built (to meet the Group B requirements), and Ford's mainstream factories could not cope, the company leased a redundant Reliant building at Shenstone to do the assembly job. Starting late, but with the intention of producing a car which could

Below: The RS200's turbocharged engine was mid-mounted, and drove all four wheels. Twin coil spring/damper units for each wheel were standard.

Above: The RS200's style was by Ghia, a beautiful two-seater with roof-mounted scoop for the turbo intercooler, and with rear spoiler to add downforce.

not only win at world level, but also carry a familiar family style, Ford designed the RS200 as a mid-engined four-wheel-drive two-seater coupé, complete with Cosworth-type turbocharged BDT engine and transmission developed by FF Developments but incorporating Hewland gears.

The chassis was a combined steel/carbon fibre composite tub, with a steel tubular safety cage around the cabin, and with steel tubular front and rear sub-frame extensions. The engine itself, driving forward rather than back, was behind the two-seater cabin, but the bulky four-wheel-drive transmission was between the driver's and passenger's footwells. On rally cars it was possible to lock up the transmission (thus negating the centre differential).

Suspension was by coil springs wrapped around shock absorber units, two of them at each corner, and because this was a light car there was no power assistance for the steering, and no ABS assistance to the all-disc-brake installation. Remarkably, the road cars had a soft ride and near-neutral handling characteristics.

In standard form the 1.8-litre engine produced 250bhp, with the turbocharger affect being felt over 3,500rpm, but when fully prepared for rallying the same engine could produce between 450 and 500bhp. Engine Tune-up kits in 300 and 350 bhp were offered from new, a fair proportion of the cars produced actually having these. Even in standard form, the cabin was noisy, there being a good deal of turbocharger wastegate chatter and transmission whine to assail the driver's ears.

The style, by Ford's subsidiary Ghia, was extremely graceful, for it was difficult to realise that the same screen, and cut-down versions of the doors, had been lifted from the Sierra family car. Luggage space was restricted to a box, up front, where a second spare wheel might be placed, while ventilation was best described as basic. Major skin panels were all in glass-fibre. Even so, road cars had wind-down glass windows in the doors, carpets on the floor, and the option of comfortable recaro seats, but competition cars were more starkly equipped. A few road cars even had radio/cassette and mobile phone installations.

Production began in mid-1985, the 200th (and last) being cobbled together in January 1986. Refurbishing and preparation for delivery was finally ceded to Tickford of Coventry, who were still delivering 'new' RS200s as late as 1989.

Although Group B was cancelled in 1986, the RS200 was successful in international rallies in that year. Versions with 2.1-litre/700bhp BDT-E engines then became dominant in rallycross in the following years – until, that is, the regulations were re-written to outlaw such an effective car.

Ford later admitted to losing several millions of pounds on this project, which was nonetheless a great image raiser for the company.

Ford Thunderbird

Thunderbird two-seater cars built from 1955 to 1957 (data for 1956 model
Built by: Ford Motor Co., United States.
Engine: Eight cylinders, in 90-degree vee-formation, in five-bearing cast-iron block. Bore and stroke 96.5mm by 87.4mm, 5,113cc (3.80in × 3.44in, 312cu.in Two detachable cast iron cylinder heads. Two overhead valves per cylinder operated by pushrods and rockers from single camshaft mounted in centre of cylinder block 'vee'. Single down-draught four-choke Ford carburettor Maximum power 225bhp (gross) at 4,600rpm. Maximum torque 324lb.ft at 2,600rpm.
Transmission: Single-dry-plate clutch and three-speed, all-synchromesh manual gearbox, both in unit with front-mounted engine. Direct-acting central gearchange. Optional three-speed automatic transmission, with torque converter. Open propeller shaft to hypoid-bevel 'live' rear axle.
Chassis: Separate pressed-steel chassis frame, with box-section side members, and pressed cross bracing. Independent front suspension by coil springs, wishbones and anti-roll bar. Rear suspension by half-elliptic leaf springs Telescopic dampers all round. Four wheel, hydraulically operated drum brakes with vacuum-servo assistance. 15in pressed-steel road wheels. 6,70 × 15in tyres. Two-seat sporting bodywork by Ford, supplied with folding hood of detachable hardtop.
Dimensions: Wheelbase 8ft 6in (259cm), tracks (front and rear) 4ft 8in (142cm Overall length 15ft 5.2in (470.5cm). Unladen weight 3,450lb (1,565kg).
History: The Thunderbird took shape in 1953, and was publicly launched i

Above and below: Only in the first three years of its long life was the Ford Thunderbird a true sporting two-seater. It persisted in growing up, and from 1958 became a close-coupled four-seater 'personal car' in advertising parlance. Conceived in 1953 the Thunderbird was Ford's first sporty two-seater for many years, and aimed to beat Chevrolet's new Corvette. The T-Bird used mainly standard Ford touring parts under a sleek pressed-steel skin, had optional automatic transmission, and a big selling point was that every car had a V8 engine. More than 53,000 were built in three seasons, after which the next model was a larger four-seater type.

▶ 1954, as the first true 'sporting' two-seater Ford for many years. Although multitude of normal saloon car parts were used under the skin, the stylin was fresh, youthful in its appeal and unique to this model. The importance of the early T-Birds was that their appeal was not compromised by othe commercial considerations. Although Ford were already looking ahead to more sporting future in the early 1950s, the arrival of the deadly rival fror Chevrolet, the first of the Corvettes, was a great spur to their ambition Even though the T-Bird was – by North American standards – a sports car, was by no means small. The first cars had 4.8 litre V8 engines and weighe in at around 3,500lb (1,587kg), which put them a full size class ahead of th Jaguars even though they were no more expensive in their native Nort America.

Styling of the first two-seaters was crisp and clean, certainly by Detroit saloon car styling standards, and the first cars in particular had virtually n extraneous decoration to spoil the overall effect. The windscreen was we swept, as were all such cars from Detroit, and the lines were very low, with height of only 4ft 5in (135cm). Either manual transmission or Ford-o-Mat automatic transmission was available. Unlike the rival Corvette, and this wa thought to be a great selling point, every T-Bird was equipped with a V8 engine there was no 'cheap' six-cylinder option. A feature of 1956 and later models wa the optional external mounting of the spare wheel, atop the back bumper, to giv a 'continental' look. There was an extensive retouching of the style for 195 which included portholes in the optional hardtop, but the car's whole characte was lost in 1958 when it was rebodied into a much less sporting four-seate After that the T-Bird became just another Ford, and it was not until 1964 and th arrival of the Mustang that sporting motoring really came back to Ford's rank Even so, Thunderbird has always been a much-respected Ford model name, ar has featured in the range to this day.

Above: Small by contemporary American standards, the mid-1950s Thunderbird looked similar to other, larger, Ford family cars of the period.

Below: Exactly right for the America of the mid-1950s, the early Thunderbird had white-wall tyres, wheel spats, and its spare wheel housed on the rear bumper.

Ford Capri (Australian-built)

Ford Capri (Mercury Capri in USA), built from 1990 to 1995 (data fo definitive 16-valve model)

Built by: Ford Motor Company of Australia Ltd., Australia.

Engine: Mazda-manufactured, four cylinders, in line, in five-main-bearing ligh alloy cylinder block. Bore and stroke 78 x 83.6mm, 1,598cc (3.07 x 3.29ir 97.6cu.in). Light alloy cylinder head. Four valves per cylinder, opposed in narrov vee, operation by twin overhead camshafts: Bosch fuel injection. Maximun power 105bhp at 5,750rpm. Maximum torque 95lb.ft at 5,250rpm. [Also wit 136bhp turbocharged 16-valve engine.]

Transmission: Transverse-engine, front-wheel-drive, single-dry-plat diaphragm spring clutch and five-speed all-synchromesh manual gearbox, i unit with engine: remote control centre floor gearchange. Optional Mazd automatic transmission.

Chassis: Unitary construction steel combined body/chassis structure, wit steel body shell in 2+2 seat open top sports car style. Independent fror suspension by coil springs, wishbones and anti-roll bar, independent rea suspension by coil springs, wishbones and anti-roll bar. Telescopic hydrauli dampers. Rack-and-pinion steering, with power assistance. Disc brakes at a four wheels, with vacuum servo assistance. 14in bolt-on cast alloy road wheels with 185/60-14in tyres.

Dimensions: Wheelbase 7ft 10.7in (240.5cm), front track 4ft 6.7in (139cm rear track 4ft 7.7in (141.5cm). Overall length 13ft 10.1in (422cm). Unlade weight 2,370lb (1,075kg).

History: The world of motoring was full of complex alliances by the 1990: which explains why an American company could launch an Italian-styled spor

Below: The Australian-built Ford Capri was built on a Mazda 323 platform, with a front-engine and front-wheel-drive.

Above: This type of Capri was available in soft-top or hard-top form, with a normally aspirated or turbocharged four-cylinder engine.

car, with Japanese running gear, to be produced in an Australian factory, mainly for export to the United States.

This, in short, was the pedigree of a car known as the Ford Capri in Australia, or as the Mercury Capri when sold in the USA. The technical and commercial connection is easily explained – Ford had held a stake in Mazda since the 1970s, and been involved in several other joint projects (including the Probe coupés) since then, while several 'Ford' cars assembled and marketed in Australia were either disguised, or merely rebadged, Mazdas.

The original inspiration behind this car was a two-seater project car which

made the rounds during the late 1980s, and it was the then Ford chairman, Donald Peterson, who decided to include this rakish little two-seater sports car in the Mazda 323 revival programme which would be centred on Ford-Australia, on the outskirts of Melbourne.

The platform, and all the running gear of this car were pure Mazda 323 (in different times the 'chassis' of an Escort could also have done the same job...) with a lightly-tuned, transversely-mounted, 16-valve 1.6-litre engine driving the front wheels. The same engine, though in a different (rear-drive) application, was also used in the Mazda MX-5 sports car.

To add to the cosmopolitan nature of this project, the exterior style was by Ford's Italian subsidiary, Ghia, the interior design was by Ital Design (also of Italy), and it was Ital who also completed much of the body engineering before the whole car was signed off and handed over for manufacture in Australia.

Not everyone liked the shape, which featured a long and low nose, with flip-up headlamp, along with a sharply truncated tail on which the humped 'safety' bumper was very obvious. Unhappily, after a couple of years, not even the alternative of a turbocharged 136bhp engine could rescue the 'orphan' image which this model acquired, and it died, peacefully, after only five seasons. It is now a footnote in Ford's history.

Frazer Nash 'Chain Gang'

'Chain gang' models, built from 1924 to 1939 (data for TT Replica mode
Built by: A.F.N Ltd., Britain.

Engine: Meadows manufactured. Four cylinders, in three-bearing cast-in block/crankcase. Bore and stroke 69mm by 100mm, 1,496cc (2.72in × 3.94 91.3cu.in). Cast-iron detachable cylinder head, modified by Frazer Nash. Two overhead valves per cylinder, operated by pushrods and rockers from single block-mounted camshaft. Twin horizontal constant-vacuum SU state of tune, to normally 62bhp at 4,500rpm.

Transmission: Single-dry-plate clutch in unit with engine. Open propeller sh to bevel box. Four-speed-and-reverse transmission by chain drive, from cro shaft, with dog engagement. Chains exposed, and no differential. Remo control right-hand gearchange.

Chassis: Separate pressed-steel chassis frame, with channel-section side members, tubular and fabricated cross bracing. Tubular front axle beam. Front suspension by cantilever semi-elliptic springs and radius arms. Rear suspension ▶

Below: Full and glorious detail of the TT Replica 'chain gang', so called as cars had run successfully in the Tourist Trophy of the early 1930s. Not more than 350 'chain gang' cars, all of the same general design, were built in fifteen years. There were several different engines, but all used the unique transmission, with a separate and exposed chain and sprockets for each gear. This needed regular greasing, but put up with a lot of abuse. The cars' ride was very hard, the steering direct, and creature comforts very few. Owners loved them!

▶ by cantilever quarter-elliptic springs and radius arms. Hartford-type adjustab[le] friction damps. Rack-and-pinion steering with fore-and-aft drag link. Four-whe[el] cable operated drum brakes. 19in centre-lock wire wheels. 4.50 × 19in tyre[s]. Two-seater open sports coachwork of light-alloy on ash frame.

Dimensions: Wheelbase 8ft 6in (259cm), track (front) 4ft (122cm), track (re[ar) 3ft 6in (106.7cm). Overall length 12ft 6.3in (351cm). Unladen weight 1,80[0lb] (816kg).

History: After Archie Frazer-Nash left the defunct GN concern, he set up [in] business on his own to make two-seat sports cars carrying his own name. It [was] not surprising, therefore, to see several design points from the GN in the earli[er] Frazer Nash cars, including the extremely simple but effective chain-dri[ve] transmission. Even the first cars, however, were much more 'grown-up' th[an] the GN had ever been, as they had a proper channel-section chassis frame a[nd] always used water-cooled four-cylinder or six-cylinder engines. In spite of [his] engineering prowess, however, Frazer-Nash himself was not always a prude[nt] business man and his company was taken over by H. J. Aldington in 1929. T[he] Aldington family controlled the destinies of Frazer Nash, through AFN Ltd., u[ntil] the cars were finally taken out of production in the 1950s. Production, albeit [on] a very limited scale, was moved from Kingston-on-Thames to Islesworth [in] 1926, where it settled permanently. Even so, cars were hand-built at a very l[ow] rate. Between 1924 and 1939, no more than 350 'chain gang' cars were b[uilt] and production of these cars, now legendary, had been reduced to the mere[st] trickle after about 1936, when the Aldingtons were more interested in buildi[ng] up their British concession to sell the Fiedler-designed BMW cars.

The GN ancestry showed up in the Frazer Nash (as it did in the HRG [car] which was master-minded by GM's other partner, Godfrey). The chassis w[as] very simple and easy to repair, with cantilever springs fore and aft to keep [the] frame short and the wheels well under control. The suspension was very ha[rd] which was exactly what the sporting-minded Frazer Nash customers wante[d] and weather protection minimal. The chain-drive transmission was so simp[le] that critics often used to disbelieve its efficiency. If, however, the chains we[re] cleaned and oiled regularly – about every 500 miles was best – they operat[ed]

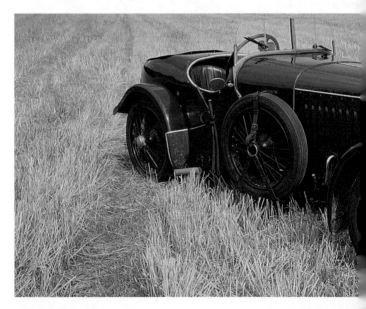

well, and the consequences of a snapped chain were not so serious as those of smashed gear wheels. There was no torque-splitting differential, because of the (literally) solid rear axle, which explains the fact that all 'chain gangs' had very narrow wheel tracks and extremely sensitive handling characteristics. Traction in all conditions, of course, was superb.

The main changes over the years centred around engines. The original cars were built with Plus Power four-cylinder engines, but after that firm closed down (with only 16 engines delivered) British Anzani engines were used for the next six years. In the early 1930s, a whole series of units were tried, including the Meadows overhead-valve engine sold in the first batch of TT Replica cars. These progressively became more of Frazer Nash and less of Meadows as their designer (Gough) developed special components. As a more refined alternative to the sporting Gough-Meadows. Aldington then began to fit the six-cylinder, ½-litre Blackburne units, redesigned to have twin overhead camshafts. However, even at the same time, the company were developing their own single-overhead cam 'Gough' engine, which was entirely special but rather under-developed.

Many of the car's variants were named after the races or circuits where competition success had been gained, which explains the naming of the 'Shelsey' and 'Boulogne' cars. TT Replicas, first built in 1931, as prototypes, were named after the cars ran in the British Tourist Trophy races of 1931, 1932 and 1934, and the first 'production' car was sold in the spring of 1932. Because of its no-nonsense specification, it became the most popular of all 'chain gangs', a total of 85 being manufactured between 1932 and 1938; 54 of the cars were equipped with the Meadows engine (complete with 'Gough' improvements. Only a few had the splendid twin-cam Blackburne engine, which in racing form and supercharged) could be persuaded to give more than 150bhp.

It might be fair to say that the Aldingtons had new ideas for improved models, but that they did not need to introduce them because the basically vintage 'chain gang' was popular as long as they needed to make it. Their ideas for post-war Frazer Nash cars, in the 1940s, were as interesting and advanced as the 'chain gangs' had been twenty years earlier.

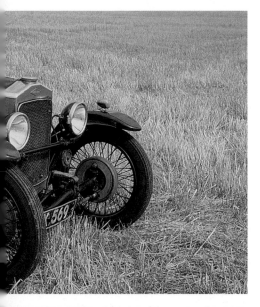

Left: The 'Chain Gang' model was expensive and exclusive, but steered and handled well, and was remarkably fast in its class. Addicts loved them then - and today.

215

Frazer Nash

Frazer Nash sports cars, Bristol-engined, built from 1948 to 1956
Built by: Frazer Nash (AFN) Ltd., Britain.
Engine: Bristol-manufactured, six cylinders, in line, in four-main-bearing cast ir
cylinder block. Bore and stroke 66 x 96mm, 1,971cc (2.60 x 3.78in, 120.3cu.i
Aluminium cylinder head. Two valves per cylinder, opposed to each other in pa
spherical combustion chambers, operation by pushrods and rockers (plus cros
pushrods for exhaust valves) from a camshaft in the cylinder block. Thr
downdraught Solex carburettors. Engine tune according to customer's wishe
Typical was maximum power 120bhp at 5,500rpm, with maximum torque 125lk
at 4,500rpm.
Transmission: Front-engine, rear-wheel-drive, single-dry-plate clutch and for
speed synchromesh manual gearbox, without synchromesh on first gear, in u
with engine, and remote control centre floor gearchange.
Chassis: Separate tubular steel chassis frame, with tubular main side membe
tubular and fabricated cross-bracing and reinforcements. Independent fro
suspension by transverse leaf spring and wishbones, suspension of beam rear ax
by torsion bars, radius arms and A-bracket. Hydraulic telescopic dampers. Rack-ar
pinion steering. Front and rear drum brakes, hydraulically operated. 16in whee
bolt-on steel disc, with 5.25-16in tyres. Choice of two-seater light-alloy panell
body style on light steel framing, some with simple style and cycle-type wing
others with full-width open-top sports car styles.
Dimensions: Wheelbase 8ft 0in (243.8cm), front track 4ft 0in (122cm), rear track
0in (122cm). Overall length (Targa Florio model) 12ft 6in (381cm). Unladen weig
(Targa Florio model) 1,940lb (880kg).
History: By the end of the 1930s, Frazer Nash, which was still owned by t
Aldington family, had given up on the manufacture of 'chain gang' models, and w
finding good business in the importation of BMWs from Germany. After the end
the Second World War, and with Germany (and BMW) in ruins, that was no long
possible, so a fresh start was needed.

The post-war Frazer Nash car evolved out of the Aldington's enterprise, not o
in luring BMW's noted engine designer, Dr. Fiedler, to come to Britain to pick up
peacetime career, but in acquiring the BMW 328 engine design as 'reparation
One of the Aldingtons, who was already a director of the Bristol Aeroplane C
persuaded them to enter the motor car manufacturing business (the Bristol 400 w
the result), and in a complicated deal agreed to design a new sports car using Bris
(BMW 328-type) engines and transmissions, while Bristol would add the Fraz
Nash name to their own new model. Although that arrangement did not prosp
what remained was an agreement to develop a new generation of Frazer Na
merely to use the new engines and transmissions.

All post-war Frazer Nash cars, therefore, dated from a 1946-1947 chas
design, which was based on two large-diameter tubes, with one or other of t
engine tunes of the 1,971cc cross-pushrod Bristol/BMW six-cylinder engine.
strong was the BMW link at first, that the 1947 prototype bore an astonishin
close resemblance to the full-width sports racing BMWs which had appeared in t
1940 Coppa Brescia race: the reason was simple, for it *was* one of those cars! T
chassis design had been to Fiedler's credit, and in 1947 he was also responsible
the definitive Frazer Nash chassis design which was to follow.

Production began in 1948, with two basic models, the stark 'cigar shape' H
Speed model, which was later renamed the 'Competition', and finally later
named as the 'Le Mans replica' (after an outstanding performance in the French
hour race classic), and with the full-width 'Fast Tourer' model, which was rather le
powerful, though better equipped to withstand the assault of wind and rain.

The use of the cigar-shaped body, complete with its cycle-type wings, in raci
brought all sorts of success, not least at Le Mans in 1949, where one of the ca

Above: This was the Targa Florio version of Frazer Nash's Bristol-powered post-war chassis. Only 14 such cars were ever produced.

driven by Norman Culpan and one of the Aldington family, finished third overall. It was such world-wide competition success that led to the naming of new derivatives, all of them with more modern two-seater coachwork, such as the Mille Miglia, the Targa Florio and the Sebring models.

Production of these fast and specialised cars was always very restricted – there were only ever three Sebrings and 14 Targa Florios, for instance – and identification of them all is made more difficult by the known fact that several Le Mans replicas were later re-bodied in the Targa Florio style after international racing outlawed the use of cars with separate wings, which were adjudged to be potentially dangerous.

According to Frazer Nash's own records, total post-war production, all types, was only 85 cars, with the Le Mans Replica the most popular, though this figure includes several prototypes, including at least one early-1950s car fitted with an Austin A90 engine, which would have had a very similar performance to the original Austin-Healey 100.

Interest in these cars had waned by 1954, which was the point at which the Aldington's took on the British import concession for Porsche cars. Incidentally, this led to the showing of a single prototype 'Continental' Frazer-Nash, which combined the existing tubular chassis and suspension, with the BMW 501/503 vee-8 engine, and a coupé body shell which used some Porsche roof, door and glass components. This never went into production.

The Porsche concession took up more and more time (and became more and more profitable), so when demand for the Bristol-engined cars dried up, no successor was either designed, or launched, and the Frazer Nash marque therefore died out.

GN Cyclecar

GN models, built from 1911 to 1925 (data for 1913 vee-twin models)
Built by: G.N. Ltd., Britain.
Engine: JAP manufactured. Two air-cooled cylinders, in 90-degree vee-formation in cast-iron cylinder barrels on light-alloy crankcase. Bore and stroke 84mm by 98mm, 1,086cc (3.31in × 3.86in, 66.3cu.in). Detachable cylinder heads. Two valves per cylinder; overhead inlets operated by pushrods and rockers, side exhausts operated direct from crankcase-mounted camshaft. Single B&B carburettor. Maximum power about 12bhp at 2,400rpm.
Transmission: Clutch on rear of engine crankcase, mounted in nose of car. Open propeller shaft drive to bevel box driving countershaft. Two-speed dog-and-chain transmission to counter shaft and final drive to solid rear axle by side-mounted belts. Remote-control right-hand gearchange.
Chassis: Separate ash chassis frame with tubular cross bracing. Tubular front axle. Front suspension by quarter-elliptic leaf springs, cantilevered forward, and lower radius arms. Rear suspension by quarter-elliptic leaf springs. No dampers. Wire-and-bobbin steering. Belt-rim brakes on rear wheels only, footbrake working on inside of rims and handbrake on outside of rims. Centre-lock wire wheels 650 × 65 tyres. Rudimentary two-seat open coachwork by GN.
Dimensions: Wheelbase 8ft (244cm), tracks (front and rear) 3ft 6in (106.7cm). Overall length 11ft (335cm). Unladen weight 670lb (304kg).
History: Viewed from the new millennium the GN is a joke, but in its day it was a popular and effective little cycle car. This type of machine was an ultra-cheap half-way house between motor cycles and light cars and most owners graduated to them from motor cycles, when they found sidecar progress too tedious. GN was founded by H. R. Godfrey and Archie Frazer-Nash in 1910 and the first cars sold a year later. To keep the price down to around 100 guineas (the cheapest of all, in 1915, sold for 88 guineas) the cars had to be as light and simple as possible. This no doubt explains the use of a wooden (ash) chassis frame, steering by wires which passed round strategically placed bobbins, and a two-speed chain-and-belt transmission, which was open to attack by the elements.

All the early models used proprietary vee-twin JAP motor cycle engines which kept the passengers' feet warm as they were set right up against the toe board. Bodywork was minimal, in line with the rest of the specification, so an early GN built in 1911 or 1912 (before the inevitable refinement process set in) weighed no more than about 400lb (181kg). In many ways a GN was crude, but

Below and below right: The GN's charm lay in its light weight, its simplicity and in its sporting potential. This two-seater was built in 1922. The radiator was a dummy as the JAP vee-twin engine was air-cooled. Final drive was by chain and there were only two forward gears. From 1923 the Austin Seven killed GN.

Above: This boat-tailed sporting GN was built in 1921, by which time it cost around £315 – and was expensive for the type of motoring offered. The weight was low, but equipment was very sparse. The chassis frame was made of wood, and body panels from aluminium alloy. Total weight was about 700lb.

it was also practical and very easy to repair when it went wrong. Almost everything in the design was simple, accessible, and with an obvious function, and the steering and (within reason) the performance were most satisfactory.

GN made very few machines before World War I (perhaps fewer than 200 in all), but in a post-war factory, production rose to the dizzy heights of 50 cars a week in the cycle-car boom, even though the price of the vee-twin-engined machines had risen to £275 or even £315. Engines were modified persistently at the start of the 1920s and right at the end an attempt was made to upgrade the car with an imported Chapuis-Dornier engine with four-cylinders and water-cooling.

In fact it was a vain hope; the GN was not only being beaten by its own price, but by the fact that the customers were demanding more weather protection and by the fact that the mass-produced Austin Seven became available in 1923 for not more than £165. Both Godfrey (with HRG) and Frazer-Nash (with cars bearing his own name) went on to build more modern and even better 'classic' cars.

Healey

Healey sports cars, built from 1946 to 1954 (data for Silverstone model)
Built by: Donald Healey Motor Co. Ltd., Britain.
Engine: Riley-manufactured, four cylinders, in line, in three-main-bearing cast iron cylinder block. Bore and stroke 80.5 x 120mm, 2,443cc (3.17 x 4.72in, 149.1cu.in). Cast iron cylinder head. Two overhead valves per cylinder, opposed in part-spherical combustion chambers, operated by pushrods and rockers from twin camshafts mounted in the cylinder block. Two horizontal SU carburettors. Maximum power 104bhp at 4,500rpm. Maximum torque 132lb.ft at 3,000rpm.
Transmission: Front engine, rear-wheel-drive, single dry plate clutch and four-speed synchromesh manual gearbox, with no synchromesh on first gear, all in unit with engine. Remote control, centre floor gearchange.
Chassis: Separate steel chassis frame, with box section side members, box, pressed and tubular bracings and reinforcements. Independent front suspension by coil springs, trailing links, anti-roll bar, and piston-type dampers. Suspension of beam rear axle by coil springs, radius arms, Panhard rod and telescopic hydraulic dampers. Worm type steering. Drum brakes at front and rear. 15in bolt-on steel wheels, with 5.50-15in tyres. Light-alloy two-seater open sports car bodywork, with cycle type wings. [Healeys were also built with four-seater saloon and drop-head-coupé bodywork.]
Dimensions: Wheelbase 8ft 6in (259cm), front track 4ft 6in (137cm), rear track 4ft 5in (135cm). Overall length 14ft 0in (426cm). Unladen weight 2,070lb (940kg).
History: Well before Donald Healey set up his business in Warwick, he had a legendary reputation. Originally a garage owner in Perranporth, Cornwall, than an international rally driver, he became technical director of Triumph in 1934.

After a war spent working with the Rootes Group, he persuaded friends and colleagues to help him design a new car. Originally he had hoped to sell the idea to Triumph, but that scheme failed after Standard bought up the rights to the name. Healey then struck out on his own in ramshackle premises.

Below: The Silverstone was at once the smallest, lightest and fastest of all the Healey derivatives: it had a 2.4-litre Riley engine.

Above: Healey Silverstones saved weight, and space, by mounting the spare wheel horizontally, and using it as a rear bumper too.

With little capital available, the new box-section chassis was designed by 'Sammy' Sampietro and Healey himself, while the original body styles by Ben Bowden (of Humber) were reputedly sketched out on the wallpaper of his house in Coventry.

Although originally intended to use Triumph Dolomite engines and transmissions, the original 'Healey' eventually used a Riley 2,443cc 'big four' engine, and its related four-speed transmission, and torque-tube back axle. There was trailing-arm independent front suspension, an expensive but effective feature.

Even at this stage, Healey made it clear that he wanted to offer a range of body shells (which he would have to buy in, from specialist coachbuilders), open and closed, sporting and touring. The first car, sold as a Westland four-seater tourer, went on sale in 1946, and almost immediately proved itself able to reach 100mph. For the next eight years every car badged as a Healey (along with the Nash-Healey, which is described separately) was based on the same rugged chassis frame, and suspension.

Almost every car, whether closed or open, could reach 100mph, which was a measure of the Riley engine's power, and of the smooth detailing of the bodies. This made the cars suitable for races and long-distance rallies, where Donald Healey, his son Geoffrey Healey, Tommy Wisdom and others enjoyed much success.

In eight years there were no fewer than seven distinct body styles offered. The original Westland was a four-seater drop-top tourer, while the Abbott and Sportsmobile models were both well-trimmed four-seater drop-head coupés. Four door saloons, with two passenger doors, came from Elliott, Duncan and Tickford, the Tickford being perhaps the most graceful.

The most distinctive Healey of all, however, was certainly the Silverstone (named after the British race circuit), which was a starkly-equipped, traditionally-styled two-seater open car, which was between 450 and 500lb (204-227kg) lighter than any other Healey, which traded comfort for flashing acceleration and roadholding. One distinctive ▶

► feature was the horizontal mounting, at the rear, of the spare wheel/tyre, which also acted as a shock-absorbing bumper. Although the long-stroke Riley engine was becoming quite old-fashioned, it was a very robust and effective power unit, which helped make the Silverstone a successful club racing machine.

One variation on the Riley-engined theme was the Sports Convertible, which combined the basic rolling chassis of the Healey, with a style like that of the first Nash-Healeys, but it was fitted with 106bhp/3-litre six-cylinder Alvis engine instead.

Because Healeys were virtually hand-built, they were unavoidably expensive, which tended to restrict sales of a fine car. It was to get round

this problem that Donald Healey conceived the Healey 100 of 1952, which immediately became the Austin-Healey 100, a most successful sports car that went on sale in 1953. Once this car had appeared, the Healey concern had little time to devote to its original models, the last of which were built in 1954.

A total of 1,287 'Warwick' Healeys were produced (of which 506 were Nash-Healeys. Only 25 had Alvis engines, the remaining 756 having Riley engines: just 105 of those were the very desirable Silverstones.

Below: Complete with an Alvis 3-litre engine, the Healey Sports Convertible was one of the rarest of all these Warwick-built cars.

Hispano-Suiza Alphonso

Alphonso model – short and long chassis, built from 1911 to 1914

Built by: S.A. Hispano-Suiza, Spain.

Engine: Four cylinders, in line, running in four-bearing light-alloy crankcase and detachable cast-iron block. Bore and stroke 80mm by 180mm, 3,620cc (3.15in × 7.09in, 220.9cu.in). Non-detachable cast-iron cylinder head. T-head valve arrangement, side inlet valves directly operated by offside camshaft, side exhaust valves by nearside camshaft. Single Hispano-Suiza carburettor, directly bolted to block/head. Maximum power 64bhp (net) at 2,300rpm.

Transmission: Multi-dry plate clutch on short-chassis cars, cone clutch on long chassis cars, and three-speed gearbox, without synchromesh (early versions), or four-speed gearbox (later versions), both in unit with engine. Right-hand gearchange. Open propeller shaft to bevel 'live' rear axle.

Chassis: Separate steel chassis frame, with channel-section side members. Forged front axle beam. Half-elliptic leaf springs at front and rear; later cars had three-quarter-elliptic leaf springs at the rear. Transmission drum footbrake, aided by rear wheel drum handbrake. Worm-and-sector steering. Centre-lock wire wheels. 815 × 105mm or 820 × 120mm tyres. Variety of sports two-seat or four-seat coachwork.

Dimensions: Wheelbase 8ft 8in or 9ft 10in (264cm or 300cm), tracks (front and rear, short chassis cars) 4ft (122cm), tracks (front and rear, long chassis cars) 4ft 3in (130cm). Overall length (short chassis) 12ft 9in (389cm). Unladen weight chassis only (short) 1,450lb (658kg), chassis only (long) 1,680lb (762kg).

History: Every Hispano-Suiza car designed between 1904 and 1934 was the work of Marc Birkigt, who also designed the first Spanish car of all, the La Cuadra. This company, along with Birkigt, was taken over by Hispano. Like many other Edwardian companies, Hispano used motor sport for publicity and were encouraged by the Spanish monarch King Alfonso XIII when he put up a cup for a voiturette race at Sitges in 1909. A team of Hispano-Suiza cars looked to be possible winners, and led at one stage, but all succumbed to troubles. The team fared better at the *Coupe de l'Auto* races at Boulogne, the best car finishing fifth overall. A year later the revised cars took third place at Sitges, but won outright at Boulogne. It was but a short step for Birkigt to decide that his customer should be able to buy near replicas. He enlarged the engine from 2.6-litres to 3.6 litres, but the basic chassis and mechanical layout was the same.

Right: In many ways the Alphonso laid down guide lines for many vintage sports cars which would follow it in the 1920s. Simple lines, an efficient engine and no excess weight were all keynotes.

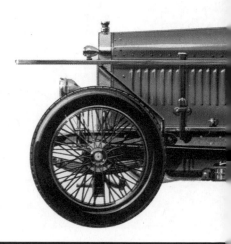

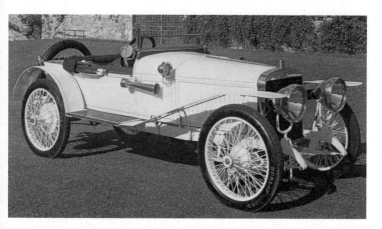

Above: Looking rather frail and spidery, the Hispano-Suiza Alphonso was a very rugged little sports car. Like all other Hispanos, it was the work of Marc Birkigt, and this model had a light-alloy 3.6-litre engine. The Alphonso raced with distinction – the name was from King Alphonso XIII.

He named his car in honour of the Spanish monarch. The Alphonso XIII, probably, was one of *the* first 'production sports cars', as opposed to pensioned-off Grand Prix cars, or vast open-bodied tourers. By our modern standards the Alphonso was not a small nor delicate car, but it was thought very advanced for 1911. By Edwardian standards it was adequately fast, with a maximum speed probably of about 80mph – this at a time when anything approaching 100mph was almost Grand Prix car pace. It was renowned for its ease of control and the very long-stroke engine made it a very easy car to drive in give-and-take country. Among its features were the engine/clutch/gearbox in unit – most cars still placed their gearboxes in isolation in the centre of the chassis – and the centre-lock wire wheels when the artillery type was more usual.

In spite of its engine size the Alphonso was not a very large car. Most Hispanos succeeding it were mechanically more complex, larger and much more expensive.

Honda S800

Honda S600 and S800 sports cars, built from 1962 to 1970
Built by: Honda Motor Co. Ltd., Japan.
Engine: Four cylinders, in line, in five-main-bearing light alloy cylinder block. Bore and stroke 60 x 70mm, 791cc (2.36 x 2.76in, 48.3cu.in). Light alloy cylinder head. Two overhead valves per cylinder, opposed at 45deg. In part-spherical combustion chambers, and operation by inverted bucket tappets and twin overhead camshafts. Two horizontal Keihin carburettors. Maximum power 70bhp at 8,000rpm. Maximum torque 49lb.ft at 6,000rpm.
Transmission: Front engine, rear-wheel-drive, single-dry-plate diaphragm spring clutch and four-speed all-synchromesh manual gearbox, all in unit with engine. Remote control, centre floor gearchange.
Chassis: Separate steel chassis frame, with box section side members, and box section cross-bracings and reinforcements, with two-seater steel body shell in open top or fastback coupé styles.. Independent front suspension by torsion bars, wishbones and anti-roll bar, suspension of the beam rear axle by coil springs, trailing arms and Panhard rod. Telescopic hydraulic dampers. Rack-and-pinion steering. Front disc, rear drum brakes. 13in wheels, steel disc. 145-13in tyres.
Dimensions: Wheelbase 6ft 6.7in (200cm), front track 3ft 9.3in (115cm), rear track 3ft 9.3in (115cm). Overall length 10ft 11.3in (333.5cm). Unladen weight 1,694lb (769kg).
History: When Honda started building cars in the 1960s, its management had one great advantage over their opposite numbers. Because they didn't have a traditional way of building cars – any cars, sports cars included – they didn't have to follow that tradition. In the 1960s, therefore, new Hondas could be totally new – and break as many unwritten rules as necessary.

Although the little S800 was the first Honda sports car known to the rest of the world, it was the third of a line that had started out in 1962. Before then, Honda had only built motorcycles, its first cars being sports cars- and a light truck. Amazingly, the high-revving twin-cam engine which so many observers admired in the sports cars was also used in Honda's original truck.

Although the style would not change throughout the 1960s, the first Honda sports cars were the S360 and S500 models, which looked like rather rounded, shrink-wrapped, versions of the current MG Midget. Under their skin was a separate, box-section chassis frame, their original four-cylinder water-cooled twin-cam engines were of 354cc and 492cc size – and final drive was by chain. The 354cc engine not only produced 33bhp, but peaked at 9,000 rpm.

Right: No larger than the MG Midget of the day, and with an engine that revved up to 9,000rpm, the Honda S800 had a frenetic character.

Some rationalisation then set in, with the 606cc S600 being announced in 1964, and with the 791cc S800 type appearing a year later, this particular type having conventional propeller shaft drive to its beam rear axle from the spring of 1966. It was that definitive type of S800 which was not only sold in Europe, but in larger numbers in North America.

Except for the light-alloy engine, which was laid over in the engine bay at an angle of 45 degrees, and produced 88bhp/litre at a time when a Midget was rated at only 55bhp/litre, the S800 was quite a conventional little car, but it was that power unit which dominated the character. It simply thrived on being revved, for at – say – 5,000rpm – when it was time to change up, the little twin-cam Honda was just getting into its stride.

Not only was it a high-revving little twin-cam jewel, with a roller-bearing crankshaft, but it seemed to relish its work, and it helped to deliver a top speed of 95mph – which was itself better than the Midget, or even the faster Triumph Spitfire, for which it was obvious competition in world markets. Because of ▶

▶ this, however, the S800 was low-geared – at a 70mph speed limited gait in the UK, it was already revving at nearly 6,000rpm.

The rest of the chassis was conventional enough, for there was independent front suspension and a beam axle at the rear, all with rather harshly configured springing and damping. Cars for sale in Europe featured front-wheel disc brakes, and radial ply tyres. Except for a rather cramped two-seater cockpit this was very much a car in the newly established 'MG Midget' class.

The style of the steel body (it was only later that one discovered how rust prone it was) had the sort of goggle-eyed headlamps, and rather over-ornate detailing for which Japanese cars were known at that time. Yet it was neatly done, had a swept windscreen, and wind-up windows in the doors.

By the time the S800 was established all round the world, Honda had also added a fastback hardtop coupé version – rather MGB GT-like in its proportions –and it was beginning to make a reputation for itself. By this time, though, Honda's ambitions had spread so far as to launch new mini-cars, and the first of the Civics was also on the way, so the S800 was finally dropped in 1970.

A total of 11,406 cars were eventually manufactured – and it was many years before Honda would once again build a two-seater sports car.

Below: The Honda S800 was the very first model to be exported from the Japanese company. Only 11,406 such two-seaters were produced.

Honda NSX

Honda NSX sports coupé, introduced in 1990 (original specification)
Built by: Honda Motor Co. Ltd., Japan.
Engine: Six cylinders, in 90-degree formation, in four-main-bearing light-allo
cylinder block. Bore and stroke 90 × 78mm, 2,977cc (3.54 × 3.07ir
181.7cu.in). Two light-alloy cylinder heads. Four valves per cylinder, i
narrow vee, operation by twin overhead camshafts and intermediat
rockers. PGM-F1/Honda electronic fuel injection. Maximum power 274bh
(DIN) at 7,000rpm. Maximum torque 210lb.ft at 5,300rpm.
Transmission: Rear-wheel-drive, single-dry-plate diaphragm spring clutc
and five-speed all-synchromesh manual gearbox, all in unit with transverse
mid-mounted engine. Remote-control, central gearchange. Optional fou
speed automatic transmission.
Chassis: Unitary-construction pressed and fabricated aluminium alloy body
chassis unit. Independent front suspension by coil springs, wishbones
telescopic dampers, anti-roll bar. Independent rear suspension by cc
springs, wishbones, telescopic dampers, and anti-roll bar. Rack-and-pinio
steering, electric power asistance on automatic-transmission models. Fou
wheel disc brakes, with Honda ALB anti-lock installation. Cast alloy roa
wheels, 15in front, 16in rear, 205/50-15in (front) and 225/50-16in (rear) tyres
Dimensions: Wheelbase 8ft 3.6in (253cm), front track 4ft 11.4in (151cm
rear track 5ft 0.2in (153cm). Overall length 14ft 5.4in (440.5cm). Unlade
weight 3,020lb (1,370kg).
History: At the height of the 1980s economic boom, when all things looke
possible to Japanese car makers, Honda decided to take on Ferrari at the
own game. Having studied the latest in 328GTBs, Honda decided that
could do better – and developed the new mid-engined NSX. Along with mos
other supercars of the period, the NSX's general layout was conventional
it was a two-seater, the engine was behind the seats driving the rear wheel
there was all-independent suspension, and the main air intakes for th
engine bay were on the flanks.

Honda, being Honda, then went their own way. Instead of a separat
chassis with steel tubes, there was a carefully detailed aluminium – ye
aluminium – monocoque, which ensured that the NSX was much lighter
some estimates quoted 300lb/136kg – than if it had been crafted in presse
steel. The engine, which both looked and sounded sensational, was th
already-known aluminium four-cam V6 whose smaller-capacity ancestor
had already been seen in cars such as the Honda Legend and Rover 82
executive saloons. Mounted transversely (Ferrari 308/328-style) it drove th
rear wheels through a five-speed transmission.

Compared with a Ferrari, the NSX was different in so many ways. Purist
(for which read 'Ferrari fanatics') suggested that Honda had developed a
the soul and all the passion out of the car. Even if this had been true, th
compensation was that they had also engineered in reliability, comfort,
driver-friendly cabin with good ventilation, and the sort of fail-safe handlir
which made every driver feel like Ayrton Senna. Senna? Indeed, for the grea
Brazilian Grand Prix driver, who was contracted to McLaren-Honda at th
time, had driven the car at every stage of its development.

The style was smooth rather than agressive, and had seen many hour
in Honda's own wind-tunnel. The result was a subtly rounded shape whic
needed no flashy spoilers to provide stability, though a transverse win
section was provided to make the rear aspect look more suitable for the jo
in hand.

Structurally and functionally, the NSX road car hardly ever put a foo
wrong, but it struggled constantly to make its mark. Although there wa

Above and below: When Honda developed the NSX, they set out to beat Ferrari at its own game. Did they succeed? The looks, the performance, the engine sounds and the general character were all absolutely in line with this: the rust-proof aluminium construction was a bonus.

nothing, absolutely nothing, wrong with its engineering, its behaviour or its performance (Honda claimed a top speed of 167mph though this was rarely delivered on production cars) it did have one failing which Honda could not solve – it was not a Ferrari. Not even in the USA, where cynicism about Ferrari reliability was well established, and where the NSX sold behind an 'Acura' instead of a Honda badge, could sales stand up against those of the Italians. Sales in the UK were abysmally small – once again, entirely without justification.

Honda persevered – a loss of face would have been unthinkable – adding a 'Targa roof' type in the 1990s, and a 290bhp/3.2-litre version with a six-speed transmission from 1997, though there were no changes to the long, low, sleek style. A revised version was introduced for the new century.

Honda S2000

Honda S2000, introduced in 1999
Built by: Honda Motor Co. Ltd., Japan.
Engine: Four cylinders, in line, in five main bearing light-alloy cylinder bloc
Bore and stroke 87 x 84mm, 1,997cc (3.42 x 3.31in, 122cu.in). Light allo
cylinder head. Four valves per cylinder, operation by inverted bucket tappet
from twin overhead camshafts: Honda PGM-F1 fuel injection. Maximum powe
237bhp at 8,300rpm. Maximum torque 153lb.ft at 7,500rpm.
Transmission: Front engine, rear-wheel-drive, single dry plate diaphragm sprin
clutch and six-speed, all-synchromesh manual gearbox, all in unit with engine
Remote control, centre floor gearchange.
Chassis: Unitary construction combined steel body/chassis structure, wit
steel body shell in two-seat open Roadster style, and optional lift-off ste
hardtop. Independent front suspension by coil springs, wishbones and anti-rc
bar, independent rear suspension by coil springs, wishbones and anti-roll ba
Telescopic hydraulic campers. Rack-and-pinion steering with power assistance
Disc brakes at front and rear, with vacuum servo assistance, and ABS a
standard. 16in bolt-on cast-alloy road wheels, with 205/55-16in (front) an
225/50-16in (rear) tyres.
Dimensions: Wheelbase 7ft 10.5in (240cm), front track 4ft 9.9in (147cm), rea
track 4ft 11.4in (151cm). Overall length 13ft 6in (411.5cm). Unladen weigh
2,778lb (1,260kg).
History: Amazingly, after Honda dropped the S800 model in 1970, it would b
twenty-nine years before another S-badged two-seater was introduced by th
Japanese concern. Along the way, of course, there had never been any lack c
resolve, or of technological achievement. Apart from launching the mid-engine
NSX (its much-praised Ferrari-competitor), Honda had produced sever.
Championship-winning F1 power units, and the worth of its passenger ca
engines had never been in doubt.

Before the new S2000 appeared – first as the SSM concept car at the Toky
Show of 1995, and finally as a production car in 1999 – Honda had watche
other Japanese makers launch their own two-seaters. Some, like Nissan's S
breed, were not sporting enough, but Mazda's MX-5 was an immediate, an
long-lasting success. Rather than face up, head on, to either type, Honc
decided to go its own way.

Like Mazda before it, Honda surveyed the world scene, studied ever
obvious layout – and rejected the idea of producing a car with its engine behir
the seats. Engines with light-alloy castings, they concluded, could be sma
enough and light enough to live up front. The new S2000, accordingly, wou
be what was fashionably called a 'front/mid-engined' car with the engine u
front, the gearbox alongside the driver's legs, driving the rear wheels. BMW ha
come to the same conclusion with the Z3 family of two-seaters – and Honc
agreed with them.

Although the looks, and the basic structural engineering, of the new S200
were conventional enough – in some ways the proportions of the Mazda MX
and the BMW Z3 could both be seen - Honda both shocked, and exhilarate
the rest of the world's motor industry with its new power train. Not only wa
there to be a six-speed transmission (which, at this end of the spectrum, wa
still little known), but the engine was an incredible high-output screamer.

Although the engine was a normally-aspirated 2-litre 'four' of seeming
conventional four-valve twin-cam layout, it had been conceived, detailed an
developed to produce no less than 237bhp at 8,300rpm. This rating, whic
equated to a specific output of almost 120bhp/litre, meant that this new engir
was the most efficient in the world at that time, and rivals made haste to se
how it was done.

Above: Although the style of the Honda S2000 was bland, it hid a remarkably advanced and powerful 2-litre engine, and could reach nearly 150mph.

The claimed rating, in fact, was so much higher than most other normally-aspirated road-car units that cynical pundits found it difficult to accept at first. It was only when independent road tests confirmed a 147mph top speed (from a two litre!), and 0-100mph acceleration in less than 15 seconds, that the message sank in. It was quicker than the original Porsche Boxster, yet much cheaper.

Honda, who always said that they were treating the S2000 as a 50th birthday present to themselves, had made no compromises in the engineering, maybe because it wanted to prove a point, and maybe because it was determined to use the S2000 as a technical show-piece for other new models which were to follow.

Like other Far Eastern manufacturers, however, Honda showed that they had not quite got to the heart of providing a complete sports car with character, for there was a surprising amount of detail which needed improvement, which explains why a technically facelifted model appeared in 2002.

While the performance was astonishing, the éngine had to be revved to high heaven for it to be achieved. 6,000 or 7.,000rpm had to be used all the time to have the desired effect, and the noise cocktail above those speeds had to be heard to be believed. To many customers, however, it was all worth it. So, what if the ride was hard, and what if the handling balance was not somehow sporty? It was hugely well-equipped (the retractable soft top was power-operated, for instance), and showed every sign of being reliable into old age.

But would this be the first, or the only, Honda in a new S-class?

HRG

HRG sports cars, built from 1935 to 1956 (data for later 1500)
Built by: HRG Engineering Co. Ltd., Britain.
Engine: Singer-manufactured, four cylinders, in line, in three-main-bearing cast iron cylinder block. Bore and stroke 73 x 89.4mm, 1,497cc (2.87 x 3.52in, 91.4cu.in). Cast iron cylinder head. Two overhead valves per cylinder, operated by rockers from single overhead camshaft. Two semi-downdraught SU carburettors. Maximum power 65bhp at 4,800rpm. Maximum torque 85lb.ft at 2,400rpm.
Transmission: Front engine, rear-wheel-drive, single dry plate clutch and four speed synchromesh manual gearbox, with no synchromesh on first gear, all in unit with engine. Remote control, centre floor gearchange.
Chassis: Separate steel chassis frame, with channel section side members, fabricated tubular cross-bracings. Suspension of front beam axle by forward facing quarter-elliptic leaf springs, suspension of beam rear axle by half-elliptic leaf springs. Friction-type dampers. Worm-and-wheel steering. Drum brakes at front and rear, mechanical and cable operation. 16in centre-lock wire wheels, 5.50-16in tyres. Light alloy panelling on body shell with wooden framing, in open two-seater style, with cycle type wings.
Dimensions: Wheelbase 8ft 7in (261.5cm), front track 4ft 0in (122cm), rear track 4ft 0in (122cm). Overall length 12ft 0in (366cm). Unladen weight 1,640lb (744kg).
[HRGs were also built with 1.1-litre engines, and briefly with full-width 'Aerodynamic' bodywork.]
History: Messrs Halford, Robins and Godfrey got together in 1935 to make an

Below: All HRGs were simple and rugged two-seaters. Announced in the 1930s, they were produced in small numbers until the 1950s.

bove: Although it was not very fast, the HRG could be used in races, llies, trials and – as here – in hill-climbs too, giving pleasure to the driver.

ll cars of their own design. Because Godfrey had been the 'G' of GN, Robins d been with Trojan, and Halford was a Brooklands racing enthusiast, the fluence behind the new HRG was obvious.

n many ways the HRG was an evolution of the GN, though it was clear that e 'chain gang' Frazer Nash chassis was an inspiration too. Like the 'chain ng', there was a channel-section chassis and leaf spring suspension, but this as so stiff that any flexing of springs made one wonder what had gone rong! In the HRG, at least, the drive line was conventional enough.

The design, not even contemporary in 1935, persisted to 1956, by which ne it looked positively archaic – and this was part of its charm. The style, no ubt modern by Frazer Nash and MG TA standards of the 1930s, looked old-shioned after the war because it had a narrow two-seater cockpit, and cycle pe wings.

Early cars used proprietary Meadows engines, but the vast majority of RGs used single-overhead-camshaft Singer units. A 61bhp/1.5-litre version of e Singer engine was the usual fitment in post-war years, this giving the arkly unaerodynamic machine a top speed of about 85mph.

Production was at its height in the post-war shortage days of the late 40s, when HRG delivered up to 70 cars, but only 14 cars followed in 1949, d in the early 1950s its was nearly all over. Not even an attempt to modernise e design, with the full-width 'Aerodynamic' version, of which just 45 were ilt, could revive it.

HRG never replaced this original and popular design, though in the mid-50s they dabbled both with a new car which might have used Vauxhall gines, and there was the intriguing possibility of using Singer's under-veloped twin-cam power unit. Total HRG production, including final ototypes, was just 236 cars.

Invicta

**Invicta 1½-litre, 2½-litre, 3-litre and 4½-litre, built from 1925 to 1933 (da
for 4½-litre S)**
Built by: Invicta Cars, Britain.
Engine: Meadows-manufactured. Six-cylinder, in line, in cast-iron block
detachable five-bearing light-alloy crankcase. Bore and stroke 88.5mm
120.6mm, 4,467cc (3.46in × 4.75in, 272.5cu.in). Cast-iron cylinder head. T
over-head valves per cylinder, operated by pushrods and rockers from sin
side-mounted camshaft. Two SU constant-vacuum carburettors. Maxim
power in excess of 115bhp.
Transmission: Single-dry-plate clutch and Meadows four-speed man
gearbox (without synchromesh), both in unit with engine. Right-ha
gearchange. Open propeller shaft to hypoid-bevel 'live' rear axle.
Chassis: Separate steel chassis frame, with channel-section side membe
tubular and channel-section cross-bracing members. Forged front axle bea
Front and rear suspension by half-elliptic leaf springs. Hydraulic piston-ty
dampers, with Hartford friction dampers in over-riding control. Rod-opera
drum brakes. Coachwork to choice from nominated coachbuilders, includ
Invictas' own two-seat light-alloy sports body on ash framing.

Dimensions: Wheelbase 9ft 10in (300cm), tracks (front and rear) 4ft 8in (142cm). Overall length 13ft 6in (411cm). Unladen weight 2,800lb (1,270kg).

History: Noel Mackin got together with Oliver Lyle (of sugar-making family) in 1924 to produce cars of a type new to the British market – cars that would combine British standards of quality and roadholding with American standards of performance and engine flexibility. To do this, as their company was to be very small, they had to be skilful assemblers of proprietary parts and 'bought-out' components. The first Invicta 'factory', indeed, was the three-car garage of Macklin's own home at Cobham, Surrey, south-west of London.

The first three cars, with 2½-litre six-cylinder Coventry-Climax engines did not match Macklin's high standards, so for future production he turned to Henry Meadows of Wolverhampton, who were already producing engines for various uses. From 1925, all Invictas with the exception of the 1½-litre model announced in 1932, used Meadows 'sixes'. Macklin's designer was W. G. Watson, later renowned for his post-war twin-camshaft Invicta Black Prince, and in the eight years of what are now thought of as 'vintage' Invictas he was loyal to one basic chassis layout. The 2½-litre Meadows model was succeeded a year later by the enlarged-bore 3-litre, but by 1928 the big six-cylinder unit had been further ▶

Left and below: Perhaps the most famous of all Invictas, the 'flat iron' 4½-litre of 1931. Donald Healey won the Monte Carlo Rally in one, and up to 100mph was possible. Only 77 of these cars were built, and they were as fierce as any Bentley or Bugatti, though without the glamour. The rivetted bonnet was a trademark, carried on to the Railton.

▶ stretched to give a powerful and reliable 4½-litres. Mechanically the Invicta
performance was way ahead of their brakes, and indeed of their styling. Befo
the end of the decade there was nothing very striking about the cars' lines, ev
though the radiator was simple and noble, and the bonnet rivets aped those
Rolls-Royce to a very obvious degree.

The 4½-litre NLC Invicta, often with a body as expensive and individua
produced as those for Rolls-Royce, was the company's most expensive car
all; its chassis price of £1,050 was only £50 under that of the contempor
20/25 Rolls. Unlike the Rolls, however, the Invicta had an engine not noted
smoothness or silence, even if it *was* powerful. An 85mph maximum speed w
normal for this car – far better than the average.

By 1930, the 4½-litre chassis was being supplied in two forms – the 'hic
A-Type, and an entirely different lowered S-Type. The latter, usually suppli
with lightweight sporting coachwork, formed the basis of really sensationa
effective competition cars. Though colloquially known as the '100mph' Invic
the production car was really capable of a 90-plus maximum. Neverthele
Invicta, who sold only 77 of these scarce sports cars, did nothing to discoura
the unofficial title, as it could only be good for sales. The chassis was repute
inspired by that of the successful Delage Grand Prix cars, was very rigid, a
was passed underneath the back axle. This rather limited wheel movement, a
may have contributed to the rather knife-edge road-holding for which the '
iron' Invicta was later renowned. One lurid accident involving 'Sammy' Davis
The Autocar, which happened in front of thousands of spectators at Brooklan
did nothing to help.

During the production run, really a misnomer as all cars were hand-built
Cobham, engine power was increased and the last cars probably boast
140bhp at 3,600rpm. The maximum speed of this bluff-fronted machine wo
undoubtedly have been over 100mph by then. It is worth recalling t
Meadows also sold this engine to Lagonda for their 4½-litre machines, and t
W. O. Bentley joined Lagonda in 1935, refined the installation and ensured
engine's life right up to 1939.

No attempt was ever made by Invicta to prove their products on the ra

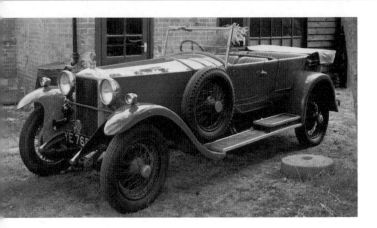

Above: A "high chassis" Invicta in four-seater tourer style.

rack, but they were keen on competition in long-distance trails of various types. In 1930 several top events in Europe were tackled with great success, and in 1931 Donald Healey astonished the motoring world by winning the Monte Carlo Rally outright. A year later the same car and driver took second overall, but as before were fastest of all on the tests where performance was at a premium. The world depression had the same effect on Invicta as on other luxury-car makers, and an entirely different 1½-litre Blackburne-engined car was briefly sold. The company stopped making cars in 1933 and Macklin turned to Railtons in their place.

Below: A Cadogan-bodied 4½-litre Invicta of 1929, with normal 'high' frame and four-seater layout. The chassis cost £1,050, body another £300.

Jaguar E-Type

E-type 3.8-litre, 4.2-litre, and Series III V12 (data for V12 car)
Built by: Jaguar Cars Ltd. (later British Leyland Motor Corporation Ltd.) Britai
Engine: Twelve cylinders, in 60-degree vee-formation, in seven-bearing ca
aluminium block. Bore and stroke 90mm by 70mm, 5,343cc (3.54 × 2.76
326cu.in). Aluminium-alloy cylinder heads. Two overhead valves per cylind
opening into 'bowl in piston' combustion chambers and operated by inverte
bucket tappets from single overhead cam per bank. Four constant-vacuum S
carburettors, positioned at the outside of the engine, feeding through verti
inlet ports. Maximum power 272bhp (DIN) at 5,850rpm. Maximum torq
304lb.ft at 3,600rpm. Exhaust emission restrictions caused both figures to dr
slightly during the model's production run.
Transmission: Single-dry-plate clutch and four-speed, all-synchromesh gearbo
both in unit with engine. Remote-control central gear-change. Open propel
shaft to subframe-mounted hypoid-bevel final drive. Limited-slip different
standard. Exposed, universally jointed drive shafts to rear wheels. Optional Bo
Warner automatic transmission.
Chassis: Front section a multi-tube 'space frame', bolted to centre/tail secti
steel monocoque tub, with rear subframe for suspension and final driv
Independent front suspension by wishbones, longitudinal torsion bars and an
roll bar. Independent rear suspension by lower wishbones, fixed-length driv
shafts, radius arms and double coil springs to each wheel. Telescopic dampe
Four-wheel hydraulically operated disc brakes, with vacuum-servo assistanc
inboard at the rear. Rack-and-pinion steering, power assisted 15in steel-di
wheels. ER70VR15in tyres. Open two-seater or closed coupé 2 + 2 seat
bodies to choice, plus optional hard-top.
Dimensions: Wheelbase 8ft 9in (267cm), track (front) 4ft 6.3in (138cm), tra
(rear) 4ft 5.3in (135cm). Overall length 15ft 4.4in (468cm). Unladen weig
3,230lb (1,453kg).
History: The E-type Jaguars, even more successful than the XK series th
replaced, were – like the XKs – popular by chance. The first E-type, designed

**Below: Although the E-Type was originally meant to be a race car, it
became an iconic road-going sports car when redeveloped and fully
equipped. This is a mid-1960s model.**

Above: One of the final batches of E-types, with the vee-12 5.3-litre engine. Early 'sixes' had short wheelbases and less passenger space. Headlamps were exposed after 1968, partly to improve lighting at night, but this marginally spoiled the sleek lines. The vast majority of all E-types were exported, many to the USA.

1956, was a racing sports car to replace the D-type. Only after Jaguar retired from racing was the order given to 'productionise' the car. It was, in all major design respects, a direct descendent of the D-type/XK-SS family, but with one major difference. It was a completely refined, docile, and roadworthy machine. It was also unbelievably cheap and used very few sophisticated special parts.

Like the D-type, the basis of the E-type (or XKE as the North Americans called it) was a combined monocoque/multi-tube chassis, covered by a sleek, aero-dynamically tested bodyshell in which the headlamps were faired into the long nose, and in which the air-intake was as small as possible. All-independent suspension was new from Jaguar. The rear suspension, hung with its differential and inboard brakes from a separate steel subframe, set a pattern followed by every other Jaguar for many years. The fixed-length drive shaft effectively formed an upper wishbone and to keep stresses in check there were *two* combined coil-spring/damper units controlling each rear wheel – one at each side of the drive shaft. The famous six-cylinder XK engine was used, in 3.8-litre 'S' tune, and specially prepared road test cars, running on Dunlop racing tyres, beat 150mph in otherwise standard form, when tested in 1961. ▶

▶   The racing E-type project had been for an open car, but for production a slee fast-back coupé with what we would now call a 'third door', was offered. Thi the afterthought, was by far more the more popular version. The first *pub* appearance of a prototype was at Le Mans in 1960, when the Cunningham racing team were asked to run a works-built light-alloy version. This, althoug fast, did not finish the race.

    The early cars were none-too-large inside, and had poor ventilation. Th United States market also found that they overheated too rapidly in heavy traff and summer conditions. These, and other minor problems, were all rectified. 1964, the engine was enlarged to 4,235cc and the first of the all-synchromes gearboxes was fitted. Over the years the engine power dropped a little (due having to meet US exhaust emission limits), the headlamp cowls we discarded and the interior was revised. Disc wheels supplanted wire-spok 'knock-ons', and power steering was made optional.

    The big change, however, was in 1971, when the six-cylinder E-type wa dropped and replaced by a brutal and very rapid V12 car! This, like the XK engine was a quantity-production 'first' in the whole world, at least of any V12 tha could be called modern and technically advanced. Jaguar intended the V12, als for their saloon cars, and for their long-term future. The rest of the E-typ basically unchanged, was extensively redeveloped to cope with the V12 power. Fatter wheels and tyres from the XJ6 were fitted, which meant that th bodywork had to be altered to suit. Early cars had had a 96in (244cm wheelbase, supplemented by a 105in wheelbase (267cm) for the 2 + 2 coup announced in 1966. For the Series III cars, the longer wheelbase wa standardised, which made the open version that much more spacious. A si cylinder version of the Series III was announced, but none was ever produce The last of the V12s were produced in the winter of 1974/75 (the last fifty we painted black, and specially plaqued) and the E-type had been replaced by th XJ-S. A total of 72,507 were made in all, more than 15,000 of them being V12

Below: All the early-model E-Types had faired-in headlamps and small front intakes. Every owner had the registration number painted onto the bonnet.

Above: The late 1960s SII cars had exposed headlamps, 4.2-litre engines, and an all-synchromesh gearbox: much better than the originals.

Above: Fixed-head coupé cars with the 3.8-litre engine were near-150mph machines and quite stunning lines. Very desirable, then and now.

Below: Final E-Types were SIIIs, with 5.3-litre V12 engines, wider grilles and wheelarches and a choice of 2+2 coupé or Roadster styles.

Jaguar SS100

**Originally known as SS100, SS90, SS100 2½-litre and 3½-litre (data fo
3½-litre)**

Built by: SS Cars Ltd., Britain.

Engine: Six cylinders, in line, in seven-bearing cast-iron block. Bore and strok
82mm by 110mm, 3,485cc (3.23in × 4.33in, 213cu.in). Cast-iron cylinder head
Two overhead valves per cylinder, operated by pushrods and rockers from
camshaft mounted in side of cylinder block. Compression ratio 7:1. Twi
constant-vacuum SU carburettors. Maximum power 125bhp (gross) a
4,250rpm.

Transmission: Single-dry-plate clutch and four-speed, synchromesh manua
gearbox (without synchromesh on first gear), both in unit with engine. Centra
remote-control gearchange. Open propeller shaft spiral-bevel 'live' rear axle.

Chassis: Separate steel chassis, with channel-section side members, and
pressed-steel cross-bracing members. Forged front axle beam. Half-elliptic lea
springs front and rear. Hydraulic piston and extra friction dampers at front
hydraulic piston-type dampers at rear. Four-wheel, rod-operated drum brakes to
all four wheels. Fly-off handbrake. Worm-and-nut steering. 18in knock-off wire
spoke wheels 5.50 × 18in tyres. Two-seaters open sports coachwork fitted, o
alloy panels on ash framing. No alternatives.

Dimensions: Wheelbase 8ft 8in (264cm), track (front) 4ft 4.5in (133cm), trac
(rear) 4ft 6in (137cm). Overall length 12ft 9in (398cm). Unladen weight 2,680lk
(1,215kg).

History: William Lyons entered the motor industry in the 1920s as a designe
and builder of special coachwork for ordinary cars like the Austin Seven and the
Standard Nine as well as for sidecars. His 'Swallow' car designs, like his

Above and below: Styled by William Lyons, the SS100 sports car was sensationally fast and attractive. There were 2½-litre and 3½-litre versions.

sidecars, were soon launched in 1931 and built in Coventry. The first SS sports car, the SS90, was an attractive short-wheelbase mechanical version of the 20hp SS1 with a side-valve 2½-litre engine. The SS100, which was born in 1935, used the same SS1 type of chassis, but with suspensions and other details from the also-new SS-Jaguar saloon cars. The engine was a Heynes-designed overhead-valve conversion of the original side-valve 2,663cc Standard six-cylinder unit.

The first SS100 was sensational enough, but the 3½-litre version, announced in 1937, was even more so. The 3,485cc engine, although keeping some Standard parentage, was largely new, and very powerful. The car, priced at a mere £445 in Britain, could achieve just over 100mph and had the looks usually associated with Italian-designed thoroughbreds. The SS100s, in 2½-litre and 3½-litre form, did much for the SS company's prestige up to the outbreak of World War II.

The car made few concessions to comfort. Style and function was considered all-important, with performance a great selling point. One has to remember that in those days a 100mph maximum speed was rare. The new engine was found to be very tuneable and a Jaguar development car eventually lapped the Brooklands oval at 125mph in tests. Only 23 of the SS90 side-valve cars were made, but SS sold 190 2½-litre SS100s and 118 3½-litres. Only one car was built up (from a partly-complete war-time state) in post-war years. In Ian Appleyard's hands it was a remarkably competitive rally car. One fixed-head coupé SS100 was built and exhibited at the 1938 Earls Court Motor Show: this car still exists.

Jaguar XJ220

Jaguar XJ220 sports coupé, previewed in 1989, on sale 1992 to 1994
Built by: Jaguarsport Ltd., Britain.
Engine: Six cylinders in 90-degree vee formation in four-main bearing cast alloy cylinder block/crankcase. Bore and stroke 94 × 84mm, 3,498cc (3.70 × 3.307in 213.5cu.in). Two light-alloy cylinder heads. Four valves per cylinder, and operation by inverted bucket tappets from twin overhead camshafts. Zytek electronic fuel injection with twin Garrett AiResearch turbochargers. Maximum power 542bhp (DIN) at 7,000rpm. Maximum torque 475lb.ft at 4,500rpm.
Transmission: Rear-wheel-drive, AP Racing diaphragm spring clutch and five-speed all-synchromesh manual gearbox, all in unit with mid-mounted engine. Remote control, central gearchange.
Chassis: Separate aluminium honeycomb chassis tub, clad in light-alloy body shell. Independent front suspension by coil springs, wishbones, telescopic dampers and anti-roll bar. Independent rear suspension by coil springs, telescopic dampers and anti-roll bar. Rack-and-pinion steering. Four-wheel disc brakes, but no anti-lock provision. Alloy road wheels, 17in at front, 18in at rear, with 255/45-17in (front) and 345/35-18in (rear) tyres.
Dimensions: Wheelbase 8ft 7.9in (264cm), front track 5ft 7.3in (171cm), rear track 5ft 2.5in (158.8cm). Overall length 16ft 2.1in (493cm). Unladen weight 3,241lb (1,470kg).
History: The mid-engined 208mph XJ220 which went on sale in 1992 was very different from the hastily completed non-running prototype which had been previewed at the Birmingham Motor Show of 1988. A car that had started out as a cost-no-object one-off by Jaguar's 'Saturday club' of engineers, was turned into a limited-production machine by Tom Walkinshaw's Jaguarsport operation. Only the styling – in truncated, and slightly simplified, form – remained. The first car, complete with a detuned version of TWR's 48-valve racing Jaguar V12, had four-wheel-drive and was enormous. At the time intended as no more than a fascinating project car, it attracted so much attention (and waving cheque books) that Jaguar then put it away to think about its future. Within months it had been farmed out for study to Tom Walkinshaw's Jaguarsport business, which was 50 per cent owned by Jaguar. Concluding that a lookalike, but mechanically different, machine *could* sell in limited numbers, Walkinshaw head-hunted Mike Moreton from Ford as his project manager to make it happen.

During 1989 the entire project was recast. Pressured by Walkinshaw, and taking the pragmatic view of costs, development headaches, and the time involved, Jaguarsport decided to ditch the V12 engine and four-wheel-drive system in favour of

a turbocharged four-camshaft V6 was smaller, the XJ220's wheelbase could be shorter, the whole car considerably lighter.

It would take more than two years to move the car from a 'For Sale' brochure to a ready-for-delivery machine.

Although the definite style looked similiar to the original, it was considerably shorter (the wheelbase was reduced by eight inches), and a lot lighter. Ex-racing car designer Richard Owen led a small design team at Bloxham – there was no input from mainstream Jaguar (or even Ford) engineers – the result being a relatively simple package which could be hand-assembled at the rate of three or four cars a week.

The aluminium honeycomb chassis tub surrounded a compact two-seater cabin, the MG Metro 6R4-derived V6 engine (complete with twin turbochargers, just as the XJR race cars had had) was behind the cabin, and transmission was through a specially-developed FF Developments five-speed transmission. Bloxham would only be an assembly plant, since the tubs and the sinuously shaped aluminium body panels would be supplied by Midlands-based specialists. Although the cabin was carefully and comfortably fitted out, and there were aerodynamic 'ground effect' tunnels under the floor of the structure, there was no place in this project for anti-lock brakes, one reason beging that a proper ABS system always takes ages to refine, and the XJ220 was always running to a very tight schedule.

By 1991 prototypes had completed their tests, and some startling top speed runs had been carried out at the superfast Nardo circuit in southern Italy, but in the meantime the world's economy had turned down into recession, many so-called rich people found their funds disappearing and, suddenly, the XJ220's order book was under pressure.

This all detracted from the worth of the £400,000 cars, which started reaching customers in mid-1992. Those who honoured their 1989 instincts found that they had a magnificent-looking, capable and amazingly fast road car, which would be outpaced by only one other machine – the McLaren F1 – later in the 1990s.

Yet everything about the XJ220 was extreme. It was large – very wide and substantially proportioned for a two-seater – far too fast to be unleashed on public roads, with the sort of gearing which made top (and sometimes fourth) gears quite redundant. Expensive to repair whenever anything went wrong – one only had to look at the 18in rear tyres, and the alloy road wheels, to realise how costly a simple kerbing incident would be – it was definitely a car for high days and holidays. Faced with reneging customners, Jaguar struggled long and hard to 'move the metal', eventually winding up the project in 1994 when just 271 cars had been built.

Left: The XJ220 was a massive car with huge performance. The mid-mounted engine produced 542bhp, and the top speed was nearly 210mph.

Jaguar XK Series

XK120, XK140, XK150 and XK150S models (data for XK120)
Built by: Jaguar Cars Ltd., Britain.
Engine: Six-cylinders, in line, in seven-bearing cast-iron block. Bore and stroke 83mm by 106mm, 3,442cc (3,27in × 4,.17in, 210cu.in). Aluminium cylinder head. Two overhead valves per cylinder, in part-spherical combustion chambers, directly operated by inverted-bucket tappets from twin overhead camshafts. Twin SU constant-vacuum carburettors. Maximum power 160bhp (gross) at 5,000rpm. Maximum torque 195lb.ft at 2,500rpm.
Transmission: Single-dry-plate clutch and four-speed, synchromesh manual gearbox (without synchromesh on first gear), both in unit with engine. Open propeller shaft to hypoid-bevel 'live' rear axle.
Chassis: Separate steel frame, with box-section side members, braced by pressed cruciform members and pressed and tubular cross members. Independent front suspension by wishbones and longitudinal torsion bars, with anti-roll bar. Rear suspension by semi-elliptic leaf springs. Telescopic dampers at front, piston-type at rear. Recirculating-ball-steering. Four-wheel, hydraulically operated drum brakes and fly-off handbrake. 16in centre-lock wire wheels 6.00 × 16in tyres. Coachwork (first 200 cars), in light alloy on ash frame base; (all other cars) pressed-steel bodywork in two-seat drop-head, and two-seat fixed-head versions.
Dimensions: Wheelbase 8ft 6in (259cm), track (front) 4ft 3in (129cm), track

Below: Announced in 1954, the XK140 was available in three body types, this being the smart and well-equipped fixed-head coupé variety.

Above: The legendary XK120 sports car, powered by the twin-cam 3,442cc engine. It could reach 120mph at a time when most cars struggled at 80.

(rear) 4ft 2in (127cm). Overall length 14ft 5in (439cm). Unladen weight (drop-head version) 2,920lb (1,324kg).

History: The XK Jaguars are rightly, legendary. Announced in 1948, they combined smooth and ultra-modern styling with fine engineering and were powered by an advanced twin-overhead-camshaft engine. This last, incidentally, was the first quantity-production 'twin cam' in the world.

The XK's success was all rather accidental. The engine and longer-wheelbase version of the chassis were intended for Jaguar's new Mark VII saloon car and William Lyons planned his XK sports car as a small-production publicity project. The customers thought otherwise. In six years, more than 12,000 XK120s were sold. The XK140 (9,000 sold) and the XK150 (9,400 sold) all added to the reputation. XK140s had better steering and more power. XK150s had revised styling, even more power and four-wheel disc brakes. The last versions also had 3.8-litre engines. Apart from looking beautiful, the XKs were always very good value for money and very fast. The twin-cam engine, although quite an oil-slinger, lasted for ever.

XKs were great rally cars and successful race cars, although they were really too heavy to take on the specialised French and Italian machines. Production eventually ceased in 1961, 13 years after launch. The XKs, successor – the E-type – made as much of a stir as its ancestor.

Jaguar XJS

Jaguar XJS sports car family, built from 1975 to 1996 (data for original V12 model)

Built by: Jaguar Cars Ltd., Britain.

Engine: V12 cylinders, in 60-degree vee, in seven-main-bearing light alloy cylinder block. Bore and stroke 90 x 70mm, 5,343cc (3.54x 2.75in, 326cu.in). Two cast alloy cylinder heads. Two overhead valves per cylinder, operated by inverted bucket tappets from single overhead camshaft per cylinder head. Bosch-Lucas fuel injection. Maximum power 285bhp at 5,500rpm. Maximum torque 294lb.ft at 3,500rpm.

Transmission: Front engine, rear-wheel-drive, with three-speed Borg Warner automatic transmission, in unit with engine. Remote control, centre floor gearchange. Optional on early cars, single dry plate, diaphragm spring clutch, and four-speed all-synchromesh manual gearbox, in unit with engine.

Chassis: Unitary construction steel combined chassis/body structure, with 2+2 seater steel body shell, in hardtop coupé style. Independent front suspension by coil springs, wishbones, and anti-roll bar, independent rear suspension by double coil springs, fixed length drive shafts, wishbones and trailing arms. Hydraulic telescopic dampers, double at rear wheels. Rack-and-pinion steering, with power assistance. Disc brakes at front and rear, with vacuum servo assistance. 15in bolt-on cast alloy wheels, and 205/70-15in tyres.

Dimensions: Wheelbase 8ft 6in (259cm), front track 4ft 10in (147.5cm), rear track 4ft 10.3in (148cm). Overall length 15ft 11.7in (487cm). Unladen weight 3,859lb (1,750kg).

[Later models had Cabriolet or Convertible bodies, 6.0-litre V12 engines, 3.6 or 4.0-litre six-cylinder engines.]

History: Because it would have been impossible to replace, and to improve upon, the legendary E-Type, Jaguar never attempted that. Instead, soon after E-Type assembly had ended, Jaguar introduced a completely different type of sporty Jaguar – the ever-controversial XJS.

Except that both cars had the same type of front-mounted V12 engines driving the rear wheels, the difference in engineering was total. The essence of an E-Type was that of an open-top two-seater, with aerodynamically-smooth lines and a multi-tube front frame, whereas the original XJS was a close-coupled four-seater coupé, built up around a conventional pressed-steel structure.

Jaguar, in fact, had saved themselves years, and many millions, by electing to develop the XJS around a short-wheelbase version of the XJ12 saloon's platform, on to which a long and rakish coupé shell had been blended, Original work was in the hands of Sir William Lyons, before he retired, the XJS being noted for its lengthy 'flying buttresses' which linked the rear window to the tail lamps.

In all major respects the XJS's running gear was shared with the XJ12 saloon, including the 285bhp/5.3-litre V12 engine, the automatic transmission, and the soft, long-travel, all-independent rear suspension: a few early cars were fitted with manual gearboxes, but were very rare.   ▶

Below: Although the XJS was built from 1975, it did not receive a facelift (including a smoother tail) until 1991. The convertible was launched in 1988.

▶ The result, a sports coupé aimed fairly and squarely at the North American market where the majority of Jaguar's sales were being secured, was a big, soft, and undoubtedly quirky-looking machine which seemed to fight fair-and-square with Mercedes-Benz and various American rather than with any other European competitors.

Functionally this was quite an amazingly capable machine, for the V12 engine had immense torque, and Jaguar's ride-and-handling package was one of the world's best, but in the early years the 150mph XJS was let down by two problems – one being its immense thirst, the other being the doubtful product quality of all the cars which came out of Browns Lane at this time.

The turn round – slow at first but gaining momentum as the 1980s progressed – started in 1981, when the more fuel-efficient 299bhp 'High Efficiency' V12 engine was standardised, and intensified in 1983 when Jaguar not only introduced a Cabriolet derivative, but the alternative of a brand new 3.6-litre twin-cam engine. Sales, which had been down to no more than 1,057 in 1980, rose steeply thereafter, and would breach 10,000 in 1988.

This was also a period when the company's image was boosted by a successful TWR-inspired race-car programme (including Le Mans victories), and with the arrival of the TWR-engineered XJR-S models.

In the meantime a private-enterprise full convertible had sold well in the USA, so a genuine factory-built convertible was put on sale in 1988. This was a huge success, and took over as the model's best seller in the USA thereafter. Ford then took over Jaguar in 1989 and, with development capital once again abundant, a major facelift took place in 1991, with a modified cabin, the loss of the 'buttresses', and a different tail profile. At the same time the six-cylinder engine went up to 4.0-litres/223bhp.

There was still time for more, as Jaguar mixed and matched its body and engine options. More and more people had come to terms with the long, low and wide style, though by early 1990s standards this was becoming to look like an over-large car. In 1993 the final product update followed, when the V12 engine was enlarged to a formidable 6.0-litre/308bhp, and a year later the 4.0-litre 'six' was boosted to 243bhp.

Even in its final years Jaguar could sell more than five thousand XJSs (mainly convertibles), and theXJS did not give way to the curvaceous new XK8 until 1996. A total of 115,413 XJSs of all types were made.

Below: This early-1990s face-lifted XJS was available with 6-cylinder or V12 engines, and with a coupé or (this car) a convertible style.

Jaguar XK8 and XKR

Jaguar XK8 sports coupé and convertible, introduced in 1996, with supercharged XKR type added in 1998

Built by: Jaguar Cars Ltd (a subsidiary of Ford Motor Co. Ltd.), Britain.

Engine: Eight cylinders, in 90-deg vee, in five-main-bearing cast alloy cylinder block. Bore and stroke 86 × 86mm, 3,995cc (3.385 × 3.385in, 243.9cu.in). Two light-alloy cylinder heads. Four valves per cylinder, in vee, operation by two overhead camshafts and hydraulic tappets. Electronic fuel injection. Maximum power 290bhp (DIN) at 6,100rpm. Maximum torque 290lb.ft at 4,250rpm. (The XKR derivative, introduced in 1998, had a supercharged engine, with 370bhp (DIN) at 6,150rpm, and 387lb.ft. at 3,600rpm.)

Transmission: Rear-wheel-drive, torque converter and five-speed automatic transmission, all in unit with front-mounted engine. Remote-control, central gearchange.

Chassis: Unitary-construction pressed-steel body-chassis unit, made as 2+2-seater fastback coupe or cabriolet. Independent front suspension by coil springs, wishbones, telescopic dampers, anti-roll bar. Independent rear suspension by coil springs, wishbones, telescopics, and anti-roll bar. Rack-and-pinion steering, with hydraulic power assistance. Four-wheel disc brakes, with ABS as standard. Cast alloy 17in road wheels, 245/50-17in tyres.

Dimensions: Wheelbase 8ft 5.9in (258.8cm), front track 4ft 11.2in (150.4cm), rear track 4ft 11in (149.8cm). Overall length 15ft 7.4in (476cm). Unladen weight 3,645lb (1,653kg).

Below: The XK8 replaced the long-serving XJS in 1996, and was a much smoother and more elegant car, powered by Jaguar's new V8 engine.

Above: The XK8 was available in fixed-head coupé or convertible form, both sharing the same sleek lines, 290bhp engine, and soft ride.

► **History:** Although the Jaguar XK8 of 1996 was broadly based on the platform an chassis engineering of the long-running XJS, the earlier car's controversial look always precluded it from being seen as an out-and-out classic. Of the engineerin heritage, though, there were never any doubts. The original XJS Coupé of 1975 ha evolved from the shortened platform of the XJ6 saloon, and in a 21-year career it ha evolved through different engine families, a restyle, and two different convertib versions, but by the early 1990s it was time for a change. In the 1980s there ha already been one false start (Project XJ41), and four-wheel-drive had been mootee but after a lot of work had been carried out, this was abandoned.

Fortunately for Jaguar, Ford had taken control in 1989, the funds were final available for a new start – styling and mechanically engineering – and, in particular, brand-new V8 engine was designed. A new car to be called XK8 was previewed March 1996, and was widely praised for its sleek good looks, and its quality.

Compared with the old XJS, the XK8 used the same basic (though much-refine 102in/259.1cm wheelbase platform and suspension systems (though much of th front-end componentry was new), but not only had the new four-cam 4-litre V engine (which was also to be used in the XJ8 saloons) been perfected, but there wa a choice of coupé or full convertible body styles.

Where the XJS had been craggy, the XK8 was sleek and rounded, for there wa a low nose with a wide-mouth oval grille, specially sculptured headlamps and line which rose gently, but persistently, towards a rounded tail. There was space in th cabin for 2+2 seating – or, to be honest, for generous two-seater accomodation wi very occasional rear seats for legless adults or willing children . . .

The equipment was as carefully detailed as expected, with airbags ahead of bot front-seats, and a full display of instruments and controls in the traditional walnu dashboard, though every car was to be built with ZF five-speed automat transmission. ABS brakes were standard, there was electronic traction control, th soft top was power-operated, and the new 290bhp V8 guaranteed instant ar seamless acceleration, and a top speed of at least 155mph. This was all done silence, with a soft yet well-controlled ride, and in a quality atmosphere that loy Jaguar buyers from the 1960s might never recognise.

Above: Fifty years of Jaguar sports car development separate the styling of these two models - the late 1990s XK8 and the late 1940s XK120.

As if this was not enough for an impressed market-place (particularly in the USA, where most Jaguars were being sold), Jaguar then set out to develop an even more colossally performing version, the XKR, which made its debut in 1998. The already lusty V8 was treated to an Eaton-type supercharger (not, please note, a turbocharger), which pushed the power up to 370bhp. Although this car's top speed was electronically limited to 155mph, the acceleration and general behaviour was even more outstanding before. By the end of the 1990s, the XK8 was selling faster than its predecessor had ever done, and more innovation was expected in the early years of the new century.

Left: The secret hidden away under the bonnet of the XKR of 1998 was a 370bhp supercharged version of Jaguar's modern 4-litre V8 engine. The top speed was electronically limited to 155mph.

Jensen-Healey

Jensen-Healey and Jensen GT models, built from 1972 to 1976
Built by: Jensen Motors Ltd., Britain.
Engine: Lotus-manufactured, four cylinders, in line, in five main bearing ligh
alloy cylinder block. Bore and stroke 95.2 x 69.3mm, 1,973cc (3.75 x 2.73i
120.5cu.in). Light alloy cylinder head. Four valves per cylinder, operated by tw
overhead camshafts and bucket-type tappets. Two horizontal twin-chol
Dell'Orto carburettors. Maximum power 140bhp at 6,500rpm. Maximum torqu
130lb.ft at 5,000rpm.
Transmission: Front engine, rear-wheel-drive, single dry plate diaphrag
spring clutch and four-speed all-synchromesh manual gearbox, all in unit wi
engine. Remote control, centre floor gearchange. (Later models had five-spee
all-synchromesh manual gearbox.)
Chassis: Unitary construction combined steel body/chassis structure, in tw
seater open sports car style or (late models, as Jensen GT) as 2+2-seat
sporting estate style. Independent front suspension by coil springs ar
wishbones, suspension of beam rear axle by coil springs and radius arm
Hydraulic telescopic dampers. Rack-and-pinion steering. Front disc, rear dru
brakes, with vacuum servo assistance. 13in cast-alloy road wheels, wi
185/70-13in tyres.
Dimensions: Wheelbase 7ft 8in (233.5cm), front track 4ft 5.2in (135cm), re
track 4ft 4.5in (133.3cm). Overall length 13ft 6in (411.5cm). Unladen weig
2,128lb (965kg).
History: The Jensen-Healey project was set up after Donald Healey lost h
links with British Leyland (when the Austin-Healey marque was killed off), a
when the American, Kjell Qvale, bought Jensen Motors of West Bromwich.
The deal was that the Healey family would design a new car, that Jens

**Below: Engineering by Healey, engine by Lotus, and manufacture by
Jensen gave the Jensen-Healey a rather complex heritage. The neat
style was not changed in four years.**

Above: Although of MGB size, the Jensen-Healey was a much more powerful (140bhp) and faster sports car, for it could reach 120mph.

would build it, and that Qvale's US interests would sell most of the cars. First thoughts centred on using Vauxhall running gear (including that company's 2.3-litre overhead-cam engine). But these foundered when the engine could not meet US emission laws, though Vauxhall front and rear suspension was always to be used.

Healey finally elected to use the brand-new 16-valve Lotus twin-cam engine (which Lotus would use later in the decade), match it to a Chrysler UK gearbox,

and fit the whole to a steel monocoque two-seater, as a front-engined/rear-drive model of MGB size.

The result was a smart, if not sensationally so, 140bhp two-seater, which started to sell well, but which was hit hard by the after effects of the Energy Crisis. With a top speed of nearly 120mph, this was a crisply styled and appealing two-seater, but one which was never well known in the USA, its principal market place.

Jensen were unlucky. The engine was by no means completely developed when used in early cars, and Jensen's own production methods could not repel early corrosion problems, but gradually the ensemble improved.

In 1974 a major transmission change saw a five-speed German Getrag gearbox replace the Chrysler unit, and in mid-1975 Jensen moved the car firmly up-market with the launch of the 'sporting estate' type, known as the Jensen GT.

Unhappily for this model, however, the parent company (which was making vast, 7.2-litre V8 engined Interceptors) struck unsolvable final problems, and ceased trading early in 1976. In a life of less than four years, therefore, just 10,504 Jensen-Healeys and 507 Jensen GTs were produced.

Lagonda V12

V12 model, built from 1937 to 1939
Built by: Lagonda Ltd., Britain.
Mechanical specification as for Lagonda LG45 six-cylinder model, except for th
following.
Engine: Twelve cylinders, in 60-degree vee-formation, in four-bearing cast-iro
block/crankcase. Bore and stroke 75mm by 84.5mm, 4,480cc (2.95in × 3.33i
273cu.in). Detachable light-alloy cylinder heads. Two overhead valves p
cylinder, operated by adjustable tappets from single overhead camshaft p
cylinder head. Two vertical single-choke Solex carburettors. Maximum pow
180bhp (gross) at 5,500rpm.
Transmission and chassis: The transmission and the chassis, wi
independent front suspension, were shared with the LG6 and the same type
coachwork could be fitted to either motor car.
History: W. O. Bentley's first job after joining Lagonda was to refine the existin
six-cylinder 4½-litre car, but once this was achieved he designed a magnifice
new V12 engine – apart from Rolls-Royce's Phantom III unit, the only su
1930s British design – and an independently sprung chassis to suit it. The engi
was actually shown at the 1936 motor show, fitted to an existing LG45 fram
but the car did not go into production until the end of 1937. The engine itself wa
everything one could have expected from the designer of great Bentleys, an
though it was never developed properly (the war saw to that) it was go
enough for special Lagondas to finish third and fourth overall at Le Mans in 193

The design was at once advanced and behind the times. Each cylinder ba
had single-overhead camshaft valve gear, which was ahead of the times, b
there was only a four-bearing crankshaft and rather rudimentary breathi
arrangements. The maximum speed of a V12 was at least 100mph, but som
cars were fitted with elephantine coachwork, which rather hamper
acceleration.

The engine found naval use in the war, but the jigs and tools were destroy
later and the magnificent V12 car and engine were never built again. They we
arguably W. O. Bentley's finest products.

Above: Lagonda's vee-12 car was designed by W. O. Bentley, no less. No car needs any other recommendation. It was fast, expensive, and exclusive. This standard saloon model was registered in 1938, and its owner is Mr David Wall.

Below: The LG6 of 1938 shared frame and body with the rarer vee-12, and had a 4½-litre six-cylinder Meadows engine.

Lamborghini Diablo

Lamborghini Diablo sports coupé, built from 1990 to 2001 (original specification)

Built by: Automobile Ferruccio Lamborghini, Italy.

Engine: Twelve cylinders, in 60-degree formation, in seven-bearing cast-alloy cylinder block/crankcase. Bore and stroke 87 x 80mm, 5,729cc (3.42 × 3.15in, 350cu.in). Two light-alloy cylinder heads. Four valves per cylinder, in narrow angle vee, operation by twin overhead camshafts and inverted bucket-type tappets. Maximum power 492bhp (DIN) at 7,000rpm. Maximum torque 428lb.ft at 5,200rpm.

Transmission: Rear-drive (four-wheel-drive version also available), diaphragm spring clutch and five-speed all-synchromesh manual gearbox, all in unit with mid-mounted engine. Remote-control, central gearchange.

Chassis: Separate multi-tubular and reinforced steel chassis frame, topped by light-alloy two-seater body shell. Independent front suspension by coil springs, wishbones, telescopic dampers, anti-roll bar. Independent rear suspension by coil springs, wishbones, telescopic dampers, anti-roll bar. Rack-and-pinion steering, no power assistance. Four-wheel disc brakes, with vacuum-servo assistance. Cast-alloy 17in road wheels, 245/40-17in (front) and 335/35-17 (rear) tyres.

Dimensions: Wheelbase 8ft 8.3in (265cm), front track 5ft 0.6in (154cm), rear track 5ft 4.6in (164cm). Overall length 14ft 7.6in (446cm). Unladen weight 3,474lb (1,576kg).

History: Lamborghini had upset the Supercar establishment (Ferrari and Maserati) way back in the mid-1960s with the launch of the mid-engined Miura, had followed it up in the early 1970s with the extreme Countach, and then moved such machinery into an entirely new dimension in 1990 with the introduction of the Diablo. It was not merely that the Diablo was so powerful, so wickedly styled, and so demonstrably special – it was that it laid down a 'beat this for power' challenge to Ferrari, and that it was also to be made available with

Below: Wickedly purposeful from any angle, the Diablo was the fastest Lamborghini. There were rear wheel and (this 'VT' version) four-wheel-drive types.

Above: Lamborghini hired Marcello Gandini to shape the Diablo for them, and he produced this unique wedge-nose/high-tail layout.

a choice of rear-wheel-drive or four-wheel-drive. What must have depressed Ferrari even more was that Lamborghini was now controlled by Chrysler of the USA, so the technical and financial muscle behind the new venture was assured.

Like its predecessors, the Diablo (Devil, in Italian, of course) was a mid-engined beast, its styling being in the capable hands of Marcello Gandini, who had already shaped the Miura and Countach models. Like the Countach, it was based on a multi-tube chassis layout (this time, though, in square-tube instead of round-tube form), with the hugely powerful V12 engine mounted longitudinally behind the two-seater cabin. Like the Countach too, the five-speed gearbox was ahead of the engine (between the seats), and the transaxle behind it, the two being neatly linked by a final drive shaft located neatly alongside the engine sump. About the engine, one needed to say no more than – V12, four overhead camshafts and four valves per cylinder, 5.7-litres and a colossal 492bhp.

The looks, complete with doors which swung forwards and upwards, coleopter-insect-fashion, when opened, rather than outwards, with a low snout, extrovert air intakes in the flanks, and with garden-roller-width rear tyres, all told a story, which was backed up by the amazing V12 sounds – and a top speed of more than 200mph. Exciting enough in rear-drive form, the Diablo was even more impressive in four-wheel-drive VT guise, with a package that not even Ferrari's Testarossa developments could offer. Lamborghini, though, always had to work hard to maintaiun their image, especially as Chrysler's resolve weakened in the early 1990s, and before VW-Audi came in to offer financial stability again in the late 1990s.

The need to impress perhaps explains why later Diablos had 6.0-litre engines with up to 550bhp, why an open-top version (think of the wind chill factor at very high speeds!) was eventually offered, and why extreme competition GT2 types were offered with no less than 630bhp, which was more than any other car in the world.

Throughout this process, the style remained basically unchanged, and it is a tribute to Gandini's experience that a Diablo seemed to be stable even as speeds approached 200mph. The fact that it was still in production in 2000, at the rate of more than 200 cars a year, proved that the concept had always been right, and that VW-Audi was going to have great difficulty in making the Murcielago a better successor.

Lamborghini Miura and Countach

Miura models, built from 1966 to 1972 (data for P400S)

Built by: Automobili Ferruccio Lamborghini S.p.A., Italy.

Engine: Twelve cylinders, in 60-degree vee-formation, in seven-bearing light alloy block. Bore and stroke 82mm by 62mm, 3,929cc (3.23in × 2.44in 240cu.in). Two detachable light-alloy cylinder heads. Two overhead valves per cylinder, opposed to each other at 70 degrees and operated camshafts per bank Six down-draught twin-choke Weber carburettors. Maximum power 370bh (DIN) at 7,700rpm. Maximum torque 286lb.ft at 5,500rpm.

Transmission: Transverse, mid-mounted engine ahead of line of rear wheels Single-dry-plate clutch and gear-driven connection to five-speed, transverse mounted, all-synchromesh gearbox, also ahead of rear wheel line. Spur-gear final-drive unit, with limited-slip differential. Exposed universally joint driv shafts to rear wheels.

Chassis: Pressed and fabricated punt-type steel floor pan/chassis, clothed by ligh alloy two-seat coupé body from Bertone. Independent suspension on all for wheels, by coil springs, wishbones and anti-roll bars. Telescopic dampers. Rac and-pinion steering. Four-wheel, hydraulically operated disc brakes, with vacuur servo assistance. 7 × 15in centre-lock cast-alloy wheels. GR70VR15 tyres.

Dimensions: Wheelbase 8ft 2.6in (250cm), tracks (front and rear) 4ft 7.8 (141.7cm). Overall length 14ft 3.5in (435.6cm) Unladen weight 2,860lb (1,300kg

History: Italian industrialist Ferruccio Lamborghini, a fast-car enthusiast, wa unhappy about the reliability of his Ferraris, and decided to do the job bett himself. His timing, in 1963, was ideal, as the Supercar market was boomin

Below: The Miura was the most sensational Italian Supercar of the 1960 not only for its looks, but for its specification, which featured a mid-mounted four-cam, 4-litre vee-12 engine. Its top speed was more than 170mph.

Above: In the 1970s, Lamborghini's vee-12-engined Countach was the first sports car to use this eye-catching but totally practical method of opening doors.

The first Lamborghini coupés – the 350GT and 400GT models – were bulbous front-engined cars, with shattering performance provided by a brand new twin-cam engine. This masterpiece, by Giotti Bizzarrini, was a beautiful and enormously powerful 60-degree vee-12, machined at a new factory at Sant'Agata Bolognese, not far from the Ferrari and Maserati factories.

At the end of 1965 Lamborghini caused a sensation by showing a rolling chassis with the vee-12 engine mid-mounted across the car, behind the seats. The design was by Gianpaolo Dallara, and was topped by an unforgettable

Bertone coupé body style in 1966. Too many cynics thought that the new car (called Miura, which was a type of Spanish fighting bull) was a one-off indulgence, but deliveries began later that year. The Miura was strictly a two-seater, but it was extremely fast (British machines achieved more than 170mph), had extremely good handling, and it was practical into the bargain. Not only that, but it was unique, for no other Italian maker of Supercars had a mid-engined car to sell for a couple of years.

Bertone's body style made the Miura memorable, for the entire nose and tail sections could be lifted up for access to the mechanical equipment, and in the daytime the pop-up headlamps laid back, flush with the bonnet lines, looking up into the sky. It was a car which appealed particularly to the "Beautiful People", for no car came more beautiful than this, and merely to look at it evoked visions of fast, high-speed dashes down the hot autoroutes or autostradas of Europe.

Lamborghini never found it necessary to ▶

▶ enlarge the engine from its original size of 3,929cc, but the original Miura P400 with 350bhp was later boosted to 370bhp for the P400S, and to an amazin 385bhp for the P400SV of 1971, by which time the top speed was under three once the new Countach prototype had been shown in 1971, but a total of 77 Miuras of all types had been built when production ceased in 1973.

COUNTACH

Announced in 1971, in production from 1974. Many components as for Miura except engine mounted in fore-and-aft position behind driver. 375bhp (DIN) a 8,000rpm. Maximum torque 266lb ft at 5,500rpm. Five-speed box in unit wit engine and hypoid-bevel final drive trans-axle. Multi-tube chassis frame, an coupe body style by Bertone, 7.5 × 15in (front) and 9 × 15in (rear) wheels, wit 205 (F) or 215 (R /70VR14 tyres.

Dimensions: Wheelbase 8ft 5.0in (245cm), track (front) 4ft 1.9in (125cm), trac (rear) 4ft 1.8in (126cm). Overall length 13ft 7in (414cm). Unladen weight 3,000l (1,360kg).

History: To improve on the Miura, Lamborghini needed something tru remarkable, and this duly arrived in 1971 as the Countach. Compared with th Miura, the Countach production car had a multi-tube chassis, and the vee-1 engine was now placed fore-and-aft, with the gearbox ahead of it, and almos between the two seats. The styling, by Bertone as it had been for the Miura was not so much 'sexy' as brutally powerful, with a marked wedge front style and with NACA-style air intakes in the flanks to channel cooling air into th engine bay. The official explanation of the title 'Countach', incidentally, is tha this is a Piemontese slang expression suggesting astonishment and admiratio – and had been used by a craftsman putting finishing touches to the firs prototype.

The prototype, incidentally, had a 5-litre Lamborghini vee-12 engine, but th production cars (which started to emerge in 1974, after a long delay fo development of the concept) reverted to 4 litres when the true top speed (wh knows...?) was between 170mph and 190mph. The most controversial featur of the body construction, apart from the looks themselves, was that the door were arranged to open forward from a front bottom hinge, rather than sideway or upwards, which apparently made safety-conscious authorities think twic about the after-effects of a serious accident.

Above: The Countach's wedge-nose style by Bertone, and a peerless 375bhp V12 engine all helped to guarantee top speeds of more than 170mph.

Countach was badly affected by the social and financial changes occurring after the 1973-1974 Suez energy crisis, and by Lamborghini's own financial traumas of the 1970s. Signor Lamborghini himself sold out during the decade, and there were other changes of ownership, at least one of which resulted in production being stopped. A total of 1111 Countachs had been built by the end of 1990 when production ended.

Left: The two-seater Countach, styled for Lamborghini by Bertone, looked startlingly attractive from any angle. The massive V12 engine was mounted 'in-line', ahead of the rear wheels.

Lamborghini Urraco

Lamborghini Urraco and Jalpa family, built from 1970 to 1991 (data for Urraco P300)

Built by: Automobili Ferruccio Lamborghini S.p.A, Italy.

Engine: Eight cylinders, in 90-degree vee formation, in five-main-bearing light alloy cylinder block. Bore and stroke 86 x 64.5mm, 2,995cc (3.39 x 2.54in, 182.8cu.in). Light-alloy cylinder heads. Two valves per cylinder, opposed in part spherical combustion chambers, operated by inverted bucket tappets from twin overhead camshafts per head. Four downdraught dual-choke Weber carburettors. Maximum power 250bhp at 7,500rpm. Maximum torque 195lb.ft at 5,750rpm.

Transmission: Transversely-positioned, mid-mounted engine, rear-wheel-drive, single dry plate diaphragm spring clutch and five-speed all-synchromesh manual gearbox, in unit with engine. Remote control, centre floor gearchange.

Chassis: Separate steel platform/punt-type chassis frame, with steel body shell in two-seater fastback coupé style welded in place on manufacture. Independent front suspension by coil springs, MacPherson struts and anti-roll bar, independent rear suspension by coil springs, MacPherson struts and anti-roll bar. Telescopic hydraluic dampers. Rack-and-pinion steering. Disc brakes at all four wheels, with vacuum servo assistance. 14in cast-alloy bolt-on wheels, with 195/70-14in (front) and 205/70-14in (rear) tyres.

Dimensions: Wheelbase 8ft 0.5in (245cm), front track 4ft 9.5in (146cm), rear track 4ft 9.5in (146cm). Overall length 13ft 1.3in (425cm). Unladen weight 3,060lb (1,388kg).

Below: The Urraco of 1970 was so beautifully styled by Bertone that few realised that the V8 engine was mounted behind the cabin.

Above: The V8-engined Urraco was arranged to have 2+2 seating, but there was little space, or head-room, in the rear.

History: Although the Urraco was not the first-ever 'small' Lamborghini to be designed, it was the only such car to be put on sale. Although it arrived at the right time, to cope with the effects of the Energy Crisis, it had a somewhat chequered career before being replaced by the closely related Jalpa model in 1979

Philosophically, if not in engineering, the Urraco counts as 'son of Miura', for it was the second mid-engined Lamborghini to be put on the market. It was,

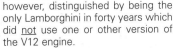

however, distinguished by being the only Lamborghini in forty years which did <u>not</u> use one or other version of the V12 engine.

The 'little' Uracco – whose Bertone style looked small and neat, in spite of its significant size, and 2+2-seater coupé cabin, was originally shown as the P250 in 1970, when it was fitted with a brand-new type of 2.5-litre, 90-degree, single-overhead-cam, V8 engine. rated originally at 220bhp, it was mounted transversely behind the cabin, where it was neatly integrated with a five-speed transmission.

Ferruccio Lamborghini, flushed with the sales success of his earlier cars (including the profit-making front-engined coupés and saloons) had allowed his engineers to develop a completely new car. Here was a unique pressed/fabricated steel platform frame, here was the new engine and transmission, and here was the sharply detailed body which somehow crammed 'almost' four seats under its roof. Because he ▶

▶ intended this car to be around for years (and to sell in relatively large numbers)
Lamborghini authorised the use of a pressed-steel body, which was welded t
the platform on assembly, which effectively made this car into a solid littl
monocoque.

Due to its size, and its potential performance (the original P250 could reac
143mph), here was a car aimed at taking sales from the Porsche 911 and the Ferra
Dino 246GT, and it certainly handled as well, and had just as much street cred.

Unfortunately the Urraco was a lot more costly than either rival and, in th
beginning, it was neither well-built, nor yet totally reliable. Lamborghini, n
doubt, were unlucky to be faced with the Energy Crisis in 1973/1974, and nc
even the arrival of a smaller-engined (182bhp/2.0-litre) P200 could solve tha
problem.

A major re-design, unveiled in 1974, saw the arrival of the Urraco P300
which had a twin-overhead-camshaft 3.0-litre/265bhp engine, but this too sol
slowly, because it was faced with the Ferrari Dino 308GTB in all its newly
launched glory.

Lamborghini, however, was determined to get the best out of this layout
First, towards the end of the 1970s, there was the 3000 Silhouette, whicl

featured a much-changed body style from Bertone, including a 'Targa' top, a two-seater cabin, along with more sporting suspension, wheel widths and tyres

Then came the 1980s, when the Urraco was dropped in favour of the two-seater Jalpa, which retained the same platform, suspension, and 3-litre V8 engine, but had a Bertone style which was really an amalgam of Silhouette and Urraco shapes and proportions. Many thought that the original Urraco of the early 1970s had been the prettiest of all these types, yet the Jalpa, complete with wheelarch bulges and engine bay scoops behind the passenger doors, sold slowly and steadily until 1991.

Sales of cars of this type and price are always restricted, so Lamborghini achieved much by selling 776 Urracos (only 190 of which were P300s, and 66 P200s), 410 Jalpas and 52 Silhouettes. Even so, mindful of the cost and complication of developing another such product line, the company did not try again, and all late-twentieth-century Lamborghinis therefore took shape around the successful V12 engine.

Below: Bertone styled the Urraco for Lamborghini on a chassis with a transverse V8 engine positioned just ahead of the rear wheels.

Lamborghini Murcielago

Lamborghini Murcielago, introduced in 2001
Built by: Nuova Automobili Ferruccio Lamborghini SpA, Italy.
Engine: Twelve cylinders, in 60-degree vee, in seven main-bearing cast alloy cylinder block. Bore and stroke 87 x 86.8mm, 6,192cc (3.42 x 3.42in, 378cu.in) Two cast alloy cylinder heads. Four valves per cylinder, in narrow angle vee operation by twin overhead camshafts and inverted bucket tappets Lamborghini fuel injection. Maximum power 571bhp at 7,500rpm. Maximum torque 479lb.ft at 5,400rpm.
Transmission: Mid-engine, four-wheel-drive, diaphragm spring clutch and six-speed all-synchromesh manual gearbox, all in unit with engine and final drive Remote control centre floor gearchange.
Chassis: Separate multi-tubular steel chassis frame, with steel and carbon fibre reinforcements, topped by steel/carbon-fibre two-seater body in fastback coupé style. Independent front suspension by coil springs, wishbones and anti roll bar, independent rear suspension by coil springs, wishbones and anti-roll bar. Hydraulic/electronically sensed telescopic dampers, with adaptive ride control. Rack-and-pinion steering, with power assistance. Disc brakes at all four wheels, with vacuum servo assistance, and ABS as standard. 18in bolt-on cast alloy wheels, with 245/35-18in (front) and 335/30-18in (rear) tyres.
Dimensions: Wheelbase 8ft 9in (266.5cm). Overall length 15ft 0.3in (458cm) Unladen weight 3,638lb (1,650kg).
History: By the end of the 1990s, Lamborghini watchers began to wonder if a replacement for the Diablo would ever go on sale. Projects had come and gone backers had appeared, then faded away – and the Diablo had kept on selling. It was not until 1998, when Audi purchased Lamborghini, that serious project work began

If a new car was to be better than the Diablo, it would not only need to be more powerful, even faster than before, and would have to look good too. Mechanically, Lamborghini's engineers were always confident that they could deliver performance, but it apparently took years for the final shape to be agreed.

The first L147 style concepts were drawn up in 1995 and prototypes first ran in 1996, but Audi then rejected the style, and initiated a 'design competition' to reach a new conclusion. By 1999 Audi's own designer, Luc Donckerwolke, produced the shape which Audi-VW's CEO Ferdinand Piech finally signed off, and committed to production. Even so, it took nearly three years (an age, by previous Lamborghini standards) before the new car, now proudly named Murcielago, was revealed. The name, incidentally, is Spanish for 'bat'.

Like the Diablo which it replaced, the Murcielago was a massive, very wide, and of course hugely powerful mid-engined two-seater, with a revised version of the famous V12 engine mounted amidships, and with the transmission actually ahead of it between the seats. Like the last of the Diablos, four-wheel-drive was standard, but this time there were six forward speeds, and the engine was significantly changed.

When L147 was originally planned, it was due to have a 6.0-litre version of the V12 (this engine also going into the last of the Diablos), but a 6.2-litre version (with a 2.8mm longer stroke, but the same on-the-limit bore of 87mm) was finally developed. As expected, this 6.2-litre V12 is one of the finest of all fine Italian supercar power units, for pride (and the need to out-do Ferrari) was ▶

Below: Practice makes perfect – this being the 2001 production version of the Murcielago, which had been much-modified at the testing stage.

▶ always at stake. Not only was its peak power an amazing 571bhp, but this was significantly better than that of the 6-litre Diablo (543bhp), and well in advance of the 485bhp of the contemporary 5.5-litre Ferrari V12.

Like the Diablo, the Murcielago used a steel multi-tube space frame chassis, but this time there was much reinforcement from a carbon fibre centre tunnel, and under-body, while almost all the exterior body panels were also in carbon fibre. Not surprisingly, Lamborghini claimed that the structure was 60 per cent stiffer than ever before.

Amazingly, when the car was announced there were comments that it did not look special enough – compared with the Diablo there were no extrovert spoilers, aerofoils, sill extensions or flutes – but there was no doubting its integrated visual appeal – or its promise of performance. Like the Diablo, it had passenger doors that opened upwards and forwards, coleopter-like.

And there was plenty of that. Lamborghini claimed a top speed of at least 205mph/330kph, and although there had been much chassis development work (which included the use of ABS braking on enormously wide 18in tyres) there seemed to be an airy disdain for matters of fuel economy. With a car like this, it seems, the performance, and the image, was always going to be vital – and the rest could safely be ignored.

The new Murcielago, in any case, seemed set for a long career. 2,884 Diablos had been produced, and Audi was determined to beat that with its new toy. In the early 2000s, for the time being, the Murcielago was one of the world's very fastest sports cars.

Above: This detail of the Murcielago's rear quarters, shows the way that fresh air scoops were neatly integrated into the profile above the rear wheels.

Below: Real engine, real horsepower – for the Murcielago's 6.2-litre vee-12 produced no less than 571bhp.

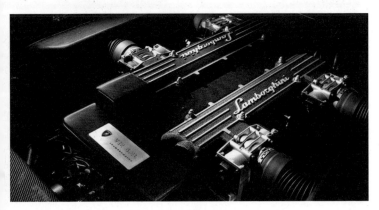

Lancia Lambda

Lambda Series 1 to 9, built from 1923 to 1931 (data for Series 1 Lambda)
Built by: Fabbrica Automobili Lancia e Cia., Italy.
Engine: Four cylinders, in 13-degree vee-formation, in three-bearing light-alloy block/crankcase. Bore and stroke 75mm by 120mm, 2,120cc (2.95in × 4.72in, 129.4cu.in). Single detachable cast-iron cylinder head. Two overhead valves per cylinder, operated by rockers and cam followers from single overhead camshaft. Single Zenith carburettor at rear of head, feeding to middle of engine. Maximum power 50bhp at 3,000rpm. Maximum torque 38lb.ft at 2,125rpm.
Transmission: Multiple-dry-plate clutch and three-speed manual gearbox (without synchromesh) both in unit with engine, direct-acting central gearchange. Two-piece open propeller shaft to spiral-bevel 'live' rear axle unit.
Chassis: Separate sheet-steel chassis, really a unitary structure forming frame and basic body structure in one. Independent front suspension by Lancia-type coil springs and sliding pillar linkage, with vertical telescopic dampers. Rear suspension by semi-elliptic leaf springs, with Hartford friction-type dampers. Worm-and-wheel steering. Centre-lock wire wheels. 765 × 105 tyres. Four-wheel drum brakes. Coachwork to choice – tourer, sports, or saloon. Structural boot compartment supplied as part of Lancia unitary-construction chassis structure.
Dimensions: Wheelbase 10ft 2in (310cm), tracks (front and rear) 4ft 4in (132cm), overall length 14ft 4in (437cm). Unladen weight (depending on coachwork) about 2,400lb (1,088kg).

History: Narrow-angle vee-formation engines had been an obsession in Vincenzo Lancia's plans for many years before his Lambda was announced in 1921, but the Lambda will also be remembered for its remarkable, unique, and rigid chassis. The engine, with only 13 degrees between banks (the block casting was actually almost cubic) was very short and stubby, with no attempt to deal with the out of balance dynamic forces. It is interesting to note that later Lambdas used 14-degree engines and final versions a 13-degree 40-minute layout.

The chassis was even more remarkable. It was a skeleton framework of flanged pressed-steel members, riveted together in ship fashion, with cut-outs for doors and for lightening. Cross bracing for these deep side members was provided by scuttle and bulkhead panels, and a rigid backbone, which included the propeller shaft tunnel. Suspension and steering were hung from strategically placed tubular cross members. Front suspension was independent, by coil springs bearing above and below on to the sliding pillar stub axles – an arrangement used by Lancia for another thirty years. The firm was even forced to invent its own type of hydraulic dampers, integral with the 'king pin' housing.

The Lambda, made in nine series between 1923 and 1931, was at once light, low, and with exceptional roadholding, by any standards. More than 12,000 were made and Lancia's reputation for making 'way out' engineering work was established.

Left: Lancia's famous Lambda model was introduced in 1923 and ran through to 1931. The example shown was a 1928 version, mechanically very similar to the originals, and with that unique type of narrow-angle vee-4 light-alloy engine. The chassis frame was the other Lambda advance – of sheet steel and very deep – really an early example of unit-construction, now universal.

Lancia Stratos

Stratos model, built from 1974 to 1975

Built by: Fabbrica Automobili Lancia e Cia. (now part of Fiat), Italy.

Engine: Ferrari manufactured. Six cylinders, in 65-degree vee-formation, in fou bearing light-alloy block, transversely mounted behind seats. Bore and strok 92.5mm by 60mm, 2,418cc (3.64in × 2.36in, 147.5cu.in). Light-alloy cylinder head Two overhead valves per cylinder, inclined to each other in part-spherical combustic chambers and operated by twin overhead camshafts. Three down-draught twi choke Weber carburettors. Maximum power 190bhp (DIN) at 7,000rpm. Maximui torque 159lb.ft at 4,500rpm. Four-valve cylinder heads also available for competitic purposes, along with fuel injection in some applications.

Transmission: Single-dry-plate clutch and five-speed, all-synchromesh manu gearbox, behind and below the main engine block. Remote-control centr gearchange. Direct gearbox shaft to hypoid-bevel final-drive unit. Expose universally jointed drive shafts to rear wheels.

Chassis: Fabricated sheet-steel chassis structure, with tubular and othe fabricated cross-bracing members. Glassfibre body skin panels, non-loa bearing. Engine/transmission behind driving compartment. Two seats in close coupé layout. All independent suspension, by coil springs, wishbones, and an roll bars. Telescopic dampers. Rack-and-pinion steering. Four-whee hydraulically operated disc brakes. 14in bolt-on cast-alloy wheels. 205/70VR1 tyres. Wider wheels optional.

Dimensions: Wheelbase 7ft 1.8in (218cm), track (front) 4ft 8.2in (143cm), trac (rear) 4ft 9.5in (146cm). Overall length 12ft 2in (371cm). Unladen weight abo 2,160lb (980kg).

History: The Stratos was born out of Lancia's desire to dominate internation production car motor sport, and particularly rallying. Cesare Fiorio, at once sale director and competition chief at Lancia, knew that the front-drive Fulvia coupé were no longer competitive and co-operated with Bertone in evolving a ve special machine. It was nothing less than a full-blown mid-engined competitic car, of which the minimum number (400 in a 12-month period) would be mad to ensure approval for Group 4 competition. The first 'show car' by Bertone wa a non-runner and was fitted with a Lancia Fulvia V4 engine, but as Lancia ar

Below: The Lancia Stratos was a purpose built competition car, of which on a few hundred were made between 1974 and 1975. It could win races or survive the roughest and toughest rallies, with a combination of over powerful 2.4-litre vee-4 Ferrari engine, and a light but rigid structure.

Above: The Stratos's style was by Bertone, the rear-drive engine was behind the seats, and rally-tuned 24-valve engines produced up to 280bhp.

Ferrari were now both controlled by Fiat it seemed reasonable to go the whole way to domination. The 'production' Stratos, therefore, was given a straight transplant, without any need for modification, of the 2.4-litre, four-cam, V6 Ferrari Dino engine and transmission, which was already engineered for mid-mounting. The Stratos, although stubby, low, and wickedly purposeful-looking, was also very strong. It had to be – it was meant to win not only the fastest tarmac rallies, and road races to be found in Europe, but also to tackle the rough events like the East African Safari, the Moroccan rally and the RAC rally. After some development problems, speedily solved because the solution could be applied to the small batch of production machines, the Stratos soon began to win, more or less as it pleased. It has to be said that the 'works' machines were usually stronger and more reliable than those supplied to private owners, but this is only to be expected.

The production Stratos disposed of 190bhp, but competition versions usually had 240bhp, and – once the four-valve cylinder heads were homologated – up to 280bhp was available. This along with the splendid traction and road-holding of the cars, allied with the bravery of factory-hired drivers, made the cars almost unbeatable. Only the Safari (where dust in the engines is a major hazard) has really defeated the arrow-shaped projectile from Turin. The Stratos was never a serious road car, although some wealthy enthusiasts use the cars in this way. The factory continued to campaign the machines years after production ceased.

Lotus Elan SE

Lotus Elan, with front-wheel-drive, built from 1989 to 1994 (data for original SE model)

Built by: Lotus Cars Ltd., Britain.

Engine: Isuzu, four cylinders, in line, in five-main-bearing cast-iron cylinder block. Bore and stroke 80 × 79mm, 1,588cc (3.15 × 3.11in, 96.9cu.in). Light-alloy cylinder head. Four valves per cylinder, in narrow vee, operation by twin overhead camshaft and inverted hydraulic tappets. Rochester fuel injection and IHi turbocharger. Maximum power 165bhp (DIN) at 6,600rpm. Maximum torque 148lb.ft at 4,200rpm (Non-turbocharged version, with 130bhp and 105lb.ft, available on entry level Elan not badged as 'SE'.)

Transmission: Front-wheel-drive, single-dry-plate diaphragm spring clutch and five-speed all-synchromesh manual gearbox, all in unit with transverse front-mounted engine. Remote-control, central gearchange.

Chassis: Separate chassis frame, backbone shape, in presswed and fabricated steel, clad in glassfibre/advanced composite two-seater style, open roadster or with hardtop. Independent front suspension by coil springs, wishbones, telescopic dampers and anti-roll bar. Independent rear suspension by coil springs, wishbone and transverse links, telescopic dampers, and anti-roll bar. Rack-and-pinion steering with hydraulic power assistance. Four-wheel disc brakes, no ABS. Cast alloy 15in wheels, 205/50-15in. tyres.

Dimensions: Wheelbase 7ft 4.6in (225cm), front track 4ft 10.5in (148.6cm), rear track 4ft 10.5in (148.6cm). Overall length 12ft 5.7in (380.2cm). Unladen weight 2,253lb (1,022kg).

History: During the 1980s, Lotus went through agonies in trying to develop a new 'small' sports car to slot into a product range under the existing Esprit models. It was not until General Motors took control, and provided finance to underpin development and investment, that a new car, the Elan, was finalised. Although this was traditional Lotus in many ways – including the use of the stubby steel backbone type chassis, and the VARI-patented way of manufacturing a glass-fibre body shell – there was sensation in other aspects. Not only was this the first (and only) Lotus to use

Below: From this view the Elan's style had similarities with earlier Lotus sports cars. The turbocharged SE delivered a 136mph top speed.

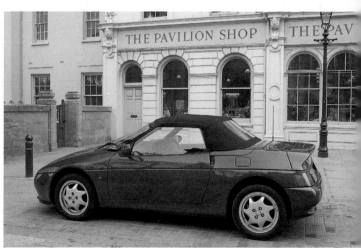

Above: Wide, squat but above all purposeful, the 1989 Elan was the first-ever front-wheel-drive Lotus, with remarkable steering and handling.

Japanese Isuzu engine, but it also had front-wheel-drive.

The choice of front-wheel-drive, with a transverse engine and five-speed gearbox, went hand in hand with the use of the Isuzu power pack, this being provided courtesy of General Motors, who also had a controlling interest in the Japanese concern. The engine itself was a sturdy 16-valve 1.6-litre twin-cam unit being developed for use in front-drive Isuzus of the 1990s, and was ideal for this purpose. Although Isuzu had never previously been known for producing fine engines, this was a typical, smooth, high-revving, Japanese 16-valver, which worked well in the Lotus. Two engine tunes were to be offered – a normally aspired unit with 130bhp, and an IHi-turbocharged version with no less than 165bhp – but sales experience showed that few people took up the low-powered option. With 165bhp the new Elan SE (without a turbo, it was not an SE either . . .) could reach 136mph.

Naturally there was independent front and rear suspension, but a front-end novelty was that the suspension was mounted on a separate 'raft' or sub-frame, which allowed the Lotus engineers to provide peerless refinement to go with the steering and suspension accuracy all such Hethel-built cars always had. Here was a short-wheelbase car with wide tracks, which could so easily have looked stubby, but Peter Stevens (who would later go on to shape the McLaren F1 road car) did a marvellous design job to prevent this possibility. Neat, rounded, with a front-to-rear wing line rising steadily towards the tail, and with a vast multi-curvature windscreen, this was an unmistakeable Lotus which could never be taken for anything else.

UK sales began in 1989, with USA sales starting in 1991, but orders were always disappointingly low. Although this was a fast car which handled superbly, it was always expensive. This, and the fact that Lotus's once-unreliable build quality reputation took ages to be killed off, did not help.

At the development stage Lotus had made sure that the engineering, and the behaviour, was right, at the (to them) laudable expense of neglecting product cost. This Elan, too, was difficult to build and (in view of the finicky nature of the front suspension system) time-consuming to set up. Faced with an on-going loss-maker, General Motors pulled the plug in 1992, closed down the assembly lines, and shortly after decided to sell off the entire company. Kia, of South Korea, bought the design and manufacturing rights to the Elan, installed its own normally aspirated engine, and called it a Roadster from 1995, but it was no Lotus, and sales ended in 2000.

Lotus Elise

Lotus Elise two-seater sports car, introduced in 1995
Built by: Lotus Cars Ltd., Britain.
Engine: Rover K-Series four cylinders, in line, in five-main-bearing light-allo
cylinder block/crankcase. Bore and stroke 80 × 89.3mm, 1,796cc (3.15 × 3.51i
109.6cu.in). Light-alloy cylinder head. Four valves per cylinder, in narrow ve
operation by twin overhead camshafts and inverted bucket tappets. MEM
electronic fuel injection. Maximum power 118bhp (DIN) at 5,500rpm. Maximu
torque 122lb.ft at 3,000rpm.
Transmission: Rear-wheel-drive, single-dry-plate diaphragm spring clutch ar
five-speed all-synchromesh manual gearbox, all in unit with transverse-mounte
mid engine. Remote-control, central gearchange.
Chassis: Separate extruded aluminum tub, bonded together from section
clothed in a glassfibre advanced composite two-seater body style. Independe
front suspension by coil springs, wishbones, telescopic dampers, anti-roll ba
Independent rear suspension by coil springs, wishbones and telescop
dampers. Rack-and-pinion steering. Four-wheel disc brakes without ABS. Ligt
alloy 15in and 16in road wheels, 185/55-15in (front) and 205/50-16in (rear) tyre
Dimensions: Wheelbase 7ft 6.5in (230cm), front track 4ft 8.7in (144cm), re
track 4ft 9.2in (145.3cm). Overall length 12ft 2.7in (372.6cm). Unladen weig
1,594lb (723kg).
History: The miracle is not that the lightweight and appealing Lotus Elise ev
became a success, but that it ever went into production at all, for it wa
conceived when Lotus's entire business was in turmoil, and when comple
closure was forecast on more than one occasion. Lotus, at one time a Gener
Motors subsidiary, had been sold off to Romeo Artioli's business empire (he wa
also trying to revive Bugatti) in 1993, and although he always talked big, neith
the financial backing nor the deeds ever backed this up. After a great deal
strife, which included the aborted sale to other interests, Lotus was finally so
to Proton of Malaysia in 1996.

In the meantime, the Elise project had stuttered into life, a light, back-t

**Below: Not a line out of place, and not a kilo of surplus weight – that wa
the philosophy behind the mid-engined Elise.**

Above: The basis of the Elise was a bonded-together extruded aluminium tub, with a Rover K-Series engine mounted behind the seats – ultra-light, and very effective.

basics two-seater being built around a bonded-together aluminium chassis/tub whose technology and original execution hailed from Denmark. The engine/transmission unit, mounted behind the starkly trimmed two-seater cabin, was the modern Rover K-series installation, where the aluminium engine had a 16-valve twin-cam cylinder head, and where 118bhp was developed from 1.8-litres.

Linked to a neat five-speed transmission, this all looked very familiar, and so it should, for the same combination was also to be found in the also-new MG MGF. The body itself was in glass-fibre, as was every modern Lotus of the 20th Century, but trim was almost non-existent, there were no carpets on the floor, and the 'all-weather' equipment could best be described as skimpy. Yet this was precisely the type of car, it seemed, that sporty young customers were seeking, expecially as the initial price – originally set at £18,950 in the UK – looked to be so reasonable. Previewed in September 1995, the Elise was ready for sale by mid-1996, but deliveries were originally hampered because many suppliers (especially Rover) demanded cash-on-delivery before they would release components, and it was not until Proton took charge towards the end of 1996 that continuity was assured.

Once the first independent road tests were published, the Elise's charm became common knowledge. Fast (124mph) but not astonishing, it was light and possessed of simply incredible mid-engine-type road holding. Its natural rival, the new mid-engined Renault Spider, had no answer to its capabilities which, in one tester's opinion, 'Rewrites the book on driver appeal.'

With more unpainted aluminium on show in the cabin that trim materials, one would not expect it to sell to the staid, and the pernickety, but Lotus never expected that. Within two years, in any case, 3,000 Elise types were being delivered every year, which was more than Lotus had ever sold, of any one model, at any time. By 2000 the range had been further expanded, not only with 145bhp Elise 111S derivative, but there was also talk of an Exige model with permanent hardtop and a bigger, more powerful engine. For the first time in decades, it seemed, Lotus had a sure-fire winner on its hands, the back-to-basics decision of 1994 having been responsible for this.

Lotus Elite (1950s Type)

Lotus Elite, built from 1957 to 1963 (data for 1959 car)
Built by: Lotus Cars Ltd., Britain.
Engine: Coventry Climax manufactured. Four cylinders, in line, in three-beari█
light-alloy block. Bore and stroke 76.2mm by 66.6mm, 1,216cc (3.0in × 2.62█
74.2cu.in). Light-alloy cylinder head. Two overhead valves per cylinder, in line█
wedge-shaped combustion chamber, operated by inverted-bucket tappets fro█
single overhead camshaft. Single or twin side-draught constant-vacuum S█
carburettors to choice. Maximum power with single carburettor 71bhp (net)█
6,100rpm. Maximum torque with single carburettor 77lb.ft at 3,500rpm█
Maximum power with twin carburettors 83bhp at 6,300rpm.
Transmission: Single-dry-plate clutch and four-speed, synchromesh manu█
gearbox (no synchromesh on first gear), both in unit with engine. Remo█
control central gearchange. Exposed propeller shaft to chassis-mounted hypo█
bevel differential. Exposed, universally jointed drive shafts to rear wheels.
Chassis: Three main piece glassfibre monocoque, with steel-tu█
reinforcements. No separate chassis frame. Independent front suspension █
coil springs, wishbones and anti-roll bar. Independent rear suspension █
Chapman strut and coil springs. Telescopic dampers. Rack-and-pinion steerir█
Four-wheel, hydraulically operated disc brakes, inboard at rear. 15in centre-lo█
wire wheels, with 4.90 × 15in tyres.
Dimensions: Wheelbase 7ft 4in (224cm), tracks (front and rear) 3ft 1█
(119cm). Overall length 12ft (366cm). Unladen weight 1,200lb (544kg).
History: Colin Chapman had established Lotus's reputation on the race track █
1956, but the Elite coupé, conceived in 1956 and revealed in 1957, was his fi█
true road car. Nearly 1,000 were made between 1959, when full producti█
began, and 1963 when it ceased, but although it was attractive and ve█
functional the Elite was never a profit-maker for the company. In particular █
cost of making the bodies became prohibitive, which is one reason why the E█
sports car had a steel chassis.
The Elite's concept was of a glassfibre monocoque – made in three ma█

284

Above: The Elite, revealed in 1957, was beautiful and technically clever. A unit-construction shell in glassfibre was unique, the car was very light, and used a Climax engine.

sections, floor, structural centre section and one-piece outer skin – on to which all mechanical and suspension parts would be mounted. This worked remarkably well, even if there were refinement problems in bolting the axle and engine units to the shell, and it certainly made the whole car very light. The shape was sleek, and the fuel company therefore very good. Series II cars, produced in the 1960s, incorporated revised rear suspension and other improvements, and late in life Coventry-Climax engines of up to 100bhp were offered.

Perhaps the Elite's biggest disadvantage was that the roof was stressed and a convertible version was therefore impossible. Ventilation was also poor, because door shape did not allow for opening side windows. It is already a collector's piece in many countries.

Left: Inspired by Peter Kirwin-Taylor, the two-seater monocoque Elite was sinuous and sleek from every angle.

Lotus Elan and Plus 2 (1962-1974)

Lotus Elan and Elan Plus 2 family, built from 1962 to 1974 (data for origina Elan of 1963)

Built by: Lotus Cars Ltd., Britain.

Engine: Four cylinders, in line, in five-main-bearing cast iron cylinder bloc Bore and stroke 82.55 x 72.75mm, 1,558cc (3.25x 2.86in, 95.1cu.in). Light allo cylinder head. Two valves per cylinder, opposed to each other in part-spheric combustion chamber, operation by inverted bucket tappets and twin overhea camshafts. Two horizontal twin-choke Weber carburettors. Maximum pow 105bhp at 5,500rpm. Maximum torque 108lb.ft at 4,000rpm.

Transmission: Front engine, rear-wheel-drive, single dry plate clutch and fou speed all-synchromesh manual gearbox, all in unit with engine. Remote contr centre floor gearchange.

Chassis: Separate steel backbone chassis frame, with pressed and fabricated ste reinforcements. Independent front suspension by coil springs, wishbones and an roll bar, independent rear suspension by coil springs, Chapman struts an wishbones. Hydraulic telescopic dampers. Rack-and-pinion steering. Disc brakes all four wheels. 13in wheels, bolt on steel disc, with 5.20-13in tyres. Glass-fib body shell in two-seater, open top Roadster style, with optional removable hardto or in alternative fixed-head coupé style. [Elan Plus 2 had a longer chassis w. 12in/30.5cm longer wheelbase, wider wheel tracks, and a fixed-head coupé bo style. Later Elans had more power, up to 126bhp/6,500rpm.]

Dimensions: Wheelbase 7ft 0in (213cm), front track 3ft 11in (119.5cm), re track 4ft 0.5in (123cm). Overall length 12ft 1in (368.3cm). Unladen weig 1,515lb (687kg).

History: To follow the original Elite, Lotus started again with a much simp concept, but with its own, in-house, twin-cam engine. For the 1960s the id of using a glass-fibre monocoque was abandoned, in favour of a simple, ea to produce, steel backbone frame, though the body shells continued to be glass-fibre.

Between 1962 and 1974, two different types of Elan – the original car w a small, taut, two-seater style, and a larger, longer, and wider version called t Elan Plus 2, sold in their thousands. Although the LOTUS acronym (Lots Trouble, Usually Serious) still applied at times – quality control was alwa doubtful in this fast-expanding business – the performance, the handling, a above all the looks of these cars were never in doubt.

Below: Two versions of the two-seater Elan – a 1970 S4 on the right, and 1972 Sprint coupé on the left, showing off the tiny two-seater proportion

Above: The Elan Plus 2, announced in 1967, was longer and wider than the original Elan, with 2+2 seating and a new body style.

For these cars Lotus, in particular, had mastered the trick of providing its machines with soft suspension, very firmly damped, which gave an appealing and effective package of road manners. This, combined with finger-light and accurate steering, and lightweight construction, made the cars very responsive to the driver's wishes. Unhappily, the same light weight often led to reliability breakdowns and quality failings.

The new twin-cam engine, which was based on the Ford Cortina's cylinder block and details, was central to the layout of all these cars. Originally tweaked by Cosworth, and rated at 105bhp, it was torquey and lively. In motorsport it could eventually be made to produce more than 170bhp, while the final Elan road cars had an equally impressive 126bhp.

The first Elan two-seater was simply trimmed and equipped, but because of its 115mph top speed and 0-60mph acceleration in less than nine seconds, it hit the popularity jackpot at once. Over the years, the Elan two-seater grew up through S2, S3 and S4, to culminated in the 'Big Valve' Sprint model of the early 1970s. Along the way, the car's equipment was gradually improved – centre-lock wheels took over from bolt-on types, wind-up windows were improved, a removable hardtop became optional, and there was also a permanent coupé derivative too. Even to the end, this two-seater was lean, responsive, and super-fast on ordinary roads.

The Elan Plus Two, which was announced in 1967, used a stretched and widened version of the same backbone chassis (the wheelbase went up by 12in/30.5cm), and had a totally new coupé body style, into which 2+2-seating had somehow been squeezed.

Like the two-seater, the Elan Plus 2 had all the latest Lotus virtues of soft but well controlled suspension, and was (according to Lotus'' advertising, at least) ideal for the sporting 'young family' man. In a seven year life, its evolution and development tracked that of the two-seater, though in the case of the Plus 2, towards the end of its career, it also inherited a newly-developed five-speed gearbox too.

Sprint models, 126bhp-equipped, and with that gearbox, could beat 120mph, and this, by any standards, was one of the fastest all-condition road cars of the time. Like all previous Elans, they were popular, and remained so, there being so much animal appeal in their design that customers put up with all manner of minor failings for which Lotus became famous.

Although Lotus archives were always notoriously vague, it seems that 9,659 two-seater Elan, and 4,798 Plus Twos were produced. It was, and still is, one of the most profitable programmes Lotus ever tackled. Later in the 1970s and 1980s, Lotus road cars became heavier, and more 'touring', so the appeal of these original types was lost.

Lotus Esprit (all types)

Lotus Esprit family, introduced 1975, re-styled 1987 (data for origin **Turbo of 1980/1981)**
Built by: Lotus Cars Ltd., Britain.
Engine: Four cylinders, in line, in five-main-bearing light alloy cylinder bloc Bore and stroke 95.28 x 76.2 mm, 2,174cc (3.75 x 3.00in, 132.7cu.in). Lig alloy cylinder head. Four valves per cylinder, opposed to each other in narro vee, operation by bucket tappets from twin overhead camshafts. Two tw choke Dell'Orto carburettors with Garrett Airesearch turbocharger. Maximu power 210bhp at 6,000rpm. Maximum torque 200lb.ft at 4,000rpm. [Espr also available with 2.2-litre/4-cylinder engine up to 243bhp, and with 3.5-litre \ engine, up to 354bhp.]
Transmission: Mid-engine, rear-wheel-drive, single dry plate diaphragm sprir clutch and five-speed all-synchromesh manual gearbox, all in unit with engi and final drive. Remote control centre floor gearchange.
Chassis: Separate pressed-steel chassis frame, backbone constriction, wi pressed and fabricated steel reinforcements. Independent front suspension coil springs, wishbones and anti-roll bar, independent rear suspension by c springs, fixed-length drive shafts, transverse and longitudinal links. Hydrau telescopic dampers. Rack-and-pinion steering. Disc brakes for all four whee with vacuum servo assistance. 15in bolt-on cast alloy wheels, with 195/60-15 (front) and 235/60-15in (rear) tyres. Glass-fibre body in two-seater, fastba coupé style.
Dimensions: Wheelbase 8ft 0in (244cm), front track 5ft 0.5in (154cm), re track 5ft 1.2in (155.5cm). Overall length 13ft 9in (419cm). Unladen weig 2,650lb (1,202kg).
History: To replace the long-running Europa, and to take full advantage of t newly generated 16-valve 2-litre engine, Lotus developed a new mid-engin

Below: From 1987 Lotus produced the Esprit with this rather more rounded body style, still a two-seater, still with a mid-mounted engine.

Above: Styled by Giugiaro in 1972, but re-shaped by Lotus in 1987, the mid-engined Esprit has always been a design classic.

two-seater. Called the Esprit, it finally went on sale in mid-1976, and in much-developed form, but still recognisably the same product, it was still on sale in the early 2000s.

As with all contemporary Lotus road cars, the Esprit used a steel backbone frame, with soft, long-travel, all-independent suspension, and a glass-fibre body shell. The 160bhp engine was the same as that used in the new-generation Elite, but in this new model it was placed amidships, behind the two-seater cabin, and drove the rear wheels through a modified Citroen SM transmission.

For the first time, too, Lotus went overseas for its styling, and contracted Giorgetto Giugiaro to provide a neat, distinctive, and totally recognisable fast-back style. That style matured very well indeed, and did not need a complete reskin until 1987, when the Lotus-evolved 'X180' came along. In all cases, the Esprit had a very compact two-seater cabin (leg-room was restricted at first, but improved over the years), and there was little attempt to provide much stowage space.

Almost by tradition, there were quality problems with the earlier Esprits, but they car sold well, nevertheless, and there was never any doubting the performance levels. S2 and S3 models came along during the late 1970s/early 1980s, not only with real chassis and suspension improvements, but with attention to reliability and to equipment. S3s could certainly reach 135mph, and because this was still only a 2.2-litre car the clientele was highly impressed.

Although this was the sort of car which ought to have offered head-to-head competition with Ferrari's 'little' Dino types, the Esprit never gained that sort of image. Efforts to establish the brand in North America always foundered because of difficulties in setting up a viable dealer network: Lotus always regretted this, especially as the American market was usually so receptive to this type of sports car..

Yet there was more to come. By 1980, not only was the beefy 16-valve twin-cam engine ready to be enlarged to 2.2-litres, but Lotus also produced a 210bhp turbocharged version. Then, and now, the Turbo never needed an intercooler to produce its power, though this was eventually raised to more than 240bhp in its final version. Turbos were very fast – 150mph was possible – which for such a compact and small-engined car was quite remarkable. ▶

►   Lotus finally re-styled the Esprit in 1987, retaining the basic style and outline, but making it slightly and definitely more rounded in the detail, and it was this style which then carried on successfully into the early 2000s. At first the revised normally-aspirated 'four' produced 172bhp, the turbocharged version 215bhp.

Along the way, though, there always seemed to be the need for more performance, so the normally aspirated four-cylinder type was dropped in 1990, and from 1996 a twin-turbocharged vee-8 3.5-litre type was finally introduced. This engine, in effect, was a direct evolution of the long-running 'four', and was not only compact but light and fuel efficient.

With no less than 354bhp available, this put the latest Esprit up into real 'supercar' territory, for it had an easily-achieved top speed of more than

Above: All Esprits feature a steel backbone frame, a mid-mounted engine, and a wedge-nosed glass-fibre body shell. The spoiler on this version was completely functional.

170mph, and the acceleration to match.

By the late 1990s, though, the arrival of new Lotus models such as the Elise and Exige meant that the old Esprit had almost become a forgotten car, and not even a cosmetic facelift in the early 2000s could do more than keep sales ticking over.

Even before the turbocharged models were introduced in 1980, well over 4,000 Esprits had been produced, and after another twenty years the total must have been approaching the 10,000 mark.

Lozier Type I 50hp

Type I 50hp, built from 1907 to 1911 (data for 1910 model)
Built by: Lozier Motor Co., United States.
Engine: Six cylinders, in line, in three cast-iron blocks, with four-bearing light-alloy crankcase. Bore and stroke 117.5mm by 139.7mm, 9,089cc (4.62in × 5.5in, 554.6cu.in). Three non-detachable cast-iron cylinder heads. Two side valves per cylinder, in T-head layout with exposed valve stems and springs, operated via tappets from two camshafts mounted in sides of crankcase. Single up-draught carburettor.
Transmission: Multiple-dry-plate clutch, in unit with front-mounted engine, and shaft drive to separate four-speed manual gearbox (without synchromesh) – third gear direct and fourth gear an overdrive. Remote-control right-hand gear-change. Propeller shaft, enclosed in torque tube, driving straight-bevel 'live' rear axle.
Chassis: Separate pressed-steel chassis frame, with channel-section side members and pressed and tubular cross bracing. Forged front axle beam. Front suspension by semi-elliptic leaf springs. Rear suspension by semi-elliptic leaf springs, with transverse 'platform' leaf spring picking up rear of these springs, plus torque tube and radius arm location. Friction-type dampers. Worm-and-sector steering. Foot-operated transmission drum brake. Hand brake on rear

wheel drums. Artillery-style road wheels. 36 × 4½in tyres. Choice of coachwork.
Dimensions: Wheelbase 10ft 11in (333cm), tracks (front and rear) 4ft 8in (142cm).

History: Lozier cars, like Pierce-Arrows and Packards, were among the finest American cars of the highest quality in the halcyon days before the outbreak of World War I. Unhappily, like many other firms around them, the social and financial changes which followed this conflict served to kill off many of the bespoke car makers. Lozier was one of the unlucky ones. The original Loziers had 'conventional American' T-head engines and chain drive, but only two years later they adopted shaft drive, and the 'platform' type of leaf spring suspension so beloved of the American designers. The engines had alloy crankcases and paired cast-iron blocks, which made it easy and straightforward to build fours or sixes. The 1907 range was precisely that – a high-quality mixture of components and a 40hp four alongside a 50hp six. Aids to luxury motoring were the chassis-long cast-alloy undertray (which protected the mechanicals from the dust of the era's unmade roads), and, in the case of the Type I, the geared-up fourth speed, which gave an 'overdrive' effect. It was no wonder that the Lozier marque was active in motor sport – in 1910 they won the National Stock car championship, and in 1911 the Vanderbilt Cup, with a second place overall in the Indianapolis 500.

Left: Lozier's Type I was one of North America's finest cars. Only a few were built, and raced successfully.

Marcos 1800/3-litre/ Mantula family

Marcos sports car range, built from 1964 to 1971, then 1981 to 2001 (data for 3-Litre Volvo-engined type of late 1960s)

Built by: Marcos Cars Ltd., Britain.

Engine: Volvo-manufactured, six cylinders, in line, in seven main-bearing cast iron cylinder block. Bore and stroke 88.9 x 80mm, 2,978cc (3.50 x 3.18in, 181.7cu.in). cast iron cylinder head. Two overhead valves per cylinder, operation by pushrods and rockers from a camshaft in the cylinder block. Two semi-downdraught Zenith-Stromberg carburettors. Maximum power 130bhp at 5,000rpm. Maximum torque 152lb.ft at 2,500rpm.

Transmission: Front engine, rear-wheel-drive, single dry plate diaphragm spring clutch and four-speed all-synchromesh manual gearbox. Remote control centre floor gearchange.

Chassis: Separate steel chassis frame, with tubular main side members, tubular and fabricated reinforcements, topped by two-seater glass-fibre body shell in fastback coupé style. (Early cars, pre-1968, had laminated wood chassis.) Independent front suspension by coil springs, wishbones and anti-roll bar, suspension of beam rear axle by coil springs, trailing arms and Panhard rod. Hydraulic telescopic dampers. Rack-and-pinion steering. Front disc, rear drum brakes. 13in bolt-on cast alloy road wheels, with 175-13in tyres.

Dimensions: Wheelbase 7ft 5in (226cm), front track 4ft 2.5in (128.3cm), rear track 4ft 4.0in (132cm). Overall length 13ft 4.5in (407.7cm). Unladen weight 2,028lb (920kg).

[This family built with different Ford V4 and V6, Volvo 4-cyl and 6-cyl and Rover V8 engines over the years. Some late models also built with convertible body styles.]

History: Although the Marcos GT's career resembled that of the Morgan in so

Below: By the 1980s, Marcos GT styling, as on this Mantula, had been changed slightly, to accommodate wider tyres, but the basic proportions were never lost.

Above: 1980s Marcos styles (like the Mantula) featured the familiar cowled headlamp layout, and a long snout, which hid a variety of engines.

many ways – the same basic design went on, and on, modified slightly over the years, but still recognisably developed from an original theme, the two cars could not have been more different. Whereas the Morgan was intentionally traditional, the Marcos always set out to be modern, to look modern, and to provide innovation.

In 37 years, this design evolved into all manner of different sub-types, and the company only closed down when demand for its cars finally fried up.

Jem Marsh (engineer) and Frank Costin (aerodynamicist) first got together in the late 1950s to develop a prototype GT car, endowing it – MarCos – with a diminution of their two names. Early cars featured strange but effective styling, and used a chassis/body unit made from box-sections of marine plywood, and though traditionalists scoffed these proved to be remarkable efficient little cars, especially on the race track.

The first true production Marcos – the GT – came along in 1964, this being the spring from which almost all derivatives came along in later years. The original GT not only used a marine-ply chassis (this was unique in the motor industry, and distrusted by almost every one) but was fitted with a 1.8-litre engine out of the Volvo P1800, and had a complex type of De Dion rear suspension.

Almost every mechanical element would change inside five years, but the original body style – long and low, with a big snout, faired-in headlamps, and a two-door fastback cabin, all made out of glass fibre – would persist until the early 2000s. Not only did the new GT look totally distinctive, but it proved to be a very effective machine and sales – of kits to be completed by the customer – gradually built up.

Within two years the complex rear suspension had been dropped – it was replaced by a beam rear axle, properly located and suspended on coil springs – and by the late 1960s the choice of engines was beginning to mount up. Because Jem Marsh was reluctant to drop any particular option completely (in case a customer might offer him some profitable business!), the four-cylinder Volvo engine disappeared, and it wasn't long before the same structure/style was on sale with a choice of 1.5-litre or 1.6-litre Ford, 2-litre V4 or 3.0-litre V6 ▶

▶ Ford, or even a straight-six Volvo 3-litre power unit.

Along the way – not only for credibility reasons, but because it would make the car easier to meet proposed barrier-crash tests, especially in north America – the marine-ply chassis was dropped in favour of a simple but sturdy square-section tube frame instead. That frame, in later years with independent rear suspension to match the already independent front, would continue to the end.

Attempts to sell lots of big Volvo-engined cars in the USA failed, causing Marcos to stop building cars at the end of 1971, but Jem Marsh kept up a spares service, and eventually production began again in 1981s. Jem Marsh, like his rival TVR, had decided to ignore the USA thereafter.

Although early-1980s GTs were much the same as those discontinued a

decade earlier, after a time the product began to diversify, and with a great deal of extra decoration, and add on scoops, spoilers and sills, the shape became more extrovert.

First with light-alloy V8 engines, as the Mantula, Mantara and Mantaray types, then with Ford-USA four-camshaft V8s, with an open-top convertible option from the mid-1980s, the cars got gradually faster and more expensive. With 350bhp from the Ford-USA unit, their top speed was up into the 170s, and prices were reaching towards Porsche levels, but this was the end for Marcos, who could no longer sell the cars.

Below: Jem Marsh designed the GT in the early 1960s, with small four-cylinder engines in mind, but by the 1980s 350bhp V8s were being used.

Maserati Bora and Merak

Bora V8 model and Merak V6 model, built from 1971 to 1983 (data for Bora of 1972-3)

Built by: Officine Alfieri Maserati SpA, Italy.

Engine: Eight cylinders, in 90-degree V8 formation, five-bearing light-alloy block. Bore and stroke 93.9mm by 85mm, 4,719cc (3.70in × 3.34in, 290cu.in). Light alloy cylinder heads. Two overhead valves per cylinder, inclined to each other in part-spherical combustion chambers and operated by inverted-bucket tappets from twin-choke Weber carburettors. Maximum power 310bhp (DIN) at 6,000rpm. Maximum torque 340lb.ft at 4,200rpm.

Transmission: Mid-mounted engine ahead of final drive and five-speed, all synchromesh manual gearbox behind final drive. Single-dry-plate clutch, all in direct gearbox · and straight-bevel final drive, all in unit with the engine. Remote-control central gearchange. Exposed, universally jointed drive shafts to rear wheels.

Chassis: Unitary-construction fabricated steel (sheet and tubular) structure, with tubular extensions to support engine and transmission. Engine mid mounted between two-seat closed passenger cabin and transaxle. All-independent suspension by coil springs, wishbones, anti-roll bars and telescopic dampers. Rack-and-pinion steering. Four-wheel, hydraulically operated disc brakes, with vacuum-servo assistance. 15in bolt-on cast-alloy wheels. 215/70VR15 tyres.

Dimensions: Wheelbase 8ft 6.2in (260cm), track (front) 4ft 9.9in (147cm), track (rear) 4ft 9.1in (145cm). Overall length 14ft 2.4in (433cm). Unladen weight 3,090lb (1,400kg).

History: It was Citroën, which had taken a controlling interest in Maserati in 1968, who provided the inspiration, and the impetus, for the mid-engined Maseratis built in the 1970s. The Bora evolved around a 4.7-litre V8 engine which Maserati had steadily been refining since the days when it had powered

Below: Maserati's mid-engined Bora was a fine two-seater machine, powered by the mid-mounted 310bhp/4.7-litre V8 engine.

Above: Recognition points on the vee-6 Merak are the road wheels and the more sloping rear quarters. There is also a very occasional rear seat.

the lusty 4½-litre two-seat racing sports cars. Mid-engined cars were not new to them (their first rear-engined 'birdcage' racing two-seaters had been used in 1961), although they knew little about the unitary-construction techniques which went with them. The Bora, revealed at Geneva in March 1971, was at once a gamble and a technical triumph. Like other supercars to come from the Modena region (such as the soon to follow Ferrari Boxer and Lamborghini Countach), it followed a predictable trend, with mid-mounted in-line engine, five-speed gearbox and transaxle bolted to it, and a wedge-shaped two-seater body.

The performance – 160mph was a perfectly usable maximum speed – was sensational, and the roadholding and response for experienced and skilful drivers was also superb. Not that the Bora was by any means an excuse for a road-going racing car, not by any means. Air-conditioning and electric windows were standard, along with adjustable pedals and many other creature comforts. Styling was by Giugiaro (Ital Design). Citroën influence, incidentally, was obvious in the fully powered braking circuits, with the zero-travel brake pedal. ▶

▶ To supplement the Bora, Maserati next revealed the Merak, which once again owed its existence to Citroën. The kernel of the Merak was the V6 engine, a Maserati development which the Italian firm could never have afforded to put into production without a contract also to supply it to Citroën for their SM coupé. In effect the V6 engine (3 litres in the Merak but 2.7 litres in the Citroën SM) was developed from the ageing Maserati V8, but was very different in detail. The overhead-camshaft drives, for instance, were taken up the centre of the engine, between one end pair and the centre pair of cylinders. The angle between banks, at 90 degrees, was unusual for a V6, but allowed the V8's production tooling, such as it was, to be used in another application. The Merak itself looked virtually identical to the Bora, except in detail, but because the engine was substantially shorter than the V8, Maserati managed to insert a pair of almost useless 'jump seats' behind the existing front seats. Even with only a 3-litre engine installed, the Merak had a maximum speed of around 140mph, together with much improved operating economy. Maserati struck financial difficulties soon after their agreement with Citroën had been dissolved in 1973 and stopped trading for a time in 1975. With government finance, Alejandro de Tomaso made a take-over bid and restored the factory to activity during the year. Boras and Meraks were still being made at the end of the 1970s, in developed form, the Bora boasting a full 5-litre engine and the Merak more power than ever before. Some Citroën influence was still present – both cars having the Citroën brakes, the Merak having the SM's gearbox and the Bora having hydraulic adjustment to seats and pedals. The Merak incidentally, had inboard rear brakes (Citroën SM style) while the Bora's were outboard. These two cars were joined by a new front-engined Quattroporte four-door saloon.

Above and below: Both Merak (vee-6 engine) and Bora (vee-8 engine and 4.7-litres) share the same basic chassis. In each case the unit is mid-mounted, behind the seats, with all-independent suspension. The Bora (below) is a strict two-seater; the Merak has a shorter engine, set back, and room for a bit more space in the shape of an upholstered shelf. The Merak (above) has craggy wheels and sloping rear, the Bora a squared-off tail.

Maserati 4200 Spyder

Maserati 4200 Spyder, introduced in 2001
Built by: Maserati S.p.A, Italy.
Engine: Eight cylinders, in 90-degree vee formation, in five-bearing cast alloy cylinder block. Bore and stroke 92 x 80mm, 4,244cc (3.62 x 3.15in, 259cu.in) Two light-alloy cylinder heads. Four valves per cylinder, opposed in narrow vee operation by inverted bucket tappets and twin overhead camshafts per cylinder head. Bosch Motoronic fuel injection. Maximum power 385bhp at 7,000rpm Maximum torque 333lb.ft at 4,500rpm.
Transmission: Front engine, rear-wheel-drive, Twin-dry-plate clutch and six speed all-synchromesh manual gearbox. Remote control gearchange, either centre floor location, or behind-steering-wheel paddle control. Optional BTF automatic transmission.
Chassis: Unitary construction combined steel body/chassis structure, with two seater steel (with some aluminium panels) body shell in open sports car style Independent front suspension by coil springs, wishbones and anti-roll bar independent rear suspension by coil springs and anti-roll bar Hydraulic/electronic telescopic dampers, with adaptive ride control. Rack and pinion steering, with power assistance. Disc brakes at all four wheels, with vacuum servo assistance, and ABS. 18in bolt-on cast alloy road wheels, with 235/40-18in (front) and 265/35-18in (rear) tyres.
Dimensions: Wheelbase 8ft 0.6in (244m), front track 5ft 0in (152.5cm), rear track 5ft 0.6in (154cm). Overall length 14ft 1.4in (430.3cm). Unladen weight 3,793lb (1,720kg).
History: Maserati in the 1970s had been a great company, but under DeTomaso rule in the 1980s and early 1990s its reputation slumped alarmingly. It was no

Below: With the launch of the magnificent Spyder of 2001, Maserati regained its once glorious reputation. With 385bhp, this car could reach 175mph.

Above: For its chassis and running gear, the Spider of 2001 used a shortened version of the 3200GT coupe, and had a much more powerful engine.

until Fiat took over in 1993 that the turn-round began, and it was not until Ferrari (another Fiat subsidiary) took full control, in 1997, that this Italian marque returned to greatness.

Work on a new generation of Maseratis was well advanced before Ferrari management arrived, but it was their capital, and their expertise, which saw two fine new front-engined cars come to market. First, in 1998, there was a sturdily-built 2+2-seater with a turbocharged V8 engine, and three years later this was joined by a related, but very different V8-engined open-top Spyder.

Here was the new generation of cars which Maserati needed to re-launch itself. With no ancient hand-over pieces from the old models, with smart new styling by Giugiaro, and with investment now being spent, by Ferrari, on the Modena factory, there was novelty on all sides. Here was a brand new, and conventional, steel monocoque, with the all-independent coil spring/wishbone layout which seemed to be normal on all such Italian supercars – and then, of course, there was the V8 engine.

Maserati had been making brawny vee-8 engines since the 1950s, but this was a design which had been conceived in the 1990s, not only to be powerful (and to sound powerful, make no mistake) but to be able to meet all known, and projected, noise and exhaust emissions regulations. Complete with its narrow-angle layout of four valves per cylinder, it started life in the last of the Quattroporte saloons in 1995, as a 3.2-litre with twin turbochargers.

The same twin-turbo unit powered the Giugiaro-styled 3200GT, but for the Spyder which followed, it would be enlarged to 4.2-litres, and be a massively capable normally-aspirated 385bhp engine. Backed by the choice of Getrag six- ▶

▶ speed manual gearboxes - with a floor-mounted change lever, or Cambiocorsa 'paddle control' behind the steering wheel – clearly this was a power pack to guarantee a 175mph top speed. Within months, incidentally, it was no surprise to see this 4.2-litre engine was also adopted in the Coupé.

Although 4200 Spyder and 3200GT shared the same basic engineering, the same steel structural members, and identical front-end styling, the Spyder had a drastically shortened wheelbase (by 8.7in/22cm), and a truncated two-seate open-top cabin. There was no space, no provision even, for extra 'occasional seats, for the bulk and mechanism of the electrically-operated soft-top made sure of that.

The Spyder was not only colossally fast in a straight line – it was, after all the most powerful Maserati road car of all time, even in its initial specification – but it was trimmed, furnished, and intended, to be ultra-comfortable and well equipped too. A look around the cabin showed wall-to-wall leather, a full array of instruments, and such good-to-have features as ABS anti-lock braking, air

conditioning, and the availability of satellite navigation too.

Although the two cars were currently being built by the same stable, the Spyder was totally different in every way from the Ferrari F360 Modena, and both Maserati and Ferrari were happy about that. Although the Spyder was still demonstrably a sports car, it leaned more towards the Mercedes-Benz SLK way of doing things than to the Ferrari's more obvious V12-engined appeal. Although it was a remarkable performer – cruising at 130-140mph was easy enough, provided that the lawmakers did not interfere – the Spyder was much more of a gentleman's carriage than its stable mate.

That, in fact, was exactly what was intended, as the Fiat Group thought it high time that Maserati regained its place in the supercar firmament.

Below: With a style mainly by Giugiaro, the Maserati Spyder reminded everyone of the marque's great days of the 1960s and 1970s. Were the good times rolling again?

Mazda MX-5

Mazda MX-5 (known as 'Miata' in some markets) introduced in 1989 (dat‍
for original model)
Built by: Toyo Kogyo Co. Ltd., Japan.
Engine: Four cylinders, in line, in five-main-bearing cast iron cylinder block‍
Bore and stroke 78 x 84mm, 1,598cc (3.07 x 3.31in, 97.5cu.in). Light allo‍
cylinder head. Four verhead valves per cylinder, operation by twin overhea‍
camshafts: Mazda fuel injection. Maximum power 114bhp at 6,500rpm‍
Maximum torque 100lb.ft at 5,500rpm. [Later models with 1.6-litre/88bhp an‍
1.8-litre/140bhp engines, with six-speed gearboxes, and with optiona‍
automatic transmission.]
Transmission: Front engine, rear-wheel-drive, single dry plate diaphragr‍
spring clutch and five-speed all-synchromesh manual gearbox, all in unit wit‍
engine. Remote control centre floor gearchange.
Chassis: Unitary construction combined steel body/chassis structure, wit‍
steel body shell (some aluminium some composite panels), two-seater oper‍
top style. Independent front suspension by coil springs, wishbones and anti-ro‍
bar, independent rear suspension by coil springs, wishbones and anti-roll ba‍
Hydraulic telescopic dampers. Rack-and-pinion steering, with powe‍
assistance. Disc brakes at all four wheels, with vacuum servo assistance, an‍
optional ABS on later models. 14in bolt-on cast alloy road wheels, with 185/6(‍
14in tyres.
Dimensions: Wheelbase 7ft 5.2in (226.5cm), front track 4ft 7.5in (141cm), rea‍
track 4ft 8.2in (143cm). Overall length 12ft 11.5in (395cm). Unladen weigh‍
2,093lb (950kg).
History: If ever one car changed the face of sports car motoring, Mazda‍
appealing little MX-5 (or 'Miata', as it was known in the USA) was it. Not on‍
was this the first time that Mazda had produced such a sports car, but‍
seemed to take the layout of small two-seater motoring back to basics.

Before the MX-5 appeared, small sports cars had become thin on th‍
ground, and in general it was thought that such machines needed to have fron‍
wheel-drive, or should have their engines behind the seats, to drive the rea‍
wheels. Mazda's design team did not agree, and in what many pundits called‍
'Back to the Future' move, they developed a re-statement of the familiar of‍
MG Midget/Triumph Spitfire theme, though with engineering at least equal t‍
that of the 1960s-style Lotus Elan. Here, for the first time in ages, was a sma‍
neat, two-seater sports car, in which the engine lived up front, and drove th‍
rear wheels.

Mazda made no bones about their ambition for the MX-5. It was to re‍
create the character and appeal of the traditional-style, budget-price, two-seate‍
sports car. Being thorough, it is said, they purchased several well-kep‍
examples of old-style European two-seaters, stripped them right down, an‍
assessed their appeal – and how it could be improved. The secret to all th‍
work was that it was mostly carried out at Mazda's 'satellite' design an‍
product-planning department in California, USA, where some of the staff and a‍
the local influences were North American.

And they never deviated from that aim. To quote one pundit: 'There's r‍
four-wheel steering, no four-wheel-drive, no electronic damper control, no tr‍
control ....' – which was true in 1989 when the MX-5 first appeared, and wa‍
still true in the early 2000s when it carried on selling in big numbers.

Except that they chose to use the latest 16-valve twin-cam derivative of‍
well-established Mazda four-cylinder engine, the MX-5's design was essentia‍
not backward looking in any way, but as straightforward as possible. Th‍
structure was a unique sturdy steel monocoque, the style was so simple as ‍
be close to anonymous, and the layout was as totally 'retro' as possible.

There had been no attempt to base the structure on that of an existing Mazda passenger car (Ford-USA had just done this, with the Australian-built Capri, and it had not been a success), nor to break any technological barriers. Under the tiny, smooth, somehow anonymous shape, the twin-cam engine sat up front, driving the rear wheels through a five-speed gearbox, and there was conventional coil spring/wishbone suspension all round. Mazda even styled the road wheels so that they looked rather like Minilites, which were icons seen on so many 1960s and 1970s rally cars ! The only real concession to modern (for which, read 'American') tastes, was that power-assisted rack-and-pinion steering was optional.

The interior, on the other hand, was thoroughly modern, with a well-trimmed cabin, a full display of instruments, and well-contoured sports seats.

The original car looked good, was priced competitively, and soon started to sell at the rate of 50,000 a year. In the territories for which it was intended – North America's West Coast, for instance – it was a huge and lasting success. While the Mazda's delight it also sold well in Europe's traditional' 'sporting' countries like Britain, France and Italy.

Although the MX-5 was not a very fast car at first – a top speed of 114mph was competitive, but not outstanding – it was simply bursting with character, and appealed to all types of buyer. As the 1990s progressed, Mazda not only announced more powerful 1.8-litre types, but even cheekily added an 88bhp 'entry-level' model.

Even before a major facelift arrived in 1998, when headlamps were finally exposed behind glass cowls, and eventually when a six-speed transmission was made available, the MX-5 was on its way to becoming a world's best seller. By the early 2000s, there was never any doubt about that, for more people had already bought MX-5s than any other make and model of sports car.

Below: Small, neat and carefully engineered, the Mazda Miata/MX-5 eventually became the world's best-selling sports car.

Mazda RX-7

Mazda RX-7, built from 1978 to 1985 (data for original type)
Built by: Toyo Kogyo Co. Ltd., Japan.
Engine: Wankel rotary type, with two rotors, back-to-back, in light-alloy casin
Nominal capacity 2,292cc (140cu.in). No separate cylinder head, ports in ea
chamber opened and closed by rotation of rotors. One downdraught four-cho
Nippon carburettor. Maximum power 105bhp at 6,000rpm. Maximum torq
106lb.ft at 4,000rpm. [Later models had 115bhp (normally aspirated) or 165b
when fitted with a turbocharger.]
Transmission: Front engine, rear-wheel-drive, single dry plate diaphrag
spring clutch and five-speed all-synchromesh manual gearbox, all in unit w
engine. Remote control centre floor gearchange. Optional three-spe
automatic transmission.
Chassis: Unitary construction steel body/chassis construction, with steel bo
shell in 2+2 fastback coupé style. Independent front suspension by coil sprin
MacPherson struts and anti-roll bar, suspension of beam rear axle by c
springs, trailing links and Watts linkage. Hydraulic telescopic dampe
Recirculating ball steering, with optional power assistance. Front disc, re
drum brakes, with vacuum servo assistance. 13in bolt-on cast alloy whee
with 185/70-13in tyres.
Dimensions: Wheelbase 7ft 11.3in (242cm), front track 4ft 7.9in (142cm), re
track 4ft 7.1in (140cm). Overall length 14ft 0.7in (428.5cm). Unladen weig

,258lb (1,024kg).

History: More than a century after the first spindly motor cars took to the roads
n Germany, the same type of piston engine is still in use, all round the world.
t was not until the 1960s that a viable alternative – Felix Wankel's fascinating
otary engine – came on the scene.

There were far fewer moving parts in the Wankel engine, which could
heoretically rev much higher than any piston power unit had ever done.
Combustion relied on a triangular rotor spinning inside a complex toroidal
hamber, which not only opened and closed appropriate inlet and exhaust
orts, but effectively moved a combustion chamber into place where a
onventional sparking plug did the rest. Because combustion took place every
evolution, instead of every two revolutions, the agreed capacity of such
ngines was double that of the 'nominal' capacity.

This sounded seductive to companies as diverse as Rolls-Royce and
General Motors, so in the next twenty years, fortunes were made and lost all
ound the world, in the search for reliable Wankel power. Having started in the
970s, Mazda of Japan was the most persistent of all, and in the early 2000s it ▶

**Below: Although the RX-7 used a compact rotary engine, this was never
obvious from the badging. The small engine, though, allowed a low
ose to be styled**

▶ was the only car-maker still using these rotary power units.

In 1978, therefore, Mazda pulled off a double first – not only by launchin dedicated series-production sports coupé, the RX7, but by using a twin-ro Wankel power unit. In this Porsche 924-sized package the RX7, therefore, a mixture of innovation and tradition, for it combined a smart front engine/r drive layout with the use of the rotary engine, all covered in a neat, curvaceous two-seater hatchback coupé style.

It was the engine, its smooth, high-revving qualities and (in due course, Mazda found to their cost) its struggle to deliver true reliable long life wh made all the headlines. Yet behind all the 'Wankel' headlines was a car wh not only looked good, but handled well, and which behaved in every way lik 1970s sports car.

Although Mazda eventually defeated its Wankel problems (rotor tip w was the most important), it could never produce these engines at the same cost as a piston engine, which meant that the RX7 always cost more than obvious rivals, from Porsche (924) and from Nissan.

Even so, this type of engine was clearly capable of more, which Ma proved by lifting the power from 105bhp to 115bhp in 1981, and e offered 165bhp in turbocharged form (with the second-generation mod

bove: The RX-7 was a very smart closed two-seater and, like the MGB GT, had a large, lift-up rear window - sports car motoring with practicality.

hich took over in 1985, an enlarged power unit produced 255bhp with
rbocharging).

Without this engine, the RX7 might merely have been see as another
nventional coupé, but it was its own best publicity campaign, and its most
ffective talking point. The RX7's chassis, after all, was simple enough, for
ere was rear wheel drive of a beam axle which was located only by coil
rings and locating links, and at its initial 105bhp rating its top speed was no
ore than 113mph. Think modernised MGB, therefore, but with a sensational
wer unit tucked away under that needle-sharp nose.

The initial RX7 was a promising car which eventually came good, which
ld in tens of thousands (especially in North America, where all such novelties
ere being welcomed at the time), and was clearly profitable, for Mazda did not
esitate to replace it in 1985 with a second-generation model.

RX7s have sold well ever since, for a third-generation model appeared in
e 1990s, and in the early 2000s a fourth type of this two-seater was already
n sale.

McLaren F1

McLaren F1 sports coupé, built 1993 to 1997
Built by: McLaren Cars Ltd., Britain.
Engine: Twelve cylinders, in 60-degree vee-formation, in seven-bearing lig
alloy cylinder block. Bore and stroke 86 × 87mm, 6,064cc (3.38 × 3.42
370cu.in). Two light-alloy cylinder heads. Four valves per cylinder, operation
twin overhead camshafts. Bosch/BMW fuel injection. Maximum power 627b
(DIN) at 7,400rpm. Maximum torque 479lb.ft at 4,000rpm.
Transmission: Rear-wheel-drive, triple-plate carbon clutch and six-speed
synchromesh manual gearbox, all in unit with mid-mounted engine. Remo
control, central gearchange.
Chassis: Unitary-construction carbon fibre advanced composite monocoq
structure and combined bodyshell with three-seater accommodation. Front a
rear suspension mounted on subframes. Independent front suspension by c
springs, wishbones, telescopic dampers and anti-roll bar. Independent re
suspension by coil springs, wishbones, telescopic dampers and anti-roll b
Rack-and-pinion steering. Four-wheel disc brakes with vacuum ser
assistance, but no ABS. 17in cast-alloy wheels, 235/45-17in (front) and 315/4
17in (rear) tyres.
Dimensions: Wheelbase 8ft 11in (271.8cm), front track 5ft 1.7in (157cm), re
track 4ft 10in (147cm). Overall length 14ft 0.8in (429cm). Unladen weig
2,509lb (1,138kg).
History: Vaunting ambition is often thwarted, as it was with McLaren and th
incredibly fast F1 road car. Conceived in 1990 when it was thought that th
could easily sell cars priced at £540,000, it did not go on sale until 1993. By t
time the world's economy had turned down, potential customers fled for cov
and sales were extremely sluggish. In the end the project had to be wou
down in 1997, after only 100 machines (a proportion of them GTR competiti
cars, and LM types) had been built.

Technically, however, the F1 was superb. Because of the way that wo
attitudes to motoring changed so much in the last years of the 20th Centu
(when enjoying high performance became politically incorrect), its top speed
231mph will probably never be bettered by a rival.

Gordon Murray, poached from the Brabham F1 team to head McLare
design team, was allowed to indulge himself with the F1 road car. There we
effectively, no limits to what he might specify, for this car had to be the best, 1
fastest and the most desirable: it was always understood that it could also be t
most exclusive, and the most expensive. Like the Jaguar XJ220, which it followe
and surpassed, it was to have amazingly high performance, but lack several pa
expected amenities. There was, for instance, no provision for four-wheel-dri
none for traction control, and none for ABS anti-lock brakes. Nor was there a
power assistance for the rack-and-pinion steering, or even a spare wheel.

Murray was, above all, a deep thinker, so the layout of the Supercar wh
he conceived was unique. Although, like many other such machines, it had
mid-mounted engine driving the rear wheels, it had a wide cabin with not tv
but three, seats, the driver occupying the central seat, which was set ahead
the others. Although the F1 was neither light enough or small enough to
considered as a single-seater with a roof, the (wealthy) driver might fantas
that he was in just such a car.

Structurally, the F1 was built up around a full F1-race-style carbon fi
monocoque, and was powered by a brand-new engine. McLaren went to BN
of Germany, explained its need for a normally aspirated engine with more th
550bhp, and placed a contract. BMW therefore designed a brand-new V
(which, in detail, had much in common with their latest M3 straight-six), a
within 18 months had it thrumming away on their test beds in Munich. It v

Above: The McLaren F1 road car, immensely fast and very expensive, was the world's fastest car in the 1990s.

altogether typical of BMW that it not only surpassed every contract requirement, but produced a stunningly civilised, refined and reliable engine too. Having settled on a capacity of 6,064cc, it then delivered no less than 627bhp at 7,400rpm – this from a normally aspirated layout which had to pass every one of the world's exhaust emission tests.

The rest of the car lived up to these standards. With carbon fibre body panels, doors which (when opened) swung upwards and forwards, Lamborghini Diablo-fashion, and without the need for a single aerodynamic spoiler to keep it stable at 200mph-plus speeds (except a discreet, flush-mounted, spoiler on the tail which popped up when the brakes were applied from high speed), the style was stunning. But this had always been expected, for the F1 had been shaped by Peter Stevens, whose reputation (for designing cars like the front-wheel-drive Lotus Elan) had already been made.

The sheer, mind-boggling, record-breaking performance of this car caused every jaw to drop, especially as it was linked to impeccable stability, roadholding and general behaviour. Only a handful of the owners were ever likely to see the speedometer indicate more than 200mph (with a lot more to come, please note . . .), but most of them would revel in the acceleration.

Tyre wear, for sure, from those massive 315/45-17in 'rollers' at the rear might be expensive, but rich men would not mind, preferring to bury the throttle from a standing start, see 60mph come up in 3.2 seconds, 100mph in a mere 6.3 seconds, and 150mph in 12.8 seconds. The quarter-mile post would be passed in 11.1 seconds.

▶

▶ All such figures completely annihilated the opposition from any other car in the '200-Club', and not even recognised iconic Supercars like the Ferrari F40 and the Jaguar XJ220 could match them. And there was more. Every one of the world's open road speed limits could be passed in the second (of six gears), where 95mph was possible; fourth gear was good for 150mph; and, before changing up out of fifth gear, the F1 could be passing most Ferraris (which would be flat out) at 180mph.

Put another way, if an owner was content to trundle through towns and cities with a 30mph speed limit, he would be obliged to change down to fifth or even fourth gear so that the magnificent BMW V12 was not turning over too slowly. At sensible speeds, all this, mind you, was delivered in near silence – to witness an unmodified F1 at speed on a test track was almost to watch a silent movie – and, if it mattered to the sort of driver this car would attract, the fuel consumption was a totally acceptable 15mpg.

Part of the F1's attraction, however, was not in its style, or its performance, but in its detailing. Gordon Murray and Peter Stevens, having been given their head, did not skimp on a single detail. To keep the flanks smooth (or, at least, to ensure that the style was not compromised), the

engine air intake was in the roof, immediately behind the top of the screen, with a long, carbon fibre, channel leading back from there and dividing the rear window glass.

The six-speed gearbox, especially designed for McLaren by Traction Products of America, had a magnesium casing, while the final drive was packaged alongside the clutch. Like the XJ220, the carbon body shell included under-floor venturi sections to add downforce at high road speeds. The engine silencer had a volume of no less than 65 litres. Discs, by Brembo, were Formula 1 type, massive, light and incredibly effective.

The GTR, developed as a racing car for Le Mans, was even more extreme, and the incredibly rare Lm type, with all the GTR chassis, but in road-legal form, was a £799,000 indulgence. The F1 was that sort of car, unsurpassed, and unsurpassable. At the end of the day, it must have been a big loss-making project, but for McLaren the prestige bonus was immeasurable. We may never see another car like it.

Below: The F1's 6.1-litre V12 BMW engine was behind the cabin, which had three seats, with the driver sitting in the centre.

Mercédès 60 Model

60 models, built from 1903 to 1904 (data for 1903 model)

Built by: Daimler Motoren Gesellschaft, Germany.

Engine: Four cylinders, in line, in two cast-iron blocks, with three-bearing light-alloy crankcase. Bore and stroke 140mm by 151mm, 9,293cc (5.52in × 5.94in, 567cu.in). Non-detachable cylinder heads. Two valves per cylinder: over-head inlet valves, with special Mercédès annular construction, operated by pushrods and rockers, and side exhaust valves; both valves operated from single camshaft in side of crankcase. Single up-draught Mercédès-Simplex carburettor. Maximum power about 65bhp at 1,100rpm.

Transmission: Scroll clutch in unit with front-mounted engine and separate four-speed manual gearbox (without synchromesh) and straight-bevel differential in rear of gear case. Final drive by countershaft from transmission to sprockets. Drive to rear wheels by chains.

Chassis: Separate pressed-steel chassis frame, with channel-section side members and tubular cross bracing. Forged front axle beam. Front and rear suspension by semi-elliptic leaf springs. No dampers. Worm-and-nut steering. Externally contracting drum brake, foot-pedal and mechanically operated, on gearbox counter shaft. Hand lever operating drums on rear wheel hubs. Wooden artillery style wheels. 910 × 90mm tyres (front) and 920 × 120mm tyres (rear). Open two-seat or four-seat bodywork.

Dimensions: Wheelbase 9ft 0.2in (275cm), tracks (front and rear) 4ft 7.5in (141cm). Overall length 12ft 3.5in (375cm). Unladen weight 2,204lb (1,000kg).

History: Emil Jellinek was a wealthy admirer of the German Daimlers and ordered a series of cars to his own requirements at the end of the 19th century. For 1901, he persuaded Daimler's Wilhelm Maybach to design him a completely new type of car, one which is now recognised as the forerunner of modern designs. The chassis, much lower than before, was of pressed steel and the layout and detail represented a complete change from 19th century practice. These Mercédès-Simplex cars were progressively developed in racing after

1901, until Mercédès 60 cars were announced for 1903. The name Mercédès, incidentally, is that of Jellinek's own daughter.

For the infamous 1903 Paris-Madrid race a 90bhp car was produced, but it was beaten by the 60s and a fire at Cannstatt destroyed all five special racing cars. For the Gordon Bennett races in Ireland the factory appealed for owners to return their cars on loan. The American Clarence Gray Dinsmore lent his car, and Camille Jenatzy duly won the race in it, achieving 49.2mph in average speed, and notching up a 66mph maximum speed.

The transmission, with countershaft and chain drive to the rear wheels, was typical of the period, as was the braking system, with foot brake operating on the transmission drum. The engine, with its cast-alloy crankcase and paired cast-iron cylinders, had an integral cylinder head and overhead inlet valves which, admitted mixture through annular slots. The basic design of these cars was so good that the 12.7-litre 90 and the 14-litre models used virtually the same chassis and details, and all used the same robust family of four-cylinder engines. The success of the predecessors of the famous 60 cars caused the name Mercédès to be applied to all private cars built at Cannstatt from 1902. Jellinek himself had been on the board of the company since 1900. By 1908, however, when Mercédès won the Grand Prix, their cars had become even more advanced and with repeat wins in 1914 (with overhead-camshaft engines) they were established as leading makers of really fast cars.

Left and above: Sheer exciting modern engineering in the Mercédès 60. It is hard to believe that this splendid car was built as early as 1903. Most truly modern cars seem to have evolved from this brilliant design. A Mercédès 60 won the Gordon Bennett race in 1903.

Mercedes-Benz 38/250

36/220 and 38/250 models, built from 1927 to 1933 (data for 1929/30 SS model)
Built by: Daimler-Benz A.G., Germany.
Engine: Six cylinders, in line, in four-bearing light-alloy combined block/crankcase. Bore and stroke 100mm by 150mm, 7,069cc (3.94in × 5.91in, 431.4cu.in). Detachable cast-iron cylinder head. Two overhead valves per cylinder, vertically mounted, but staggered, and operated by fingers from single overhead camshaft. Two up-draught single-choke Mercédés-Benz carburettors, with or without assistance from Roots-type supercharger driven from nose of crankshaft. Maximum power (supercharged) 200bhp at 3,000rpm (140bhp if not supercharged).
Transmission: Multi-dry-plate clutch and four-speed manual gearbox (without synchromesh), both in unit with front-mounted engine. Direct-acting central gearchange. Propeller shaft enclosed in torque tube, driving spiral-bevel 'live' rear axle.
Chassis: Separate pressed-steel chassis frame, with channel-section side members and pressed and tubular cross bracing. Forged front axle beam. Front suspension by semi-elliptic leaf springs. Rear suspension by semi-elliptic leaf springs and torque tube. Lever-arm hydraulic dampers or friction-type dampers (depending on customer). Four-wheel, shaft and rod-operated drum brakes (some cars with vacuum-servo assistance). Centre-lock wire wheels. 6.50 × 20 tyres. Two-seat or four-seat open coachwork.
Dimensions: Wheelbase 11ft 4in (345.4cm), tracks (front and rear) 4ft 10in (147.3cm). Overall length 15ft 5in (470cm). Unladen weight 2,800lb (1,270kg).
History: Following the completion of the merger between Mercédès and Benz, in 1926 (the accents on the name were dropped thereafter), the new combine continued to develop a fabulously fast, brutally impressive, starkly attractive and very successful series of supercharged sports cars. These cars are, in the beginning, to the credit of Dr. Ferdinand Porsche, who worked for the company after leaving Austro-Daimler earlier in the 1920s and before leaving to set up his own engineering consultancy business. The origins of a remarkable series of cars lie in the Mercédès (pre-merger, that is) 24/100/14PS of 1924. This car was designed around a vast new six-cylinder unit and the three figures, respectively, referred to the tax horsepower, the unsupercharged peak power output and the supercharged peak power. The blower itself was mounted at the nose of the engine, in an upright position, and could be clutched in or out of engagement (by friction clutches at the front end of the crankshaft) by the driver. Mercedes were at pains to point out to owners that the supercharger should be used only when needed, as it vastly increased the stresses on the engine and on the transmission. The engagement linkage was connected to the throttle pedal. Newer and faster models followed with great industry. First came the 36/220S, with its engine enlarged to 6/8-litres and that 220 referring to supercharged peak horsepower; this then paved the way for the 7-litre 38/250. This last car, in more and yet more developed form, was the basis of all the Mercedes sports racing two-seaters of the late 1920s and early 1930s, which culminated in the very rare SSKL cars with their 300bhp and a top speed of more than 145mph in

Below: The 38/250 (or SSK) was typical of late-1920s Mercedes-Benz design, complete with an outside exhaust system.

Above: Dr. Ferdinand Porsche's masterpiece of design for Mercedes was the six-cylinder supercharged car, built up to 1933.

streamlined form. After the Mercédès and Benz merger, the 'basic' 140bhp supercharged car was given a shorter chassis and became the K (K = Kurz). This car was fast, but was not yet nimble enough, so it was reengineered for an S version to be built alongside it. The S had a new chassis frame dropped considerably by comparison with the K, and with the engine moved back by about 12in along with a lowered radiator. This car, in German numbering, was the 26/120/180PS, which indicated how the power was being increased. The 1928 cars which, among other things, won the German Grand Prix, were SSs (27/140/200PS), and had 7.1 litres compared with 6.8 litres for the original S. The cars were now becoming very specialised and a series of SSK cars (K = Kruz again, for shortened chassis) were raced with great success. These, in German terms, were 27/170/225PS cars. There was now only one more development to come – the SSKL – which was incredibly expensive to build, very specialised, much lightened, even more highly tuned, and intended for factory use only. The SSKLs were 27/170/300PS cars – which gives an idea of the engine boost they were asked to withstand from the latest enlarged elephant blowers. No doubt Mercedes-Benz could have improved the cars still further, but by then they were committed to a large-scale single-seater racing programme, with cars being built for the new 750kg Grand Prix formula, and the sports car programme was dropped. Perhaps even more than the much-vaunted Bentleys and Hispano-Suizas, and certainly more so than the bigger Bugattis, the Mercedes supercharged sports cars said everything about the magnificence of the vintage era. The cars were, frankly, expensive, fast and exhilarating toys for their rich buyers; with usually more than 200bhp on tap and often only a token four-seater body shell without much weather protection provided, they were hardly practical every-day machines. Their 'optional' supercharging was a unique way of providing, at one and the same time, a potential race-winning car which could also be cruised around when the pressure was off and which could also be used on the road in its less forceful state. Even if the supercharger could not be used with impunity, the howl emitted when it was in use must have made quite an impact on its opposition. Strangely enough, a weak point with these cars was the brakes, which is hardly surprising when one considers that they were, relatively speaking, faster in their day than a Ferrari or Lamborghini road car is today *and* cable-operated drum brakes were all that could be provided. Such performance, too, was achieved without any pretence to streamlining. Cycle type wings, which did not turn with the front wheels, were the order of the day, and between them was the bluff and legendary vee-shape of the Mercedes radiator, with the equally famous three-pointed star fixed to its apex. Yet this immense performance, much feared by any rival met on road or track, was mostly to the credit of Dr. Porsche's splendid engine, the rest of the chassis engineering, although carried out with great care and in high-quality materials, was entirely conventional, and was on a par with cars like the W.O. Bentleys and the Hispanos.

Mercedes-Benz 300SL

300SL models, built from 1954 to 1963 (data for 1954 model)
Built by: Daimler-Benz AG. West Germany.
Engine: Six cylinders, in line, in seven-bearing cast-iron block, installed in car at angle of 45 degrees. Bore and stroke 85mm by 88mm, 2,996cc (3.35in × 3.46in, 182.8cu.in.) Detachable light-alloy cylinder head with joint not perpendicular to cylinder bores. Combustion chamber formed in top of piston and top of cylinder block. Two overhead valves per cylinder, staggered (with inlet valves in one line and exhaust valves in other line) and operated by rockers from single overhead camshaft. Dry-sump lubrication. Bosch direct fuel injection. Maximum power 215bhp (net) at 5,800rpm. Maximum torque 228lb.ft at 5,000rpm.
Transmission: Single-dry-plate clutch and four-speed, all-synchromesh manual gearbox, both in unit with engine. Direct-acting central gearchange. Open propeller shaft to chassis-mounted hypoid bevel final drive.
Chassis: Separate multi-tubular spaceframe, with many small-diameter steel tubes linking points of stress. Lightweight aluminium two-seater body shell – coupé with gull-wing doors or open 'roadster' with conventional doors. Independent front suspension by coil springs, wishbones and anti-roll bar. Independent rear suspension by coil springs and swing axles. Telescopic dampers. Steering wheel hinged for access to driving seat and steering by recirculating-ball unit. Four wheel, hydraulically operated drum brakes, vacuum-servo assistance. 15in pressed-steel road wheels. 6.70 × 15in tyres.
Dimensions: Wheelbase 7ft 10.5in (240cm), track (front) 4ft 9in (145cm). Overall length 15ft (457cm). Unladen weight 3,000lb (1,364kg).
History: Mercedes-Benz began to introduce a new series of passenger cars in 1950 and 1951, among which was a big and impressive six-cylinder 3-litre car, but they made a sensation when re-entering motor sport in 1952 with the futuristic 300SL sports-racing car. The fact that this car won its very first Le Mans race was startling enough, but that Mercedes were proposing to put it into some sort of quantity production was even more astonishing. Apart from the

Above: Hidden under the skin of this 300SL was a complex lattice of slim steel tubes – the world's first automotive space-frame chassis.

Below: From 1954 to 1957 the 300SL was sold as a coupé, with lift-up 'gullwing' doors. By any standards, at this time it was the fastest road car in the world.

▶ obvious facts that it was at the same time very fast and very attractive, it was also exceedingly complex, mechanically, and was not really designed for quantity production. The heart of the car's performance lay in its engine, which had direct fuel injection on production cars (although the Le Mans winner had used an engine with conventional carburettors), but the main interest was in the structure. Mercedes had gone all the way towards a theoretically perfect multi-tube 'spaceframe' structure, where all tubes were slim and absolutely straight and none had to withstand bending or torsional stresses of any nature. Taken to extremes, this would deny access to the car altogether, so there were inevitable compromises in the region of the passenger compartment. To ease this problem as much as possible, the frame was very deep along the sills and the doors were arranged to hinge along their top edge and open upwards in 'gull-wing' fashion. The car's only failing, more noticeable at very high speeds than at touring speeds, was that Mercedes were then wedded to swing-axle independent rear suspension. This allowed large (driven) rear wheel camber changes and produced serious and possibly dangerous oversteer at times. To handle a 300SL at really high speeds required good 'racing-driver' reflexes. Far more of the 300SLs were ordered than Mercedes had bargained for and in 1957 they introduced the open-topped 300SL Roadster, which was a little easier to make and handled better by virtue of its low-pivot swing-axle rear suspension. This model continued to be made at Stuttgart until the early 1960s and a total of 3,250 of both types were eventually sold.

There was no doubt that a suitably-geared 300SL, particularly in the more-streamlined coupé condition, had a very high maximum speed. The original publicity claims were that the car could accelerate from 15mph to no less than 165mph in top gear (which said a lot for the flexibility of the fuel-injected engine).

but the higher figure was not attainable by a normally equipped road car. In British tune the cars could certainly beat 130mph, which made them supreme; however, with very high gearing it was possible for something like 150mph to be passed. The 300SL was forecast to start a new trend in sports car design, but even Mercedes themselves did not really want to have to build a spaceframe chassis in quantity and they were not copied by any other serious production-car concern. The multi-tube layout was very expensive and very difficult to build properly, as Mercedes soon found out. Neither did the gull-wing doors find favour elsewhere and when the Roadster 300SL was announced it was seen to have a modified frame with conventionally hinged doors.

The 300SL's descendants, truly, were the W196 Grand Prix car, which had many family resemblances, and the 300SLR sports-racing-car (which in unique closed-coupé guise looked astonishingly similar to the 300SL). A car does not have to be a commercial success to be an all-time 'classic'. In looks, in performance and in the sheer exuberance of its complex engineering, the 300SL stood quite apart from any really fast supercar of the 1950s. Not even Ferrari, with exotic V12 engines in more mundane chassis, could match their ambience. The 300SL's engine, in less highly tuned form, was a mainstay of the Mercedes production car range until the end of the 1960s, when it was at last replaced by a new 3½-litre/4½-litre V8 unit. The direct-injection system in the 300SL was unique for many years.

Below: Striking comparison between the world-famous gull-wing Mercedes 300SL (on the right), and the mid-engined four-rotor Wankel engined Mercedes C111 Coupé. Both are from the same stable, but the progress made in less than 20 years is obvious. The 300SL engine is front-mounted, on its side; the Wankel is mid-mounted.

Mercedes-Benz 500K/540K

Mercedes-Benz 380K, 500K and 540K family, built from 1933 to 1939 (data for 540K)

Built by: Daimler-Benz AG, Germany.

Engine: Eight cylinders, in line, in nine-main-bearing cast iron cylinder block. Bore and stroke 88 x 111mm, 5,401cc (3.46 x 4.37in, 329.6cu.in). Cast iron cylinder head. Two overhead valves per cylinder, operation by pushrods and rockers from a camshaft in the cylinder block. Single up-draught Mercedes-Benz carburettor, with optionally-engaged Roots supercharger. Maximum power 180bhp (supercharged) or 115bhp (normally aspirated) at 3,600rpm. Maximum torque not quoted. [380Ks had 3.8-litre engines, and 500Ks had 5.0-litre engines, both small versions of the 540K.]

Transmission: Front engine, rear-wheel-drive, single dry plate clutch and four-speed synchromesh manual gearbox, with no synchromesh on first gear, all in unit with engine. Direct-acting centre floor gearchange.

Chassis: Separate steel chassis frame, with box-section main side members, and box-section cross-bracings. Independent front suspension by coil springs and wishbones, independent rear suspension by double coil springs and swing axles. Lever-arm hydraulic dampers. Worm-type steering. Drum brakes at all four wheels, hydraulically operated, with vacuum servo assistance. 17in bolt-on wire spoke wheels, with 7.00-17in tyres. Choice of aluminium/steel bodywork, on a wooden skeleton, in open two-seater, cabriolet or sports saloon forms.

Dimensions: (Typical) Wheelbase 10ft 9.5in (329cm), front track 4ft 11.5in (151cm), rear track 4ft 11in (150cm). Overall length 17ft 2.5in (525cm). Unladen weight 5,000lb (2,268kg).

History: Starting with the Type 380K of 1933, and culminating in the still-born 580K of 1939, this was a design which typified everything that was grand, assertive, pompous and spectacular about Germany under the influence of

Adolf Hitler. Although there was no direct relationship, this family was certainly the spiritual descendant of the S/SS/SSK models of the 1920s, though with much more flamboyance, and more sumptuous style and equipment than those cars.

The 380K of 1933 may only have produced 90bhp from its 3.8-litre eight-cylinder engine (or 120bhp when the supercharger was clutched into action), but it set all the markers for the rest of the decade. It didn't matter that the 'blower' was for limited use only, or that it only kicked in when the throttle pedal was buried to the floor – it made a magnificent noise and certainly had an effect!

The chassis specification not only featured coil spring independent front suspension, but an independent rear end by coil springs and swing axles too. Even so, it was not the chassis, but the choice of bodywork, which immediately made these cars so outstanding. A whole variety of styles, most built by Mercedes-Benz at Sindelfingen, some closed, some with drop-head coupé styles, some with four-seats, and some with only two-seats, all shared the same type of character.

The proudly displaced, almost arrogant, radiator grille was always flanked by long, sweeping, front wings, which were matched by shapely tails, and the soft-top cars often featured hoods with exposed, chrome-plated, frames behind the side glass. Spare wheels were usually mounted alongside the engine bay, recessed into a front wing pressing. There seemed to be no attempt to keep down the weight, for most shells featured big and heavy doors, with drop-glass in the doors, and with sumptuous trim. With an unladen weight of at least 5,000lb/2,268kg, these cars carried as much metal as a Rolls-Royce.

In its early days, therefore, this original K-series model (K for *kurz* or 'short') was by no means outstanding, as it could certainly be outpaced by cars like the ▶

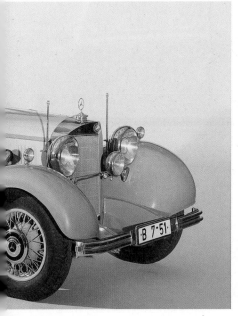

Left: 500Ks and 540Ks usually had the same style features – including a long bonnet, exposed exhaust pipes, and a spare wheel mounted alongside the engine.

▶ Bentley 3 1/2-litre, and Lagonda's latest 4 1/2-litre models. Accordingly, in 1934, the 380K gave way to the longer-wheelbase 500K, in which the engine had been enlarged to 5.0-litres, and no less than 160bhp with the supercharger engaged. This was more like it, for up to 100mph was now available, which made the 500K one of Europe's fastest (if not the most manageable) two-seaters.

Two years later, though, Mercedes-Benz went better, with the launch of the 540K, in which the engine had been enlarged yet again, this time to 5.4-litres. Now, with 180bhp when the supercharger was being used, here was a magnificently arrogant machine which could sometimes reach and exceed 105mph. By 1930s standards this was quite outstanding, Germany's new autobahns might have been designed to show off this pace – and who cared that such cars could rarely beat 10mpg (Imperial)?

The sort of people who bought such cars (they were produced in tiny numbers), were either very wealthy, or had other people to pay their bills.

Production figures of 114 (380K), 354 (500K) and 447 (540K) tell their own story, as does the fact they they were invariably among the most costly of any car listings, in any territory.

As far as Mercedes-Benz was concerned, these cars (and the simply gargantuan 'Grosser 770' saloon/limo/landaulette types which were being built at the same time) were not only effective publicity flagships, but were also the place for technological innovation to be tried out.

If war had not come in 1939 and brought an end to K-series production, there would have been one further expansion of this type – the 5.8-litre 580K, which also had a five-speed gearbox – but in the end only a dozen such cars were ever built.

Below: 540Ks were not only vast, heavy, and very powerful, but even with this bodywork they could exceed 100mph – sensational for the 1930s.

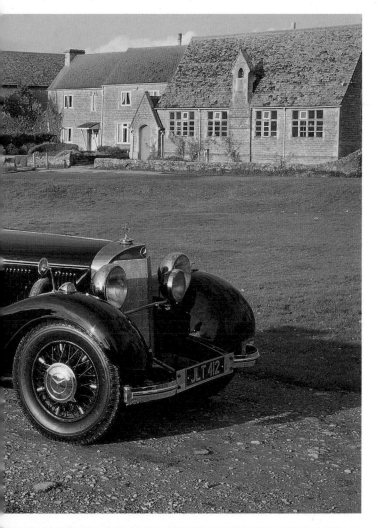

Mercedes-Benz
230SL/250SL/280SL

**Mercedes-Benz 230SL, 250SL and 280SL family, built from 1963 to 197[
(data for 230SL)**

Built by: Mercedes-Benz AG, Germany.

Engine: Six cylinders, in line, in four-main-bearing cast-iron cylinder block. Bor
and stroke 82 x 72.8mm, 2,306cc (3.23 x 2.87in, 140.7cu.in). Light-alloy cylinde
head. Two valves per cylinder, operation by fingers from single overhea
camshaft in cylinder head. Bosch fuel injection. Maximum power 170bhp a
5,600rpm. Maximum torque 159lb.ft at 4,500rpm.

Transmission: Front engine, rear-wheel-drive, single dry plate diaphragm sprin
clutch and four-speed all-synchromesh manual gearbox, remote control centr
floor gearchange. Optional Mercedes-Benz four-speed automatic transmissior

Chassis: Unitary construction steel combined body/chassis structure, wit
steel body shell in 2+2 seater open top style, or with removable steel hardtor
Independent front suspension by coil springs, wishbones and anti-roll ba
independent rear suspension by coil springs, low-pivot swing axles centr
compensating spring and radius arms. Hydraulic telescopic dampers
Recirculating ball steering, with optional power assistance. Front disc, rea
drum brakes, with vacuum servo assistance. 14in bolt-on steel disc wheels
with 185-14in tyres.

Dimensions: Wheelbase 7ft 10in (249cm), front track 4ft 10.5in (151cm), rea
track 4ft 10.5in (151cm). Overall length 14ft 1.5in (430cm). Unladen weigh
2,700lb (1,224kg).

History: By the 1960s, Mercedes-Benz had expanded so much that it neede
to rationalise the way it made all its cars. Turning its attention to its sportin

**Below: The 230SL family of sports cars was available as an open
roadster (this car) or with a removable steel hardtop.**

Above: The 'pagoda roof' 230SL was built for eight years, and was available with three different six-cylinder engines.

models, it concluded that the 180-based 190SL was beginning to look old-fashioned, while the 300SL, as ever, was still far too complex and specialised to sell in any numbers. From 1963, therefore, the company retired both old models and effectively replaced them both with a single new design, the 230SL.

If for no other reason, the hardtop version of the 230SL will always be remembered for its unique 'pagoda roof' style. This, Mercedes-Benz point out with truth, was not adopted to lower the roof line, but to make the side vision and the glass area larger than would otherwise have been possible. One must note, in any case, that this car was also sold with a folding-roof open-top style – though the majority seem to have had the 'pagoda roof' fitted.

Like the 190SL before it, the 230SL was closely based on touring-car engineering. In this case, much of the chassis was derived from the well- ▶

► known, successful, and popular 220SE saloon, along with the enlarged engine and the choice of manual or automatic transmissions. Unlike the earlier mode though, the new car had the later type of low-pivot swing-axle rear suspension which made cornering behaviour 'on the limit' more predictable. The new ca too, was much sleeker, more stylish, better equipped and considerably faste than before. By comparison with the 300SL it might have been rather slowe but was mechanically more simple and considerably easier to service an maintain.

The 230SL was an immediate success, and in the gruelling Liege-Sofia Liege rally later in the year a factory entered example was driven to a conclusiv victory by Eugen Bohringer. This served to prove both performance an strength. The styling, meantime, rapidly gained acceptance, and the car bega to sell all over the world.

In that the 230SL was much more of a mature man's sports car than it predecessor, the 190SL, it is not surprising that it had softer and more 'touring habits than the ultra-specialised 300SL had enjoyed, though no-one eve complained about the 120mph performance. Many examples were built wit the optional automatic transmission. This, incidentally, was Mercedes-Benz own design, which combined a simple fluid-flywheel coupling with a four-spee epicyclic gearbox.

During the early life of this car, however, the 230SL rapidly began to b

verhauled in performance by some of its competitors, particularly those sold most strongly in the United States. Fortunately, larger capacity and more powerful versions of the six-cylinder overhead-camshaft engine were already becoming available for Mercedes-Benz's own saloon models, so there was never any big problem in adapting them for use in the 2+2-seater 230SL's chassis.

Even so, it was very puzzling that the factory should adopt what is now generally recognised as an 'interim' engine of 2,496cc (this, therefore, became the 250SL model) for only one year, and then follow it by fitting the definitive 2,778cc engine (and thus making the 280SL), a combination which would then carry on successfully for three more seasons.

If the 280SL had a fault, it was that it was perhaps a touch less 'sporting', and a touch more 'touring' than the original 230SL, for its soft, ultra-civilised and (admittedly) well-developed character backed this up. As the 1970s opened, however, and with all the opposition seemingly committed to building even faster cars, it was no surprise that the 280SL had to give way to another new Mercedes-Benz family, the V8-engined 350SL types. Between 1963 and 1971, no fewer than 48,912 of these cars were produced.

Below: The 280SL was the third and final derivative of this family, complete with a 2.8-litre engine, and four-wheel disc brakes.

Mercedes-Benz
350SL to 560SL family

**Mercedes-Benz 350SL to 560SL family, built from 1971 to 1989 (data f
original 350SL)**
Built by: Daimler-Benz AG, Germany.
Engine: Eight cylinders, in 90-degree vee-8 formation, in cast iron cylind
block. Bore and stroke 92 x 65.8mm, 3,499cc (3.62 x 2.59in, 213.6cu.in). Tv
aluminium cylinder heads. Two valves per cylinder, operation by rockers an
single overhead camshafts per head. Bosch Jetronic fuel injection. Maximu
power 200bhp at 5,800rpm. Maximum torque 211lb.ft at 4,000rpm.
Transmission: Front engine, rear-wheel-drive, with single dry plate diaphrag
spring clutch and four-speed all-synchromesh manual gearbox, all in unit wi
engine. Remote control centre floor gearchange. Optional four-speed (lat
three-speed) Mercedes-Benz automatic transmission.
Chassis: Unitary construction combined steel body/chassis structure, wi
steel body shell in two-seat open top style and optional removable hardto
Independent front suspension by coil springs, wishbones and anti-roll b
independent rear suspension by coil springs, semi-trailing arms, and anti-roll b
Auxiliary rubber springs. Hydraulic telescopic dampers. Recirculating b

steering with power-assistance. Disc brakes at all four wheels, with vacuum servo assistance. 14in bolt-on steel disc wheels, with 205/70-14in tyres.

Dimensions: Wheelbase 8ft 0.9in (246cm), front track 4ft 9.2in (145.3cm), rear track 4ft 8.7in (144cm). Overall length 14ft 4.4in (437.9cm). Unladen weight 3,487lb (1,581kg). [Range also built with 3.8, 4.2, 4.5, 5.0 and 5.6-litre V8 engines, up to 245bhp, with 2.8 and 3.0-litre six-cylinder engines up to 190bhp, and as SLC Types with 14.1in (35.8cm) longer wheelbase, 2+2 seating and permanent coupé roof.]

History: The successor to the 230/250/280SL of civilised sports cars was a bigger car of rather different character. Although it was easy to decry the boulevard manners of such a machine, Mercedes-Benz could also point at the huge sales achieved by this range in 18 profitable years. Originally as a 3.5-litre-engined 350SL, this range eventually grew so far that the definitive model, sold in the late 1980s, was the 5.6-litre V8 560SL. ▶

Below: The original car in this family had a 3.5-litre V8 engine, but final mid-1980s models were produced with a massive 5.6-litre unit.

The first appeared in 1971, but most of the original range was launched within two years. Like the superseded 280SLs, these cars shared their chassis and power-train engineering with a touring car, in this case the new S-Class saloons and coupés, though with a special floorpan, and special styling and body superstructures. Both of the original new-generation V8 engines sizes 3.5 and 4.5-litres – rapidly became available.

Apart from the out-and-out sports cars, this was always meant to be a complete range. Not only was there a choice of engines, but there were two wheelbases. SL types were available as open-top Roadsters, or with massive removable hardtops, while the longer-wheelbase models were only built with permanent coupé roofs. The latter, by no means as sporting, were the 350SLC/450SLC models, which also had close-coupled four-seat accommodation.

The Energy Crisis of 1973 then encouraged the arrival of the 280SL, which shared its name with the obsolete model, but used the new-generation twin-cam six-cylinder engine from the latest saloon cars. On the other hand,, before the end of the 1970s, the 450SLC 5.0 arrived, this having a light-alloy litre/240bhp version of the V8 engine, an event which signalled a complete upheaval of the model range.

During the 1980s the range changed gradually, but persistently. First the long-wheelbase type was dropped, leaving the sporting SL 2+2 seater all on own, but engines changed gradually, and inexorably. 3.8-litre 300SL and 5 500SL became the mainstream cars from 1980, a 4.2-litre 420SL appeared 1985, as did a 3-litre six-cylinder-engined 300SL, and before long a 5.6-litre

560SL (sold only in North America) was also added to the range.

In every way, all these cars were massive, typically Teutonic, strong and very reliable, but not at all as ponderous as their bare specification might suggest. Although they had soft suspension, power-assisted steering, and saloon-car standards of equipment, they could be very fast, and very effective. 450SLs, after all, dominated the 1978 Round South America Marathon, and at the end of the 1970s won World Championship rallies like Bandama against the best of all opposition. Not only did they have extremely well-engineered, well-developed, running gear, but they were built according to Mercedes-Benz's passenger car standards. Standards, and requirements, having changed inexorably over the years, the vast majority of these V8-engined machines had automatic gearboxes, along with air-conditioning, which was even used with the soft-top folded back !

Even with the six-cylinder engines, they were fast and flexible machines – and with the best of the V8s they could reach more than 140mph in great comfort and safety.

Mercedes-Benz were, and still are, interested only in building the best possible car for a job, and this was their interpretation of what high-class, high-price, sports car motoring should be all about. The buying public, particularly those in North America, agreed with their conclusions – so it is no wonder that 300,175 such machines were delivered in eighteen years.

Below: The imposition of harsh North American crash test rules meant that Mercedes-Benz had to add vast bumpers to the 560SL.

Mercedes-Benz SLK

Mercedes-Banz SLK, two-seater convertible/hardtop, introduced in 199(
(data for original Kompressor model)
Built by: Daimler-Benz AG, Germany.
Engine: Four cylinders, in line, in five-bearing cast iron cylinder block. Bore ar
stroke 90.9 × 88.4mm, 2,295cc (3.58 × 3.48in, 140.1cu.in). Light-alloy cylind
head. Four valves per cylinder, in vee, operation by twin overhead camshaft
and hydraulic inverted bucket tappets. Electronic fuel injection ar
supercharger. Maximum power 190bhp (DIN) at 5,300rpm. Maximum torqu
206lb.ft at 2,500rpm.
Transmission: Rear-wheel-drive, torque converter and five-speed manual
automatic transmissions, all in unit with front-mounted engine. Remote-contr
central gearchange.
Chassis: Unitary-construction pressed-steel body-chassis unit, in combine
two-seater roadster or hardtop style. Independent front suspension by c
springs, wishbones, telescopic dampers, and anti-roll bar. Independent re
suspension by coil springs, multi-link location, and telescopic damper
Recirculating ball steering with hydraulic power assistance. Four-wheel dis
brakes, servo assisted, with ABS as standard. Cast alloy 16in road whee
205/55-16in (front) and 225/50-16in (rear) tyres.
Dimensions: Wheelbase 7ft 10.4in (240cm), front track 4ft 10.6in (148.8cm
rear track 4ft 10.3in (148cm). Overall length 13ft 1.3in (399.5cm). Unlade
weight 2,950lb (1,338kg).
History: In the 1990s, as in many previous decades, Mercedes-Benz was ade
at squeezing every possible derivative from a particular model range. Althoug
the two-seater SLK roadster of 1996 looked completely new, therefore, it hid
great deal of existing technology under the skin. It may have appeared to b
related to the existing, longer, heavier and much more upmarket SL series, b
it was actually based on the pressed-steel platform of the latest C-Class saloon
which had been launched in 1993. The use of 'K' (for Kurz, or 'short' in th
German language) showed that it had a shorter wheelbase, but the bas
suspension, steering and running gear were all lifted from that car.

Because it was a Mercedes-Benz model, of course, there was no sign

**Below: The SLK, introduced in 1996, was a compact and carefully
detailed two-seater, with an electric fold-up hardtop feature.**

Above: The SLK, naturally, had a strong family resemblance to the longer and larger SL, but at first was available only with 4-cylinder engines. A V6-engined derivative was added in 2000.

compromise in this design, for it had all been carefully developed, integrated, and tested. The new R170 style (to use Mercedes-Benz's own internal description of this model) not only had a family resemblance to other current cars from Stuttgart, but it was as rigid and as wind-cheating as possible.

More than that, this was a car which could be used as an open roadster or as a snug two-seater coupé, for it incorporated a clever fold-away steel roof feature, which might have made the boot space rather restricted, but was an extremely neat and versatile way of providing two cars in one. One interesting feature, which caused a great deal of worry among customers, was that there was no spare wheel (no space in the tail, apparently), but instead the car was supplied with tyre sealant and an electric pump.

Although it was small by other Mercedes-Benz standards (it was only 157.3in/399.5cm long), it was also sturdily built, so powerful engines were needed to push it along. In the beginning there were to be two types of the ubiquitous four-cylinder C-Class unit – a normally aspirated 135bhp two-litre and an Eaton-supercharged 193bhp 2.3-litre, badged 'Kompressor' for obvious reasons. Although this car was offered with a choice of five-speed manual or automatic transmissions in continental Europe, only the automatic was available in the UK. The lower powered car, frankly, was not fast enough for what its customers required, most of whom chose the blown example.

The car's initial reception was friendly, but not ecstatic, reflecting the balance of Mercedes-Benz build quality against a certain lack of refinement (the four-cylinder engine did not help) and sporting character. Early in 2000, therefore, without changing the car's style, or its clever packaging, there was a major reshuffle of engines and transmissions. The 'entry level' machine became a supercharged 2.0-litre/163bhp unit, the 2.3-litre 'Kompressor' was slightly uprated to 197bhp, while a range-topping 218bhp 3.2-litre V6 engine was also added. Newly developed six-speed manual transmissions were introduced, the five-speed automatic box was continued, and all of a sudden the SLK began to look like a more integrated package. In the meantime, none of the hewn-from-solid build quality feel was destroyed, nor was the full range of safety equipment, and the SLK became one of Mercedes-Benz's best-selling roadsters ever.

MG 14/28 and 14/40

MG 14/28 and 14/40 models, built from 1924 to 1929 (data for 'flat radiator' models)

Built by: Morris Garages Ltd., Britain.

Engine: Morris-manufactured, four cylinders, in line, in cast iron cylinder block. Bore and stroke 75 x 101.6mm, 1,802cc (2.95 x 4.0in, 110cu.in). Cast iron cylinder head. Two side valves per cylinder, operation directly by tappets from a camshaft mounted in the cylinder block. One horizontal Solex carburettor. Maximum power 35bhp at 4,000rpm. Maximum torque not quoted.

Transmission: Front engine, rear-wheel-drive, single plate cork clutch running in oil, and three-speed manual gearbox, with no synchromesh. Direct acting centre gear change.

Chassis: Separate steel chassis frame, with channel section side members, pressed and tubular reinforcement and cross-bracings, with aluminium/steel panelled, on wood framing two-seat or four-seat tourer bodies, and some saloons. Suspension of beam front axle by half-elliptic leaf springs, and of beam rear axle by half-elliptic leaf springs. Friction dampers. Worm type steering. Drum brakes at all four wheels, mechanically operated by rods, levers and links, with Claydon Dewandre vacuum servo assistance. 4.95 x 28in tyres on bolt-on wire spoke wheels.

Dimensions: Wheelbase 8ft 10.5in (270.5cm), front track 4ft 0in (122cm), rear track 4ft 0in (122cm). Overall length 12ft 3in (373cm). Unladen weight 2,129lb (965.5kg).

History: Although the first-ever MGs were built in Oxford in 1923, the marque did not become generally known until the mid-1920s. The first series production machine was the 14/28 Super Sports, which was little more than a tuned-up and re-decorated Morris 'Bullnose' model. However, after Cecil Kimber, who inspired the growth of the marque, showed that he could sell 400 of these cars in two years, the boss of Morris Garages, William Morris, authorised the birth of a second new car – the 'flat-nose' 14/28. This was the first MG to have its own distinctive radiator style, though it was not for another two years that the famous, and distinctive, MG style first appeared, on the M-Type Midget.

Like the 'Bullnose' 14/28, the 'flat-nose' 14/28 was derived from the latest Morris Oxford chassis. William Morris, of course, not only owned Morris Motors, but he also owned Morris Garages. Since the 'MG' (which was an acronym for 'Morris Garages') made money for the garage business, it also helped boost sales of Oxfords, which meant that he approved of the entire enterprise.

Between 1926 and 1929, at least 900 such cars would be produced, but during that time the model name (which never appeared on the cars, but only in advertising) advanced from 14/28 to 14/40, and on to 'Mk IV' with no more than minor changes along the way. Dedicated MG historians point to the much-boosted power of Morris Garages-tuned engines, and prefer to call them all 14/40s anyway !

To turn what was a very mundane Morris into a sporting 14/40, MG engineers used flatter road springs, stiffer dampers, and substituted Marles steering for the original Morris layout. At the same the braking system was revised, and beefed up, with a vacuum servo to add to the driver's efforts. In addition, MG engineers also tuned the side-valve engine (this was not easy, for the side-valve engine was one of the simplest designs known to man, more useful for mass production than for producing much power) by modifying the cylinder head, matching up the ports, and fitting a special carburettor – the final tune being estimated at a mere 35bhp.

Open and closed body types were listed, the so-called 'Super Sports' tourer

Above: Original MGs had 'bullnose' type noses, but from late 1926 the 14/28 inherited a new flat-nose type of grille. The 1.8-litre engine produced 35bhp.

being a two-seater with an extra dickey seat which was exposed when the luggage lid was opened. For 1927, prices started at £340, and when *The Autocar* magazine tested one of the cars in 1927 it recorded a top speed of 65mph, could cruise around all day at perhaps 45mph, with all-in fuel economy at about 29mpg (Imperial). Seventy years on, such figures might sound positively derisory, but in the 1920s they definitely placed the new MG into the sports car category. It was certainly enough to encourage private owners to go motor racing, one of the earliest successes being in Argentina.

That, and the smart style of the cars (a four-seater tourer was also popular, and there was a closed 'Salonette' model too) meant that sales leapt upwards. More than 400 were sold in the first year, and in some weeks between ten and fifteen cars were despatched – this being very encouraging for such a small concern.

Demand was such that the factory had to move from Bainton Road, to a new building in Edmund Road, and there is no doubt that the new model's reception made Cecil Kimber very ambitious: it was now some time since he had been able to give any attention to the servicing side of Morris Garages, where he had conceived the first MGs.

As an honest sports car with no obvious failings, the 14/40 helped found a great dynasty, one which has survived into the twentieth century. Like almost every MG which followed it, it had distinctive looks, and before the end of the run, the now-legendary MG octagon not only appeared on the radiator badge, but was also beginning to back the instruments, and to appear on the body's running boards.

By 1929, it was time for a bigger, more expensive MG, the 18/80, to take over, so 14/40 production came to end after 900 cars had been sold.

MG M-Type Midget

M-Type Midget, built from 1929 to 1932
Built by: M.G. Car Co. Ltd., Britain.
Engier: Four cylinders, in line, in two-bearing cast-iron block. Bore and stroke 57mm by 83mm, 847cc (2.24 × 3.27in, 51.8cu.in). Cast-iron cylinder head. Two overhead valves per cylinder, operated by single overhead camshaft. Single SU side-draught carburettor. 5.4:1 compression ratio. Maximum power 20bhp at 4,000rpm (raised to about 27bhp at 4,500rpm after 2,000 cars had been built). Engine (like chassis) derived from that of Morris Minor saloon.
Transmission: Single-dry-plate clutch and three-speed manual gearbox (without synchromesh), both in unit with engine. Optional four-speed gearbox (also without synchromesh) from autumn 1930. Open propeller shaft to spiral-bevel 'live' rear axle.
Chassis: Simple channel-section frame with five pressed cross members, Semi-elliptic leaf springs at front and rear, with Hartford friction-type dampers. Four-wheel, cable-operated drum brakes. 19in wire wheels. 4 × 19in tyres. Original coachwork was light and simple two-seat sports car layout with pointed tail, framed in ash and fabric covered. First cars had rear-hinged doors (changed in 1930, but later versions had metal panels with a folding hood. A closed two-door

Above: The standard production Midget M-Type, built from 1929 to 1932. This car is a 1930 example, with appropriate 'MG' registration plate found on many such London-sold Midgets in the 1930s. The chassis and engine were developed form the Morris Minor. Note fabric body.

Left and below: M-Type Midgets prepared for competition had tiny and lightweight bodies. This 1930 Double-12 car averaged 60.23mph for 24 hours at Brooklands, and was the highest-placed of the Team Prize winning cars, driven by C.J. Randall and F.M. Montgomery.

▶ 'Sportsman's coupé was also offered as an extremely attractive alternative.

Dimensions: Wheelbase 6ft 6in (198cm), track (front) 3ft 6in (106.7cm), track (rear) 3ft 6in (106.7cm). Overall length 10ft 3in (312cm). Unladen weight 1,120lb (508kg).

History: The very first MGs were built in 1924 and were no more than lightly modified and rebodied 'Bullnose' Morris Cowleys. They were inspired by Cecil Kimber at Morris Garages Ltd. In Oxford, which was owned by William Morris himself. The M.G. Car Co. Ltd. was formally established in 1928, by which time Kimber was already planning to build a tiny new two-seater sports car. Morris, having bought Wolseley Motors of Birmingham, were proposing to announce their new Morris Minor in the autumn and Kimber decided that this car's little chassis and Hispano-inspired overhead-camshaft engine would be an ideal starting point.

Mechanically, therefore, the M-Type MG Midget, announced in 1928, first sold in April 1929 and withdrawn in June 1932 after 3,235 examples had been delivered, was almost pure Morris Minor. To make it a proper MG, the suspension was lowered, the steering column was re-angled and that distinctive MG radiator was added. The initial bodies were simplicity themselves, having a very light plywood and ash frame mainly covered by fabric. The ensemble was completed by cycle-type wings, a neat little vee-shaped windscreen and a very elementary hood.

Apart from its cheekily attractive lines, the car's main attraction was the price – £175 in Britain – much lower than for almost any other sportscar in the world. Performance was good for its size, with maximum speed of more than 60mph and an average fuel consumption of around 40mpg. The brakes were not very efficient, but the handling and roadholding made up for this.

The press and the first customers loved the car and it was not long before it started to appear in competition, being used equally in sporting trials and on

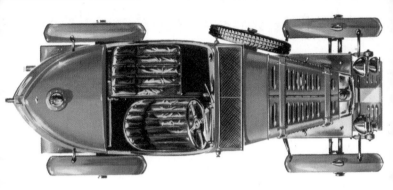

Above: Not much space for the riding mechanic in the Double-12, whose seat was set back. Note bonnet straps and wire mesh screen.

the Brooklands race track. Camshaft changes intended to make the car competitive boosted the power from 20bhp to 27bhp and several factory-backed cars raced with distinction in 1930. The C-Type Montlhéry Midgets, out-and-out competition cars, were derived directly from the M-Type and its racing experiences.

Even with the optional four-speed gearbox and a tuned engine, the M-Type was not quite competitive enough in international racing, although it established the pedigree of all other MGs built before 1950. Production moved from Oxford to Abingdon in September 1929.

Below: 1930 Le Mans M-Type Midget.

MG Midgets–'Overhead Cam' Types

D-Type, J-Type four-cylinder models, built from 1931 to 1936 (data for 1934 PA two-seater)

Built by: MG Car Co. Ltd., Britain.

Engine: Four-cylinder, in line, with three-bearing cast-iron cylinder block. Bore and stroke 57mm by 83mm, 847cc (2.24 × 3.27in, 51.8cu in). Cast-iron cylinder head. Two overhead valves per cylinder, operated by single overhead camshaft. Twin semi-downdraught SU constant-vacuum carburettors. Maximum power 35bhp at 5,600rpm.

Transmission: Single-dry-plate clutch, with four-speed non-synchromesh manual gearbox, both in unit with engine. Open propeller shaft to spiral-bevel 'live' rear axle.

Chassis: Simple channel section pressed steel frame with pressed and tubular cross-members. Semi-elliptic leaf springs at front and rear, with Hartford friction-type dampers at front, and lever-arm hydraulic dampers at rear. Bishop cam steering. Four-wheel, 12in diameter, cable-operated drum brakes. 19in centre-lock wire-spoke wheels, with 4 × 19in tyres. Choice of coachbuilt bodywork, or steel panels on ash framing – two-seat open sports, four-seat open tourer, and two-seater closed 'Airline' coupé.

Dimensions: Wheelbase 7ft 3.3in (221.7cm), track (front and rear) 3ft 6in (106.7cm). Overall length (two-seat sports) 11ft 3in (343cm). Unladen weight (two-seat) 1,568lb (711kg).

History: After the original small MG sports car, the M-Type, had made its mark, there was never much doubt that it would have successors. Even so, nobody could have forecast that there would be a continuous and recognisable strain of MG Midgets in production until 1955, when the last of the TFs was finally replaced by the first of the Midgets built between 1931 and 1936 were all designed around the same basic mechanical layout (only the very rare R-Type single-seater racing Midget had all-independent suspension), with progressive

Below: The PA Midget of 1934 was one of the last Midgets to be sold with an overhead-cam engine. Separate simple steel frames meant that other styles were offered – including four-seaters. The engine size was 847cc and four-cyl.

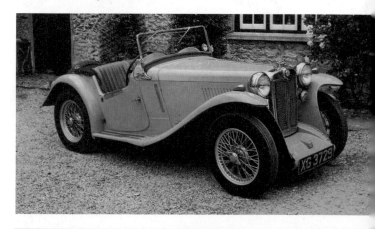

Above: Perhaps not the copybook way to corner a racing Midget, but at least we get a good view of the front end and the good steering lock! This particular car is a TC, built in large numbers immediately after the Second World War. By then all of MG's design traditions were thoroughly established and the car sold well in export markets.

development of the four-cylinder overhead camshaft engine originally designed for the humble little Morris Minor of 1928. All had narrow, flexible, channel-section chassis frames with the rear slung under the spiral bevel back axle, and with rock-hard half-elliptic front and rear suspension, three- or four-speed manual gearboxes without synchro-mesh, cable brakes, centre-lock wire wheels, and a fly-off handbrake. Most of them had narrow, starkly trimmed, British-traditional styling, with separate front wings and free-standing head-lamps, most were open sports two-seaters, and all were enormous fun to drive. Bodies were cheap and simple, with ash frames supporting pressed or hand-formed steel panels; creature comforts were few, and not demanded by customers.

The M-Type's successor was the short-lived D-Type of 1931 and 1932, with 27bhp and a three-speed box, of which only 250 were built, but it was followed by the J1/J2 models of 1932-1934 (2,463 built in two years), and finally by the PA and PB cars of 1934-1936 (which sold to the tune of 2,526 cars. Compared with the D-Type, the J-model had 36bhp, a four-speed gearbox and rather more rakish styling, which included the use of cutaway doors to allow driver and passenger more elbow room. Like the D-Type, J1 and J2 models, the original P-series cars of 1934 and 1935 (retrospectively known as PAs) still retained an 847cc overhead camshaft engine, but now allied to a three-bearing block and crankshaft. There was no more power than before, but this was rectified for the PB of 1935-1936, which had 939cc, 43bhp, and a top speed of nearly 80mph.

Other MG models were built during the same incredibly prolific period, under the direction of Cecil Kimber, but other Midgets like the C-Type Montlhery, ▶

▶ J3, J4, Q-Type and R-Type models were all strictly for competition, and the complex series of Magnas and Magnettes all had six-cylinder engines of the same basic design, related to the original Midget 'fours'.

MG's problem, at Abingdon, was that although success upon success was being gained by the competition cars, the road cars were becoming more and more expensive and (by Morris Motors standards) more and more specialised. Lord Nuffield, who personally owned MG throughout this period, saw that sales were dropping steadily, as losses began to mount. In 1935 he sold MG to his corporate Nuffield Group, where they came under the direct control of Morris Motors. Immediately the competitions programme was cancelled, and a new and cheaper-to-build Midget was put in hand. The last PB was built in 1936, when it was replaced by the entirely different TA model.

It is worth noting that although the MG Midget was *the* most popular British sports car, in fact and in legend, of the early 1930s, a total of only 8,474 overhead-camshaft engined road cars were sold in eight years.

Right: A TC fully modified for circuit racing in Britain, with a roll cage and fat non-standard tyres on 16 inch wheels (a popular modification).

Below: The well-known overhead-cam 847cc or 939cc PA/PB engine, with twin SU carburettors, and three main bearings.

Below: The PA Midget of 1934, with a full range of instruments, and much evidence of Cecile Kimber's well-loved style feature on MGs, the octagonal emblem.

MG Midgets – T-Series Models

TA, TB, TC, TD and TF models, built 1936 to 1955 (data for 1946 model TC)

Built by: MG Car Co. Ltd., Britain.

Engine: Four-cylinder, in-line, based on three-bearing cast-iron block. Bore and stroke 66.5mm by 90mm, 1,250cc (2.62 × 3.54in, 76.3cu in). Cast-iron cylinder head. Two overhead valves per cylinder, operated by pushrods and rockers from single side-mounted camshaft. Twin semi-downdraught SU constant-vacuum carburettors. Maximum power 54bhp (net) at 5,200rpm.

Transmission: Single-dry-plate clutch and four-speed, synchromesh manual gearbox (un-synchronised first gear), both in unit with engine. Remote-control central gearchange. Open propeller shaft to spiral-bevel 'live' rear axle.

Chassis: Separate channel-section steel chassis, with two main longitudinal members, braced by pressed and tubular cross members. Semi-elliptic front and rear springs. Luvax-Girling piston type dampers. Bishop cam-and-lever steering. Four-wheel, hydraulically operated drum brakes. Fly-off handbrake. 19in centre lock wire wheels. 4.50 × 19in tyres. Two seat open sports bodywork, of steel panels on an ash frame. No alternative coachwork.

Dimensions: Wheelbase 7ft 10in (239cm), tacks (front and rear) 3ft 9in (114cm). Overall length 11ft 7.5in (354cm). Unladen weight 1,736lb (787kg).

History: The T-Series MG Midget was conceived as a direct result of the sale of MG by Lord Nuffield to his own Nuffield Group, which was effectively passing control of the finances from one hand to another. The obsolete, and displaced PB had an overhead-camshaft engine, and a special 'crash' gearbox, whereas the original TA of 1936 had a more mundane overhead-

Top right and below: The last of the T-Series Midgets was the TF of 1953-1955, which had a slightly updated styling, and 85mph performance.

valve engine, and a synchromesh gearbox.

Although, in its general layout and design philosophy, the TA was like the PB, which is to say that it had a channel-section frame, a two-seater open sports body style panelling on a simple ash frame, sweeping front wings and free-standing headlamps, it was a larger, simpler, and altogether more pragmatic machine. Whereas the PB had been the final, and far-removed derivative of the 1928-1932 Morris Minor, the TA leaned heavily on the Wolseley 10/40 power train and transmission, a car that was itself a more advanced update of the Morris 10hp model.

The instant reaction of enthusiasts was that the TA was not a *true* Midget, but experience showed that it was a better, faster, and more roomy car in all respects, and that it offered remarkable value for money with a 1,292cc engine and 54bhp it sold for £222. The TA became the TB in 1939, with a new design of short-stroke 1,250cc engine, and in 1945 it became TC, with a rather wider cockpit but little modernisation. The TC was MG's first successful export-market car, and a total of exactly 10,000 were sold before the end of 1949.

In the meantime, Nuffield had produced the MG Y-Type, which was an amalgam of Morris 8hp Series E body, a new independent front suspension chassis, and the 1,250cc engine. This sold well, and in 1950 it led to the launch of the TD Midget, which was a much modified version of that chassis, the TC's running gear, and a wider, cobbier, but still essentially 1930s body style. It also had steel disc wheels (the firs Midget so to be equipped), but it was also available in left-hand drive, and the USA customer loved it. Nearly 30,000 TDs were built up to the summer of 1953.

By this time, MG were ready to replace the TD with a new modern car, but this (which later became the MGA of 1955) was frozen out by the new company management, called BMC (British Motor Corporation). In place of the new design, MG were only allowed to face-lift the TD into the TF of 1953-1955, which retained the same centre body and doors, but incorporated a slightly smoothed out nose and a more sloping tail, still on the same 7ft 10in wheelbase of all T-Series MGs.

The TF was not a car which was liked, even when the enlarged 1,466cc engine was made available in the autumn of 1954. The public had been offered old-style MGs in a modernising world for too long, and had eventually rebelled against this. Poor aerodynamics meant that even a TF1500 could only reach 85mph, which was so much slower than Triumph were offering with the TR2 that it was embarrassing. Like all other T-Series cars, however, the TF had excellent road manners.

MG MGA and Twin-Cam

MG MGA family, built from 1955 to 1962 (data for MGA 1500)
Built by: MG Car Co. Ltd., Britain.
Engine: Four cylinders, in line, in three-main-bearing cast iron cylinder block. Bore and stroke 73.02 x 88.9mm, 1,489cc (2.87 x 3.50in, 90.9cu.in). Cast iron cylinder head. Two overhead valves per cylinder, operation by pushrods and rockers from a camshaft in the cylinder block. Two semi-downdraught SU carburettors. Maximum power 72bhp at 5,500rpm. Maximum torque 77lb.ft at 3,500rpm.
Transmission: Front engine, rear-wheel-drive, single dry plate clutch and four-speed synchromesh manual gearbox, no synchromesh on first gear, all in unit with engine. Remote control centre floor gearchange.
Chassis: Separate steel chassis frame, with box section side members, cross-bracings and reinforcements, with steel (some aluminium panels) body shell in two seat open sports car style, or with permanent bubble-top hardtop. Independent front suspension by coil springs and wishbones, suspension of beam rear axle by half-elliptic leaf springs. Hydraulic lever-arm dampers. Rack-and-pinion steering. Drum brakes at front and rear. 15in wheels, bolt-on steel disc or centre-lock wires, with 5.50-15in tyres.
Dimensions: Wheelbase 7ft 10in (238.8cm), front track 3ft 11.5in (120.6cm), rear track 4ft 0.75in (123.8cm). Overall length 13ft 0in (396.2cm). Unladen weight 1,988lb (901.5kg).
[MGA Twin-Cams, built 1958 to 1960, had 108bhp/1.6-litre twin-cam engines and four-wheel disc brakes. Other MGAs had 80bhp and 86bhp 1.6-litre engines.]
History: MG's range of traditionally-styled T-Series sports cars had such a long

Below: From 1956, all versions of the MGA, whether push-rod or twin-cam engined, were available with this smart bubble-top coupé body style.

Above: The MGA was the first all-enveloping style to be put on sale from MG's famous Abingdon factory in England.

▶ pedigree – it started in 1936 with the TA – that it was well overdue for replacement in the 1950s. The origins of a new-generation car, however, date from 1951, when MG provided a specially-streamlined body for George Phillips to clothe a TD for the Le Mans 24 Hour race. The style, if not the chassis, inspired the MGA which would be launched in 1955, and would be built for seven years.

To match the sleek new all-enveloping style, MG designed a sturdy new box-section chassis frame, which picked up the coil spring independent suspension of the TF. The new body shell was an expensively tooled steel structure, which (for financial reasons) meant that it was bound to be in production for some years.

Originally MG hoped that it could use improved 1.5-litre versions of the TF's engine, but corporate policy dictated the use of the new BMC 'B' Series engine, gearbox and back axle. These, though distrusted at first, proved to be very suitable, the engine being particularly receptive to power-tuning.

Original launch plans were that a team of light-alloy versions would race at Le Mans in June 1955, and that the production car would be launched at the same time. Unhappily, tooling delays meant that this scheme had to be abandoned, and steel bodied Roadsters actually went on sale in September of the same year.

The new MGA not only looked beautiful, but it handled very well, and was at least 15-20mph faster than the TF which it replaced. It had a larger cabin, better equipment, and (for the first time in an MG sports car) a closed luggage boot. No wonder that it was an immediate and enormous success which would break every previous MG sales record.

The original car, with 72bhp, drum brakes and an open-top style, was just the first of a family which would expand successfully. Each and every MGA was a smart, civilised, roadworthy and effective sports car, possessed of much

more modern-feeling behaviour than its predecessors. If anything, it was over-engineered and somewhat heavy, which meant that it did not have flashing acceleration, though it later had great success in races and rallies.

Only a year after launch the smart coupé, complete with bubbletop steel roof and wind-up windows, appeared, and would stay in production to the end. Then, in 1959, the original car was replaced by the 1600, which had an 80bhp/1.6-litre engine and front disc brakes, and in 1961 the final version was the 86bhp/1.6-litre 1600 Mk II.

The most exciting version of all was the MGA Twin-Cam model, launched in 1958 after protracted development, and available either as a roadster or as a coupé. Although based on the original, it had a new 8-valve twin-cam 1.6-litre with 108bhp, disc brakes at all wheels, and used racy centre-lock steel wheels. With its 115mph top speed, and acceleration to match, it was a spirited (though expensive) performer: unfortunately, early and well-known engine reliability problems meant that it sold slowly – and only 2,111 were produced. The tragedy of this is the BMC simply could not find time to solve the problems – that work being done by classic car specialists in later years.

The 'half-way' house model which took over in 1960 was the 1600 'De Luxe', which used the disc braked/centre-lock wheeled chassis, but a conventional pushrod engine. Although this was rarely even publicised, several hundred such cars were sold by word of mouth, thus disposing of the redundant Twin-Cam chassis.

Because no fewer than 101,470 of all MGA types were produced, it would need an even better MG sports car to improve on it. That car duly arrived in 1962 – the MGB.

Below: Even the original 72bhp version of the MGA could reach nearly 100mph – thanks to the sleek shape of the new body.

MG Midget

MG Midget, built from 1961 to 1979 (includes Austin-Healey Sprite) (data for original 1961 model)
Built by: MG Car Co. Ltd., Britain.
Engine: Four cylinders, in line, in cast iron cylinder block. Bore and stroke 62.94 x 76.2mm, 948cc (2.48 x 3.0in, 57.9cu.in). cast iron cylinder head. Two overhead valves per cylinder, operation by pushrods and rockers from camshaft mounted in the cylinder block. Two semi-downdraught SU carburettors. Maximum power 46bhp at 5,500rpm. Maximum torque 53lb.ft at 3,000rpm. [Later Midgets had 1.1 and 1.3-litre engines, up to 65bhp by 1974, then 1.5-litre/66bhp Triumph engines until 1979.]
Transmission: Front engine, rear-wheel-drive, single dry plate clutch and four-speed synchromesh manual gearbox, no synchromesh on first gear: remote control, centre floor gearchange.
Chassis: Unitary construction steel combined body/chassis structure, with steel two-seater open roadster body style, with optional removable hard top. Independent front suspension by coil springs and wishbones, suspension of beam rear axle by cantilever quarter-elliptic leaf springs and radius arms. Lever-arm hydraulic dampers. Rack-and-pinion steering. Drum brakes at all four wheels. 13in wheels, bolt-on steel disc or centre-lock wires, with 5.20-13in tyres.
Dimensions: Wheelbase 6ft 8in (203cm), front track 3ft 9.7in (116cm), rear track 3ft 8.7in (114cm). Overall length 11ft 5.9in (350cm). Unladen weight 1,525lb (692kg).
    [Later Midgets had 1.1 and 1.3-litre engines, up to 65bhp by 1974, then 1.5-litre/66bhp Triumph engines until 1979.]
History: Although the MG Midget revived a famous name in 1961, and sold strongly until 1979, it was really born as an Austin-Healey Sprite in 1958. Twin

Below: By 1973 the MG Midget had been on sale for twelve years. This 'round wheelarch' variety was a short-lived derivative.

**bove: Among MG enthusiasts, the most fashionable Midgets were
ese 1.3-litre models of 1966-1974. Until 1970 there was also an Austin-
ealey Sprite version too.**

ports cars from 1961 to 1971, almost all of them being built at Abingdon, these
ars were formidably successful two-seaters in the BMC line up.

To follow up the successful Austin-Healey 100, the Sprite had been
onceived by the prolific Healey family, in response to BMC's request for a
mall and inexpensive sports car to be designed, to sell alongside the MGA and
ustin-Healey sports cars. In its original Austin-Healey form, its unit-
onstruction bodyshell had no external access to the luggage compartment,
nd had a cheeky frontal style with protruding 'frog eye' headlamps.

Not only did this hard-riding little car (which used a mixture of Austin A35
nd Morris Minor 1000 chassis components) exude great charm, but it was also
neat, good-handling little machine, which could be made to go much faster if
e engine was power-tuned. It was excellent value for money, and simple to
pair too. All had good racing records, and appeared with honour in long-
stance races at Le Mans and Sebring.

From June 1961, however, the range was re-designed and widened. This
me there were Sprite and MG Midget versions, mechanically and bodily
entical, except for minor cosmetic differences. The restyled cars looked
onventional, with wing-positioned headlamps, and with a boot compartment
aving an access lid. Optional hardtops were available, along with many other
xtras including wire-spoke wheels.

Over the years, progressive changes were made to align these cars with
MC mass-production cars. The engine was enlarged to 1,098cc in autumn
962 at the same time as it appeared in the Morris 1100, and in the autumn of
966 the latest 1,275cc power unit took over. Although all those engines had ▶

▶ different bores and strokes, there were based on the A-Series engines whi⸋ would be built from 1952 to 2001.

Then, from the autumn of 1974, and six years after the formation of Briti⸋ Leyland, a Triumph Spitfire 1500 engine and gearbox was adopted, commonisation specifications, this being because the A-Series engine could ⸋ longer cope with ever-tightening North American exhaust emission regulatio⸋

The only significant chassis changes ever made came in the spring of 19⸋ when the rear suspension was re-designed. Half-elliptic leaf springs we⸋ adopted, to replace the cantilever springs and radius arms used up to that poi⸋ Front wheel disc brakes, too, were standardised when the 1,098cc engi⸋ arrived in late 1962.

Apart from the fitment of controversial black rubber bumpers (needed ⸋ meet USA crash test regulations) to the Spitfire 1500-engined type in late 197⸋ there were no major style changes in eighteen years, though there was regu⸋ attention to the interior, and wind-up windows were opted in the spring 19⸋ reshuffle. By the mid-1970s, the cramped Midget interior looked far more ⸌ market, and was much better-equipped and furnished, than had the origin⸋ rather stark, Sprite of 1958-1961.

Midgets and Sprites always sold in very large quantities, though Bℕ⸋ always leaned sentimentally to favouring the MG-badged car. For that reas⸋ alone, the Sprite was allowed to wither in the late 1960s, and was dropped⸋ 1970: for 1971 alone, an orphan, the 'Austin Sprite' was briefly built.

Even the Midget gradually lost its charm in North America, so producti⸋ was gradually phased out before the end of 1979, which left British Leyla⸋ making only the Triumph Spitfire 1500 for that market sector.

More than 226,000 Midgets and nearly 130,000 Sprites of all typ⸋ (49,000 of them 'frog-eyes') were made – each and every one of the⸋ having a cheeky, bright, character: all behave exactly as a traditional spo⸋ car should.

Right: The original 'frog-eye' Austin-Healey Sprite was built from 1958-196⸋ the MG Midget, with more conventional styling, evolved from that car.

Below: These 'frog-eye' headlamps were typical of the original Austin-Healey Sprite, which pre-dated the definitive MG Midgets.

MG MGB

MGB sports car and GT coupé, built from 1962 to 1980

Built by: BMC (later British Leyland), Britain.

Engine: Four cylinders, in line, in three-main-bearing (later five-main-bearir cast iron cylinder block. Bore and stroke 80.26 × 88.9mm, 1,798cc (3.16 3.50in, 109.8cu.in). cast iron cylinder head. Two overhead valves per cylinder, line, operation by pushrods and rockers from a camshaft in the cylinder blo Two semi-downdraught SU carburettors. Maximum power 95bhp (DIN) 5,400rpm. Maximum torque 110lb.ft at 3,000rpm.

Transmission: Rear-wheel-drive, single-dry-plate diaphragm spring clutch and fo speed manual gearbox, no synchromesh on first gear originally, all-synchrome from 1967, all in unit with engine. Remote-control, central gearchange.

Chassis: Unitary-construction pressed-steel body-chassis unit in two-sea style, open Roadster or fastback/hatchback GT. Independent front suspens by coil springs, wishbones, lever arm dampers, and optional anti-roll bar. Be axle rear suspension by half-elliptic leaf springs and lever-arm dampers. Ra and-pinion steering. Front disc, rear drum brakes, no servo assistance. 1 wheels, steel disc or centre-lock wires, 5.60-14in tyres.

Dimensions: Wheelbase 7ft 7.0in (231cm), front track 4ft 1.0in (124.5cm), r track 4ft 1.25in (125cm). Overall length 12ft 9.3in (389.4cm). Unladen weig (Roadster) 2,030lb (921kg), (GT) 2,190lb (993kg).

History: Is there anyone in the world who has not seen, admired, driven owned an MGB? Until Japanese cars like the Datsun Z-class, and the Maz MX-5/Miata finally racked up higher figures in the 1990s, the MGB was world's best-selling sports car. Announced in 1962, made steadily until 1980, recognisably the same at the end, as in its beginning, the four-cylinder M notched up sales of 513,272. Along the way, another nine thousand six-cylin MGCs, and 2,591 MGB GT V8s were also built. Nor was that all, for in the ea 1990s the Rover group briefly revived a restyled, V8-engined version of the calling in the MG RV8, and selling most of them to Japan.

Below: The elegant MGB was, and is, Britain's best-selling sports car, with more than half a million built in eighteen years.

bove: The smart MGB GT style, complete with hatchback, was ntroduced in 1965. Most were 1.8-litre, but from 1973-1976 there was lso a V8-engined car.

Conceived as BMC's mass-production sports car for the 1960s, and to eplace the successful MGA, the MGB had a sturdy new monocoque shell, and style devised by Abingdon (Italian influence was not needed), the running gear eing a developed version of that used in the old MGA. With 95bhp from 1.8-tres, and a more slippery shape, the original roadster was capable of more than 00mph. Overdrive was optional (it would not be standardised until the 1970s), utomatic transmission eventually became a short-lived option, and from 1965 ere was even a smart and extremely successfull fastback coupé/hatchback ersion called the MGB GT.

Like many a previous MG, the sporty, stylish two-seater shape hid positively undane running gear. Properly maintained by any competent mechanic or MC dealer (which was one charm of this car, especially when being run ousands of miles from Britain), an MGB could go on forever, with saloon-type nning costs. Engine and transmission were both shared with other mass-roduction BMC (later, British Leyland) cars, while the chassis, with its coil oring front suspension and beam axle/leaf-spring rear was extremely onventional, but here was a sports car which was more than the sum of its arts. The fabled 'Abingdon Touch' was certainly applied to this model.

Not only did it look good, but it handled well, and tuners soon found that ce-prepared cars could be made to go very fast too. Although not outstanding n the track, the MGB still figured in endurance racing – the 'works' motorsport epartment, for instance, preparing a succession of long-nosed cars to contend, nd complete, the legendary Le Mans 24 Hour race.

Although a new all-synchromesh gearbox was fitted from late 1967, and ere were regular cosmetic retouchings in the 1970s, the MGB was really lowed to go on too long without a major update. For 1975 it was necessary to t vast, controversially styled, rubber bumpers for the car to go on selling in orth America, at which point the ride height went up and the roadholding uffered. By the late 1970s British Leyland had lost faith in it (they also favoured e in-house rival, Triumph, at this time), American emission rules had strangled e engine too far, and an overhead-camshaft engine transplant was ruled out. e consequence was that the MGB finally died of senile decay. The good ews, though, is that body shells were later remanufactured in numbers, all arts were available through the 1990s, and the MGB was as much of an icon the 2000s as it was all those years ago.

MG MGC/BGT V8 and RV8

MG C, BGT V8 and RV8, built 1967-1969, 1973-1976, 1992-1995 (data for GT V8)

Built by: MG Car Co. Ltd., Britain.

Engine: Rover manufactured, eight cylinders, in 90-degree vee, in light al cylinder block. Bore and stroke 88.9 x 71.1mm, 3,528cc (3.5 x 2.8 215.3cu.in). Two light-alloy cylinder heads. Two overhead valves per cylinc operation by pushrods and rockers from a camshaft in the cylinder block v Two horizontal SU carburettors. Maximum power 137bhp at 5,000rp Maximum torque 193lb.ft at 2,900rpm. [The MGC had a straight-six 2.9-li engine, the RV8 had a 190bhp 4.0-litre V8.]

Transmission: Front engine, rear-wheel-drive, single dry plate diaphrag spring clutch and four-speed all-synchromesh manual gearbox, and Layco overdrive operating on top gear, all in unit with the engine. Remote cont centre floor gearchange.

Chassis: Unitary construction steel combined body/chassis structure, w steel body shell in 2+2-seater fastback style. Independent front suspension coil springs, wishbones and anti-roll bar, suspension of beam rear axle by h elliptic leaf springs. Hydraulic lever-arm dampers. Rack-and-pinion steeri Front disc, rear drum brakes, with vacuum servo assistance. 14in bolt-

Above: The MGC evolved from the classic MGB, with a six-cylinder engine, and a bonnet bulge needed to clear the engine – plus 15in wheels.

steel/cast alloy road wheels, and 175-14in tyres.

Dimensions: Wheelbase 7ft 7in (231cm), front track 4ft 1in (124.5cm), rear track 4ft 1.25in (125cm). Overall length 12ft 10.7in (393cm). Unladen weight 2,387lb (1,081kg).

History: During and after the long career of the MGB, there were three

different types of large-engined derivatives: all were made in limited quantities for a limited period of time. In all cases, the same basic style and structure of the four-cylinder car was retained, the most wide-ranging and significant changes being made under the skin.

MGC: In the mid-1960s, MG's parent company, BMC, wanted to replace the ageing Austin-Healey 3000, and elected to do this with a re-engineered MGB (there were proposals to build 'badge-engineered' Austin-Healey versions too, but these were squashed by the Healey family), which was called MGC. Somehow or other, a lengthy six-cylinder engine was squeezed into the MGB's engine bay.

A much-re-engineered version of the Austin-Healey 3000 engine was chosen, but this was so bulky that a new type of front suspension, with longitudinal torsion bars, rather like that of the Jaguar E-Type, had to be employed, and clearance bulges had to be pressed into the bonnet.

Except for the use of 15in wheels, the 120mph MGC looked just like the MGB, but did not behave in the same way The engine was slow to rev, the front-heavy weight distribution made the handling less responsive, and the four-cylinder car's balance had been lost. Just 8,999 were sold in two years.

MGB GT V8: The V8-engined MGB GT was inspired by a private-enterprise conversion by Ken Costello, but it was only ever marketed in fastback/hatchback GT guise, and was only ever sold as a right-hand-drive machine in the UK.

British Leyland, which controlled MG at this time, ▶

Left: The MGB GT V8 was on sale from 1973 to 1976. The rubber bumper style, caused by US legislation, was introduced in 1974.

▶ rejected the idea of building open-top V8s, thinking that they could sell the GT version as a 'Grand Tourer' rather than a sports car. Unhappily, they also asked a high price, and sales would be disappointing. Technically this was quite a simple conversion, for the Rover V8 engine (BL also controlled Rover) was lightweight and a snug fit, while the MG GT's structure, transmission and chassis could easily cope with 137bhp. Except for special wheels, exterior and cabin styling was unchanged, the only V8 evidence being the badging on the tail and flanks.

Sales of this 125mph sports car began well in 1973, but faded as inflation (and the effects of the Energy Crisis, and petrol price rises) increased. For 1975, the addition of the black rubber-bumper front and rear end style looked well on the GT, but was disliked by many. As it was only being sold at home, sales died out in 1976, after 2,591 cars had been produced.

R-V8: This oddity was conceived by a Rover (as British Leyland had become) special projects department, who wanted to preserve the MG name at a time when there was no other 'modern' MG in the product range, and to prepare the ground for the forthcoming MGF.

By this time the long-serving Rover V8 engine had been enlarged to 4.0-litres, 190bhjp, and emissions-reducing fuel injection, and this time the company decided only to produce Roadsters, but no GTs. Twelve years after it had died, the reason the MGB structure could still be used was that British Motor Heritage (a small re-manufacturing enterprise) was still able to produce the body shells.

Third time around, much more attention was given to the style, which featured flared wheelarches, different front and rear end treatment, and a plushy interior with a wooden fascia. Although there was no lack of performance – the R-V8 could reach 136mph – the handling no longer met 1990s standards, and there was a struggle for sales.

A high proportion were sold to MG-mad Japan, but only 2,000 R-V8s, all of them with right-hand-drive, were ever built.

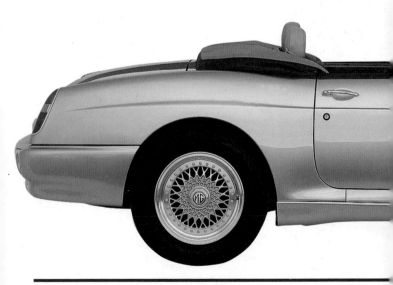

Above: The Rover V8-engined RV8 was a limited-production model, which had flared wing pressings, and a new front-end style.

Below: The RV8 of the early 1990s was developed from the MGB roadster, with different skin styling, and with a 4.0-litre V8 engine.

MG MGF

MG MGF sports car, built from 1995 to 2002
Built by: Rover Group (originally BMW-owned), Britain.
Engine: Four cylinders, in line, in five-main-bearing light-alloy cylinder block. Bore and stroke 80 × 89mm, 1,796cc (3.15 × 3.50in, 109.6cu.in). Aluminium cylinder head. Four valves per cylinder, operation by twin overhead camshafts and inverted bucket tappets. MEMS electronic fuel injection. Maximum power 118bhp (DIN) at 5,500rpm. Maximum torque 122lb.ft at 3,000rpm, or 143bhp (DIN) at 7.000rpm. Maximum torque 128lb.ft. at 4,500rpm.
Transmission: Rear-wheel-drive, single-plate diaphragm spring clutch and five-speed all-synchromesh manual gearbox, all in unit with transverse mid-mounted engine. Remote-control, central gearchange. Optional Steptronic automatic on 118bhp versions.
Chassis: Unitary-construction pressed-steel body-chassis unit, in two-seater roadster style, with optional hardtop. Independent front suspension by Hydragas springs, wishbones, and anti-roll bar, with self-levelling connection to independent rear suspension by Hydragas springs, wishbones and anti-roll bar. Rack-and-pinion steering, with optional electric power assistance. Four-wheel disc brakes. Cast alloy 15in road wheels, 185/55-15in (front), 205/50-15in (rear) tyres.
Dimensions: Wheelbase 7ft 9.5in (237.5cm), front track 4ft 7.1in (140cm), rear track 4ft 7.5in (141cm). Overall length 12ft 10in (391.4cm). Unladen weight 2,366lb (1,073kg).
History: After the MGB died away in1980, British Leyland and its successors kept the MG badge alive on a series of lack-lustre, hotted-up Austin hatchbacks. Yet for many years in the 1980s and 1990s it looked as if no new sports car would ever be developed. Then came the period when the Rover Group was owned by BMW, who invested heavily in their new acquisition, saw the merits of MG, and commissioned a neat new two-seater, the MGF. It was, of course, too late to make this new car at Abingdon (which had been flattened after the MGB was killed off), so it was manufactured at Longbridge, alongside the Minis and Metros.

Below: The mid-engined MGF, first seen in 1995, had smart and timeless styling. This was the first-ever MG sports car to be built at Longbridge.

Above: The MGF was a curvaceous and roomy two-seater, with the transverse engine mounted behind the seats. A hardtop was also available.

In basic layout – it was a steel monocoque-shelled two-seater, with a transversely mounted four-cylinder engine positioned immediately behind the seats – the MGF followed other such successful cars as the Fiat X1/9 and the Toyota MR2, but there were many unique touches. Almost as expected, the chassis borrowed heavily from Rover 100 (as the Austin Metro had been renamed) and Rover 200 models.

In an interesting commercial deal, Mayflower of Coventry agreed to manufacture the body shells, take the commercial risk in producing tools, but also take an enhanced proportion of the profits. Rover engineers then slotted in an enlarged version of the modern K-series 16-valve – which boasted 1,796cc and a choice of 118bhp or 143bhp, all mated to the latest 5-speed transmission from the 200. (The same engine/transmission package, incidentally, would also be adapted by the Lotus Elise.)

Independent suspension at front and rear was by wishbones, with springing by interconnected Hydragas units, as previously used on cars like the Metro/100 and, before that, on the Austin Allegro and Princess 18/22 ranges. Rack-and-pinion steering was standard, shortly to be augmented by the option of electric power assistance, and there were disc brakes at all corners.

The style, stubby but rounded, was of a pure two-seater, with space for stowage ahead of the toeboard (not much) and also behind the transverse engine. Wind-up door glasses were standard, there was a vast, steeply sloping windscreen, and the cabin was well furnished with inviting-looking seats. A removable hardtop soon became optional.

The new car, in other words, was no more pure-bred than the previous MGB, or the Midget, had ever been, but the engineers somehow melded the whole into an appealing package, and the use of the traditional MG octagon badge was all-important. Even though it had a rear-based weight distribution, the new car proved to handle well (if a little biased towards safe-but-not-exciting understeer), and even in lower-power (118bhp) guise it was a brisk performer.

The 143bhp version, complete with its high-revving variable valve timing feature, was capable of 130mph, which was one extreme, while the 118bhp type, with the optional Steptronic transmission which was later added, was the other. Five years after its launch, with up to 15,000 MGFs being produced every year, the company's gamble in re-introducing an MG sports car had clearly paid off. A much-revised version, the MGTF, was introduced in 2002.

Morgan 4/4

Morgan 4/4, second generation, introduced in 1955 (data for 1600 model of (1968-1982)

Built by: Morgan Motor Co. Ltd., Britain

Engine: Ford-manufactured, four cylinders, in line, in cast iron cylinder block. Bore and stroke 81 x 77.62mm, 1,599cc (3.19x 3.06in, 97.6cu.in). Cast iron cylinder head. Two overhead valves per cylinder, operation by pushrods and rockers from camshaft in side of cylinder block. One downdraught dual-choke Weber carburettor. Maximum power 88bhp at 5,400rpm. Maximum torque 96lb.ft at 3,600rpm. [4/4s were also built with various 4-cylinder engines and related gearboxes, from Ford and Fiat, from 36bhp to 121bhp.]

Transmission: Front engine, rear-wheel-drive, single dry plate diaphragm spring clutch and four-speed all-synchromesh manual gearbox, all in unit with engine. Remote **Chassis:** Separate steel chassis frame, with Z-section main

side members, and with tubular and fabricated cross-bracings and reinforcements. Steel-panelled body shell on wooden framing, in two-seater open-top sports car style, with separate front wings. Independent front suspension by sliding pillars and coil springs, and telescopic hydraulic dampers. Suspension of beam rear axle by half-elliptic leaf springs, with lever-arm hydraulic dampers. Worm-and-nut steering. Front disc, rear drum brakes. 15in wheels, either bolt-on steel disc or centre-lock wires. 5.60-15in tyres.

Dimensions: Wheelbase 8ft 0in (244cm), front track 3ft 11in (119.4cm), rear track 3ft 11in (119.4cm). Overall length 12ft 6in (381cm). Unladen weight 1,560lb (708kg). ▶

Below: This was the original style of 4/4, late 1930s, which would change little in the next 70 years.

▶ **History:** The twenty-first century Morgan 4/4 had much in common with the *original* 4/4 of 1936, which is just the way that Morgan wanted it to be. The Malvern-based company has never believed in changing a car which is still selling well, and the long waiting lists for what at first look like archaic machines proves their point.

First there were Morgan three-wheelers, then (from 1935) the first of the 4/4s. The Standard-engined Plus 4 followed in 1950, and a new-generation 4/4 was finally launched in 1955. Direct descendants of that mid-1950s 4/4 were still being made in the early 2000s, and there was no sign of demand drying up

All these cars were based on the same simple and rather flexible ladder style chassis frame, with its Z-section side members, and its stiff coil spring/pillar front suspension. Bodies were built up on wooden skeletons, mainly with steel panels, but with aluminium wherever weight could be saved

Two-seater or four-seater open tourers were on offer over the years. Floors, made of wood, would leak in heavy weather, the ride of the suspension was very hard, creature comforts were absolutely minimal- yet the clientele loved every minute of it.

Original 4/4 Series IIs used puny 36bhp side-valve Ford engines of 1,172cc matched to a three-speed gearbox, and over the years it was those components, not the chassis or body styles, which received attention. First of all, from 1960, Ford's brand-new short-stroke 997cc overhead-valve engine

complete with its four-speed gearbox, was adopted, then as that engine was enlarged by Ford, so it was adopted by Morgan. By 1968, when the engine had reached 1.6-litres, and 88bhp, the 4/4 1600, as it was called, had become a spirited performer.

Even though a much larger-engined Morgan, the vee-8-engined Plus 8 which was based on the same traditional chassis design, was now on the market, the four-cylinder-engined 4/4 types sold well. Morgan's cottage industry factory could not build more then ten cars a week, of which seven or eight would be 4/4s. This was sufficient to keep the waiting list well up, with customers willing to put down money as a deposit several *years* before their new toy would be ready.

The design seemed to be stable until the early 1980s, though changes were regular thereafter. First (and because Morgan could see an impending famine of Ford engines) the 4/4 was offered with a 98bhp/1.6-litre twin-cam Fiat engine, but Ford then began to supply new CVH (Escort-type) engines of 96bhp/1.6-litres, that engine being upgraded to 98bhp with fuel injection in the 1990s. From 1993 a new type of Ford engine, the 16-valve twin-cam 121bhp/1.8-litre 'Zetec' (Escort/Mondeo type) was standardised, and such 4/4s were capable of about 118mph.

In the same period, incidentally, Morgan had also re-introduced what they called a 'Plus 4' model. This was effectively a 4/4, but with more power and

larger 2-litre engines, originally from Fiat, but latterly from Rover, with the 134bhp fuel injected T16 type, though this range did not see out the 1990s.

Although the styling, and construction, had changed little over the years, much of the detail engineering had been upgraded to suit the four-fold increase in power. Five-speed transmissions were standardised in the 1990s, galvanised bodywork became optional from 1986, powder-coating was added to the chassis from the same period, disc front brakes were standardised from the early 1960s, and the tyre size crept up, all the way from 5.00-16in cross-ply in 1955 to 195/60VR15in radial-ply tyres in the mid-1990s.

Well over 8,000 4/4s had been produced by the opening of the twentieth century, and other retro-chic customers were still ready to join them.

Left: Morgans of all types gathered together for a club meeting. The 4/4 closest to the camera has an early type of drop-head-coupé style.

Morgan Plus-Four and Plus-Eight

Morgan Plus-Four and Plus-Eight, built from 1950 (data for 1954 Plus-Four)
Built by: Morgan Motor Co. Ltd., Britain.
Engine: Triumph manufactured. Four cylinders, in line, in three-bearing cast-iron block. Bore and stroke 83mm by 92mm, 1,991cc (3.27in × 3.62in, 121.5cu.in) Cast-iron cylinder head. Two overhead valves per cylinder operated by pushrods and rockers from single camshaft mounted in side of cylinder block. Twin semi-downdraught constant-vacuum SU carburettors. Maximum power 90bhp (net) at 4,800rpm. Maximum torque 130lb.ft at 2,600rpm.
Transmission: Single-dry-plate clutch in unit with engine. Moss four-speed Synchromesh manual gearbox (no synchromesh on first gear) mounted separately. Direct-acting central gear-change. Open propeller shaft to hypoid-bevel 'live' rear axle.
Chassis: Separate steel chassis frame, with A-section boxed side members and tubular and pressed cross-bracing members. Independent front suspension by sliding pillars and coil springs, with telescopic dampers. Rear suspension by semi-elliptic leaf springs, with lever-type hydraulic dampers. Worm-and-nut steering. Four-wheel hydraulically operated drum brakes (later models had front discs). Fly-off handbrake. 16in pressed steel-disc road wheels (optional centre-lock wire wheels). 5.25 × 16in tyres. Morgan-built two-seat sports, two-seat DH coupé or four-seat tourer coachwork to choice.
Dimensions: Wheelbase 8ft (244cvm), tracks (front and rear) 3ft 11in. (119cm) Overall length 11ft 8in (356cm). Unladen weight 1,900lb (862kg).

Above: Like other aspects of the design, the instrument panel display of the traditional Morgan changed little over the years. This was a late 1980s model.

Below: A separate chassis frame, separate wings and running boards, and wooden frames for the body shell have been typical Morgan features for more than 50 years.

▶ **History:** The present-day Morgan has, fairly accurately, been described as the only vintage car still in production. Like all *bon mots* this tends to be an exaggeration, but there is no doubt that the philosophy of Morgan design is entrenched in the 1930s. Although the engines, the performance and the details receive regular attention, the chassis, ride, roadholding, body style and construction are old designs with old fashioned results. The modern Plus Eight Morgan, with its 155bhp Rover-made 3½-litre engine and five-speed gearbox, was good for nearly 130mph with acceleration to match. Weather protection, noise-suppression and refinement do not match this, however.

Morgan machines have been built in the same Malvern Link factory, under the direction of the Morgan family, since Edwardian times. Up to 1936, however, every Morgan was a three-wheeler, with a single, driven, rear wheel – and three-wheeler production carried on into the early 1950s. In 1936, the first four-wheel Morgan, the four-seat 4/4, was revealed in a form which would be very familiar to present-day Morgan buyers. The sliding-pillar independent suspension used today was on that first 4/4, but it had been on the 1910 three-wheeler too! The Z section side members of the chassis frame are still a feature and the bodies, erected by Morgan themselves, were of simple steel foldings on an ash wood frame. Engines of the first 4/4s were side-valve Fords. Other pre-war 4/4 engines used were overhead-inlet, side-exhaust Coventry Climax 1100s and overhead-valve-converted Standard Ten engines of 1,267cc. After the war, the standard unit was used for a time, but when Standard decided to follow a 'one-model' (or rather a 'one-engine') policy, Morgan had to think again. Because of their links with Standard they decided to upgrade the 4/4 by fitting the big and heavy Standard Vangaurd unit of 2,088cc, along with a proprietary Moss gearbox.

The Plus-Four, as the new two-seat car was named, arrived in 1950, and soon made a name for itself in competition. Compared with the little 4/4 the new car was very much faster and more rugged. Even so, once Triumph had developed their TR2 sports car, it made sense for Morgan to use the tuned-up 2-litre engine. This, then, was the definitive Plus-Four, a car lighter and more accelerative than

either the Triumph TR2 or the Austin-Healy 100. During the life of the car, Morgan made few concessions to modernisation, although they improved the body style with a cowled nose and a sleeker tail. Disc front brakes were standardised late in the 1950s and when Triumph increased their TR engine size to 2,138cc Morgan followed them. For a time too they offered a 'Competition' model with Lawrence-tune TR engine and light-alloy body panels. In the meantime, from 1955, the 4/4 was re-introduced as a Series II, powered by Ford's side valve 1,172cc engine and matching gearbox. The 4/4 continues to this day, uprated regularly with the latest Ford engines – over-head-valve units being adopted in 1960.

With Triumph dropping the four-cylinder engine completely in 1967, it was clearly only a matter of time before supplies to Morgan ran out. From the autumn of 1968, then, it was no surprise to see that the Plus-Four was equipped with the 1,600cc Ford Cortina engine, and that the exciting Plus-Eight, was added to the range. This car is powered by the ex-Buick Rover 3½-litre V8 engine. When Rover introduced a manual gearbox for their engine, this replaced the old Moss gearbox, but it has itself been dropped in favour of the 'new' Rover 3500 five-speed box. Many features of the Plus-Four are evident in the Plus-Eight models. To take account of the greatly increased performance since the first Vanguard engine was fitted in 1950 (there is more than twice the power nowadays) the wheel tracks have been increased and fatter tyres and wider wheel rims introduced, along with better and more powerful brakes. Interior appointments have been improved, but the cockpit's size is little larger than it was a quarter of a century ago. More important than anything – the car's character had been maintained. Orders exceed the ten-per-week production capability and waiting lists still stretch ahead for years.

Below: Today's Morgan is the very fast vee-eight engined Plus Eight. The engine and gearbox are from Rover, but the rest is pure Morgan, built now to the standards and tastes of yester-year. Along with the 4/4, only about ten cars a week are built and sold.

Morgan Aero 8

Morgan Aero 8, introduced in 2000
Built by: Morgan Motor Co. Ltd., Britain.
Engine: BMW-manufactured, eight cylinders, in 90-degree vee, in five-main-bearing cast alloy cylinder block. Bore and stroke 92 x 82.7mm, 4,398cc (3.62 x 3.26in, 268.5cu.in). Two cast aluminium cylinder heads. Four valves per cylinder, operation by inverted bucket tappets and twin overhead camshafts per cylinder head. Bosch fuel injection. Maximum power 286bhp at 5,400rpm. Maximum torque 324lb.ft at 3,600rpm.
Transmission: Front engine, rear-wheel-drive, single dry plate diaphragm spring clutch and six-speed all-synchromesh manual gearbox, all in unit with front-mounted engine. Remote control, centre floor gearchange.
Chassis: Separate semi-monocoque aluminium chassis frame, glued from sub-assemblies, with aluminium-panelled wooden framed two-seater body, with separate front wings, in two-seater open Roadster style. Independent front suspension by coil springs and wishbones, independent rear suspension by coil springs and double wishbones. No anti-roll bars. Telescopic hydraulic dampers. Rack and pinion steering, with power assistance. Disc brakes for all four wheels, with vacuum servo assistance and ABS as standard. 18in centre-lock cast alloy road wheels, with 225/40-18in tyres.
Dimensions: Wheelbase 8ft 3.6in (253cm), front track 4ft 11.4in (151cm), rear track 4ft 11.4in (151cm). Overall length 13ft 6.2in (412cm). Unladen weight 2,503lb (1,135kg).
History: When Morgan launched the Aero 8 in 2000, it caused a real sensation. Not only was this the first genuine all-new Morgan of all time, but it was one whose quirky body style hid a genuinely advanced new assemblage of engineering features. Pundits were agreed that this would either make, or thoroughly break, the fiercely independent little British company.

Until then the Morgan pedigree had been continuous, as 4/4s had led to Plus 4s, back to 4/4s again, and on to Plus 8s, all with the same archaic suspension, body construction, and rock-hard ride. Here, now, was a new car which owed nothing to the past, looking at once old-fashioned and modern, yet hiding ultra-modern power train and chassis engineering.

Chief executive Charles Morgan, great-grandson of the original founder, was finally persuaded of the need for a new model in the mid-1990s, and his tiny team delivered precisely that. To lead the engineers, Morgan brought in Chris Lawrence, whose links went back to the time when Lawrencetune breathed on Morgans to go motor racing.

Wrapped around a bonded and riveted aluminium chassis by Alcoa was a

aluminium-panelled body shell on a wooden frame, which still had long sweeping wings, and running boards, but featured a pair of faired-in headlamps which, from some angles, appeared to be peering inwards rather than straight ahead.

Power was by BMW's ultra-modern four-valves per cylinder 4.4-litre V8 engine, backed by a six-speed Getrag gearbox: Somehow, in a very limited space under the frame, Morgan had even been able to include the catalytic converters normally fitted to equivalent BMWs. With 286bhp (and a lot more to come, one day, no doubt), this guaranteed a top speed of more than 150mph, which was a speed regime where Morgan had never visited before.

It also meant that the suspension would, at least, have to be modernised to suit, and so it was, for there was coil spring independent suspension at front *and* rear. To match all this, the rack-and-pinion steering had power assistance, there were disc brakes at all four wheels and, wonder of wonders for such a tiny company, ABS anti-lock braking was standard.

Morgan's on-going problem, which no family member had previously wanted to tackle, was that it had large and traditional client base to consider, and because they had always demonstrated a liking for the old-fashioned, there had never been any impetus to change. Charles Morgan, however, was looking to expand the business, which automatically meant finding new customers, and committed the company to producing this new model.

For all these reasons, the Aero 8 was vastly different from its predecessors. Although it looked somewhat like those cars – somehow it was more 'pastiche' then 'evolution' – it behaved in a completely different manner. It was colossally fast, of course – 0-100mph in 11.7 seconds was extremely impressive – but this was achieved with great smoothness and panache, as the engine was in precisely the same tune as fitted to BMW's own 5-Series saloons.

Because of its independent rear suspension, and the use of a limited-slip differential, traction was immeasurably better than that of the old rigid-axle Plus 8s, and the ride was softer than before, but by no means as limousine-like as some of its ultra-modern competitors.

In other words, here was a fascinating, and promising new Morgan which would take time (which in Morgan language means years) to settle down and mature. With production to be limited to not more than six cars a week, and with an instant two-year waiting list from the day the car went on sale, it would be years before the company needed to make further improvements. For the time being, though, it was enough to bask in the pleasure of producing an all-new Morgan four-wheeler – at last, after more than 65 years!

Left: The Aero 8 was the first all-new Morgan to be launched since the 1930s, yet retained a traditional style – but had modern engineering hidden away.

Mosler MT 900S

Mosler MT900S, introduced in 2000
Built by: Mosler Automotive, USA.
Engine: Chevrolet-manufactured, eight cylinders, in 90-degree vee, in five-main-bearing cast aluminium cylinder block. Bore and stroke 99.1 x 91.95mm, 5,665cc (3.90 x 3.62in, 346cu.in). Two aluminium cylinder heads. Two overhead valves per cylinder, operation by pushrods and rockers from camshaft mounted in the cylinder block vee: Bosch fuel injection. Maximum power 425bhp at unquoted rpm. Maximum torque not quoted.
Transmission: Mid engine, rear-wheel-drive, five-speed all-synchromesh manual gearbox, in unit with engine and final drive unit. Remote control, centre floor gearchange.
Chassis: Monocoque aluminium honeycomb/vac-formed glass-fibre composite chassis frame. Independent front suspension by coil springs, wishbones and anti-roll bar, independent rear suspension by coil springs, wishbones and anti-roll bar. Telescopic hydraulic dampers. Rack and pinion steering, with power assistance. Disc brakes at all four wheels, with vacuum servo assistance, and ABS brakes. Bolt-on cast alloy road wheels, 19in and 20in, with 255/40-19in (front) and 295/40-20in (rear) tyres. Body shell and skin panels manufactured from advanced composite materials, in two-seater fastback coupé style.
Dimensions: Wheelbase 9ft 1in (273.5cm), front track 5ft 8in (172.7cm), rear track 5ft 8in (172.7cm). Overall length 15ft 9in (480cm). Unladen weight 2,200lb (998kg).
History: Although North Americans buy many of them, their automotive industry does not normally design supercars. When the Mosler MT900 arrived in 2000, with a potential top speed of 200mph, and looking for all the world like a cross between a Jaguar XJ220 and a McLaren F1, it was the only such type in the USA.

The MT900 project began in 1998, when engineer Rod Trenne first approached Florida millionaire and inventor Warren Mosler, with the idea of producing a genuine, new, all-American supercar, mid-engined with rear-wheel-drive, and able to meet all regulations. Although Americans had never been besotted by the mid-engined layout (icons like the Dodge Viper, and every generation of the Corvette had classic front-engine/rear-drive installations), they were happy to accept it on true, dedicated, high-performance machinery like this.

Below: Modern technology was blended with aerospace engineering in evolving the mid-engined Mosler MT 900 model, which used a 5.7-litre Chevrolet engine.

Above: Although the Mosler MT 900 was all-American, its style, including the fold-forward doors, nodded to contemporary Italian trends.

Except for the use of a highly tuned Chevrolet Corvette engine (developed by US tuner Lingenfelter), this would be specially evolved. The company's pre-launch publicity, too, made much of its design 'in cyberspace' – which meant that computer-aided design, rather than drawing boards and pencils, had been used to lay it out.

Mosler Automotive, though small, had been in business since 1985, its original product being the Consulier GTP. This had been designed to win races, and to be a street-legal machine, though some considered it ugly, and only a handful were ever produced. The MT900 was intended to be prettier, more practical, and altogether more saleable than that.

Mosler wanted the new 900 to be a race car and a road car too – denoting the two types as 'S' for 'street' and 'R' for 'race car. Except that race cars would be even more powerful, and sit lower to the ground, with dedicated wheels and tyres, the two types were remarkably similar. The new car was blessed with stunning looks, rounded, and ultra-low, so if the running gear matched up it was bound to be an intriguing proposition.

Trenne's chassis layout was at once advanced, yet practical. The use of aluminium honeycomb and glass-fibre for the chassis, topped by carbon fibre body panels, was well-established, and of course the entire North American high-performance industry had been in love with Chevrolet Corvette engines for many years.

Although the chassis layout, and in particular the materials chosen, were unique to this car, much of the chassis engineering – suspension and brakes in particular – we based on that of the latest Chevrolet Corvette. At a price that was bound to approach $200,000 in finalised form, this car would have to be effective *and* well-equipped. Immense performance would be a given (Mosler, in any case, intended it to be the 'R' version for GT racing in the USA), and for the street-car (S) derivative it was good to see that air conditioning, electric window lifts, traction control, power-assisted steering and anti-lock brakes would all be standard..

Perhaps it was well that Mosler's owner, Warren Mosler, was an out-and-out petrol head, for this was bound to be a very ambitious venture. Mosler himself still liked to go motor racing, but would he find enough customers to keep his small company alive? With sales beginning only in 2002, it will take time for this to become clear.

Nash-Healey

Nash-Healey, built from 1950 to 1954 (data for original model)

Built by: Donald Healey Motor Co. Ltd., Britain.

Engine: Nash manufactured, six cylinders, in line, in four-main-bearing cast iron cylinder block. Bore and stroke 85.72 x 111.1mm, 3,848cc (3.37 x 4.37in 235cu.in). Cast iron cylinder head. Two overhead valves per cylinder, operation by pushrods and rockers from a camshaft in the cylinder block. Twin horizontal SU carburettors. Maximum power 125bhp at 4,000rpm. Maximum torque 210lb.ft at 1,600rpm. [From 1952, this model was sold with 135bhp/4.2-litre engine.]

Transmission: Front engine, rear-wheel-drive, single dry plate clutch and three speed synchromesh manual gearbox, with mechanical overdrive on top gear, all in unit with engine. Direct action centre floor gearchange.

Chassis: Separate steel chassis frame, with box-section side members, box and fabricated reinforcements. Aluminium and steel panels on wooden skeleton body shell, in two-seater open roadster style. Independent front suspension by coil springs and trailing links, anti-roll bar and piston-type hydraulic dampers, suspension of beam rear axle by coil springs, radius arms

and Panhard rod, with telescopic hydraulic dampers. Worm type steering. Drum brakes at all four wheels. 15in bolt-on steel wheels, with 6.40-15in tyres.

Dimensions: Wheelbase 8ft 6in (259cm), front track 4ft 5in (134.6cm), rear track 4ft 7in (139.7cm). Overall length 14ft 4in (386cm). Unladen weight 2,688lb 1,219kg).

History: Certainly the only sports car to be born after a chance meeting on the *Queen_Elizabeth* liner, the Nash-Healey was conceived by Donald Healey and George Mason (of the Nash motor car business in the USA). The object, basically, was to produce a new sports car, which would combine Healey chassis engineering and know-how with Nash's own engine and transmission. It would be sold only in the USA.

The process sounded simple enough, but it was only Healey's small-company know-how which made it possible. Nash provided the long, heavy and bulky 3.8-litre six-cylinder engine, and its related gearbox, Healey somehow mated it with its existing (usually Riley-engined) chassis, and a new two-seater sports car body style by Panelcraft completed the transformation.

In 1950 this new car's reception was so favourable that almost all  production of Riley-engined Healeys had to be suspended to make space for it at Warwick. 'Works' cars raced successfully in the Mille Miglia, and at Le Mans, the two companies garnering great publicity.

More than 100 such cars were produced in 1951 before assembly was suspended. At this point an agreement was forged with Farina of Italy (who already had agreements with Nash), who agreed to rework the body style, to take over production of shells, and deliver complete cars directly to the USA.. Such cars, henceforth with 4.2-litre engines, went on sale in 1952, and would be built until 1954.

The Italian-styled cars not only looked smarter than the original British types (the revised machines had headlamps inset from the wings, in the extremities of the grilles), but they were more completely equipped too. All this, a reported top speed of around 110mph, and a racing record which included third place at Le Mans, made this unique machine a great success.

By 1954, however, Healey was totally bound up in evolving the new Austin-Healey 100, and the Nash-Healey had to be abandoned; a total of 506 such cars had been built.

Left: This Nash-Healey, with British chassis, American engine, and Italian body by Pininfarina, was truly a multi-national automotive effort.

Nissan 300ZX family

Nissan 300ZX family, built from 1983 to 1990 (data for 2+2-seater)
Built by: Nissan Motor Co. Ltd., Japan.

Engine: Six cylinders, in 60-degree vee formation, in four-main-bearing cast ir
cylinder block. Bore and stroke 87 x 83mm, 2,960cc (3.42 x 3.27in, 180.7cu.i
Two aluminium cylinder heads Two valves per cylinder, opposed in pa
spherical cylinder heads, operation by rockers from single overhead camsh
in each cylinder head. Bosch fuel injection. Maximum power 170bhp
5,600rpm. Maximum torque 175lb.ft at 4,400rpm.

Transmission: Front engine, rear-wheel-drive, single dry plate diaphrag
spring clutch and five-speed all-synchromesh manual gearbox, all in unit wi
engine. Remote control centre floor gearchange. Optional four-speed automa
transmission.

Chassis: Unitary construction combined steel body/chassis structure, w
steel body shell in 2+2-seat fastback coupé style. Independent fro
suspension by coil springs, MacPherson struts, and anti-roll bar, independe
rear suspension by coil springs, semi-trailing links, and anti-roll bar. Rack-ar
pinion steering, with power assistance. Disc brakes for all four wheels, wi
vacuum servo assistance and optional ABS anti-lock. 15in bolt-on cast-alloy ro
wheels, with 215/60-15in tyres.

Dimensions: Wheelbase 8ft 3.2in (cm), front track 4ft 7.7in (141.5cm), re
track 4ft 8.5in (143.5cm). Overall length 14ft 10.5in (453cm). Unladen weic
3,055lb (1,385kg).

[Turbocharged engine also available, with 228bhp at 5,400rpm. As befo
also available as two-seater, with shorter by 7.9in/20cm wheelbase and cabi

History: Stand by for a short, but headache-inducing history lesson. First of
in the late 1960s, there had been Datsun 240Zs, the same car also being kno
as a Nissan Fairlady in some markets. Then, from 1975, there were the secor
generation types, more often known as Nissan 280Zs, sometimes 280ZXs, a
only occasionally as Datsuns. These were bigger, heavier, but not as integrat
as the original types – yet they sold in large numbers.

By 1983 Nissan was ready to launch a third-generation car, marketing it o
as a Nissan-badged car, making sure that it had ZX in its title at all times, a

equipping it with a brand-new corporate V6 engine. Later, in the 1990s, there would be another generation of 'Z-Cars', which would be heavier, and less sporting, than before.

The third-generation Z-Car, known as ZX, and available in two-seater or 2+2-seater coupé form, might have looked rather like the ousted 280ZX, but was totally different in every way. Not only did have a completely new and much more aerodynamically efficient body structure, but because of its new 170bhp – 228bhp with turbocharging – engine it had moved into a higher-performance bracket.

Built on the same 91.3in/232cm (two-seater) or 99.2in/252cm (2+2-seater) wheelbases as before, the 300ZX's chassis platform looked very familiar, for it had MacPherson strut suspension up front, and coil spring/semi-trailing links at the rear. It was the engine, of course, which made all the difference. Nissan, like other major manufacturers, had concluded that a 60-degree vee-6 engine – one which was, effectively, as broad as it was long – would best fill their large-car needs, for such an engine could be mounted either in line, or transversely in a front-wheel-drive car. Although Nissan still had no front-drive plans at this level, they were looking a long way ahead.

Most of these engines were 3-litre units, but (for fiscal reasons) there was also to be a turbocharged unit in Japan. All types were compact, and neatly detailed, the cylinder heads featuring opposed valves, each line being operated by rockers from a single, centrally mounted camshaft in each cylinder head.

In moving from 280ZX to 300ZX, Nissan had also moved the character of these cars. They were all sports cars, for sure, most of them being built with permanently fixed roof structures, but in an attempt to provide open-air motoring there was also an opening-panel 'T-bar' derivative too. The cabin was the important bit more capacious than before. Most importantly, the aerodynamic performance of what was quite a bulky shell had been improved considerably. Changes, all of which had an effect, included a re-raked windscreen, a more drooping nose, differently positioned rectangular headlamps which were semi-retractable (it was as if there were half-permanent lids over them), while the screen itself was flush-mounted.

The new car was given a significantly softer ride than its predecessors, an evolution apparently requested by those customers (a majority) who lived in North America. As a trade-off, however, Nissan equipped the turbocharged version with adjustable dampers, they setting of which were controlled from a switch on the centre console between the seats.

This, by any standards, was a fast car. Although Nissan talked wistfully of 150mph top speeds, a pace of 140mph was rarely exceeded. Even so, the 300ZX sold at least as well as its ancestors. In the early 1970s, 45,000 – 50,000 240Z types were being sold every year, and in the early 1980s this had risen to 65,000 – 70,000 a year. Now, with the 300ZX, Nissan was looking for sales in advance of 70,000 every year – a figure of which any of its rivals would have been proud to achieve.

Left: Although the mid-1980s Nissan 300ZX was purely Japanese, it was aimed to sell well in North America, the styling influences being obvious.

Noble M12 GTO

Noble M12 GTO, introduced in 2001
Built by: Noble Moy Automotive Ltd., Britain.
Engine: Ford-USA manufactured, six cylinders, in 60-degree vee, in ca
aluminium cylinder block. Bore and stroke 82.4 x 79.5mm, 2,595cc (3.24
3.13in, 158.4cu.in). Two light-alloy cylinder heads. Four valves per cylind
opposed in narrow vee, operation by inverted bucket tappets and tw
overhead camshafts per cylinder head. Magnetti Marelli fuel injection and tw
Garrett turbochargers. Maximum power 310bhp at 6,000rpm. Maximum torq
320lb.ft at 3,500rpm.
Transmission: Transverse mid-engine, rear-wheel-drive, single dry pla
diaphragm spring clutch and five-speed all-synchromesh manual gearbox, all
unit with engine. Remote control, centre floor gearchange.
Chassis: Separate steel multi-tube chassis space-frame, with steel body sh
in two-seat seat fastback coupé style . Independent front suspension by c
springs and wishbones, independent rear suspension by coil springs a
wishbones. Telescopic hydraulic dampers. Rack-and-pinion steering, w
power assistance. Disc brakes at all four wheels, with vacuum ser
assistance, but no ABS. 18in centre-lock cast alloy wheels, with 225/50-18
(front) and 265/35-18in (rear) tyres.
Dimensions: Wheelbase 8ft 0in (243.8cm), front track 5ft 0in (152cm), re
track 4ft 11in (150cm). Overall length 13ft 5in (408.9cm). Unladen weig
2,161lb (980kg).

**Below: Lee Noble's M12 Supercar featured a transverse-positions Ford
V6 engine, which was mounted behind the two-seater cabin.**

Above: Although the M12 GTO only had 310bhp – a modest figure by 2000s-standards – it was extremely fast, and handled like a race car.

History: Far too many fine prototypes have to be abandoned, and become no more than footnotes in motoring history. At one time the earlier Noble products looked likely to join that long list, but as the M12 of 2001 slowly got into production, its future looked sound. Designed by Lee Noble, with backing from Tony Moy, a notable figure in the travel agency business, here was a mid-engined sports coupé which seemed to be reliable, and well-detailed, right from the start. ▶

▶ Noble himself already had a good reputation in the sports car business, f
it was his previous Ultima car which was used as an early 'mule' whe
McLaren needed to get early prototype experience for their F1 road car proje
Accordingly, with new backing, the use of a multi-tube space frame, and
mid/rear-engine position, was expected.

But not this combination. Having studied the availability of 'building block
Noble chose to use the new four-cam V6 engine normally seen in front-whe
drive Ford Mondeos, linked it to the five-speed manual transmission of t
same car and – Fiat X1/9 fashion – then positioned the whole package behi
the two-seater cabin. That, on its own, would not have been enough, for t
standard engine produced less than 170bhp, so Noble then arranged to give t
engine the twin-turbo tune-up treatment, the result being 310bhp in what w
only a 2,160lb/980kg motor car.

Above: The Noble M12 GTO was a compact and neatly detailed mid-engined two-seater, whose proportions were similar to those of the Lotus Esprit.

So far so good, and once a good-handling car (to race-car standards, some say) had been clothed in an extremely smart two-seater fastback coupé body, the M12 was ready for production.

The big free-standing transverse aerofoil above the engine lid was there for a purpose, to trim the high-speed handling, and all the signs were that the aerodynamic drag was low, and that a 150mph-plus top speed was assured.

Yet this was a car that cost £44,950 at the very beginning of its career – it would need a growing list of satisfied customers to turn a Great Idea into an established marque.

Pagani Zonda C12

Pagani Zonda C12, introduced in 1999
Built by: Pagani Automobili SrL, Italy.
Engine: Mercedes-Benz manufactured, 12 cylinders, in 60-degree vee
formation, in seven-main-bearing light alloy cylinder block. Capacity 7,291cc
(445cu.in). Two light-alloy cylinder heads. Four valves per cylinder, in narrow vee
formation, operation by twin overhead camshafts in each cylinder head. Bosch
fuel injection. Maximum power 555bhp at 5,900rpm. Maximum torque 553lb.ft
at 4,050rpm.
Transmission: Mid-engine, rear-wheel-drive, dry multi-plate clutch and six-
speed all-synchromesh manual gearbox, in unit with engine and final drive.
Remote control, centre floor gearchange.
Chassis: Separate carbon fibre centre chassis frame, with multi-tubular space-
frame attachments, clothed in carbon fibre (some light-alloy) two-seater body
shell in fastback coupé style. Independent front suspension by coil springs,
wishbones and anti-roll bar, independent rear suspension by coil springs,
wishbones and anti-roll bar. Telescopic hydraulic dampers. Rack-and-pinion
steering, with power assistance. Disc brakes for all four wheels, with vacuum
servo assistance, but no ABS. 18in bolt-on cast alloy road wheels, with 245/35-
18in (front) and 335/30-18in (rear) tyres.
Dimensions: Wheelbase 8ft 11.4in (273cm), front track 5ft 6.0in (167.5cm),
rear track 5ft 5.3in (166cm). Overall length 14ft 5in (439.5cm). Unladen weight
2,756lb (1,250kg).

**Below: Although the Pagani name was not well-known in 1999, its
engineer (Horacio Pagani) had already done much work on Lamborghini
models.**

Above: Not much space inside the cabin of the Pagani Zonda C12, for this was a short-wheelbase two-seater, with much race car heritage built in.

History: When Horacio Pagani's personal dream car, the C12, first broke cover in 1999, testers described it as an old-fashioned supercar, one where sheer brute power, and an uncompromising cabin-forward two-seater style shouted its aim for supremacy. If cars like the ageing Lamborghini Diablo were ever to face competition, this surely was it?

It wasn't merely that the engine came with the best possible pedigree – it was to be an AMG-prepared, 7.3-litre, Mercedes-Benz V12 with no less than 555bhp – but that the proprietor did so too. Pagani himself was no mere rich romantic, but an Argentine-born engineer and long-time friend of Juan-Manuel Fangio, who had moved to Italy, and was already credited with much work at Lamborghini on the Countach Evoluzione and on Diablo concepts.

Having set up his own little company, Modena Design, in the late 1980s, Pagani specialised in carbon composites and engineering, and picked up much consultance from Ferrari, Dallara, Lamborghini and Renault.

According to Pagani himself, the C12 is a tribute to Fangio (which, maybe, explains the use of a Mercedes-Benz engine and some ▶

▶ resemblance to a Group C Mercedes-Benz race car, for at the height of his fame Fangio was always linked to the mighty German concern), while the style was reputedly influenced by Pagani's wife's hour-glass figure: so Pagani was a romantic after all!

Because Pagani Automobili SrL was small, and self-financed, the C12 had to be a relatively simple machine. This explains why there was no four-wheel-drive to compete with the Lamborghini, no own-brand engine, no ABS braking, and a simple rather than a totally equipped cabin. Even so, it looked fiercely functional, brutally effective, and there was no doubt that it was amazingly fast. Those detecting a Group C racing character were backed-up by the very

Above: Like the Ferraris and Lamborghinis with which it fought, the Pagani was a fierce, ultra-powerful, 220mph animal, deserving great respect.

aggressive style, by the wonderful noise of the AMG-tuned vee-12, and by the way it seemed to promise 200mph even when standing still.

Yet the C12 certainly delivered all that it promised – and much more. Pagani himself said that 210mph was available, and no-one disbelieved that, and though this was a man's car, with heavy controls, a notchy gearchange, and no ABS brakes because Pagani himself preferred it that way, it was still an astonishing complete car.

▶ It was not merely that it looked fast, and was *very* fast, but that the car was obviously engineered well, with every detail worked out. More important, especially at the price asked, which was in the order of £275,000/$400,000, was that it was obviously carefully built, No loose panels, no raw edges, no silly leaks or rattles – this was a car meant to offer real value. And there was more – every slot, every air intake, every aerofoil section, and every super-wide tyre had a function.

Pagani didn't expect to sell more than 20 cars a year, and the company directors were adamant that they could not build more than 25, even if big cheques were waved in front of their noses. This was a car, maybe, which did not have the cachet of a world-renowned badge on its nose (not yet anyway), and it wasn't being sold at a bargain price – but it was already one of the most accomplished two-seater supercars the world had ever seen.

And where did it come from? From Modena, of course. Where else?

Right: Pagani Zonda C12 power was by a 7.3-litre Mercedes-Benz vee-12 engine, which guaranteed a top speed of 220mph.

Below: Like all Supercars of the late 1990s, the Zonda C12 had huge rear tyres to deal with colossal horsepower, with a transverse spoiler to trim the downforce.

Panoz Esperante

Panoz Esperante, introduced in 2000
Built by: Panoz Auto Development Co., USA.
Engine: Ford-USA manufactured, eight cylinders, in 90-degree vee, in five-main-bearing light alloy cylinder block. Bore and stroke 90.2 x 90mm, 4,601cc (3.55 x 3.54in, 280cu.in). Two light-alloy cylinder heads. Four valves per cylinder, opposed in narrow vee, operation by bucket tappets from twin overhead camshafts in each cylinder head. Ford electronic fuel injection. Maximum power 320bhp at 6,000rpm. Maximum torque 315lb.ft at 4,750rpm.
Transmission: Front engine, rear-wheel-drive, single dry plate diaphragm spring clutch and five-speed all-synchromesh manual gearbox, in unit with engine. Remote control centre floor gearchange.
Chassis: Extruded aluminium separate chassis frame, with steel subframes bolted and boned to the assembly. Independent front suspension by coil springs, wishbones and anti-roll bar, independent rear suspension by coil springs, wishbones and anti-roll bar. Telescopic, hydraulic, gas-filled, dampers. Rack-and-pinion steering, power-assisted. Disc brakes for all four wheels, with vacuum servo assistance, and ABS. 17in bolt-on cast alloy road wheels, with 255/45-17in tyres. Aluminium panelled two-seater coupé body style.
Dimensions: Wheelbase 8ft 10in (269cm), front track 5ft 1in (154.6cm), rear track 5ft 3.2in (158cm). Overall length 14ft 8.3in (447.5cm). Unladen weight 3,263lb (1,480kg).

Above: Because the Esperante was a limited-production car, it relied on many Ford Mustang parts, though the ensemble was very appealing.

History: North American millionaire and sports-car racing enthusiast Don Panoz, whose base was in Atlanta, elected to build on the reputation of his race cars by launching a production sports car which would use mainly American pieces, but still be a domestic product. The result was the Esperante, which was previewed in 1999, went into production in 2000, and was delivered in slow, but steady numbers, thereafter.

For a vignette of its size and market intention, think of a Jaguar XK8 or Mercedes-Benz SL type of sports car, well-trimmed and equipped (the soft-top was electrically retracted), with excellent sporting character, and a top speed which would exceed 150mph. The Esperante, in other words, was an indulgence for most of its buyers, who would be North American, for there was nowhere on the public highway that it could be unleashed. Not that Don Panoz minded too much – for his strategy also included building lightweight, more powerful, versions to go motor racing in North American events.

Designed by the DZN Studio in ▶

Left: In so many ways the Panoz Esperante set out to be a more civilised alternative to the Dodge Viper, but used a Ford Mustang engine.

▶ California, the Esperante carried a neat and somehow understated style – it was certainly no more flamboyant than the Jaguars and Mercedes-Benz types which have already been mentioned. Although Panoz's own literature described it as 'front/mid-engined', this merely meant that the 4.6-litre Ford V8 engine (the most modern variety, with four-valves per cylinder and twin-cam cylinder heads, as used in Ford Mustangs and various Lincolns) was set well-back in the engine bay at the front

The chassis layout, too, was conventional by 2000s standards for there were various extruded aluminium sections, all bonded and bolted together according to aerospace methods. The body shell, too, was in aluminium hand-crafted and very carefully detailed. Suspension – independent at front and rear, the rear lifted from the Mustang Cobra – had been engineered and detailed with advice from Panoz's own race-car designers, for this car had already been raced before the public got its hands on the road cars.

Unlike his contemporary sports car rivals in the USA, such as Mosler and Saleen, Panoz was aiming at an 'affordable' rather than a 'supercar' marketing sector. In fact, having taken a look at the style, a detailed study of the specification soon proved that point.

Not only was the 320bhp engine, and its matching five-speed gearbox lifted straight out of the Ford Mustang Cobra, but so was the Mustang windscreen, its brakes, and quite a lot of that car's instrumentation and switch-gear. Panoz's point, crisply and repeatedly made, was that he was aiming at a particular type of buyer, who would pay a certain amount of money (Porsche

customers, in particular, were being targeted), and to get down to that price, he needed to raid the parts bin of a benevolent car company. Not only that, but if he found a customer in Smallville, Mid-West, USA, he wanted that customer to be able to drive down to his local Ford dealer for parts and service – at Ford prices.

If the quality of this new model could be kept up, it was a philosophy which might just work, as the Esperante's technical and visual merit was matched by good financial backing, and by a growing reputation. Once one studied the essence of the Esperante, and dug into its character, it certainly lived up to all that. The impression of broad-shouldered power, a vee-8 rumble, and brash character was backed up by the delivery, and the fact that here was an engine quite unstressed by contemporary sports car standards. Panos claimed that they had spent countless hours, not only on getting the performance right, but on making it sound right too.

With a top speed of at least 155mph, and 0-60mph in only 5.0sec, they had certainly achieved as much as their long-established rivals, and experience showed that the rear-drive handling was well up to expectations too. But, when faced up against the 911, the XK8 and the SL, would it attract enough custom? With sales in Europe promised for 2003, Don Panoz was determined that it should.

Below: The Panoz Esperante's aluminium body hides Ford Mustang engine, transmissions, brakes and suspension, but its character was quite unique.

Pegaso Z102

Z102 cars, built from 1951 to 1958 (data for 1951 Z102)

Built by: Empresa Nacional de Autocamiones SA., Spain.

Engine: Eight cylinders, in 90-degree vee-formation, in five-bearing light-alloy block/crankcase. Bore and stroke 75mm by 70mm, 2,474cc (2.75in, 151cu.in). Two over-head valves per cylinder, opposed to each other at 90-degrees in part-spherical combustion chambers and operated by twin overhead cam-shafts per cylinder head. Dry-sump lubrication. Single down-draught twin-choke. Webber carburettor. Maximum power 140bhp at 6,000rpm. Maximum torque 135lb.ft at 3,900rpm. Alternative engines, either with higher-compression heads and twin Weber carburettors, or bored-out to 2.8 litres and with original carburation, were available.

Transmission: Single-dry-plate clutch, in unit with front-mounted engine. Open propeller shaft to five-speed manual gearbox (without synchromesh), in unit with spiral-bevel final drive. Remote-control central gearchange.

Chassis: Unitary-construction pressed-steel and light-alloy body/chassis structure. Independent front suspension by wishbones and longitudinal torsion bars. De Dion rear suspension, with transverse torsion bars, radius arms, and sideways slide-block location. Telescopic dampers. Four-wheel hydraulically operated rum brakes, inboard at rear. 16in centre-lock wire wheels. 6.00 × 16in tyres.

Dimensions: Wheelbase 7ft 8in (234cm), track (front) 4ft 4in (132cm), track (rear) 4ft 2.7in (128.8cm). Overall length 13ft 4in (406cm). Unladen weight 2,160lb (980kg).

History: The only post-war Spanish car to achieve international 'super car' fame in the 1950s was the Pegaso, designed by Wilfredo Ricart (ex-Alfa Romeo) and built in a factory once occupied by Hispano-Suiza. The Z102 was first shown in 1951 and was a thoroughly exotic and modern design, obviously meant for small-scale production at high cost. The company was government-backed and had already

Below: Just about every Pegaso Z102 coupé was hand-built. Both these 1953 models have Touring of Milan body styles, but differ considerably in tail treatment. Hidden away is the unique Spanish twin-cam vee-8 engine, in this case of 2.8-litre capacity, along with a five-speed gearbox, and advanced De Dion rear suspension.

Above: The Pegaso out-ran Ferrari in many respects, even performance, and the body styles (this was from Touring) were always elegant.

made its name with unitary-construction coaches of more than 9-litres.

The original car had a 2½-litre V8 engine, with four overhead camshafts, dry-sump lubrication, a five-speed gearbox in unit with the back axle and De Dion rear suspension. Later developments, also at a very low rate of production, were the Z102B (with 2.8-litres and 210bhp), the Z102SS (with 3.2-litres and up to 280bhp) and finally the Z103 series (which had a rather different overhead valve engine of 4.0, 4.5 or 4.7-litres). The cars were supplied with a bewildering variety of engine tunes, including a few with superchargers, and one or two sprint records were taken in 1953. The cars were strikingly styled in the Italian-coupé manner. When Ricart retired in 1958, car production ceased. Only about 125 Pegasos were made in all.

Porsche 356

Porsche 356 cars, built from 1948 to 1965 (data for 1960-type S90)
Built by: Dr. Ing.h.c. F. Porsche KG., West Germany.
Engine: Four cylinders, horizontally opposed, in three-bearing, light-alloy block/crankcase, air cooled. Bore and stroke 82.5mm by 74mm, 1,582cc (3.25in × 2.91in, 96.5cu.in). Two light-alloy cylinder heads. Two overhead valves per cylinder operated by pushrods and rockers from single camshaft, centrally mounted in crankcase. Two downdraught Zenith carburettors. Maximum power 90bhp (net) at 5,500rpm. Maximum torque 89lb.ft at 4,300rpm.

Transmission: Single-dry-plate clutch, and four-speed, all-synchromesh manual gearbox, both in unit with rear-mounted engine. Engine behind line of rear wheels and gearbox ahead of it. Remote-control central gearchange. Spiral-bevel final drive, and exposed, universally jointed drive shafts to rear wheels.

Chassis: Pressed-steel punt-type chassis frame, topped by pressed-steel and light-alloy-panelled coupé or convertible bodyshells. Independent VW-type front suspension by trailing arms, transverse torsion bars and anti-roll bar. Independent rear suspension by swinging half-axles, radius arms and transverse torsion bars. Telescopic dampers. Worm-and-roller steering. Four-wheel, hydraulically operated drum brakes. 15in pressed-steel-disc wheels. 5.60 × 15in tyres.

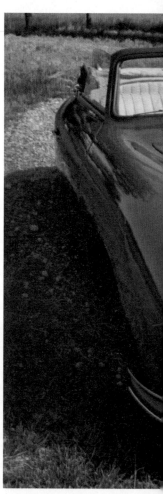

Dimensions: Wheelbase 6ft 10.7in (210cm), track (front) 4ft 3.4in (130.5cm), track (rear) 4ft 2.1in (127cm). Overall length 13ft 1.9in (401cm). Unladen weight 1,985lb (900kg).

History: Dr. Porsche had been in the centre of modern motor car development since Edwardian times, but it was son Ferry who laid out the bare bones of the Porsche car project after World War II. Using VW Beetle mechanical equipment – engines, transmissions and suspensions – Porsche built their very first car in 1948 and this had the engine ahead of the rear wheel line. However, all production cars reverted to the familiar VW-style layout, with the air-cooled flat-four engine overhanging the rear wheels.

Type 356, incidentally, indicates that this was the 356th project undertaken by the Porsche design office since its formation in 1930. Early Porsches were 1100s, with very nearly standard VW

Right: Only an expert can tell the age and pedigree of a Porsche 356 from a picture. This is a 1951 Cabriolet – note the divided screen and flush-fitting headlamps. Engines from 1,100cc to 2,000cc were supplied, and the last of all 356s was built in 1964.

engines, but they very rapidly found success in motor racing and proved to be surprisingly strong rally cars.

Production was well under way by 1950, when steel-bodied cars were phased in at the new Zuffenhausen works, to replace the original light-alloy. Enlargement began in 1951 when the 1,286cc car was announced, 1,488cc Porsches were revealed in 1951 and the first 1,582cc car followed in 1955. This engine, developed from its original 60bhp output to 95bhp in 1965, was standardised for the last ten years of the 356's life. In all this time there was only one significant restyling operation – in 1959 when headlamps and bumpers were raised, the windscreen enlarged and trim updated. The Porsche's shape was always aerodynamically efficient, and the last of the Super 90s was good for 115mph, with excellent fuel economy. Although the 356 carried on until 1965, it was effectively replaced by the 911 series, which went into series production in 1964.

Porsche 911

Porsche 911 and 912 models, built from 1963 to 1999 (data for 1976 3-litre Turbo)

Built by: Dr. Ing.h.c. F. Porsche KG., Germany.

Engine: Six cylinders, horizontally opposed, in detachable finned light-alloy barrels, with two-piece, eight-bearing magnesium crankcase. Air cooled. Bore and stroke 95mm by 70.4mm, 2,994cc (3.74in × 2.77in, 182.7cu.in). Detachable light-alloy cylinder heads. Two overhead valves per cylinder, inclined to each other in part-spherical combustion chambers and operated by rockers from single overhead camshafts; Bosch fuel injection and KKK turbocharger. Dry sump lubrication. Maximum power 260bhp (DIN) at 5,500rpm. Maximum torque 253lg.ft at 4,000rpm.

Transmission: Single-dry-plate clutch and four-speed, all-synchromesh manual gearbox, in transaxle assembly. Engine behind line of rear wheels, gearbox ahead of it. Remote-control central gearchange. Hypoid-bevel final drive. Exposed universally jointed drive shafts to rear wheels.

Chassis: Unitary-construction pressed-steel body-chassis unit. Rear-mounted engine/transmission, engine overhung to rear of car. All-independent

suspension, front by lower wishbones, torsion bars and anti-roll bar, rear by semi-trailing links, transverse torsion bars and anti-roll bar. Telescopic dampers. Rack-and-pinion steering. Four-wheel hydraulically operated disc brakes. 15in forged aluminium-alloy road wheels, 205 × 15in front tyres, 225 × 15in rear tyres.
Dimensions: Wheelbase 7ft 5in (226cm), track (front) 4ft 8.5in (143cm), track (rear) 5ft 1in (155cm). Overall length 14ft 2in (432cm). Unladen weight 2,700lb (1,224kg).
History: To replace the legendary Type 356 family, Porsche embarked on an entirely new design. Although no old component was carried forward the design philosophy was not changed – the car still had a rear-mounted, horizontally opposed, air-cooled engine, a 2+2 seating arrangement and a sleek closed coupé body style. In case of the 911, the engine was a flat-six, with a single overhead cam-shaft per bank, and there was a five-speed or four-speed gearbox according to the model. Although the 911 was in a different, higher, price class than the 356 once this had been drawn a 912 model was sold with the 1,582cc Super 90's flat-four unit installed. Even in this guise the car could clock up 120mph, but 130 was quite normal for the sixes. The 911 was launched as a 2-

litre in 1963, and was in production by the following summer. The 911S was a highly tuned version with 160bhp, and was immediately successful in en-durance racing and rallying. Over the years the car was further developed: the 2-litre engine became 2.2-litres in 1969, 2.4-litres in 1971, and 2.7-litres in 1973. There have been 3.0-litres since 1975 and 3.3-litres since 1977.

Also introduced in the model's long life span had been the removable-roof 'Targa' body style, and the semi-automatic 'Sportomatic' transmission, but the most sensational development of all was the 3-litre Porsche Turbo. This installation, proved first in prototype racing, had an exhaust-gas-driven turbocharger to boost the inlet mixture, is very tractable, and endows the car with a maximum speed of more than 160mph. Even with twice as much power as the original 911 had, the Porsche Turbo's handling is probably safer and more predictable than ever and the aerodynamic aids (including the large engine-lid spoiler) make it very stable at high speeds. All 911s have an impressive reliability record, and recent versions use galvanised structural panels, a seven-year guarantee being offered accordingly.

Left: Announced in 1963, the Porsche 911 sold well ever since. Engines have been enlarged from 2-litre to 3.3-litre over the years. The basic two-door fastback always looks good.

Porsche 959

Porsche 959 sports coupé, built in 1987 and 1988
Built by: Dr. Ing. h.c. F. Porsche KG, Germany.
Engine: Six cylinders, in 'boxer' horizontally opposed formation, in seven bearing light-alloy cylinder block/crankcase. Bore and stroke 95 × 67mm, 2,851cc (3.74 × 2.64in, 174cu.in). Two light-alloy cylinder heads. Four valves per cylinder, in vee, operation by twin overhead camshafts and inverted bucket tappets. Bosch fuel injection and twin KKK turbochargers. Maximum power 450bhp (DIN) at 6,500rpm. Maximum torque 370lb.ft at 5,500rpm.
Transmission: Four-wheel-drive, single-plate-diaphragm spring clutch and six-speed all-synchromesh manual gearbox, all in unit with rear-mounted engine. Remote-control, central gearchange.
Chassis: Unitary-construction pressed-steel body-chassis unit in two-door 2+2 seater coupé layout. Independent front suspension by coil springs, wishbones, telescopic dampers, and anti-roll bar. Independent rear suspension by coil springs, wishbones, telescopic dampers, anti-roll bar. Electronic ride control at front and rear. Rack-and-pinion steering with hydraulic power assistance. Four-wheel disc brakes with power assistance and anti-lock. Cast light alloy 17in road wheels, 235/45-17in (front) and 255/45-17in (rear) tyres.
Dimensions: Wheelbase 7ft 5.4in (227.2cm), front track 4ft 11.2in (150.4cm) rear track 5ft 1.0in (155cm). Overall length 13ft 11.7in (426cm). Unladen weight 3,197lb (1,450kg).
History: Conceived in 1983 as a car with which Porsche might dominate Group B category motor racing, the 959 matured into the most complete, most sophisticated, and most capable Supercar of its period. However crude it might

Below: Even before sales began, Porsche used the 959 to win the gruelling Paris-Dakar 'Raid', where long-distance durability and four-wheel-drive were essential.

Above: Originally shown as the 'Gruppe B' project car in 1983, the turbocharged four-wheel-drive Porsche was only a distant relative of the 911.

have been when invented, when it went on sale it was the most beguiling of any rear-engined Porsche so far introduced. Although broadly based on the rear-engined/rear-drive air-cooled 911, the 959 evolved so far that it retained only the same basic body shell, yet it had precious little in common with that famous model. With four-wheel-drive instead of rear-drive, with water-cooling instead of air-cooling to the cylinder heads, it had moved on a long way.

The story began in the early 1980s when the authorities introduced Group B motorsport, demanding only that 200 cars needed to be built to qualify for homologation (while allowing manufacturers to make a further 20 'Evolution' examples of an even more special type). Most car-makers chose to go rallying, but Porsche, at least at first, had circuit motor racing in mind. The 'Gruppe B' concept car was shown in 1983, when it was not nearly ready to go out on to the tracks, let alone go on sale, and in 1984 the first normally aspirated four-wheel-drive 'Gruppe B' 911s competed in the Paris-Dakar marathon rally, winning at their first attempt. Porsche meantime, in its own methodical way, then evolved the definitive car, taking so long to do it that the first examples would not be put on sale until 1987. The wait, however, was worth it, for every possible snag had been ironed out, and every possible ability added in.

Starting on the basis of an existing 911 monocoque body shell, with the flat-six engine in its usual position, way out in the tail, but retaining no more than that, the engineers then changed, improved and upgraded everything. First of all the engine, chosen in 2,851cc form, was given four-valves-per-cylinder water-cooled twin-cam cylinder heads, a KKK turbocharger and an intercooler to each bank – and produced a rock-solid 450bhp. Much more was available in racing form, for this was a unit which had evolved from that already being used in the fabulously successful 956 racing two-seater.

Next, and integral to the entire design, was the four-wheel-drive system (the first ever to have been developed at Porsche), where there was a massive six- ▶

▶ speed all-syncromesh manual gearbox ahead of the engine, in the usual Porsche position (under the rear seats), which was linked to the front axle casing by propeller shaft inside a solid aluminium torque tube.

Next there was the chassis, with an ultra-wide-track coil spring/wishbone independent suspension at each corner, and with rack-and-pinion steering, naturally enough with hydraulic power-assistance. Vast ventilated disc brakes (with electronic ABS, even though some of the test drivers felt that competition-inclined drivers would not want this feature) completed the chassis set up. But there was more. Computer sensing controls helped the transmission decide what proportion of the torque should be fed to the front wheels, while the suspension ride height could be adjusted to allow for smooth or rough roads: computers, in any case, looked after ride levelling at high speeds, allowing the car to sink further towards the ground to improve the aerodynamic balance.

To complete the picture, there was the styling, at once 911-related, but at the same totally separate, and instantly recognisable. Each difference, it seemed, had a good reason to be there – the faired-headlamp nose to reduce the drag, the bulging wheelarches to cover the wide-track suspension and ultra-wide tyres, the wide sills under the doors to link those arches, and the cool air intakes to feed the brakes (front corners) and the twin intercoolers (rear). There were exhaust vents behind the rear wheels, which allowed the two turbochargers to 'breathe', and finally there was the full-width, fixed-incidence aerofoil, across the tail to trim the high-speed handling.

Could anything have been more beguiling? Porsche thought not, which is why they confidently put the car on sale at an ex-factory price of DM 420,000 (which was roughly equivalent to £150,000 at that time). At this point there were two road-going 959s on offer, one of them the normal car, the Sport, which came without a rear seat, and a higher-specified, higher-priced type called the

959 Comfort, which had electric window lifts, air-conditioning and central locking. With motorsport in mind, a 961 version was also planned, but since Group B motorsport had already gone past its best by 1987 such cars were not seriously marketed.

When customers took delivery of their 959s, its reputation had already been made, for a trio of fully specified 'works' cars had competed in the Paris–Dakar marathon (all the way across the Sahara desert, flat out), to a 1-2 finish, while Claude Ballot-Lena's car had won the IMSA class and taken seventh place overall at Le Mans in the same year.

The 959's straightline performance, of course, was astonishing, for its top speed was almost 200mph – and a comfortable all-day cruising speed of 170–180mph seemed to be acceptable – while, aided by the tenacious grip of the four-wheel-drive system, the 450bhp car could sprint up to 100mph in about nine seconds. That, though, could only tell half of the story, for those lucky enough to drive 959s found that they not only looked good, and sprinted well, but that they were cool and comfortable to drive, the ride was as fluid as any other Porsche, and they seemed to be as well-built as any of the world's most expensive limousines.

No other company, it was generally agreed, would have taken so much trouble to finalise such a limited-production car, and since sales were limited to 250 cars, the 959 can surely not have made a profit for Porsche. No matter. It was the best 911-based car of all, and even as the new century opened, it had still not been surpassed by a better and more complete machine.

Below: Although the 959 shared its cabin with the 911, the floor pan, four-wheel-drive running gear, engine, chassis, and front and rear-end styles were all unique.

Porsche 924/944/968

Porsche 924, 944, and 968 family, built from 1975 to 1995 (data for origina 944)

Built by: Dr. Ing. h.c.F.Porsche KG, Germany.

Engine: Four cylinders, in line, in five-main-bearing cast alloy cylinder block Bore and stroke 100 x 79mm, 2,479cc (3.94 x 3.11in, 151.3cu.in). Cas aluminium cylinder head. Two valves per cylinder, operation by inverted bucke tappets from single overhead camshaft. Bosch Motronic fuel injectior Maximum power 163bhp at 5,800rpm. Maximum torque 151lb.ft at 3,500rpm [Original 924 models had 125bhp/2-litre Audi 4-cyl engine, later 944s and 968 had 16-valve/twin-cam versions of the 944 engine, up to 250bhp/6500rpm.]

Transmission: Front engine, rear-wheel-drive, with single dry diaphragm sprin plate clutch and five-speed all-synchromesh manual gearbox, in the rear, in un with the final drive casing. Remote control, centre-floor gearchange. Optiona three-speed autumatic transmission.

Chassis: Unitary construction steel combined body/chassis structure, wit steel 2+2 body shell in sports fastback style. Independent front suspension b coil springs, MacPherson struts, wishbones and anti-roll bar, independent rea suspension by transverse torsion bars, semi-trailing arms, and anti-roll ba Telescopic hydraulic dampers. Rack-and-pinion steering. Disc brakes at all fou wheels, with vacuum servo assistance. 15in bolt on cast alloy road wheels with 215./60-15in tyres.

Dimensions: Wheelbase 7ft 10.5in (240cm), front track 4ft 10.2

Below: The 924, introduced in 1975, was Porsche's first to have a front-mounted, water-cooled engine. It would sell in large numbers.

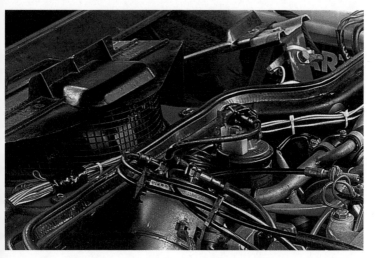

Above: Four-cylinder engines in 924s – whether Audi or Porsche-designed – were laid over at a considerable angle, to aid engine bay packaging.

(147.7cm), rear track 4ft 9.1in (145cm). Overall length 12ft 11.3in (420cm). Unladen weight 2,632lb (1,195kg).

History: Because Porsche had previously built nothing but cars with air-cooled engines, mounted behind the seats, in 1975 the arrival of the all-new

924 was a real shock to everyone's perceptions. Not only was the 924 a front-engined car which drove the rear wheels, but it had a conventional water-cooled power unit.

The 924, in fact, had started life as a VW-Audi project, designed on their behalf by Porsche, but at a fairly late stage the client cancelled it. Accordingly, it was then adopted as a 'Porsche', even though it was to be built in an ex-NSU factory at Neckarsulm which VW owned, and would include no special Porsche hardware.

The 924, in fact, was laid out to use many existing VW and Audi components, including a fuel-injected 2-litre Audi engine, VW Golf front suspension and VW Beetle-derived rear suspension. However, although the body style was a conventional-looking 2+2 sports hatchback, it hid a combined transaxle [four-speed gearbox and final drive] at the rear, which was actually the transposed component from a <u>front</u>-wheel drive Audi 100! Engine and transaxle were connected by a propeller shaft inside a rigid steel tube, the result being a very well-balanced piece of engineering which worked well.

The first 924 was the mildest of all the cars in this family which were to follow, for its single-cam Audi engine produced only 125bhp, and provided a 126mph top speed, though each and every type that followed was fiercer and faster than that.

These cars were different, in every possible way, from the 911s which were – and remain – Porsche's lifeblood, there being no common components, nor any common design philosophy. With the 924, Porsche set out to ▶

▶ produce an entirely new, simple, type of 'entry-level' sports car, one which would handle like many other conventional sports cars, and one which might attract clients from other makes of cars.

This was a range which soon expanded, later changed, and finally became very different from the original, though a family resemblance also remained. The original rather rounded style of the 924, complete with its droop-snoot nose, and its rather hump-backed 2+2 hatchback cabin, was merely widened and refined for the 944, and given a new nose and different decoration for the 968.

First-generation 924s all had the same Audi-based engine, but later versions had a turbocharged engine, five-speed manual and automatic transmissions also appeared, along with a host of options and special editions.

According to Porsche fanatics, the 944, which first appeared in 1981 was what the 924 should always have been. At first with a genuine Porsche four-cylinder single-cam 2.5-litre/163bhp, and later with engines of up to 3.0 litre/211bhp, it was much faster and more specialised than the 924, with a wide-arched body and more aggressive character to suit. Once again, development was continuous, so engines eventually became twin-cam, with 16 valves, and the capacity crept up from 2.5, to 2.7, and on to the full 3-litres, by which time the

slightly rough character of such a larger 'four' was becoming obvious.

The fastest 944s of all were the Turbos, with 250bhp, and a top speed of more than 150mph. By this time, too, the 924 had evolved into the 924S of 1985-1988, which actually used what had been the original 944 engine, though years after time had moved on for that original car: the last 924-badged car, therefore, died in 1988.

The final derivative of this family was, according to many enthusiasts, a model too far, for it extended the life of an already old-fashioned model. The 968, when previewed, sounded promising, but when launched in 1991 it was seen as a heavily facelifted 944 (with exposed headlamps), with a 240bhp/3.0-litre engine, while the 968 Turbo had 305bhp and could reach 175mph.

This range, even so, was a best-seller by any standards, with nearly 327,000 of all types built, 135,000 of these being Audi-engined cars.

Below: One of the best-balanced of all 944 types was the Turbo model of the mid-1980s, which had low-mounted aerodynamic spoilers in the rear to balance the handling.

Porsche Boxster

Porsche Boxster two-seater sports car, introduced in 1996 (data for the original model)

Built by: Dr. Ing. h.c. F. Porsche KG, Germany.

Engine: Six cylinders, in horizontally-opposed formation, in four-bearing light-alloy cylinder block/crankcase. Bore and stroke 86 × 72mm, 2,480cc (3.39 × 2.83in, 151.4cu.in). Two light-alloy cylinder heads. Four valves per cylinder, in vee, operation by twin overhead camshafts, with variable camshaft timing. Bosch Motronic fuel injection. Maximum power 204bhp (DIN) at 6,000rpm. Maximum torque 181lb.ft at 4,500rpm.

Transmission: Rear-wheel-drive, single-dry-plate diaphragm spring clutch and five-speed all-synchromesh manual gearbox, all in unit with mid-mounted engine. Remote-control, central gearchange. Tiptronic semi-automatic transmission also available as an option.

Chassis: Unitary-construction pressed-steel body-chassis unit with some aluminium panels, as two-seater open sports car style. Independent front suspension by MacPherson struts, coil springs, wishbones, telescopic dampers,

and anti-roll bar. Independent rear suspension by MacPherson struts, coil springs, trailing arms and lower wishbones, telescopic dampers, and anti-roll bar. Rack-and-pinion steering with hydraulic power assistance. Four-wheel disc brakes with power assistance and ABS. cast alloy, 16in road wheels, 205/55-16in (front) and 225/50-16in (rear) tyres.

Dimensions: Wheelbase 7ft 11in (241.5cm), front track 4ft 9.3in (145.5cm), rear track 4ft 11.4in (150.8cm). Overall length 14ft 1.9in (431.5cm). Unladen weight 2,739lb (1,242kg).

History: In the late 1980s and early 1990s, Porsche had a troubled existence. Management came and went, new models were started, then cancelled, sales peaked in 1990 then plummeted in the next few years, and for a time the company made big financial losses.

▶

Below: The all-new Boxster was the first Porsche ever to have a new-generation water-cooled flat-six engine. The entire front end was shared with the new-generation 911.

▶   It was not until 1992 that a solid new strategy was adopted, one cornerstone of which was to develop a new 'entry-level' two-seater roadster. The reason was that Porsche prices, in general, had drifted gradually but firmly upwards in the previous decade, and many enthusiastic drivers could no longer afford to buy. It was not feasible to get down to a truly stripped-out car, but it was certainly possible to claw back to a smaller, and cheaper base. The result was the Boxster of 1996 – except for its choice of a flat-six engine layout a car with no links at all with Porsche's illustrious past.

From the windscreen forward, the Boxster was to be common with the still-secret new-generation 911 (Porsche would later claim that 35 per cent of the two cars were the same in every detail), but aft of that it was unique. Whereas the next-generation 911 would have a rear-mounted engine, the new flat-six engine of the Boxster was water-cooled (cylinder heads *and* cylinder blocks – a real novelty for Porsche), and was positioned ahead of the line of the back axle. By definition, this meant that the 'chassis' platform of the Boxster was unique, as was the transmission and the rear suspension which was all linked to it. The pressed-steel body style itself was rounded, and sleek, without a trace of so-called fashionable wedge, or of folded edges in it, with twin roll-over hoops behind the seats, a flat rear deck to emphasis the compact engine – and space for stowage at front and rear.

The engine itself was at once all-new (water-cooled, don't forget) yet instantly recognisably Porsche. Compact, with all its fuel injection and auxiliary drives packaged above it, it sat ahead of its transmission, and was effectively underneath where the '+2' seats might otherwise have been found. Initially it was rated at 204bhp/2,480cc, but it was clear that much more power (and enlargement) was possible – this being proved within a year when the first 300bhp/3,387cc version of the same engine appeared in the new-type 911!

Complete with all-round MacPherson strut suspension, and big four-wheel disc brakes, the first Boxster looked appealing, and capable – and so it was. Handling better than any previous Porsche had ever done, it was already capable of nearly 140mph, but by existing Porsche standards this was milk-and-water

Below: The new Boxster was so carefully proportioned that it was difficult to realise that the engine was actually behind the seats, but ahead of the rear axle line.

Above: Compared with the obsolete 911, the fascia/instrument layout of the late-1990s Boxster was a huge advance. Tiptronic transmission was an option.

stuff, so demands for higher-powered versions were soon made. Porsche, of course, had already thought about this, and within three years they had introduced a 220bhp/2.7-litre/150mph version of the original Boxster, along with a 252bhp/3.2-litre/161mph Boxster S. All this, note, was with a still-young and normally aspirated engine – so prospects for the 2000s, when turbocharging might be applied, were intriguing.

413

Porsche 911 Carrera (new 996 generation)

Porsche 911, new water-cooled engine generation, introduced in 1997 (data for the original model)

Built by: Dr. Ing. h.c. F.Porsche KG, Germany.

Engine: Six cylinders, in horizontally opposed formation, in four-main-bearing cylinder block/crankcase. Bore and stroke 96 x 78mm, 3,387cc (3.80 x 3.07in, 206.8cu.in). Two light-alloy cylinder heads. Four overhead valves per cylinder, operated by twin overhead camshafts per cylinder head, with variable valve timing. Bosch Motronic fuel injection. Maximum power 296bhp at 6,800rpm. Maximum torque 251lb.ft at 4,600rpm. [By 2002, normally aspirated 911s had 320bhp/3.6-litres, whereas the new Turbo had 420bhp/3.6-litres.]

Transmission: Rear-mounted engine, rear-wheel-drive (or, optional, four-wheel-drive), single-dry-plate diaphragm spring clutch, and six-speed all-synchromesh manual gearbox, all in unit with rear-mounted engine. Remote control, centre floor gearchange. Tiptronic semi-automatic transmission also available as an option.

Chassis: Unitary construction pressed-steel body/chassis structure, with some aluminium panels, as 2+2-seater closed coupé (convertible later available as an option). Independent front suspension by coil springs, MacPherson struts, and anti-roll bar, independent rear suspension by coil springs, multi-link location, and anti-roll bar. Hydraulic, telescopic, dampers. Rack-and-pinion steering, with power assistance. Disc brakes at all four wheels, with vacuum servo assistance, and ABS (anti-lock) as standard. 17in bolt-on cast-alloy wheels, with 225/50-17in (front) and 255/40-17in (rear) tyres.

Dimensions: Wheelbase 7ft 8.5in (235cm), front track 4ft 9.2in (145.5cm), rear track 4ft 11in (150cm). Overall length 14ft 6.4in (443cm). Unladen weight 2,911lb (1,320kg).

Below: The second-generation 911, announced in 1997, was different in every detail from the original, but kept the same general proportions.

Above: New-type 911s, coded 996, were smoothly detailed, and had uniquely proportioned headlamps and turn indicators.

History: Although it had taken Porsche no less than 34 years to come up with an entirely new 911 model, the wait had been worth it. Although the new car was entirely different in detail from the old, both the layout and philosophy of the original type had been retained.

In particular, the two cars shared the same basic layout, of having a flat-six engine tucked into the tail with a transmission ahead of it. As ever, the structure was a sturdy steel monocoque, with much of the stiffness and rigidity in the floor, sills and central tunnel. As ever, there would be normally aspirated and

turbocharged versions of the engine, two-wheel-drive or four-wheel-drive, and a choice of body styles which encompassed fastback coupé (most of the cars built would be like this), a convertible, and derivatives of both types.

It is a measure of the work put in by Porsche on their own behalf, and for prestigious clients, that the new car's internal project code was '996', compared with that of '901' for what the world still knows as the original 911. Each and every number which intervened was a major project of one type or another.

The time around, however, there were two important changes, both of them absolutely ▶

▶ central to the design. One was that the entire front end of the new 911 was shared with that of the Boxster which had gone on sale a year earlier (Porsche actually claimed 35 per cent commonality in every detail). The other was that for the first time in a rear-engined Porsche road car, the engine would be water cooled.

Having spent years considering the future of the 911, Porsche decided on a safe strategy – more of the same, and better of the same. The new generation car would use a proven variety of all-steel monocoque structure (it would be 45 per cent stiffer in torsional rigidity), and would carry a new interpretation of the famous fastback coupé style. Longer, wider, heavier and aerodynamically smoother than before, the new-type 911 would be altogether more delicately shaped, though none-the-less recognisable. The headlamp shapes, in particular, would be styled, rather than circular – and everything forward of the doors – body panels, structure and front suspension – would be shared with the Boxster.

Unavoidably, the new 911 would be heavier than ever (2,911lb/1,320kg) and would carry 61 per cent of that weight over its rear wheels. However, half a-century of rear-engined car experience, allied to the use of multi-link coil spring rear suspension, meant that Porsche was sure it would handle ever better than before.

The engine itself was all-new, but exactly as expected, not only

because of its flat-six 'Boxer' layout, but because of its four-valve, twin-cam, water-cooled layout. In the Boxster it was originally a 2.5-litre unit, in this 911 it was initially a 300bhp/3.4-litre type, and it was already known that 3.6-litre capacities, and well over 400bhp in turbocharged form, was going to be available. Even in its original state, the 300bhp 911 could reach 174mph.

Everywhere else in the chassis, Porsche built on what they knew – six-speeds instead of five-speeds in the latest manual gearbox, a five-speed Tiptronic box as an option, and the choice between two and four-wheel-drive, a fixed-head coupé or a complete drop-top Cabriolet type of body style, and a positivre raft of options, and specially-derived models yet to come.

The new-generation Turbo of 1999 not only had 420bhp, but permanent four-wheel-drive, so a top speed of 190mph, complete with awesome stability and control, immediately set new standards for Porsche's rivals

But this was just the beginning for what was sure to be a lengthy and exciting development programme. How long could the 996-generation 911 go on? Maybe not as long as its illustrious forbear, but certainly with as much variety, and as much innovation.

Below: Customers for new-type 911s had many choices, including two or four-wheel drive, coupé or convertible styles, normal or turbo engines.

Renault Alpine A110

Alpines 1955 to 1977 (data for 1600S model of 1970)
Built by: Automobiles Alpine srl., France.
Engine: Renault-manufactured, four cylinders, in line, in five-bearing light-alloy block. Bore and stroke 77mm by 84mm, 1,565cc (3.03in × 3.31in, 95.5cu.in). Light-alloy cylinder head. Two overhead valves per cylinder, operated by pushrods and rockers from single camshaft, high-mounted in cylinder block. One twin-choke Weber carburettor. Maximum power 138bhp (gross) at 6,000rpm. Maximum torque 106lb.ft at 5,000rpm.
Transmission: Engine mounted longitudinally behind line of rear wheels, driving through gearbox, ahead of rear wheels, and transaxle. Single-dry-plate clutch, and five-speed, all synchromesh manual gearbox. Central, remote-control gearchange. Drive forward over final drive to gearbox, then back to hypoid-bevel final drive. Exposed universally jointed drive shafts to rear wheels.
Chassis: Separate tubular backbone chassis frame, with square-section and circular-section built-up frames supporting suspensions and power pack. Independent front suspension by coil springs, wishbones and anti-roll bar. Independent rear suspension by swinging half axles, coil springs, radius arms and anti-roll bar. Telescopic dampers. Rack-and-pinion steering. Four-wheel disc brakes, with optional vacuum servo. Cast-alloy, 15in road wheels. 145 × 15in, or 165 × 13in tyres. Two-door, two-seat, closed glassfibre bodywork by Alpine.
Dimensions: Wheelbase 6ft 10.6in (210cm), track (front) 4ft 3in (129.5cm),

Right: Alpine-Renaults are really rally cars which can be used on the road. With a tubular chassis, light glassfibre bodies, and powerful modified Renault engines, the A110 was an outright winner for years. This was Pat Moss-Carlsson's Monte example.

track (rear) 4ft 2.2in (127.5cm). Overall length 12ft 7.5in (385cm). Unladen weight 1,400lb (635kg).

History: Jean Redélé worked in the family Renault dealership when young, and started competition motoring in the not-very-sporting 4CV saloon model. From this he progressed to building a glassfibre special using mainly 4CV parts – the very first Alpine-Renault sports car. From very small beginnings, this dumpy little machine was built in limited quantities; it was given a larger engine and refined and it gradually built up a loyal clientele. The breakthrough came in 1961, when the A108 Tour de France machine was introduced, visually very similar to the cars to be made for the next fifteen years, with a steel backbone chassis and steel platform floor, with the Renault Dauphine 956cc engine. Development thereafter was rapid, with first an 1,108cc and later a 1,255cc engine.

Alpines were very successful class and 'Index' performers on the race track and in smooth-road rallies, but it was not until the light-alloy Renault 16 unit was made available that outright victories became possible. From the end of the 1960s, the cars were also strengthened, until by the early 1970s they could win rallies through the Alps, in the dust and sand of Morocco, and continue to shine on the race tracks. As a production car the Alpine was only a compromise, for its very lightweight and flexible glassfibre body shell and tail-out handling was strictly competition-inspired. The company is now financially controlled by Renault, the French giant.

Renault Alpine A610 GTA

Renault Alpine A610, built from 1985 to 1995 (data for new 1991 A610)
Built by: Regie Nationale des Usines Renault, France.
Engine: Mid-mounted, six-cylinders, in 90-degree vee, in light alloy cylinder block. Bore and stroke 93 x 73mm, 2,975cc (3.66 x 2.87in, 181.6cu.in). Two light alloy cylinder heads. Two overhead valves per cylinder, operated by rockers from single overhead camshafts mounted in each cylinder head. Renix fuel injection and Garrett turbocharger. Maximum power 250bhp at 6,750rpm. Maximum torque 258lb.ft at 2,900rpm.
Transmission: Rear-mounted engine, rear-wheel-drive, with single dry plate diaphragm spring clutch and all-synchromesh five-speed manual gearbox, all in unit with engine. Remote control central floor gearchange.
Chassis: Separate steel backbone-style chassis frame, with box, pressed and fabricated cross-bracing, and stiffeners. Independent front suspension by coil springs, wishbones and anti-roll bar, independent rear suspension by coil springs, wishbones and anti-roll bar. Telescopic, hydraulic, dampers. Rack-and-pinion steering, with power assistance. Disc brakes at all four wheels, with vacuum servo assistance. 16in cast alloy bolt on wheels, with 205/45-16in (front) and 245/45-16in (rear) tyres. Glass-fibre and composite bodyshell, 2+2 seating, in fastback coupé style.
Dimensions: Wheelbase 7ft 8.1in (234cm), front track 4ft 11.2in (150.5cm), rear track 4ft 10in (147cm). Overall length 14ft 5.8in (441.5cm). Unladen weight 3,042lb(1,380kg).
History: By the 1970s, Alpine and Renault fortunes were becoming integrated, especially after the independent Dieppe-based concern was purchased by Renault in 1974. Specialist Renault models (like the 5 Alpine) would be assembled at Dieppe, and Renault's financial muscle then allowed new Alpine models to became larger, more sophisticated, and better engineered. By the 1980s such cars had different names for different markets, and by the 1990s the 'Alpine' had become a model, rather than a marque name.

Below: Like other V6-derivatives which were to follow, the mid-1980s Alpine GTA V6 had a rear-mounted engine, and a backbone chassis.

Above: The original V6 GT (also known as the GTA V6) was a graceful 2+2-seater sports coupé, with the engine mounted in the extreme tail.

From the 1970s, too, Renault made more and more use of a new 90-degree vee-6 engine, which was actually a joint PRV (Peugeot-Renault-Volvo) project, built at Douvrin in Northern France. Not only did this find a home in Renault saloons, but in a series of rear-engined (*not* mid-engined) Alpines.

First of all, in 1976, there had been the Alpine Renault A310 V6, yet this was only a sighting shot, or a half-way house, for the next-generation type was launched in 1984, as a Renault Alpine V6GT (or as a GTA in certain markets). Not only was this a newly engineered rear-engined sports coupé, but it was officially called a Renault-Alpine, rather than an Alpine-Renault. Although it would be heavily-modified and re-launched as the Renault Alpine A610 in 1991, this was effectively Renault's long-lived and determined attempt to fight the Porsche 911, head-to-head, for domination of the rear-engined sector.

Renault always insisted, and must be taken on trust in this regard, that in moving from V6GT/GTA to A610, that some 80 per cent of the design was either completely new, or was substantially revised. Statistically this may be true, but the fact is that the two cars shared the same basic layout, and the same glass-fibre/composite body style throughout their eleven year life. In some ways the A610 was subtly more rounded in some details, but the cabin, the proportions, and the outline (from top, front, or side) was never changed. One easy way to 'pick' one car from the other was that originals had fixed headlamps behind glass, while A310s had pop-up headlamps normally hidden behind plastic panels.

Central to the design was the complex pressed and fabricated steel backbone chassis frame, where the engine was mounted in the extreme tail, with its five-speed trans-axle ahead of it, and where there were sturdy sill members linked to the backbone by outriggers. Front and rear suspension were both by coil springs and wishbones, and the smart 2+2-seater body shell was manufactured from glass-fibre.

Renault, like Porsche, was so wedded to rear-engined installations that all its engineering, and the development of the layout, was concentrated on making the layout acceptable, for it would never be perfect. Even on the A610, where Renault insisted that they had improved the layout of the chassis, 57 per cent of the weight was concentrated over the rear wheels, these very cannily ▶

▶ being provided with wider tread tyres to balance up the handling.

Original V6GTs had 160bhp/2.85-litre or (as V6 Turbos) turbocharged 200bhp/2.5-litre, whereas A310s of the 1990s had turbocharged 3.0-litre/250bhp derivatives of the same power unit. The latter car, which came complete with ABS braking, and a top speed of nearly 160mph, was a great car by any standards, but it was always let down by a single factor – that it did not carry a Porsche badge.

Life is not fair sometimes, particularly in the motor industry, where 'image'

often goes ahead of the truth, for the truth was that the A310 was at least as stylish as the last of the rear-engined, air-cooled Porsches, yet it never sold in the same numbers. Even so, Renault were sorry to see it go, when it had to clear the decks to make way for the entirely different little Spider which followed.

Below: Alpine GTAs had a sizeable cabin, the V6 engine was in the tail, and they could be identified by the headlamps mounted behind glass.

Renault Spider

Renault Spider, built from 1996 to 2000
Built by: Regie Nationale des Usines Renault, France.
Engine: Four cylinders, in line, in five-main-bearing cast iron cylinder block transversely-mounted in chassis. Bore and stroke 82.7 x 93mm, 1,998cc (3.25 x 3.66in, 122cu.in). Light alloy cylinder head. Four overhead valves per cylinder operated by two overhead camshafts. Renault fuel injection. Maximum power 150bhp at 6,000rpm. Maximum torque 140lb.ft at 4,500rpm.
Transmission: Mid-mounted transverse engine, rear-wheel-drive, single-dry-plate diaphragm spring clutch and five-speed all-synchromesh manual gearbox, all in unit with engine. Remote control., centre-floor, gearchange.
Chassis: Separate aluminium spaceframe-style structure, with glass-fibre two-seater open sports body shell. Independent front suspension by coil springs, wishbones and anti-roll bar, independent rear suspension by coil springs, wishbones and anti-roll bar. Hydraulic telescopic dampers. Rack-and-pinion steering. No power assistance. Disc brakes at front and rear: no ABS. 16in cast alloy wheels, with 205/50-16 (front) and 225/50-16in.(rear) tyres.
Dimensions: Wheelbase 7ft 8.2in (234 cm), front track 5ft 0.7in (154.3cm), rear track 5ft 0.5in (153.6cm). Overall length 12ft 5.4in (379.5cm). Unladen weight 2,106lb (955kg).
History: Sometimes, in automotive engineering, there is a lull in innovation after which similar novelties arrive at once. And so it was in the mid-1990s. Sports car engineering seemed to have settled, until two new cars – the Renault Spider and the Lotus Elise – both broke cover in the same period.

Although there had been no collusion, in styling or in engineering, the two cars were remarkably similar. Both had ultra-modern chassis engineering, both had mid-mounted engines driving the rear wheels, both had glass-fibre bodies and both were dedicated to providing no-frills, low-weight, performance and

character. Lotus had the advantage of forty years of sports car heritage behind them, while Renault was a vastly larger and more profitable organisation which could use all of its own running gear.

One car, however – the Elise – went on to prosper, to sell in considerable numbers by Lotus standards, and to re-create its company's image, while the Renault was, at best, a well-liked curiosity, which disappeared after less than four years on the market. Looking back, the Spider might almost have been a mirage, for it left no lasting trace on the Renault scene.

The first Spiders. shown in 1995, seemed like de-tuned racing sports cars, for Renault insisted that they would go into production without windscreens, and no heaters, that there would be no spare wheel, and that buyers would be well advised to wear full-face helmets when driving them on the public highway. Without soft tops, fold-back hoods or even optional hardtops, and without bumpers of any sort, these seemed to be no-compromise machines that would have to sell on their dynamic merit. The fact that this was one of those rare cars with fold-forward doors (Lamborghini Diablo-style) almost seemed irrelevant, as young and vigorous owners would be tempted to vault aboard without troubling the latch mechanism!

At least Renault eventually softened their stance, and agreed to supply a windscreen and wipers (along with what they called an 'optional emergency soft-top' which would tear off at more than 40mph) when right-hand-drive cars went into production. None of this abrasive, he-man's car character was ever abandoned, which made the Spider more saleable, even though the weight had crept up considerably during development. Whenever or wherever the Renault ▶

Below: The Renault Spider had its Clio Williams engine mounted behind the seats, the chassis was aluminium, the body glass-fibre.

▶ had to sell against the Elise, it was much more expensive.

It was, in any case, an expensively engineered mid-engined machine. Although the 16-valve engine and five-speed gearbox were pure Clio Williams (which was a front-wheel-drive hatchback), the chassis was an aluminium space frame where many sections were high-tech. Extrusions. The all-independent suspension with racing-car style horizontal coil-over-dampers, which featured Rose joints, owed more to race track methods than to road-car practice. Anyone who drove the Spider agreed that its handling and response were, simply, superb. Since there were no airbags for safety, and no ABS braking, perhaps this was just as well. Although the brakes were huge (they had been lifted from the Renault A610), and the tyres wider even than an enthusiast might have desired, the interior was positively spartan (and would,

n any case, get soaked when it rained), and the instrument package distinctly basic.

In launching a car like this, Renault took a huge gamble, which failed, for not even the hardy well-to-do young enthusiasts seemed to like paying so much for a car in which they could be so obviously and unstoppably uncomfortable. A 124mph top speed from 150bhp was, in any case, no better than expected, for this did not put the Spider out of reach of its obvious rivals. For Renault the bald, unpalatable, truth was that the Spider would became a 'classic' machine, but that the Lotus Elise would have much more success.

Below: The Spider was all function, and all form, with no concessions to comfort. Original cars did not even have a windscreen.

Saab Sonett

Saab Sonetts built from 1966 (II, then V4), and 1970 (III) to 1974 (data f‹ Sonett III)

Built by: SAAB Actiebolag, Sweden.

Engine: Ford-Germany-manufactured, four cylinders, in 60-degree vee, three-main-bearing cast iron cylinder block. Bore and stroke 90 x 66.8mr 1,699cc (3.54 x 2.63in, 103.7cu.in). Cast iron cylinder heads. Two overhea valves per cylinder, operated by pushrods and rockers from a camshaft in th cylinder block vee: One downdraught Solex carburettor. Maximum pow‹ 75bhp at 5,000rpm. Maximum torque 94lb.ft at 2,500rpm.

Transmission: Front-engine, front-wheel-drive, single dry plate, diaphrag‹ spring clutch and four-speed all-synchromesh manual gearbox, all in unit wi‹ engine. Remote control, centre floor gearchange.

Chassis: Separate steel platform-type chassis frame and internal structur‹ Independent front suspension by coil springs and wishbones, suspension ‹ rear 'dead' axle by coil springs, radius arms, and locating brackets. Telescopi‹ hydraulic, dampers. Rack and pinion steering. Front disc, rear drum brakes. 15 cast alloy wheels, with 155-15in tyres. Bodyshell of glass-fibre, in two-seat‹ fastback coupé style.

Dimensions: Wheelbase 7ft 0.6in (215cm), front track 4ft 0.4in (123cm), re track 4ft 0.4in (123cm). Overall length 12ft 9.5in (390cm). Unladen weig 1,785lb (820kg).

History: Saab started out as aircraft manufacturers in Sweden, then beg‹ making two-stroke-engined cars in the late 1940s, and soon built up reputation for making strong and versatile little front-wheel-drive saloons.

Rally successes (not least by Erik Carlsson) gave the marque a spor image, and to build on this it decided to market coupés. The Sonett II of 196 (there was a Sonett I which never went on sale), combined the front-dri‹ platform of the latest 96 saloon with a smart little GRP coupé body style, t‹ shell being built by ASJ (a Swedish railway carriage specialist).

Below: The Sonett III was powered by a Ford-Germany V4 engine mounted in the nose, driving the front wheels.

Above: The 100mph Sonett III was building up its reputation in the USA when new safety rules proved too onerous to make it worth continuing.

Like the saloons from which had evolved, it handled well, the front-wheel-drive feeling very secure, and considering that this company had never before built a sports machine, it was an encouraging first effort. However, although it was smaller and lighter than the saloon, with only 60bhp from 841cc it was rather underpowered, so when the Ford-Germany V4 engine was fitted to Saab saloons from 1966, it was soon adopted for the little coupé too. With a torquey 65bhp four-stroke engine, it was more viable than before, and Saab claimed a top speed of 100mph.

The next generation model, the Sonett III, arrived in 1970. Although it retained the same 96 V4 steel platform and front-wheel-drive, it not only had a more stylish GRP body style by Coggiola of Italy, but it was fitted with the enlarged, 75bhp/1.7-litre version of the V4 engine.

Thus equipped it sold well, if not sensationally, especially in North America, for which market it was chiefly intended, but the onset of ever-more-fierce safety and exhaust emission regulations killed it off in 1974. All in all, 10,236 Sonetts of all types were built, no fewer than 8,351 of these being Sonett IIIs.

Saleen S7

Saleen S7 sports coupé, introduced in 2000
Built by: Saleen, USA.

Engine: Modified Ford manufacture, eight cylinders, in 90-degree vee, in five main-bearing light-alloy cylinder block. Bore and stroke 104.8 x 101.6mm 7,011cc (4.09 x 4.00 in, 428cu.in). Two aluminium cylinder heads. Two overhead valves per cylinder, operated by pushrods and rockers from a camshaft in the cylinder block vee, and EGR fuel injection. Maximum power 558bhp at 6,400rpm. Maximum torque 525lb.ft at 4,000rpm.

Transmission: Mid-mounted engine, rear-wheel-drive, Dry plate clutch and six-speed all-synchromesh manual gearbox, all in unit with engine and final drive unit. Remote control, centre floor gearchange.

Chassis: Separate chassis frame/underframe, with tubular main members steel and composite structural members. Independent front suspension by coil springs, wishbones and anti-roll bar, independent rear suspension by coil springs, wishbones, and anti-roll bar. Telescopic hydraulic dampers. Rack-and-pinion steering. Disc brakes at front and rear, with vacuum servo assistance. 19 in cast alloy wheels. 275/30-19 (front) and 355/25-19 (rear) tyres. Two-seater coupé body shell in glass-fibre, with coleopter-style lift-up/lift-forward doors.

Dimensions: Wheelbase 8ft 10.3in (270cm), front track 5ft 8.9in (175cm), rear track 5ft 7.3in (171cm). Overall length 15ft 8in (477.5cm). Unladen weight 2,756lb (1,250kg).

History: Even though the market for very expensive supercars was, and always will be, very restricted, any number of romantics, and millionaires, fall for the temptation of trying to break into a market that may not be there in number. Supercars rarely succeed for long unless than use their own, or a very

Above: Amazing how many makers of limited-production cars look to McLaren or Lamborghini for inspiration on door operation.

Below: The S7, announced in 2000, was an ultra-limited-production dream car, with ground-effect bodywork and a 7-litre Ford V8 engine.

▶ prestigious supplier's, engine, but this never deters the entrepreneurs who like to see their own name on a new product.

Such a car was the Saleen S7, which was launched in mid-2000, received rave reviews from everyone who saw it, or sampled it, but then struggled to get into production, or to make the sort of sales it would need for a long life. One problem, perhaps, that it was yet another mid-engined/rear-drive fastback coupé, yet another which used an American vee-8 engine, and yet another which – at £234,000/$400,000 – would only be bought by those rejecting the most expensive Ferraris and Lamborghinis which were already on the market.

The Saleen S7 was a car with heritage both in the USA and also in Great Britain, for it had been inspired in North America, and partly engineered and developed in the UK. Original inspiration came from Steve Saleen of North America, who had already made his name as a much-respected tuner of Ford Mustangs, so there was no surprise at all when he chose Ford-USA vee-8 power. His race-car expertise was not in doubt, either, for his cars had already won several American championships, and achieved success in the French Le Mans 24 Hour race.

Much of the development and chassis engineering, particularly of the ground-effect floorpan, was completed by Ray Mallock Racing in the UK, this being a race-car constructor which a good record in sports and in saloon car events.

When the car was unveiled it was suggested that it would be built in left-hand and right-hand drive form, that some of the cars would be assembled by Ray Mallock, the balance to be produced by Saleen in Irvine, California, and that by 2003 it would be ready for assembly at the rate of 100 cars a year. At the outset Saleen forecast that between 300 and 400 cars would be built in total – a figure which would, if delivered, make this car more numerous that the Jaguar XJ220 and the McLaren F1, both of which were considered commercial failures.

In many ways the layout was conventional by early-2000s supercar

Below: The Saleen S7 of 2000 looks bulky, but was actually a neat two-seater, with a mid-mounted 7-litre/558bhp Ford engine.

Above: Saleen's strategy was always to sell the S7 as a race car (foreground) or as a more fully equipped road car version of the same chassis.

standards, for the engine was behind the seats, driving the rear wheels. Saleen had chosen a massive 428CID/7-litre Ford-US engine, and although

this was a power unit with a long history, it was updated with all-aluminium castings, and with Saleen's own specially-designed cylinder heads. With more than 550bhp, and a ground-shaking 525lb.ft. of torque, it promised to guarantee 200mph-plus performance – and to give the six-speed ZF transaxle a very hard time.

The style looked brutal, and effective (it was claimed that so much ground force was developed at high speed that it would have been able to drive along, upside down, on a ceiling without any peril), and the doors opened up forwards, scissors or 'coleopter' style, rather like those of the Lamborghini Diablo

Although the original S7 was an extremely well-equipped two-seater – the cabin was trimmed in Connolly leather and suede – and the cabin was arranged so that the driver's seat was slightly more towards the centre line than that of the passenger, there was no immediate rush to order, and the initial on-sale date of 2001 slipped considerably.

Would this be yet another 'Great Idea' which never went beyond that? The world's motoring enthusiasts hoped not.

Simplex 50HP

Simplex 50hp, built from 1907 to 1914 (data for 1907 model)
Built by: Simplex Automobile Co. Inc., United States.
Engine: Four cylinders, in line, two cast-iron blocks, with three-bearing light-alloy crankcase. Bore and stroke 146.1mm by 146.1mm, 9,797cc (5.75in × 5.75in, 598cu.in). Non-detachable cast-iron cylinder heads. Two side valves per cylinder, in T-head layout with exposed valve stems and springs, operated by tappets from two camshafts, each in separate cast tunnel on outside of crankcase. One up-draught carburettor.
Transmission: Cone clutch, in unit with front-mounted engine, separate four-speed manual gearbox (without synchromesh). Remote-control right-hand gearchange. Straight-bevel differential in tail of gearbox and countershaft to sprockets. Final drive to rear wheels by twin side chains.
Chassis: Separate pressed-steel chassis frame, with channel-section side members and pressed and tubular cross bracings. Forged front axle beam. Front and rear suspension by semi-elliptic leaf springs. Friction-type dampers. Worm-and-sector steering. Foot brake, mechanically operated, by contracting bands on gearbox countershaft drums. Hand brake, mechanically operated, on rear wheels drums. Fixed artillery-style road wheels 35 × 5in tyres. Choice of coachwork, open or closed touring or saloon.

Dimensions: Wheelbase 10ft 6in (320cm), tracks (front and rear) 4ft 8in (142cm). Unladen weight, depending on coachwork, from 3,750lb (1,701kg).

History: The Simplex car evolved from the Smith and Mabley motor agents in New York. At first they sold Mercédès, Panhard and Renault cars, but in 1904 they began to build a Smith and Mabley Simplex car, first of 18hp and later of 30hp. The company went out of business in 1907, but the moribund concern was acquired by Herman Broesel, who had a vast new 9.8-litre 50hp car designed and called it – simply – a Simplex. The company was only to live for ten years, but the original chain-drive 50 was always part of the range. It was a big, expensive ($4,500 for the chassis alone) and exclusive car, with bodies from prestigious coachbuilders. The mechanical layout was typical of the period, but the engine had a lot of potential, as stripped models proved time and time again on the American race tracks. By 1911, there was a shaft-driven 38hp model being built alongside the 50 and in 1912, the massive 75 (still with chain drive) was introduced as a faster version of the 50 model.

A change of company ownership in 1914 spelt the end for the classic Simplex car and the big 50 disappeared. No more Simplexes were built after 1917. There were two types of radiator fitted to these cars – one a conventional Mercédès-type flat unit and the other a sharply pointed vee radiator.

Below: As suggested by its name, the Simplex was mechanically simple, but sold for a very grand price. This 50hp model was built in 1909 – the 75hp car was even faster and more massive.

Singer Nine and Le Mans

Singer Nine family of sports cars, built from 1932 to 1937 (data for original 1932/1933 model)

Built by: Singer & Co. Ltd., Britain.

Engine: Four cylinders, in line, in two-main-bearing cast iron cylinder block. Bore and stroke 60 x 86mm, 972cc (2.36 x 3.39in, 59.3cu.in). Cast iron cylinder head. Two overhead valves per cylinder, operated by single overhead camshaft. Single horizontal carburettor. Maximum power not quoted (estimated 35bhp at 5,500rpm).

Transmission: Rear-wheel-drive, single dry plate, coil spring, clutch and four-speed manual gearbox, no synchromesh, all in unit with engine. Remote control, centre floor gearchange.

Chassis: Separate steel chassis frame, with channel section side members, channel and tubular cross-bracing and reinforcements. Beam axle front suspension by semi-elliptic leaf springs, suspension of beam rear axle by semi-elliptic leaf springs. Friction-type dampers. Drum brakes at front and rear wheels. 18in centre-lock wire wheels, with 4.50-18in tyres. Choice of body styles, including four-seater sports car, two-seater coupé, four-seater sports saloon.

Dimensions: (Open sports car body) Wheelbase 7ft 8in (233.7cm), front track 3ft 9in (114cm), rear track 3ft 9in (114cm). Overall length 11ft 8in (355.6cm). Unladen weight 1,638lb (743kg).

History: Until the early 1930s, MG's stranglehold on the small, simple, cheap

Below: Complete with a high-revving overhead-cam 972cc engine, the Singer Nine was real competition to the MG Midget of the day.

Above: The Singer Nine Sports had unmistakable front-end styling, this being a four-seater tourer, though a two-seater was also available.

sports car market was complete, for there was really nothing to compete against their tiny M-Type Midget, or the larger-engined F-Type Magna which followed in 1931: the J2 of 1932 was much better even than the M-Type.

Singer of Coventry, which was then one of Britain's important car makers, then decided to fight in the same market, with the appealing little Nine Sports, a car which then evolved into the Nine Le Mans, and finally to the 1½-litre Le Mans. By 1930s standards these were entertaining sports cars which soon made their name in rallies and sporting trials.

This car's pedigree stemmed from that of the Junior 9hp saloon (a car of similar size to the Morris Minor, or the Ford 8hp), which had a magnificent little four-cylinder 972cc overhead-camshaft engine (even though there was only a two-bearing crankshaft), and a four-speed gearbox as standard. The Nine Sports that followed used all the saloon's running gear, which meant that it beam axles at front and rear, small hydraulically-operated drum brakes, stiff half-elliptic leaf springs – all of which were definitely built down to a price.

On the other hand, it had a lowered frame and a series of cute body styles – tourer, coupé or saloon, and a sporty remote-control gearchange, along with a twin-carburettor version of the high-revving engine. Complete with its fold-flat windscreen, and elegantly sweeping front wings, plus cutaway doors, it looked the part, and was definite competition for the small MGs.

The original models, however, looked quicker than they actually were – for with only 35bhp and a top speed of no more than 70mph, the Nine Sports was no match for the MG J2 – but the big selling point was the choice of open or closed bodywork, and availability through a large and well-known dealer chain.

The Le Mans Speed Special of this car, which followed a year later, was a more formidable machine, for it featured the same body styles, but had a 972cc engine which had been tuned up to 42bhp (a twenty per cent improvement), and this was a competitive little 75mph car. In the model's best year, 1934, more than 2,000 were sold, which meant that the MG competition was trailing for a time.

Much more rare, but extremely desirable, was the 1½-litre type, which had a 63bhp/1,493cc six-cylinder version of the effective little 'four, with four main bearings – this engine having always been designed with a six-cylinder version in mind. The 'basic' version of this sporty 'six' produced 46bhp.

Body styles were very similar to those of the small-engined types, but a

longer wheelbase was needed to accommodate the longer engine. Even so, a top speed of 84mph was recorded in road tests, which was better than anything that MG could achieve at the time, and because this car's looks, and its price (£375 was quite a bargain in this sector) were both very attractive, it generated a real following.

Singer, though, did not pursue a consistent new model policy at this stage (and were, in any case, more interested in building family cars), so the sports car line died out in 1937 without ever being replaced. By comparison with these, the Bantam Roadsters, launched in 1939 and made in numbers after the Second World War, were neither as fast, nor as pretty. The engine, at least, was carried over to this car, and also found its way into the HRG sports cars of the same period.

Below: For Singer, the Nine Sports was just a sideline to its family cars, but models like this four-seater were very appealing.

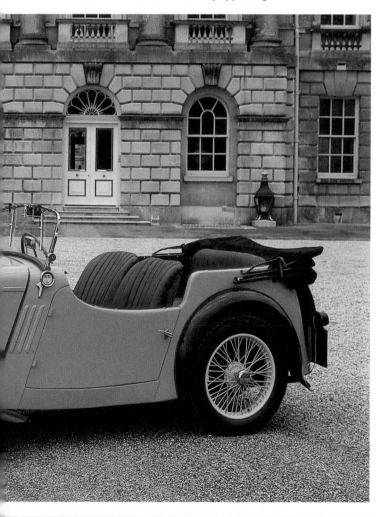

Stutz Bearcat

Bearcat, built from 1914 to 1917 in original design (data for 1914 model)
Built by: The Stutz Motor Car Co: of America, United States.

Engine: Wisconsin manufactured. Four cylinders, in line, in cast-iron block, with three-bearing light-alloy crankcase. Bore and stroke 120.6mm by 139.7mm, 6,388cc (4.75in × 5.5in, 390cu.in). Non-detachable cylinder head. Two side valves per cylinder, in T-head layout single up-draught carburettor. Maximum power about 60hp at 1,500rpm.

Transmission: Cone clutch, in unit with front-mounted engine, and shaft drive to three-speed manual gearbox (without synchromesh), in unit with straight-bevel 'live' rear axle. Remote-control right-hand gearchange.

Chassis: Separate pressed-steel chassis frame, with tubular and pressed cross bracing. Forged front axle beam. Front and rear suspension by semi-elliptic leaf springs. Optional friction-type dampers. Worm-type steering. Rear-brakes only. Choice of artillery-style wheels with detachable rims, or centre-lock wire wheels.

History: Harry C. Stutz's famous Bearcat sports car was also one of the very first cars his Indianapolis-based company ever designed. His first products were racing cars, from 1911 on-wards, but the Stutz Motor Car Co. was founded in 1913 and announced the Bearcat for 1914 production. The racing Stutz cars helped pave the way for the Bearcat, but this had also been obviously developed with an eye to the Mercer Raceabout, which it resembled visually and whose

Below: The stark and purposeful Stutz Bearcat of 1914, with that distinctive monocle windscreen for the driver. The engine was a 6.4-litre.

market it sought to invade. Like the Raceabout, the Bearcat was a big-engined rough-and-ready sports car, of the type where hairy-chested behaviour and performance was thought all-important. There were two seats, but no doors and certainly no windscreen. The driver had a 'monocle' screen to protect him from the flies and debris, but the passenger had nothing at all. The uncompromising bonnet hid a big and conventional 6.4-litre engine and really the only novel fitting in the chassis was the three-speed gearbox; this found itself in unit with the back axle, which had been a Stutz-built speciality for several years.

One reason behind the car's fame was that a team of racing cars, the White Squadron, performed well in 1915. These cars had special sixteen-valve overhead camshaft engines of 4.8-litres, and were far from standard, but this did not deter the customers. Cannonball Baker also used a Bearcat to break the Atlantic-Pacific record in 1916 – by an astonishing margin and without any mechanical problems.

More than any other, this one model reminds the world of Stutz, even though there were many other, more practical, products from that stable in Indianapolis before the last car of all was assembled in 1935. With a wheelbase of 120in, the Bearcat had space for only two seats and there was absolutely no weather protection - but this was a real sports car.

Seldom has a car become so indelibly etched in memory via a single model. Worth a fortune today, the original Bearcat retailed for only $2,000 in 1914, but even in those expansionist days sales were limited. When Stutz started making cars again after World War I, its clientele demanded more comfort, so this exposed-to-the-weather style faded from the scene.

Sunbeam Alpine

Sunbeam Alpine, built from 1953 to 1955
Built by: Rootes Ltd., Britain.
Engine: Four cylinders, in line, in cast iron cylinder block. Bore and stroke 81 x 110mm, 2,267cc (3.19 x 4.33in, 138.4cu.in). Cast iron cylinder head. Two overhead valves per cylinder, operated by pushrods and rockers from a camshaft in the cylinder block. One downdraught Stromberg carburettor. Maximum power 80bhp at 4,200rpm. Maximum torque 124lb.ft at 1,800rpm.
Transmission: Rear-wheel-drive, single-dry-plate clutch and four-speed manual gearbox, no synchromesh on first gear: optional Laycock overdrive on top gear on late models, all in unit with engine. Steering-column gearchange.
Chassis: Separate steel chassis frame, with box section side members and reinforcements, with steel body shell in two-seater roadster style. Independent front suspension by coil springs, wishbones and anti-roll bar: suspension of

beam rear axle by half-elliptic leaf springs, Panhard rod. Hydraulic lever-arm dampers. Recirculating ball steering. Drum brakes at front and rear. 16in wheels, steel disc. 5.50-16in tyres.

Dimensions: Wheelbase 8ft 1.5in (248cm), front track 3ft 11.5in (121cm), rear track 4ft 2.5in (128cm). Overall length 13ft 11.5in (425.5cm). Unladen weight 2,968lb (1,346kg).

History: Sunbeam-Talbot was a new-manufactured marque invented by Rootes when they bought up distinguished companies in the 1930s. For many future years, these would be sporty versions of the bread-and-butter Hillmans and ▶

Below: The original Sunbeam Alpine was a graceful two-seater conversion of the larger Sunbeam-Talbot 90 convertible. It was on sale for just two years.

▶ Humbers in the Group. In 1948, the Sunbeam-Talbot 80 and 90 four-door saloon types appeared. The Loewy Studio had offered styling advice, the overall effect being of much more elegant cars than contemporary Rootes saloons.

The 90 soon took on a lusty engine, had independent front suspension (from 1950) and made a reputation for itself in rallying. Early in the 1950s a Rootes dealer, George Hartwell of Bournemouth, built himself a two-seater open sports version of a 90 saloon to go rallying. Rootes bosses saw it, liked it, and adopted a similar style for a car they called the Alpine. It was revealed in the spring of 1953, and initially every example was sold in the USA.

Although it looked glamorous (do you recall Grace Kelly in *To Catch a Thief*?), the Alpine was let down by its weight, its saloon-car type soft handling, its drum brakes and such details as its steering column gearchange. Even so, it

was a very pretty two-seater, and a series of spirited performances in European rallies (Stirling Moss and Peter Collins both figured in such expeditions) gave it a certain reputation.

If it had not come on to the scene at exactly the same time as the Austin-Healey 100 and the Triumph TR2, it might have sold better. However, even with the overdrive offered on 1955 models, its weight was always against it, and production faded away after just two years, in mid-1955. About 3,000 such cars had been built. The next Alpine, of 1959, would be a completely different type of car.

Below: The 1953 Sunbeam Alpine used a sturdy separate chassis, and a 2.3-litre engine, but was only built with a steering column gearchange.

Sunbeam Alpine and Tiger

Alpines I, II, III, IV and V, Tigers I and II 1959 to 1968 (data for Tiger I)
Built by: Rootes Ltd., Britain.
Engine: Ford-of-Detroit manufactured. Eight cylinders, in 90-degree vee formation, in five-bearing cast-iron block. Bore and stroke 96.5mm by 73.0mm 4,261cc (3.80in × 2.87in, 260cu.in). Two cast-iron cylinder heads. Two overhead valves per cylinder, operated by pushrods and rockers from single camshaft mounted in centre of cylinder block 'vee'. One down-draught twin-choke Ford carburettor. Maximum power torque 258lb.ft at 2,200rpm.
Transmission: Single-dry-plate clutch and four-speed, all-synchromesh manual gearbox, both in unit with engine. Remote-control central gearchange. Open propeller shaft to hypoid-bevel 'live' rear axle.
Chassis: Unitary-construction pressed-steel two-seat sports car body/chassis unit, heavily modified by Jensen from Sunbeam Alpine shell. Independent front suspension by coil springs, wishbones and anti-roll bar. Rear suspension by semi-elliptic leaf springs and Panhard rod. Telescopic dampers. Rack-and-pinion steering. Four-wheel hydraulically operated brakes, front discs and rear drums, vacuum-servo assisted. 13in pressed-steel-disc wheels. 5.90 × 13in tyres Optional bolt-on steel hardtop.
Dimensions: Wheelbase 7ft 2in (218cm), track (front) 4ft 3.7in (131cm), track (rear) 4ft 0.5in (123cm). Overall length 12ft 11.2in (394cm). Unladen weight 2,640lb (1,197kg).
History: In the early 1950s, Rootes produced a stylish two-seater car, based on a Sunbeam-Talbot saloon, called the Sunbeam Alpine. This was too heavy and cumbersome to be very popular, although it did have some competition successes. In 1959, a new Sunbeam Alpine appeared, this being based on the sport-wheel-base Hillman Husky floorplan and fitted with Sunbeam Rapier engine and transmission. The fashionable finned body was Rootes' own work In a complex commercial deal involving Rootes having an engine like that of the Armstrong-Siddeley Sapphire for their big Humbers, the Alpine was originally assembled by Armstrong-Siddeley in Coventry. At first the car had a 1½-litre engine, but this was soon enlarged to 1.6 litres. That was the Alpine II. Alpine II came along in the early 1960s, with more refinement and a smart new stee

Left: The Sunbeam Tiger was Rootes's answer to the AC Cobra, and had a similar Ford vee-8 engine squeezed into the modified Alpine body shell. The Tiger II of 1967 had 4.7 litres and 200bhp.

hardtop, but within a year this was superseded by Alpine IV which had its rear fins cropped. In the meantime, Rootes' North American importers looked at the AC Cobra, liked what they saw and engineered a similar prototype transplant of their own. The Sunbeam Tiger, announced in the spring of 1964, was really a Sunbeam Alpine with a 4.2-lite Ford V8, a Borg-Warner four-speed gearbox and a heavy-duty back axle installed, together with many other modifications to keep the engine cool and to make the handling satisfactory and the traction sound. Pressed-Steel produced the bodies (as they did for the Alpine), then Jensen made all the Tiger changes and carried out final assembly on Rootes' behalf. Soon after this, Alpine IV became Alpine V, the engine being enlarged to 1,725cc to match the already specified all-synchromesh gearbox. Both cars were smart and sold well, but unhappily they did not make profits for Rootes. Soon after Chrysler took a financial stake in Rootes they brought political pressure to bear and the rival Ford V8 engine was dropped. This was a shame, as Tiger II, announced for 1967, had been much fiercer with its more powerful 4,727cc (289cu.in) V8 engine. The Alpine V was discontinued in 1968.

Left: The Rootes Alpine had a sleek body style hiding more humble mechanical parts. The floor was from the Hillman Husky, and the power train from the Rapier. The 1959/64 version had more pronounced tail fins. Later cars had an all-synchromesh gearbox. This final version, the 1,725cc Series V, could beat 100mph. The last was built in 1968.

Talbot 75/90/105

Talbot 75/90/105 series, built from 1930 to 1935 (data for original 105)
Built by: Clement Talbot Ltd., Britain.

Engine: Six cylinders, in line, in seven-bearing cast iron cylinder block. Bore and stroke 75 x 112mm, 2,969cc (2.95 x 4.41in, 181.1cu.in). Cast iron cylinder head. Two overhead valves per cylinder, operated by pushrods and rockers from a camshaft mounted in the cylinder block. Single up-draught Zenith carburettor. Maximum power 100bhp at 4,500rpm.

Transmission: Front-engine, rear-wheel-drive, single-dry-plate clutch and four-speed manual gearbox, with no synchromesh, in unit with engine. Remote control right-hand-gearchange. [A four-speed preselector gearbox was fitted from 1932.]

Chassis: Separate steel chassis frame, with channel section side members, pressed and tubular cross-bracings. Front suspension of forged axle beam by semi-elliptic leaf springs, of rear axle beam by quarter-elliptic leaf springs. Piston-type hydraulic dampers. Worm-and-nut steering. Drum brakes at front and rear, operated by rods and cables: no servo assistance. 18in centre-lock wire wheels. 5.5 x 29in tyres. Choice of body styles, from open two-seater sports car, to tourer and saloon types, on wooden frame with steel and light alloy skin panels.

Dimensions: Wheelbase 9ft 6in (290cm), front track 4ft 7.5in (141cm), rear track 4ft 7.5in (141cm). Overall length (depending on body style) about 14ft 9in (450cm). Unladen weight (rolling chassis, without body) 2,050lb (930kg).

History: Until the marque was taken over by the Rootes Group in the mid-1930s, all Talbot cars were made in West London, in Barlby Road, from 1904. At first the company was independently financed, and it was not until just after First World War that the company became part of the French-English Sunbeam-Talbot-Darracq combine, whose guiding light was the famous engineer, Louis Coatalen.

Georges Roesch, Swiss-born, had originally learned his craft as a motor car designer in France, before moving to Britain, where he finally became chief engineer of Talbot in 1926. This, though, was not a period of stability for him, for his ultimate boss, Coatalen, liked to move his talented staff around. After a short period with Sunbeam in Wolverhampton, and then at the Talbot concern in Paris, Roesch finally returned to London in 1925. At this time the British Talbot concern was struggling, with almost non-existent sales and a poor but honest design of car. I

Below: The original Roesch Talbots were easily recognised by their radiator grilles, and by their fine six-cylinder engine performance.

Above: BGH 23 is probably the best known of all Roesch Talbots, and was originally one of the team cars. It later became a famous Brooklands race car.

was Roesch's task to change all that.

From 1926 until the late 1930s, Roesch designed, developed, improved and (in his eyes) perfected a six-cylinder engine design, which was to serve humble saloons in the 1920s, great race cars, and Brooklands models in the late 1930s. The first of this family, the 14/45, was launched in 1926, and established its pedigree.

The chassis was conventional enough, even by simple 'vintage' standards, but the six-cylinder engine was superb. At first it had only four main bearings, and 1,665cc, but successive re-designs eventually gave it a seven-bearing crankshaft, and no less than 3,377cc (which was used in the 110 model). This was a brilliantly conventional power unit, which breathed well, and had light and efficient valve gear and only ever needed a single carburettor.

Even so, the best (racing) version of a 110 engine developed 160bhp, for racing at Brooklands, where it achieved 140mph. Talbots raced and rallied with distinction in the early 1930s, their staple models being the 75s and 90s (2,276cc) and the 105s (2,969cc).

These cars, well-built rather than skimpy, were expensive by 1930s standards, but sold steadily on their high-quality reputation – there being 2,757 of the 75s, 216 of the 90s and 335 of the 105s of all types – many of them being built as big and comfortable saloons or even limousines, but a number were very capable sports cars.

The 120bhp 3.3-litre 110 of 1934 was the apogee of this layout – which still had a conventional channel-section frame, but was at least being built with a pre-selector transmission – and was capable of up to 95mph, which put it on performance terms with Bentley's latest 3½-litre types.

But the end was near, for the STD combine went bankrupt (too much spending on racing programmes the principal cause), and the components had to be sold off. The Rootes Group, which already owned Hillman and Humber, snapped up Talbot, and started the rationalisation process (for which read, 'dumbing down') for which they were already famous.

Late-model 75, 105s and 110s were gradually Humber-ised, so when the marque was finally killed off in 1937 Talbot fans found this a merciful release. The reputation of that great engine, though, lived on, and even when Jaguar's famous twin-cam XK power unit appeared in the late 1940s, Georges Roesch found time to criticise it as being little better than his own pushrod overhead-valve masterpiece had ever been.

Toyota MR2

Toyota MR2, two-seater sports coupé, built from 1984 to 1989 (data for the original model)

Built by: Toyota Motor Co. Ltd., Japan.

Engine: Four cylinders, in line, in five-main-bearing cast-iron cylinder block. Bore and stroke 81 × 77mm, 1,587cc (3.19 × 3.03in, 96.9cu.in). Light-alloy cylinder head. Four-valves per cylinder, in vee, operation by twin overhead camshafts and inverted bucket tappets. Nippondenso electronic fuel injection. Maximum power 122bhp (DIN) at 6,600rpm. Maximum torque 105lb.ft at 5,000rpm.

Transmission: Rear-wheel-drive, single-dry-plate diaphragm spring clutch and five-speed all-synchromesh manual gearbox, all in unit with transverse mid-mounted engine. Remote-control, central gearchange.

Chassis: Unitary-construction pressed-steel body-chassis unit, in two-seater sports coupé style. Independent front suspension by MacPherson struts, coil springs, wishbones, telescopic dampers, and anti-roll bar. Independent rear suspension by MacPherson struts, coil springs, lower wishbones, telescopic dampers, and anti-roll bar. Rack-and-pinion steering. Four-wheel disc brakes with vacuum servo assistance. Cast alloy 14in road wheels, 185/60-14in tyres.

Dimensions: Wheelbase 7ft 6in (232cm), front track 4ft 6in (137.2cm), rear track 4ft 6in (137.2cm). Overall length 12ft 6in (392.5cm). Unladen weight 2,319lb (1,051kg).

History: Too many cynics have branded the Japanese motor industry as no more than expert copiers – and lived to regret this. In the case of the mid-engined Toyota MR2, though, the jibe was justified. What happened seemed to be perfectly clear. Never having been in the 1.6-litre sporting coupé market section with an appealing and well-packaged car, Toyota studied the opposition, concluded that the Fiat X1/9 was a much better car than any of the front-engine/rear-drive opposition, and designed a new car on the same lines.

Although the company boasted that it had spent a decade developing its ideas, by the time it appeared the MR2 (Toyota told us that 'MR' meant 'Midship

Below: The original MR2 of 1984-1989 had very sharp-edge styling: the removable-panel version was an option.

Above: The original MR2 of 1984-1989 had very sharp-edge styling: the removable-panel version was an option.

Runabout') was a familiar layout. Inside the all-steel, monocoque steel two-seater coupé, the 1.6-litre engine and five-speed transmission was mounted behind the cabin, positioned across the car, and drove the rear wheels. In all but detail (and the fact that the steering gear was omitted!), this power pack was lifted straight out of the front-wheel-drive Corolla GT. MacPherson strut front and rear suspension, a small space for stowage up front (ahead of the toeboard) and a larger space behind the engine, in the extreme tail, were all exactly as already well-known in the Fiat X1/9. The only significant packaging differences were that the spare wheel of the MR2 was mounted up front, and the roof panel could not be removed for summer-time motoring.

The style was still in the 'Japanese origami' trend of the day, with a wedge-nose, sharply defined edges, with a sharply cut off coupé roof, and with a sizeable spoiler across the tail to trim the handling. As on other, larger Toyotas, the headlamps were normally hidden, but could be flipped up when needed. This, though, was strictly a two-seater, for the sports seats, when pushed back to the limit of their slides, were hard against the bulkhead immediately in front of the engine – not even space to stow a briefcase being left over.

Toyota, of course, had done an extremely competent development job, and had also produced a car which looked well, handled well, and was as refined as any of its saloon car counterparts. As originally sold in Europe and the USA, with a 122bhp engine, it was good for nearly 120mph. That, though, was only one of the types available, for Toyota produced a very meek-and-mild 1.5-litre/83bhp version for home con-sumption, balancing that eventually with a 145bhp/1.6-litre supercharged type for true extroverts. Then, to round off the range, in 1986 a removable-roof derivative was launched, this allowing two small panels to be taken out (leaving a rigid T-bar still connecting the screen rail to the rear) and either stowed up front in the front 'luggage' area, or left at home.

In only five years, the original MR2 was a great success, for no fewer than 166,104 such cars were sold (many of them on the West Coast of North America) before the second-generation MR2, a much larger, somehow softer-character, and more spacious model, came along. Having established itself in this market sector, however, Toyota was not about to give in lightly, and a third-generation type was put on sale before the end of the century.

Triumph TR2-TR6

**Triumph TR2-TR6, separate-chassis series, built from 1953 to 1976 (da
for TR3A)**

Built by: Standard-Triumph Motor Co. Ltd (Leyland Motors from 1961, Briti
Leyland Motor Corporation from 1968), Britain.

Engine: Four cylinders, in line, in three-main-bearing cast iron cylinder bloc
Bore and stroke 83 x 92mm, 1,991cc (3.27 x 3.62in, 121.5cu.in). Cast ir
cylinder head. Two overhead valves per cylinder, operated by pushrods a
rockers from a camshaft in the cylinder block. Two semi-downdraught S
carburettors. Maximum power 100bhp at 5,000rpm. Maximum torque 118lb
at 3,000rpm.

Transmission: Front engine, rear-wheel-drive, single dry plate clutch w
synchromesh four-speed manual gearbox (no synchromesh on first gear), w
optional Laycock overdrive, all in unit with engine. Remote control, centre flc
gearchange.

Chassis: Separate steel chassis frame, with box section side membe
channel and tubular cross-bracing and reinforcement members. Independe
front suspension by coil springs and wishbones, suspension of beam rear a>
by semi-elliptic leaf springs. Telescopic front dampers, hydraulic lever arm re
dampers. Worm-and-peg steering. Front disc, rear drum brakes, hydrau
operation, no servo assistance. 15in wheels, steel disc or centre-lock wir
5.50-15in tyres. Open two-seater pressed-steel sports car bodywork, w
optional removable steel hardtop.

Dimensions: Wheelbase 7ft 4in (224cm), front track 3ft 9n (114cm), rear tra
3ft 10in (117cm). Overall length 12ft 7in (384cm). Unladen weight 2,17(
(984kg).

History: Triumph's famous TR sports cars established their own image a

**Below: The TR6 was built from 1969 to 1976, and had a fuel-injected
engine, but carburettors were specified for North America.**

Above: The TR2 was a simple and rugged sports car (with a developed tractor-type engine) which became more sophisticated as the years passed.

their own living reputation, from a standing start in a very short time, for before then Standard (which had owned the 'Triumph' marque since 1944) had never produced a proper sports car.

The original '20TS' prototype of 1952, which founded the dynasty, was apparently inspired by managing director John Black, piqued at his failure to take over the Morgan company. That prototype was not up to scratch, being based on a modified old-style chassis frame, with poor roadholding and not enough power from the ex-Ferguson tractor engine.

A complete redesign around a new frame, a rear-end re-style, and a boost to 90bhp all helped, but it was Ken Richardson's dedicated development efforts which turned the awful '20TS' into a saleable TR2. After starting slowly towards the end of 1953, the new car soon established itself, especially after the first race and rally victories started to flood in during 1954.

Not only was the TR2 great value for money, but optional extras such as an overdrive, wire-spoke wheels, and a neat removable hardtop were all desirable. It was also a hard-riding, if slightly uncultured 100mph-plus sports car which could easily record more than 30mpg (Imperial) in day-to-day use. It fitted neatly into the marketplace below the Austin-Healey 100, and the MG TF but within months, it seems, MG was running scared.

In the next 12 years the design changed, improved, and was transformed out of all recognition – there being new engines, chassis, suspension and body styles along the way. One model always seemed to lead logically to the next, ▶

▶ so it was no wonder that the Americans, in particular, loved what they we
offered.

To succeed the original TR2, the TR3 of 1955 had 100bhp, and a year la
front-wheel disc brakes were standardised (a 'first' for a sports car of this pric
For 1958 the TR3A took over, much like the TR3, but with a wide-mouth gri
other trim changes, and 100bhp. within a year that car was available with a 2
litre engine as option, and sales soon exceeded 20,000 cars a year. In final for
for sale only to the USA, the TR3B had an all-synchromesh transmission.

The TR4, with an all-new Michelotti style, and considerably more refin
equipment and manners, appeared in 1961, complete with wind-up windov
optional 'Surrey-top' hardtop, wider wheel tracks, rack-and-pinion steering, a
an all-synchromesh gearbox. For 1965 it then gave way to the TR4A, which h
a new chassis with coil spring independent rear suspension.

Next, in 1967, it was the turn of the engine to be changed, the old 'fo
being displaced by a 150bhp fuel-injected 2.5-litre 'six' as the TR5 or (in No

Above: Interim model TR5 (1967-1969) was first to use the six-cylinder engine, the last with 1960s-type Michelotti body style. A removable hard top was a popular option.

America) as the 105bhp carburetted TR250. Even this was only an interim change, for the new-for-1969 model was the TR6, which had similar running gear, but a new front and rear end style on the Michelotti structure.

This was the definitive separate-chassis TR, which would built continuously until mid-1976, actually overlapping the TR7 by nearly two whole seasons. Few significant changes were made in those years, for attention had to be given to meeting new USA safety and exhaust emission regulations. The final TR6s, complete with their large safety bumpers, their engines bedecked with 'de-mogging' fitments, were not as simple or as sporting as their ancestors, but were still recognisably developed from the original theme. No fewer than 53,000 of all types of these TRs were produced in 13 eventful years.

Triumph TR7/TR8

Triumph TR7 and TR8 models, built from 1975 to 1981 (data for origina USA-market TR7)

Built by: British Leyland, Britain.

Engine: Four cylinders, in line, in five-main-bearing cast iron cylinder bloc Bore and stroke 90.3 x 78mm, 1,998cc (3.55 x 3.07in, 122cu.in). Cast light-allo cylinder head. Two overhead valves per cylinder, operated by inverted bucke tappets from a single overhead camshaft. Two Zenith-Stroimberg carburettor Maximum power 92bhp at 5,000rpm. Maximum torque 115lb.ft at 3,500rpm.

Transmission: Front engine, rear-wheel-drive, single-dry-plate diaphragr spring clutch and four-speed all-synchromesh manual gearbox, all in unit wit engine. Remote control, centre floor gearchange.

Chassis: Unitary construction steel combined body/chassis structure, in tw seater hardtop coupé body shell style (a convertible became available in 1979 Independent front suspension by coil springs, MacPherson struts, and anti-rc bar, suspension of rear beam axle by coil springs, radius arms, and anti-roll ba Telescopic hydraulic dampers. Front disc, rear drum brakes, with serv assistance. 13in wheels, steel disc or optional alloy disc. 185/70-13in tyres.

Dimensions: Wheelbase 7ft 4n (216cm), front track 4ft 7.5in (141cm), re track 4ft 7.5in (141cm). Overall length 12ft 10.5in (418cm). Unladen weig 2,241lb (1,016kg).

[Rest-of-the-World TR7s had 105bhp at 5,500rpm. Maximum torque 119lb.ft. 3,500rpm. Five-speed gearboxes, and three-speed automatic transmissions, we available on later models. The TR8, introduced in 1979/1980, was closely related the TR, but with a light-alloy 133bhp/3,528cc overhead-valve vee-8 engine, and fiv speed gearbox or automatic transmission.]

Below: The convertible version of the TR7 and TR8 did not arrive until 1979, this being the most appealing in the range.

Above: Triumph TR7s were originally introduced as closed two-seater coupés, with four-cylinder engines and a simple specification.

History: The TR7 was an unlucky project, which no amount of management effort could turn into a success. This wedge-nosed sports car was certainly the most controversial sports car ever produced behind the Triumph badge, for it was not only built during British Leyland's most trouble-torn years, but it also evolved as a direct (and destructive) competitor to MG's MGB family.

Always intended as a successor to the TR6, this was a completely different type of car, not only with a unit-construction body/chassis unit, but with a much simpler specification. It was, above all, designed with the North American market in mind, and if all product plans had been achieved it would have evolved into a large family, with a wide choice of engines and body styles. The stillborn 'Lynx' derivative, with its longer wheelbase, its V8 engine, and its hatchback body, would also have displaced the Stag.

Always engineered to be simple, the design featured front engines, rear drive with beam axles, the structure originally being intended to use eight-valve and 16-valve four-cylinder engines, the Rover V8, and even British Leyland's 2-litre O-Series engine, with manual or automatic transmissions, coupé and roadster styles, and the aforesaid longer-wheelbase hatchback style. Unhappily, a combination of poor initial product quality, a rash of labour problems surrounding its assembly, and a negative image brought this programme to a premature end, with several types never introduced.

The first version, badged TR7, went on sale in the USA in 1975, with a 92bhp engine, four-speed transmission and a fixed-head coupé roof. Thoughts of producing a Roadster had been put on hold due to impending USA legislation which would have outlawed it, though when this was annulled a convertible was finalised, and launched in 1979.

The TR7 had good, well balanced handling, and was adequately fast, but its long wedge nose and short high tail were always controversial. Sales, especially in the UK, were not healthy until a five-speed gearbox arrived, and although there was eventually an automatic transmission option, this was never popular.

Although a 16-valve (Dolomite Sprint) version was in preparation, and the TR8 was almost ready, these were frozen out by the lengthy strike at the Speke factory, and the Sprint derivative was killed off. After a six-month lay-off in 1978, ▶

▶ assembly was moved to the factory in Coventry, but just two years later there was a further move, to the Rover factory at Solihull.

Along the way, the engineering had been improved in many details, the rear ride height had been reduced and – most importantly – the long-forecast convertible derivative finally went on sale in 1979. So by the end of the 1970s the TR7 had matured properly. In five-speed form, with a convertible style, and the latest suspension and handling balance, it was a good, 110mph, sports car.

To join it, the long awaited TR8 arrived for 1980, this effectively being a five-speed TR7 but with a Rover V8 engine transplant, and enhanced braking and suspension specifications. Almost all these cars were convertibles, sales were

restricted to North America, and if the second Energy Crisis had not immediately struck hard it might have been a success.

By this time, though, the TR7 and TR8's reputation and image was in such confusion – they had been built in three different assembly plants in five years – that sales began to fall away. The fact that British Leyland publicly announced that the project was not profitable did not help, so the last of all were produced in October 1981. Even so, these were the best-selling TRs of all times – 112,375 TR7s and just 2,722 TR8s were built.

Below: The '3.5-litre' decal on the side of the front wings tell us that this is a V8-engined TR8, of which only 2,722 examples were built.

Triumph Spitfire and GT6

Triumph Spitfire and GT6, Spitfire built from 1962 to 1980, GT6 from 1966 to 1973 (data for original Spitfire of 1962)

Built by: Leyland Motors (British Leyland from 1968), Britain.

Engine: Four cylinders, in line, in three-main-bearing cast-iron cylinder block. Bore and stroke 69.3 x 76mm, 1,147cc (2.73 x 3.0in, 70cu.in). Cast iron cylinder head. Two overhead valves per cylinder, operated by pushrods and rockers from a camshaft in the cylinder block. Two horizontal SU carburettors. Maximum power 63bhp at 5,750rpm. Maximum torque 67lb.ft at 3,500rpm.

Transmission: Front engine, rear-wheel-drive, single dry plate clutch and four-speed synchromesh manual gearbox (no synchromesh on first gear), optional Laycock overdrive from late 1963, all in unit with engine. Remote control, centre floor gearchange.

Chassis: Separate steel chassis frame, with box section backbone main longitudinal members, box and channel cross-bracings. Independent front suspension by coil springs, wishbones and anti-roll bar, independent rear suspension by swing axles, transverse leaf spring and radius arms. Hydraulic telescopic dampers. Rack-and-pinion steering. Front disc, rear drum brakes. 13in wheels, steel disc or centre-lock wires. 5.20-13in tyres. Two-seater open two-seater body style, with optional, removable, hardtop.

Dimensions: Wheelbase 6ft 11in (211cm), front track 4ft 1in (124.5cm), rear track 4ft 0in (122cm). Overall length 12ft 1in (368cm). Unladen weight 1,568lb (711kg).

[The GT6 had a fastback coupé version of this design, with a 1,998cc six-cylinder version of the engine, 95bhp at first, 104bhp from 1968.]

Below: Four-cylinder Spitfires (facing the camera) and six-cylinder GT6 coupés (back to the camera) were built for 18 successful years.

Above: The original Spitfire of 1962 featured a 1.1-litre engine, all-independent suspension, and an amazingly tight 24ft turning circle. Wire wheels were optional.

History: Along with the MGB, Triumph's Spitfire and GT6 family was one of the longest running and most successful of all British sports cars. Unlike the MGB, however, it received far more changes and improvements over the years. Having started life in 1960 as a sporting derivative of the Triumph herald saloon car, from 1966 it also spawned off as smart six-cylinder version called the GT6, and it remained in production for an astonishing 18 years.

The Spitfire style came from their consultant Michelotti, without specific encouragement from the factory, and until Leyland Motors took over the business Triumph could not afford to put it into production. The new car, when launched in 1962, was based on much-modified Herald running gear, though with its own type of backbone frame, and the very appealing Michelotti style.

As an obvious competitor to the MG Midget/Austin-Healey Sprite family, it was both prettier and better-specified – for it had disc brakes and wind-up windows, was just as fast, and had much-superior access to the engine bay for maintenance.

Although it was a lively little car, with a soft ride and a roomy cockpit, its only failing, which was more obvious on this sports car than the Herald, was that simple high-pivot swing axle rear suspension could sometimes behave in a very skittish manner, especially on wet roads. One feature it inherited from the Herald was an incredibly tight turning circle, of only 24 feet/7.3 metres, which when used could wreak havoc on the front tyres, but made the car amazingly manoeuvrable.

Even so, well over 20,000 cars were sold in the first full year, and once the ▶

▶ factory proved that its 'works' race and rally cars were competitive, its reputation was assured. At Le Mans, in particular, special GT6-style Spitfires could reach more than 130mph, and last for 24 hours.

Over the years, and as different Marks took over (Mk 2 in 1964, Mk 3 in 1967), the engine size and power was increased. It was late in 1970, when a new type of 'swing-spring' rear suspension was standardised, along with an all-synchromesh gearbox and a re-skinned style that included a sharply cut-off tail, that this, the Mk IV, reached maturity.

The Spitfire 1500, complete with 71bhp/1.5-litre engine, took over as a genuine 100mph Spitfire for 1975, and even though it has less power when sold in the USA (where exhaust emissions laws meant that it had to be de-tuned) it was always a great success. The engine and gearbox, in fact, were also donated to the MG Midget 1500, with the Spitfire outliving its rival by a full year, and usually out-selling it in the world-wide market place.

Once Triumph had produced the six-cylinder Vitesse as a 'big brother' to the Herald, it was clear that the same could be achieved with the Spitfire.

Accordingly, from the autumn of 1966 a smart new machine called the GT6 appeared, this having a smooth 95bhp six-cylinder in the Spitfire's structure, but distinguished by a 'mini-E-Type' style of fastback coupé style.

Although this was a compact but quick, 105mph, car, it was initially let down by poor handling due to the swing axle rear suspension. The 104bhp Mk 2, though, which appeared in 1968, had wishbone-type rear suspension and was an altogether better car, which deserved its reputation. Two years later the Mk 3 appeared, with the same style changes as the Spitfire Mk IV, and this car then continued with only minor changes until killed off at the end of 1973 by ever-encroaching USA regulations.

All in, more than 314,000 Spitfires, and nearly 41,000 GT6s were produced. Both models were extremely successful in the USA, and this project would not have been viable without such sales.

Below: The GT6 had a smooth 2-litre six-cylinder engine, and a lift-up hatchback tailgate: the cut-off tail variety arrived in 1970.

Triumph Stag

Triumph Stag, built from 1970 to 1977
Built by: British Leyland, Britain.
Engine: Eight cylinders, in 90-degree vee formation, in five-main-bearing cast iron cylinder block. Bore and stroke 86 x 64.5mm, 2,997cc (3.39 x 2.54in, 183cu.in). Light-alloy cylinder heads. Two overhead valves per cylinder, operated by inverted bucket tappets from single overhead camshafts per cylinder head, two semi-downdraught Zenith-Stromberg carburettors. Maximum power 145bhp at 5,500rpm. Maximum torque 170lb.ft at 3,500rpm.
Transmission: Front engine, rear-wheel-drive, single-dry-plate diaphragm spring clutch and four-speed all-synchromesh manual gearbox, with Laycock overdrive (optional until 1973 model), all in unit with engine. Remote control, centre floor gearchange. Borg Warner three-speed automatic transmission was optional.
Chassis: Unitary construction steel combined body/chassis structure, with 2+2-seater body shell in open or with removable hardtop styles. Independent front suspension by coil springs, MacPherson struts and anti-roll bar, independent rear suspension by coil springs and semi-trailing wishbones. Hydraulic, telescopic dampers. Rack-and-pinion steering, with power assistance. Front disc, rear drum brakes, with vacuum servo assistance. 14in wheels, steel disc or (later models) cast alloy disc. 185-14in tyres.
Dimensions: Wheelbase 8ft 4in (254cm), front track 4ft 4.5in (133cm), rear track 4ft 4.9in (134cm). Overall length 14ft 5.8in (441cm). Unladen weight 2,807lb (6,189kg).
History: Once properly developed, the Stag was a far better proposition than it seemed in the early years. Engine problems – blown head gaskets and subsequent overheating – were eventually solved, and by the end of the 1990s not only were many stags in splendid, day-in, day-out reliable state, but very well preserved, and loved by their one-make club owners.

The Stag's origins were in a 'dream car' that Triumph's consultant, Michelotti, built for himself in 1966, but this was then adopted and launched by the factory after further development. Originally based on a shortened version of the Triumph 2000 platform, inner panels, suspension and running, the production car was more specialised, but still related.

Although the Stag's structure was a conventional steel monocoque, and its style was related to that of the latest Triumph 2000 saloon, it had a unique generous 2+2 seating package, and was sold either as a drop-head coupé, or as a hardtop. The massive hardtop was removable, but needed two people to lift it, and both versions were supplied, as standard, with what Triumph called a 'T-bar', which combined a rollover hoop behind the seats with a brace forward to the screen pillar.

The engine was a 90-degree vee-8, a 3-litre with single overhead camshaft cylinder heads. Designed at the same time as the four-cylinder Dolomite/TR7/Saab 99 units, it was designed for manufacture on the same machinery. This engine, incidentally, was never used in any other Triumph model. Backed by a manual (with overdrive, later standardised) or automatic transmission, this was a sports car with valid Grand Touring pretensions.

The interior was extremely well-trimmed – the wooden fascia, the full display of instruments and the smart seating would have been a great credit to a much more expensive product – so this, combined with the soft ride and power-assisted steering, made a well-set-up Stag easy to drive, either slowly or at high speeds.

Before it was phased out in 1977 (it was to have been replaced by a TR8 derivative) a total of 25,939 Stags were produced.

Below: Based on the shortened platform and suspension of a 2000 saloon, the Stag had a 3-litre V8 engine, and this unique style of body. A removable hardtop was optional.

TVR 3000/3000M

TVR M-Types, with various engines, built from 1972 to 1979 (data for original 3000M)
Built by: TVR Engineering Ltd., Britain.
Engine: Ford-manufactured, six cylinders, in 60-degree vee, in four-main-bearing cast iron cylinder block. Bore and stroke 93.66 x 72.4mm, 2,994cc (3.69 x 2.85in, 182.8cu.in). Two cast iron cylinder heads. Two overhead valves per cylinder, operated by pushrods and rockers from a single camshaft mounted in the vee of the block. One downdraught Weber carburettor. Maximum power 138bhp at 5,000rpm. Maximum torque 174lb.ft at 3,000rpm.
Transmission: Front-engine, rear-wheel-drive, single-dry-plate diaphragm spring clutch and four-speed all-synchromesh manual gearbox, all in unit with engine. Remote-control, floor centre gearchange. Optional Laycock overdrive from late 1975.
Chassis: Separate steel chassis frame, multitubular in backbone layout, with tubular cross-bracings and reinforcements. Independent front suspension by coil springs, wishbones and anti-roll bar, independent rear suspension by coil springs and wishbones. Hydraulic, telescopic, dampers. Rack-and-pinion steering. Front disc, rear drum brakes, with vacuum servo assistance. 15in bolt-on cast alloy wheels, 165-15in tyres. Two-seater glass-fibre body shell as coupé (M), hatchback (Taimar) or convertible.
Dimensions: Wheelbase 7ft 6in (228.6cm), front track 4ft 5.75in (136.5cm), rear track 4ft 5.75in (136.5cm). Overall length 12ft 10in (391cm). Unladen weight 2,240lb (1,015kg).
History: Trevor Wilkinson started building specials in Blackpool in the 1950s, the TVR name being a diminution of his own christian name. By the late 1950s there was a Grantura, which had a multi-tube frame, a fastback glass-fibre coupé body, and used proprietary engines. By the mid-1960s, the Grantura had not only been re-engineered, and given better styling, but it soon gave way to the Vixen series and the original 1960s-type V8-engined Griffith models.

Below: The 3-litre V6-powered TVR Convertible, announced in 1978, came late in the life of this range, but was a best seller once available.

466

Above: In the 1970s TVR prided itself on the well-equipped fascia/instrument panel of the 3000M/Taimar/Convertible series. The broad tunnel hides the multi-tube chassis.

TVR, in the meantime, had gone bankrupt more than once, and was eventually rescued by the Lilley family. Under Martin Lilley, not only did Vixens and Tuscan V6s sell well, but the company then invested in a major new model family, the M (M for 'Martin') series of the 1970s. This not only pushed up sales to more than ten cars a week – the best TVR had achieved for some time – but it made the business extremely profitable.

Like previous TVRs, the M-series had a multi-tube chassis frame, the strength being concentrated in the backbone, with a fastback glass-fibre body shell, and was endowed by all-independent coil spring suspension. Supplied only as a two-seater, with sizeable luggage accommodation (but no exterior access to the stowage space), it was a smart, long-legged, machine.

Although it was originally supplied with the USA-specification Triumph TR6-six-cylinder engine, as the 106bhp 2500M which was sold mainly in North America, it was soon offered as a 1600M (with 86bhp Ford Cortina engine) or most popularly of all as the 3000M, which used the lusty and mass-produced Ford-UK V6 of 138bhp/3-litres.

This was the foundation of a prosperous and versatile TVR concern of the 1970s, which not even a disastrous factory fire could destroy. The 3000M in particular was a fast, torquey, low-revving, easy-to-drive machine, with a top speed of 120mph, and an all-day cruising gate of at least 100mph.

Three major updates followed between 1975 and 1978 – not only the arrival of a Convertible version of the 3000M, but a hatchback variant of the same car, and even a lusty turbocharged model. The Convertible looked much the same as the M from the nose, and of course retained the same rolling chassis, yet after of the windscreen it had a much different body shell (later it would be reworked yet again for the S model of the 1980s), while the Taimar used virtually the same shell as the M, but had a neat hatchback engineered into the tail.

All these cars were a cut above the average small-production sporty car built in England at the time. Although their quality was sometimes not the best, they looked very smart, were practically engineered, and (important, this) had ▶

▶ easy-to-repair GRP body shells.TVR built their own chassis frames, and their own body shells, on site, and soon became known as a versatile little operation. with which Britain's big car makers were happy to do business.

The Turbo, of which only 63 such cars were built, had a 230bhp version of the 3-litre vee-6, which made it a British turbo pioneer, and provided a top speed of nearly 140mph: this was available with any of the three current body shells.

Demand for these cars – M-Series, Taimars and Convertibles were all being built on the same assembly lines – was still strong in the late 1970s, when TVR

Above: Three models evolved on the same chassis, all sharing the same nose and general performance. This was the Convertible, which had removable side curtains.

decided to produce an entirely new range, these being the sharply-styled Tasmins of 1980 and beyond.

Between 1972 and 1979, no fewer than 2,465 of this TVR family were produced, of which 1,749 were the two-seater coupé M-series models.

TVR Griffith

TVR Griffith sports car, built from 1992 to 2001 (original specification)
Built by: TVR Engineering Ltd., Britain.
Engine: Eight cylinders, in 90-degree vee formation, in cast-alloy cylinder block/crankcase. Bore and stroke 94 × 77mm, 4,280cc (3.70 × 3.03in, 261cu.in). Two light-alloy cylinder heads. Two valves per cylinder, overhead, in line, operation by pushrods and rockers from a single camshaft mounted in the vee of the block. Lucas fuel injection. Maximum power 280bhp (DIN) at 5,500rpm. Maximum torque 305lb.ft at 4,000rpm.
Transmission: Rear-wheel-drive, single-plate diaphragm spring clutch and five-speed all-synchromesh manual gearbox, all in unit with front-mounted engine. Remote-control, central gearchange.
Chassis: Separate multi-tube chassis frame, of basic backbone profile. Glass-fibre body shell. Independent front suspension by coil springs, wishbones, telescopic dampers and anti-roll bar. Independent rear suspension by coil springs, wishbones and telescopic dampers. Rack-and-pinion steering. Four-wheel disc brakes, with vacuum-servo assistance. Cast alloy wheels, 15in at front, 16in at rear, 205/55-15in (front) and 225/50-16in (rear) tyres.
Dimensions: Wheelbase 7ft 6in (228.6cm), front track 4ft 10in (147.3cm), rear track 4ft 10.4in (148.3cm). Overall length 13ft 0in (396.2cm). Unladen weight 2,304lb (1,045kg).
History: Amazing, isn't it, how one model name can be applied to entirely different cars? The original TVR Griffith of the 1960s was a raw, crude, fast, point-and-squirt machine, whereas the beautiful 1990s-style Griffith was an extremely desirable two-seater sports car. To quote one of the British magazines which tested it at the start of its life: 'So close to greatness, it hurts . . .' – which really sums up the miracle achieved by the tiny development team in Blackpool. Yet the car they originally conceived was not the car which went on sale.

At first TVR decided to convert an V8 S chassis, with a new body style, this being what was shown at the 1990 NEC Motor Show. Second thoughts, though, bred better ideas. Having kept the same swooping, achingly sleek body style,

Below: Like all other TVRs, the Griffith had a multi-tube chassis, all-independent suspension, and very high performance. The name harked back to an earlier TVR model.

Above: The rounded lines and complete lack of stick-on features meant that the Griffith looked right from every angle. It could exceed 160mph.

this was then applied to a lightly modified version of the racing Tuscan rolling chassis instead. At a stroke, here was a much stiffer backbone frame, but one that had always been intended to deal with a lot of high-torque Rover V8 power. But the Tuscan was loud, boisterous and in-your-face, and the Griffith could be none of those. The new model, which eventually went on sale in 1993, was altogether more sophisticated.

Everyone, but everyone, raved about its looks, for there was not a straight line nor a flat plane in evidence, no bumpers to get in the way of the airflow, and not a single flaw. Instead, here was a style, designed in-house, which started with an oval grille flanked by driving lamps, flowed over faired-in headlamps, swept across the doors which had no exterior method of being opened, and reached the curvaceous rump without a hiccup, or a blemish. Hidden away inside this desirable two-seater machine, as usual for a TVR of this period, was a much-modified version of the fuel-injected light-alloy Rover V8 engine and its matching five-speed gearbox, with all-independent suspension, four-wheel disc brakes, alloy wheels, and rack-and-pinion steering.

In the beginning, Griffiths were sold as 240bhp/3.9-litre cars, or 280bhp/ 4.3-litre cars, the larger and faster type being capable of more than 160mph. Nor was that available at silly prices, for to get 280bhp in 1992 you only had to pay a mere £28,295 – and the unique looks came free. The big rush in sales came at once, for more than 600 cars – well over half of the number of TVRs being assembled at the time – were delivered in 1992. TVR then introduced the Chimaera, a larger, somehow softer, and subtly less sporty machine than the Griffith, and the emphasis shifted away from the Griffith.

But not for long. The Griffith 500 then appeared in 1993, a car which combined a full 5.0-litre version of the engine, but delivering 325bhp into the bargain, and demand continued. here was a car which could tear away tyre treads at every opportunity, but one which still had a well-balanced chassis. By that time power-assisted steering was an option, the claimed top speed was up to 170mph, yet neither the style nor the appeal had diminished. It was still in TVR's ever-expanding product range at the end of the century.

TVR Cerbera

TVR Cerbera sports car, previewed in 1993, on sale in mid-1995 (data for 4.5-litre model)

Built by: TVR Engineering Ltd., Britain.

Engine: Eight cylinders, in 75-degree vee, in five-main-bearing alloy cylinder block. Bore and stroke 91.0 x 86mm, 4,475cc (3.58 x 3.39in, 305cu.in). Two light alloy cylinder heads. Two overhead valves per cylinder, operated by inverted bucket-type tappets from single overhead camshaft per cylinder head, MBE fuel injection. Maximum power 420bhp at 6,750rpm. Maximum torque 380lb.ft at 5,500rpm. [Cerbera model also available with 350bhp/4.2-litre V8, and 355bhp/6-cylinder in-line engines.]

Transmission: Front engine, rear-wheel-drive, single-dry-plate diaphragm spring clutch and five-speed all-synchromesh manual gearbox, all in unit with engine. Remote control, centre floor gearchange.

Chassis: Separate steel chassis frame, multi-tubular backbone type, with tubular cross-bracing and reinforcements. Independent front suspension by coil springs, wishbones and anti-roll bar, independent rear suspension by coil springs, wishbones and anti-roll bar. Telescopic, hydraulic, dampers. Rack-and-pinion steering with power assistance. Disc brakes on all four wheels, with vacuum servo assistance, but no ABS. 17in cast alloy wheels. 235/40-17in (front) and 255/40-17in (rear) tyres. Glass-fibre body shell, with 2+2 seating in bubble-top coupé style.

Dimensions: Wheelbase 8ft 5.2in (257cm), front track 4ft 9.7in (146.5cm), rear track 4ft 10in (147cm). Overall length 14ft 0.5in (428cm). Unladen weight 2,600lb (1,178kg).

History: Once wedded to the very profitable business of selling brutally powerful, glass-fibre bodied, two-seaters, TVR's owner, Peter Wheeler, saw no reason to change that philosophy. As the 1990s progressed, however, TVR began to make more and more of their component parts. The biggest

Below: With a family likeness to other 1990s TVRs, the Cerbera was the only one to have a fixed-head coupé style and 2+2 seating.

Above: The Cerbera was the first-ever TVR to be powered by its own 'in-house' V8 engine; 4.5-litre types produced 420bhp.

investment of all – one which took years to perfect, but eventually came to fruition – was to invest in the design of its own new engines. It was a new 'own-brand' vee-8 which made the new Cerbera so distinctive.

Like most TVRs in the modern era, the Cerbera was previewed long before sale could begin, so although a non-running prototype was first shown in October 1993, and test cars were paraded in 1994 and 1995, it was not until the high summer of 1995 that the very first cars were ever sold to the public.

Here was the biggest, the fastest, and the most extraordinary TVR yet to be offered for sale. Previous TVRs such as the Griffith had been been lightning-fast two-seaters, and all had used one or other of the Rover V8 engine types which TVR's own engineers had improved, but none was larger, and none was so special.

Although the Cerbera (the name is that of a three-headed dog of Greek mythology) remained faithful to the current TVR philosophy – front engine/rear drive, multi-tubular chassis frame, and glass-fibre body shell – it broke the mould in two major respects. First of all, and visually, it had an 8ft 5in./256.6cm wheelbase, which made it long enough for cramped 2+2 seating to be squeezed into a rounded coupé cabin. Sensationally, though, it was the first (and until the early 2000s the only) TVR to use the TVR-financed AJP8 engine.

Commissioned from Al Melling, a shadowy figure in the high-performance engine design business, the AJP unit was all new in every respect, a 75-degree vee-8 where most had 90 degrees, with single-overhead-camshaft two valve cylinder heads where others might need four-valve/twin-cam heads, and with a flat-plane crankshaft. Even in its original 4.2-litre form it developed 350bhp – and in the 4.5-litre version which followed, it was good for no less than 420bhp.

Although the Cerbera coupé was a sizeable car, it was self-evidently very aerodynamically smooth, so the 185-200mph top speed of which it was capable (this was not accurately checked, either by the factory, nor any magazine tester !) was no surprise. When it was offered with a slightly-enlarged version of the AJP8, the 4.5-litre variety, a 100mph sprint in less than nine seconds put it way up into the 'this is ridiculous' category, and in comparative tests it blew off cars like the latest Dodge Viper GTS! ▶

▶ But then, there have been other such cars that were sensationally fast, but there have not been many which were so complete in everything else they did. Once clients had got over the fact that TVR product quality still had something to learn from other makers, there was so much more to enjoy. The ride was amazingly compliant, the styling was (to most eyes) quite astonishingly well-detailed, and right for its job, the chassis and its performance could match that of the engine, and there seemed to be no squeaks, rattles or creaks from the new chassis/body combination. It was even possible, as if you cared, to record up to 22mpg (Imperial) in everyday driving.

Although TVR charged £37,000 even for the first 4.2-litre Cerberas (the 4.5-litre model cost £46,345 in the early 2000s), this never killed off the demand. TVR, in any case, were only able to build about 400 such cars every year, and at that level the order base was very strong. Even before the first engine upgrades came along (as they must surely do) this was a simply amazing car, which might even improve as the 2000s progressed.

Below: Longer than other contemporary TVRs, the Cerbera had a unique tubular chassis, and 2+2 seating with restricted rear headroom.

Volvo P1800

P1800, 1800S, 1800E and 1800ES, built from 1960 to 1973 (data for 1800S)
Built by: AB Volvo, Sweden.
Engine: Four cylinders, in line, in five-bearing cast-iron block. Bore and stroke
84.1mm by 80mm, 1,778cc (3.31in × 3.15in, 108.6cu.in). Cast-iron cylinder head. Two
overhead valves per cylinder, operated by pushrods and rockers from single side-
mounted camshaft. Twin semi-down-draught constant-vacuum SU carburettors.
Maximum power 100bhp (net) at 5,800rpm. Maximum torque 110lb.ft at 4,000rpm.
Transmission: Single-dry-plate clutch and four-speed, all-synchromesh manual
gearbox, with electrically operated overdrive, all in unit with engine. Remote-control
central gearchange. Open propeller shaft to hypoid-bevel 'live' rear axle.
Chassis: Unitary-construction pressed-steel body chassis unit, in closed two-seat
coupé form. Bodies built by Pressed Steel in Britain. Car assembled by Jensen, but
from mid 1960s assembled by Volvo in Sweden. Independent front suspension by
coil springs, wishbones and anti-roll bar. Rear suspension by coil springs, radius arms
and Panhard rod. Cam-and-roller steering. Front disc brakes and rear drums. 15in bolt-
on pressed-steel-disc wheels. 165 × 15in tyres.
Dimensions: Wheelbase 8ft 0.5in (245cm) tracks (front and rear) 4ft 3.8in (132cm).
Overall length 14ft 5.3in (440cm). Unladen weight 2,500lb (1,140kg).
History: The Volvo 1800 sports coupé made its name all over the world as the car
chosen by The Saint in that well known TV series based on the Leslie Charteris

**Below: Although the P1800 was originally designed as a coupé, as the
1800ES, it was finally built as a smart 'sporting estate' from 1971.**

Above: The P1800 reaped world-wide publicity when used by Roger Moore as 'Simon Templar's' car in the popular 1960s TV Series 'The Saint'. Those are non-standard Minilite wheels.

novels. It was a strikingly styled closed two-seater (shaped by Volvo without outside assistance) and used a compete power train from the Amazon range of saloons which had already established Volvo's reputation for rugged, reliable and no nonsense motoring. At the end of the 1950s Volvo were short of factory space, and made a unique agreement in Britain. Pressed Steel would build the body shells, while Jensen would assemble the cars from components supplied from Sweden. The arrangement worked well for a few years, until Volvo decided to upgrade the car, improve the quality, and make it themselves. P1800s were Jensen-built, while 1800S cars were built in Sweden. The 1800 engine was enlarged to a full two litres in 1968, but from 1969 this engine was given Bosch petrol injection and developed up to 125bhp. In 1971 Volvo jumped on the three-door band-wagon by giving the car an estate car shape with a vast opening rear window. This, as the 1800ES, carried on into 1973, when it was finally discontinued. There was no sporting-car successor from Volvo until 1997.

VW-Porsche 914 and Porsche 914/6

VW-Porsche 914 family, VW and Porsche engines, built from 1969 to 1975 (data for original 914)

Built by: Dr. Ing h.c.F.Porsche KG, Germany.

Engine: Four cylinders, air cooled, in flat-four formation, line, in three-main-bearing light alloy cylinder block. Bore and stroke 90 x 66mm, 1,679cc (3.54 x 2.60in 102.5cu.in). Two light-alloy cylinder heads. Two overhead valves per cylinder operated by pushrods and rockers from a single camshaft mounted in the centre of the engine. Bosch fuel injection. Maximum power 80bhp at 4,900rpm. Maximum torque 98lb.ft at 2,700rpm.

Transmission: Mid-mounted engine, rear-wheel-drive, single-dry-plate diaphragm spring clutch and five-speed all-synchromesh manual gearbox, all in unit with engine. Remote-control, centre floor gearchange.

Chassis: Unitary construction steel combined body/chassis structure, with engine mounted behind two seats, and coupé body style with removable roof panel. Independent front suspension by torsion bars, MacPherson struts and wishbones; independent rear suspension by coil springs and semi-trailing arms. Telescopic hydraulic dampers. Rack and pinion steering, no power assistance. Disc brakes at front and rear, with no servo assistance. 15in wheels, steel disc. 155-15in tyres.

Dimensions: Wheelbase 8ft 0.5in (245cm), front track 4ft 5.5in (136cm), rear track 4ft 6.4in (138cm). Overall length 13ft 2in (401cm). Unladen weight 1,898lb (860kg).

History: Ever since Dr. Ferdinand Porsche had designed the original VW Beetle, he had retained links with that concern. His original Porsche sports car, the 356, had been based on a Beetle platform, suspensions and power train. In 1969, therefore, it was no surprise that VW and Porsche had got together to design a new sports car with a mid-engined layout, and that it was to be called a VW-Porsche 914.

In the late 1960s, sports car motoring fashion had swung towards mid-engine positions, which could give better roadholding characteristics than a rear-engined car, even though there would have to be some loss of passenger and stowage space. The 914 project, although carefully engineered and developed, was no better than most. It was a strict two-seater – which was a step-back from the generous 2+2 seat layout of the existing 911, this package being made doubly controversial by its very sharp-edged body styling. Nominally this was a closed coupé, but the roof panel could be removed, and stowed, this turning it into a real Roadster, though with what was effectively a roll-over bar behind the seats.

Compared with the handling of the familiar 911s, which liked to throw out their tails when cornered exuberantly, the 914's handling was much more precise, and in normal road use it seemed to be more forgiving. But it was difficult to satisfy ▶

Below: The 914 and 914/6 shared the same structure, but had different engines, which were mounted behind the seats, under a lift-up panel.

▶ everyone, especially Porsche 'works' rally drivers, who could not get on with it, so a promising motorsport career was cut short.

When announced in 1969, there were two versions – the pure 914 being VW-badged, and having an 80bhp VW411 type of air-cooled engine and transmission reversed in the new chassis with the engine immediately behind the seats, while the 914/6 was badged as a Porsche, with an air-cooled 110bhp/2-litre/flat-6 Porsche 911T engine in the same place. Accommodation for luggage was carefully arranged – there were front *and* rear compartments, and the engines were hidden from view under swivelling panels behind the cockpit.

Karmann of West Germany produced the body/chassis structures, and also built the complete car on Porsche's behalf. VW, on the other hand, carried all the credit for the marque's name, and there was a special company that not only marketed but distributed and sold all the cars.

Although many enthusiasts always looked on this model as a rather down market Porsche, they were evidently attracted to the VW-engined version and bought large numbers. Unfortunately the Porsche-based 914/6 was very little cheaper than the least expensive 911, and was thought to be less practical, and to handle in a less predictable manner. The 914/6, in fact, was not a success, and would be withdrawn after only three years: only 3,107 were built.

The VW-engined 914, however, was further improved, and 1973 models saw the cars being re-engineered and re-launched as the 914SC. There were no style changes – the only difference being to badges – but hidden away was a car powered by a full 2-litre flat-four VW engine of 100bhp/1,971cc, which was fitted with fuel injection as standard, and was the ultimate flowering of VW's famous (and long-lived) air-cooled engine theme.

The 914SC effectively took the place of both original models, for it combined VW engine simplicity with a 120mph top speed, not as much as the 125mph of the Porsche-engined car, but still high enough for all normal traffic conditions.

Although the roadholding was good, and the engineering competent, this was a car that never totally developed its sports car image. There is no doubt, too, that its two-seater layout was less practical than that offered on Porsches, and perhaps the style was not to everyone's taste.

It was interesting to note when the companies got together on the next joint project, it would be on a conventional-looking front-engined car, the Porsche 924. The two were definitely connected, for as the last of the 914SCs was built, the first 924 took over. No fewer than 115,600 VW-Porsches were produced in six years.

Below: The 914 and 914/6 had rather sharp-edged styles, with a lift-off panel in the roof, but with a permanent roll hoop. There were two luggage boots – one at the front, one at the rear.